EDWIN ROGERS EMBREE

PHILANTHROPIC & NONPROFIT STUDIES

Dwight F. Burlingame & David C. Hammack, editors

EDWIN ROGERS EMBREE

THE JULIUS ROSENWALD FUND FOUNDATION PHILANTHROPY AND AMERICAN RACE RELATIONS

ALFRED PERKINS

INDIANA UNIVERSITY PRESS

Bloomington & Indianapolis

This book is a publication of

Indiana University Press
601 North Morton Street
Bloomington, IN 47404-3797 USA

www.iupress.indiana.edu

Telephone orders   800-842-6796
Fax orders   812-855-7931
Orders by e-mail   iuporder@indiana.edu

⊖ The paper used in this publication
meets the minimum requirements of
the American National Standard for
Information Sciences—Permanence
of Paper for Printed Library Materials,
ANSI Z39.48-1992.

Manufactured in the United States of
America

Library of Congress Cataloging-in-
Publication Data

Perkins, Alfred, [date]
  Edwin Rogers Embree : the Julius Rosen-
wald Fund, foundation philanthropy, and
American race relations / Alfred Perkins.
    p. cm. — (Philanthropic and nonprofit
studies)
  Includes bibliographical references and
index.
  ISBN 978-0-253-35604-8 (cloth : alk. pa-
per) 1. Embree, Edwin R. (Edwin Rogers),
1883–1950. 2. Embree, Edwin R. (Edwin
Rogers), 1883–1950—Political and social
views. 3. Philanthropists—United States—
Biography. 4. Rockefeller Foundation—
Biography. 5. Julius Rosenwald Fund—
Biography. 6. Endowments—United
States—History—20th century. 7. African
Americans—Social conditions—To 1964.
8. Chicago (Ill.)—Race relations—Histo-
ry—20th century. 9. United States—Race
relations—History—20th century. I. Title.
  HV28.E348P47 2011
  361.7'4092—dc22
  [B]
                                    2010036733

1 2 3 4 5 16 15 14 13 12 11

To the Tibetan people,
whose culture Edwin Embree
would have valued, and whose cause
he would have championed

CONTENTS

PREFACE

The lives of foundation officers do not often come to public attention. Wealthy persons who endow large philanthropic trusts are commonly lionized; those who distribute that largesse are not. Though foundations have set in motion many societal advances during the last hundred years, relatively little is known about the executives whose vision and beliefs underlay those innovations. Conducting their affairs far from the public eye, they exert great influence, while remaining largely, and deliberately, anonymous. Yet there have been a few nonconformists who moved beyond this conventional practice. This is the story of one of them, Edwin Rogers Embree, a man who not only did not shrink from publicity, but came to see it as essential to the success of the organization he led.

Embree worked in philanthropy for over thirty years, first as the second-ranked officer of the young Rockefeller Foundation, then as president of the Julius Rosenwald Fund, finally as head of the twin, short-lived Liberia and Africa foundations. His career was marked by remarkable imagination and uncommon boldness, by an eagerness to push organized giving in new directions and toward greater effectiveness. On the eve of the Great Depression, he attempted to change the way foundations went about their business. Later, when the market collapse wiped out almost all of the assets of the Rosenwald Fund, he pioneered a new philanthropic model that foreshadowed the ideology-driven trusts that would emerge some forty years later.

Embree earned his bread as a foundation executive, but he was much more. A world traveler, he visited an astounding forty-five countries, producing thoughtful analyses of the social and economic conditions he observed on four continents and the islands of the Pacific. Rosenwald activity focused on the American South, and in time Embree became a leading authority on race relations, serving as President Franklin Roosevelt's principal advisor on those fraught issues. In the 1930s, he mounted a campaign that resulted in important New Deal legislation, and in the 1940s he was prominent among political liberals in Illinois. Moreover, he was a writer of consequence, publishing dozens of articles in journals and magazines, numerous essays calling for the fair treatment of all Americans, and several books introducing the nation's majority to their fellow citizens of color.

With a pronounced maverick streak and a tendency to speak his mind, Embree inevitably generated controversy. He was often in contention—with southern governors, conservative midwesterners, physicians suspicious of the neighborhood clinics he promoted, Harlem political figures, even the occasional college president. At the same time, his views attracted friends and allies from the many fields in which he was engaged: school reform, civil rights, scientific research, the arts, state and national politics, higher education, world affairs. Few of his contemporaries were as deeply involved in so many disparate arenas. Few lived a life so adventurous, productive, and full.

Beyond chronicling an interesting life, this account may also help to fill an unfortunate gap in the literature on American philanthropy. Since its demise over sixty years ago, the Julius Rosenwald Fund has fallen into obscurity, even though during Embree's tenure it was arguably the most active foundation in the United States working against racial injustice. The only comprehensive record of its activities, written by Embree and his associate Julia Waxman, was published in 1949, the year after the fund closed its doors. In the hope that some enterprising scholar will soon undertake to write a full history of this significant foundation, I have provided fairly extensive endnotes that may assist that future researcher.

A related consideration is worth noting. Without an independent history of the fund, those who wrote earlier about Embree had to work within a limited context and to draw conclusions from fragmentary evidence. That problem is further complicated by the fact that the relevant materials are widely scattered—in the South, Northeast, and Midwest, in California and Hawaii. As a result, various articles and book chapters have characterized Embree in ways that I consider ill founded and, at best, misleading. Rather than treating these points of disagreement in the text, I have chosen to address them in the endnotes for chapters 2, 4, and 7.

Writing a biography would be impossible without the assistance of many persons, and it is a pleasure to acknowledge those to whom I am most deeply indebted. Tom Rosenbaum, senior archivist of the Rockefeller Archive Center, suggested to me in 2005 that a biography of Embree could be a useful addition to the story of organized giving in the United States. In the years since, he has been an unfailing source of information, insight, and encouragement, going far beyond what any researcher has a right to expect. His RAC colleague Susan Irving Havranek provided immensely helpful guidance through the rich holdings of that indispensable depository. To Beth Howse, careful keeper of the voluminous Julius Rosenwald Fund Archives held in the John Hope and Aurelia E. Franklin Library of Fisk University, I am grateful for a warm welcome, efficient service, and pleasant working conditions during multiple research trips to Nashville.

At Berea College, two people deserve hearty thanks. Professor Steve Gowler, stalwart friend and sometime co-teacher, has in this project, as in much else, been invaluable—offering advice, checking bibliographic citations, and critiquing the manuscript, while cheerfully providing photocopied materials to a retiree foolhardy enough to undertake research in a beach town far from a major library. Shannon Wilson, Director of Special Collections and an accomplished historian, brought to my attention important documents and pictures in the Embree Papers held in Hutchins Library; I greatly appreciate his help.

Various institutions in Chicago hold Embree-related materials, and I benefited there from the assistance of several individuals. Julia Gardner of the Special Collections Research Center at the University of Chicago helped me to navigate through three extensive sets of personal papers and the records of two national organizations in which Embree was a key figure. At Roosevelt University, librarian Michael Gabriel provided access to the corporate records of that institution, which Embree cofounded and helped lead. Special appreciation is owed to Peter Ascoli of Spertus College for his essential biography of Julius Rosenwald, for arranging to talk on short notice with a complete stranger, and then, even more graciously, for agreeing to read and comment on my manuscript. To Daniel Schulman, I am grateful for inviting me to contribute to the catalog for his important exhibit of Rosenwald fellows' art; preparing that piece helped me to think about the fellowship program in a new way.

I also appreciate the aid received from Paula Johnson of the Osceola (Nebraska) Public Library and from the staffs of the Franklin Delano Roosevelt Presidential Library, the Harold Washington Public Library in Chicago, the New York Public Library, the Library of Congress, the Beinecke Rare Book and Manuscript Library of Yale University, and the Manuscripts and Archives Division of Yale's Sterling Library. To the institutions these individuals represent, I am grateful for permission to quote from documents in their possession.

This book would have been woefully incomplete, and far less lively, without the unstinting cooperation of Edwin Embree's relatives. Joanne Hill Styles of Evanston, Illinois, was good enough to share her memories from the two years she lived in the Embree household as a teenager. Bryant Rogers of Leesburg, Virginia, steered me through the Embree genealogy back to the family's U.S. progenitor in the mid-seventeenth century. In 2005, I was fortunate to have two long and fruitful conversations in Ithaca, New York, with Embree's daughter, the late Edwina Embree Devereux, then in her mid-nineties. To her son, John Devereux of Madison, Wisconsin, I am much indebted for his sustained interest in this project and for hospitality during several productive and thoroughly enjoyable days while I worked through the abundant family archive he has assembled. Embree's second daughter, Catherine Embree Harris of Honolulu, has been what her father would have called "a brick." In our frequent discussions by telephone and letter, she has been a fertile source of reminiscences, anecdotes, documents, research leads, names of additional contacts, and support of every kind. Coming to know these members of an extraordinary clan has been a true delight. Unfailingly helpful with information and commentary, they have left me entirely free to form and record my own judgments.

The book has been made more readable through the diligent efforts of editors at Indiana University Press. And it owes more than can be adequately stated to the forbearance of my wife, Barbara, who has endured my extended absences during research trips and countless hours on the computer.

Conducting research inevitably involves expense. I am grateful for travel grants from the Appalachian College Association, Berea College, and the Rockefeller Archive Center, and for the great generosity of two donors who prefer to remain anonymous.

Help from many quarters is, of course, no guarantee of a successful outcome. It is only proper, therefore, that responsibility for whatever shortcomings this work possesses should rest exclusively on the author's doorstep.

Ormond Beach, Florida
July 2010

EDWIN
ROGERS
EMBREE

ONE

FRONTIER OUTPOSTS, SINGULAR VILLAGE, PRESTIGIOUS UNIVERSITY

Polk County, Nebraska, in the mid-nineteenth century was not a hospitable place. In winter, the temperature could plunge to 20 degrees below zero. Severe blizzards were frequent, some lasting almost a week. Exposed humans struggled to keep their eyes from freezing shut, and unsheltered animals could suffocate under heavy, driven snow. Summer was no less formidable; temperatures sometimes topped 110 degrees in the shade, if shade could be found. Winds could reach gale force and, even when more moderate, could feel like air from a blast furnace. Cyclones occasionally ripped across the rolling hills. Hordes of grasshoppers were known to descend suddenly, devouring every green thing, even eating the shirt off a man's back. East of the Mississippi, many believed the region unfit for permanent human habitation.

Undeterred by such harsh conditions, white settlers began to filter into the county in the late 1860s. Arriving in covered wagons drawn by oxen, horses, or the occasional mule, they discovered little to attract the eye. Away from the bottomland along creeks and rivers, neither bush nor tree could be seen, only boundless prairie stretching to the horizon in every direction. There were bison and antelope, deer and elk, muskrat and turkey and prairie chicken, enough to sustain the small bands of Pawnee and Cheyenne that inhabited the area. Darkness brought the howling of numerous wolves. Yet to the newcomer, Polk County—all 450 square miles of it—seemed a vast emptiness.

The first census of the county, taken in 1870, revealed a population of ninety settlers. Their hastily constructed dwellings were dugouts— holes gouged into the side of a hill, with poles stretched across the top, the poles then covered with sod. The floor was likely to remain dirt, with the entrance covered only by heavy cloth or a crudely constructed door. Later, as time permitted, this primitive living space might be replaced by a sod house, with walls made of stacked squares of dirt and grass cut from the land. Wood was not easy to come by, and more substantial homes were often years away.

In 1871, the citizens of Polk County chose as the county seat a small settlement on Davis Creek, a tributary of the Blue River. The following year, when the wooden courthouse was completed, the town of Osceola could boast of its first real building. Finished that same year were the first two private residences on the town site, houses soon followed by a hotel, blacksmith shop, general store, and post office. Slow but steady growth over the decade brought the population, including families whose homesteads were miles apart, to 547, enough to justify incorporation in 1881. Central to Osceola's growth was the arrival in 1879 of a branch of the Omaha and Republican Valley Railroad. And, as happened throughout the conquest of the prairie, scarcely was the spur line laid before it was acquired by a larger railroad. Thus, this section of track, soon extended beyond Osceola, was purchased in 1882 by the Union Pacific Railroad. That acquisition brought to the town, as Union Pacific's telegrapher and depot agent, a thirty-eight-year-old Union Army veteran, William Norris Embree.

By the time Embree, his wife Laura, and their six children arrived, Osceola had begun to take on conventional aspects of town life. Three church buildings—all one-room frame structures—had been erected. Residences continued to go up. Destruction of the wooden courthouse by fire led to its replacement by a brick building, and to the purchase through private contributions of a horse-drawn fire engine. At the new courthouse in late 1882, Susan B. Anthony spoke on behalf of women's suffrage. The following spring, the town hosted a three-ring circus, complete with a giant ox "larger than an elephant" and a "unicorn—with three separate horns and three distinct eyes." For the second time, plans to open a saloon in town were turned down by the county commission. The establishment of a school led in 1888 to the first high school graduating class—four boys, two girls. Ten street lamps were planned for placement around the town square. Yet for all this progress, Osceola was still a hard-living, close-to-the-earth frontier town, much like the four earlier hamlets where Union Pacific had deposited the Embree family in the previous ten years.[1]

Only a few weeks after their arrival in Osceola, Laura Embree discovered she was pregnant. This was not entirely happy news, for there were already three girls and three boys, ranging in age from fourteen to three. The three eldest—all girls—had been born when the family was well settled in Laura's hometown, the village of Berea, Kentucky. The two youngest children had been born in the only other place the family had lived for any extended period, White Cloud, Kansas, where they had spent seven happy years. But now, they were in a totally new location and had scarcely had time to set up housekeeping. Moreover, Laura was already past her thirty-eighth birthday, a time when most mothers considered their families complete. Her uneasiness was undoubtedly intensified when the news came that, in the spring, before the baby was due, William would be transferred again. The family's new location was to be Bryan, Wyoming, an even more remote place, lacking either doctor or nurse.[2]

William, accompanied by two of the children, was forced to go on ahead, leaving Laura and the rest of their brood in Osceola to await the new arrival. When her time came, Laura was fortunate that the town doctor lived right across the road from the family's rented house. The delivery was uncomplicated, and the newborn, weighing a healthy ten pounds, arrived safely on July 31, 1883. This fourth son was given the name Edwin Rogers Embree. Three weeks after the birth, mother and children left Osceola for tiny Bryan.[3]

The Wyoming town was to be no more than another way station in the family's constant migration. As the Union Pacific extended its tracks, connecting frontier settlements to the main line, it moved its experienced station agents to the new locations, frequently and not always with much notice. By 1884, William Embree had been assigned to Ogden, Utah. Not much later, he was transferred to Cokeville, Wyoming, a town that even in the 2000 census numbered only 506 residents. Before the end of the 1880s, the family found itself in Kemmerer, another frontier outpost in Wyoming.

Such frequent moves provided little opportunity for the family to establish roots or make many acquaintances. During their brief stay at

Bryan, where they lived in the Union Pacific depot, they were befriended by cowboys from a nearby ranch, and the children came to know several Chinese railroad workers. At Cokeville, the family was housed in a log cabin on a small ranch, close to a creek where two branches of the Oregon Trail came together. There, the children found occasional diversion when wagon trains heading west from Missouri moved through, and occasional irritation when forced to drive the travelers' half-starved horses out of their pasture. Their closest neighbors, and the boys' principal playmates, were Blackfoot Indians. Frequent visitors to the home were adult Indians—some local, some itinerant—looking to trade, to sell horses, or perhaps to cadge a meal.[4]

With few neighbors in these sparse settlements, the family inevitably was focused inward. Much of the family activity centered on young Edwin. His teenage sisters doted on him, not only feeding, bathing, and caring for him, but curling his hair, sewing his clothes, dressing him up in costumes they made. As the youngest child, he received the constant attention and warm affection that commonly lead to a deep sense of security and well-being.[5]

Young Edwin's life was far from sheltered, however, and early on he displayed the curiosity and boldness that would characterize his adult years. On one occasion, when only three years old, "Winnie" was left in the care of two older brothers while his mother napped. The brothers were not particularly attentive, and Edwin, seeing a horse tethered to a post beside the house, found a chair to stand on and mounted proudly to the saddle. At that point, a sudden burst of wind blew dust and trash in the animal's face, causing it to rear, throw its would-be rider to the ground, lunge against the rope until the hitching post broke, and gallop away, trailing part of the post behind. Awakened by the commotion, Laura hurried out just in time to see the horse rapidly disappearing, dragging what she thought was her youngest child. She ran frantically after the runaway, until a passing Blackfoot managed to catch and return it. Around the corner of the house, unhurt and unfrightened, young Edwin seemed to enjoy the excitement.[6]

From the perspective of Edwin's brothers, life was idyllic. The eldest worked horses and raced against Indian ponies. The Native Americans themselves—with their ceremonies and horses and hunting weapons and brightly decorated moccasins—were endlessly fascinating. School was, at best, intermittent. The nighttime howling of wolves and barking of coyotes they took for granted. And they could look forward to taking over their eldest sister's job of shooting jackrabbits for the family table.[7] But their sojourn on the western prairie soon came to an end.

By 1888, William Embree's health had begun to fail. Captured during the Civil War, he had spent months in a Confederate prison in Richmond, Virginia. There, he had contracted tuberculosis, a disease that stayed with him the rest of his life. Thus, when only in his mid-forties, he had to resign from the Union Pacific Railroad. Left with no income, and the father too ill to work, the family was forced to break up. Leaving behind two of the daughters, who were married but still short of their twentieth birthdays, and the eldest son, the family moved to William Embree's sister's home outside Philadelphia. There, William died in the spring of 1891.[8]

Her husband's death left Laura, who suffered from malaria, with no established home of her own. Wyoming was to attain statehood that year, but life in that frontier setting held no attraction for a single woman with minor children, the youngest of whom was only six years old. Lacking any real alternative, she decided to return with her three youngest to her parental home in Berea, Kentucky, while her unmarried daughter remained in Pennsylvania to study for missionary work. His mother's decision was of enormous consequence for young Edwin, for he would spend his most formative years in his grandparents' home in a racially integrated town. There, growing up without a father, he came under the powerful influence of his grandfather, John Gregg Fee.

* * *

John G. Fee had been born in 1816 into a slave-owning family in Bracken County, Kentucky. Bracken County bordered the Ohio River, on the other side of which was the free state of Ohio. The proximity of slave-holding territory to a free state meant that pro-slavery sentiment and abolitionist ideas were heatedly discussed as young Fee was growing up. Indeed, his own family was not of one mind, for his mother came from an anti-slavery Quaker background. In his mid-twenties, Fee, having decided to devote his life to the Christian ministry, enrolled at Cincinnati's

Lane Seminary, a hotbed of abolitionist fervor but a few years earlier. Though that fervor had cooled somewhat by the time Fee arrived in 1842, anti-slavery sentiment was still present in Lane's faculty, notably in the views of the school's president, Lyman Beecher, and his son-in-law, the biblical scholar Calvin Stowe. A decade before Harriet Beecher Stowe would publish *Uncle Tom's Cabin*, Fee took classes from both her father and her husband. With classmates, he engaged in fervent discussions of the slavery question, centering on its relation to Christian doctrine. Then, following a nightlong vigil, when he prayed, "Lord, if needs be, make me an abolitionist," he was converted to the anti-slavery cause. Months later, his earnest efforts to persuade his conservative father to an abolitionist view met with failure, and the senior Fee refused to continue paying his son's tuition at Lane. Forced to leave the seminary after only a year and a half, young Fee was subsequently disowned by his father and disinherited. During those months of personal turmoil, he married Matilda Hamilton, daughter of a Bracken County family of abolitionist leanings.

Bitter estrangement from his parent was but the first of many hardships Fee would endure as a consequence of his views. Ordained in the Presbyterian Church, he preached and lectured against slavery in a number of churches in Kentucky and southern Ohio during the late 1840s and early 1850s. His insistence that slavery violated Jesus' injunction to "love one's neighbor as oneself" led first to his censure by the presbytery that ordained him, then to separation from his denomination altogether. He became the pastor of a small church in northern Kentucky which forbade membership to slaveholders. The congregation was racially integrated and, highly unusual for the time, advocated full equality for blacks. Infuriated by the radical views of the congregation and its pastor, local vigilantes in 1851 burned its building to the ground.

Increasingly convinced that his mission in life was to work for the elimination of slavery and its consequences, Fee published a series of articles and an "Anti-Slavery Manual." He urged immediate emancipation and equal rights for blacks, basing his argument on the U.S. Constitution and the New Testament. His unstinting expression of such controversial views in a southern state brought him to the attention of northern abolitionists, notably the Tappan brothers of New York, and the financial support of the American Missionary Association. It also won the patronage of Cassius Marcellus Clay, a prominent Kentucky landowner and politician.

In the mid-1850s, Clay provided Fee with extensive acreage, rolling bluegrass land within sight of the Appalachian foothills, on which to build a church and establish an anti-slavery community. As the community of Berea began to grow, a school was opened under the direction of a scholarly graduate of Oberlin College and Seminary, J. A. R. Rogers, and his teenage Quaker bride, Elizabeth Embree Rogers. From the outset, the school was devoted to "coeducation" of the races, and that commitment was extended to the college established a few years later. The presence of such a community and educational institution, together with Fee's continued preaching and circulation of anti-slavery tracts, quickly aroused the ire of slaveholders in the area.

By 1858, as tension over the slavery issue escalated across the country, the Berea community was subjected to constant harassment by pro-slavery forces. Racially integrated classes were broken up. Hostile mobs interrupted Fee's sermons and otherwise undertook to intimidate the citizenry. Fee was assaulted by ruffians almost two dozen times, and was twice left for dead. To the end of his life, he carried a large bump on his head where an irate slaveholder had broken a club over it. In spite of these attacks and repeated threats against his life, Fee never resisted physically, but remonstrated with his enemies and, even when being carried away for a beating, prayed for his tormentors. Nor did he cease to preach his anti-slavery doctrine.

The climax of the community's difficulty came late in 1859, following a sermon Fee had preached in Henry Ward Beecher's church in Brooklyn, soon after John Brown's raid at Harpers Ferry. Speaking to the largest congregation in the country, Fee, always a pacifist, called for abolitionists to be as consecrated as Brown, but to use spiritual force, not physical force or weapons, to achieve their ends. Misinterpreting Fee's words as a defense of Brown's methods, Berea's enemies assembled a posse of over 700 men, who rode on the town and demanded that its citizens leave the state within a matter of days. Under this threat of imminent violence, just before Christmas a dozen families, almost a hundred men, women, and children, fled across the Ohio River to Cincinnati.

Throughout the Civil War, most of the Bereans remained in their Ohio exile. Repeated attempts by Fee and various of his supporters to return to their homes were consistently thwarted by either troop movements or mob action. Fee spent the latter part of the war, after federal troops had established control over the state, at a Union Army post that had attracted hundreds of recently emancipated slaves. He befriended these impoverished folk, preaching to them, offering primary schooling, and generally promoting their well-being. Only with the end of hostilities, however, was return to Berea possible.[9]

Town life was renewed, the school reopened, and the college was formally chartered. A key development was the presence in Berea of a significant number of the newly free men and women, many of whom Fee had encouraged to settle in the interracial town. A novel feature of the town's layout was a provision that a home-building lot purchased by whites had to be adjacent to one owned by a black, and a black-owned property had to be next to one owned by whites. In this way, residential integration of the races was guaranteed. And, consistent with Fee's insistence on equal opportunity regardless of race, African American students were enrolled in large numbers in the college and its related schools. Indeed, until the turn of the twentieth century, there were many years when black students outnumbered white students.

*   *   *

In the closing decades of the nineteenth century, before national news agencies and radio began to move Americans toward a common base of information, many villages and small towns existed in significant separation from one another. Largely self-sufficient and self-contained, these have been described as "island communities." Such communities, though not genuinely isolated, nevertheless tended to be inward-looking, to consider their own patterns of life and outlook to be the norm. They were often marked by a kind of moral homogeneity, a tendency to see local standards as universal, to hold a common definition of virtue—emphasizing hard work, modesty, thrift, honesty in word and deed.[10] Such virtues were certainly paramount in Berea in those years, and in most ways the village fit the stereotype. What set it apart, however, and reinforced its island status was its racial composition and the values and outlooks that sprang from it.

It was in this distinctive community that Edwin Embree spent his most formative years. When he arrived in the village in 1890, social patterns across the country were moving toward rigid separation of the races. The decade saw the election to public office of the likes of James K. Vardaman in Mississippi and "Pitchfork Ben" Tilman in South Carolina, and Jim Crow legislation was spreading throughout the former Confederacy. Yet Edwin's experience of race was directly contrary to that of most Kentuckians, indeed of Americans generally. Housing patterns in the town ensured that he would grow up with black neighbors. The mixed population, totaling around 1,100, routinely interacted across racial lines. During his time in Berea, the college graduated James Bond, soon to become a human rights advocate and patriarch of one of the country's most distinguished African American families. Also enrolled in the college was Carter G. Woodson, the future father of black studies and the founder of Black History Month. At the college's preparatory school, young Embree had numerous black classmates. Later in life, he recalled, "[I]t never occurred to me that it was anything out of the ordinary to study and recite with Negroes. Some of them were brighter than I was. Some of them duller. It all seemed very natural."[11] He and his fellow students knew their circumstances differed from those in neighboring communities, but they took pride in their uniqueness and the quality of their scholarship.

No less important, Edwin had before him constantly the example of his grandfather's character and his unswerving commitment to racial equality. Fee's harrowing experiences before and during the Civil War were well known to his descendants. On occasional buggy rides around the Kentucky countryside, he would give his young grandson accounts of that difficult time. Fee's opposition to racial discrimination in all its forms was a dominating element in his thinking. Thus, it was only natural that his beliefs, and the scriptural foundation for them, would be expounded during the devotional periods that characterized his household.

For thirty minutes after both the morning and evening meals, the family engaged in Bible reading and prayer. From those sessions, the youthful Embree acquired an extensive knowledge of biblical passages on which, for the rest of his life, he often called to drive home a point. Moreover, growing up without a father, he was profoundly influenced by his grandfather's moral sense and the way he stood by his convictions no matter the consequences. Half a century later, Embree affirmed that Fee had been "the great inspiration of my life. . . . The ideas for which he stood became axioms for me." Even as a youth, he recalled, he had recognized that he was "in the presence of greatness."[12]

From his grandfather and his Berea upbringing, Edwin learned a great deal, including behaviors and outlooks that would remain with him for the rest of his life. The family stressed "habits of industry," routines of activity deemed essential in a largely self-sufficient household. With their grandfather too advanced in age for heavy labor, and with no other man in the house, care of the horses and the cow fell to Edwin and his brothers. So, too, did cultivation of the garden, which provided most of the family's food. Chopping wood for cooking and heating was also the boys' responsibility. These chores, while not overly strenuous, were unending, not often gratifying, but necessary for the family's welfare.

A break in this routine came in the summer of Edwin's tenth birthday. His three older brothers, all working at the Chicago World's Fair, urged their mother to allow the family's youngest to come and see the sights. After overcoming her serious misgivings, Laura Embree agreed to let him go, with the understanding that her own mother would accompany him as far as Cincinnati and put him on the train to Chicago. He would travel alone to that city, and his three brothers would meet him as soon as he arrived. All went as planned until the train reached the Chicago station, and Edwin discovered there was no one to meet him. Remembering that a building on the fair site was the alternative meeting place, he trudged off to the Midway on his own, carrying his little suitcase—now with a broken handle—in his arms. Yet, when he arrived at the designated building, his brothers were nowhere in sight. Already enchanted by the new world around him, he decided to see as much as he could, whether or not he found his brothers. Luckily, before he had gotten far from the building, he met his anxious siblings, hurrying up after missing him at the station. After this bumpy beginning, the rest of the visit turned out well, and the novel sights and sounds, the crowds and the excitement left Edwin wide-eyed.[13] It is not hard to imagine that this episode served to whet his lifelong thirst for adventure. And his decision to explore the fair, without guidance or supervision, is suggestive of his later pattern of venturing into situations that more cautious persons would avoid.

In Grandfather Fee's household, there was little money for such jaunts outside Berea. Cash for clothing was not readily available, and the youngest child was usually clad in hand-me-downs, even in pants made over from his sisters' skirts. But the family was by no means destitute; they owned musical instruments and enjoyed making music. As an adolescent, Embree learned to play the guitar and mandolin, and he performed with a local sextet, as well as in a family quartet with his three brothers.[14]

There is no evidence that Embree suffered from the circumstances of his upbringing. On the contrary, his ability as an adult to concentrate on the task at hand, to work problems through to realistic solutions, can be traced to these early experiences. Similarly, the straitened circumstances of his youth taught him to be comfortable with the physical goods available. Far from developing a thirst for great possessions, he lived in rented quarters for most of his adulthood, never owned a car, and often lacked even such useful accoutrements as a fountain pen or a cigarette lighter.[15]

The influence of his maternal grandfather on Embree's beliefs and outlooks, particularly in regard to racial matters, is beyond dispute. Yet on his father's side as well there were forebears who had sought to free America's black population. Family lore identifies Manhattan lawyer Lawrence Embree, who in the late eighteenth century was a member of the New York Manumission Society, one of the more important anti-slavery groups at the time.[16] Edwin's father came from a long line of Philadelphia-area Quakers, who apparently shared in the anti-slavery traditions of that group. Though no direct evidence of William Norris Embree's views on slavery has been discovered, the fact that he and his father enlisted in the Union Army, thereby violating the pacifist beliefs of most Quakers, is perhaps indicative of abolitionist convictions. Of the views of William's sister Elizabeth Embree Rogers, Edwin's aunt, there can be no doubt. Not only did she attend abolitionist Oberlin College but, knowing something of the difficulties ahead, she and her preacher husband still chose to leave a comfortable pastorate in Illinois to start a "higher school" for black and white youth in Berea. Driven out of Kentucky in 1859, she and her husband returned to the racially integrated town after the Civil War, where she was joined first by her brother, then by their father. There she remained, teaching and counseling black and white students alike, until ill health forced her to relinquish those duties in the 1880s.[17]

An even more striking example of anti-slavery sentiment involves a collateral branch of the family in eastern Tennessee. A 1797 issue of the *Knoxville Gazette* carried a letter from Pennsylvania-born Quaker Thomas Embree, calling on "public spirited citizens of every denomination" to unite in efforts to bring about "a gradual abolition of slavery of every kind."[18] Thomas Embree's son Elihu, a prominent ironmonger and industrialist, became a leading figure in the Manumission Society of Tennessee, organized in 1815. Elihu Embree was probably the author of an impassioned document sent to the state legislature, in which the Declaration of Independence and the book of Romans were quoted in support of manumission. In 1820, a decade before William Lloyd Garrison's publication of the same name, Elihu Embree began to publish the monthly *Emancipator,* the first periodical in the United States devoted entirely to opposition to slavery. The militant tone of the publication quickly attracted a subscription list of 2,000, but Elihu's death, at age thirty-eight, resulted in its cessation at the end of that year.[19]

Thus, Edwin's lineage on both sides, stretching back for several generations, included active opponents of slaveholding. Following the Civil War and emancipation, this fundamentally humane commitment found expression in efforts to counter various forms of racial discrimination. Grandfather Fee was naturally quite prominent in those efforts, and his example had a lasting effect not only on those reared in his household, but even on their descendants.[20] As the youngest grandchild, and the one who lived longest with him, Edwin was probably the most profoundly affected.

One of the things young Edwin absorbed from his grandfather was the understanding that personal attitudes are not immutable, that even the most adamant outlooks can be changed. On the occasions when the boy joined the old man as he drove his phaeton around town, Reverend

Fee would sometimes stop to chat amicably with a man encountered along the way. Moving down the road, Fee would sometimes point out that, thirty years earlier, the man had been a staunch defender of slavery, had considered Fee his archenemy, and had even threatened his life.[21] The message young Edwin picked up was that an unyielding stand on principle, coupled with exemplary behavior and persistent advocacy, could in time change both hearts and minds. That understanding, deeply etched into his character in those formative years, would undergird much of his activity later in life.

That John G. Fee was the most powerful person in young Edwin's life is beyond question. The influence of other relatives, however, is less certain. For all practical purposes, his father was out of Edwin's life well before he reached school age. While William Embree figures in the correspondence of his other children, in none of Edwin's extant writings is his father mentioned. And if he ever talked with his own children about their Grandfather Embree, they do not remember it. Edwin's mother, on the other hand, was an important presence.

Laura Fee Embree was a delicate, sweet-tempered, deeply pious woman, with the clear-eyed, direct gaze that marked her youngest son. Her letters are thickly sprinkled with biblical quotations and warnings against the evil temptations of the world. While occasionally minding the Berea store managed by her husband right after their marriage, she mused on the moral qualities of individual customers as they came in. Seeing small children, she delighted in their innocence, "their simple, sweet faces," and pondered if and how they would "fall into sin." Living an upright life according to Christian principles was her great preoccupation.[22] Such principles, and such a life pattern, she sought tirelessly to inculcate in her children, perhaps in Edwin even more than the others.

As the youngest child, Edwin was his mother's favorite. Her expectations of him were higher than those she held for her other children.[23] To the end of her life, she expected him to enter the ministry, and even after he had left home she continued to offer guidance. During his first year of college, they exchanged long, news-filled letters, establishing a pattern of family correspondence that Edwin would follow with his own children. In one such letter, written to her "dear, dear Nibsie" less than three months before her death, Laura Embree provided her "Sweet Seventh" with a litany of dos and don'ts. When considering jobs for the coming summer, he should be sure to avoid those that would require him to work on Sunday. When he later prepared for the ministry, he should be careful to select the proper kind of theological school. He should be careful "to keep company with Godly girls," avoiding those who were "worldly," for that would risk "being blinded of Satan." He should be cautious about the kind of theatrical performances he attended. She asked for reassurance that he would neither play cards nor dance. Card playing was "too much the path to gambling for the Lord's people to touch it," while dancing was "the kindling for fornication and adultery." Statistics show, she reminded him, that "three-fourths of the young women in the houses of ill fame had their start in the round dance." As much as she would have enjoyed the motion and rhythm of the dance, she had always refrained, and she feared dancing would be as detrimental to him as either whiskey or cards. No other mention was made of strong drink for, a lifelong opponent of alcohol and tobacco like her father, she probably thought that lesson had been fully learned and needed no reinforcement.[24]

Embree was as devoted to his mother as she to him. His greatest punishment as a boy, he confided to a close friend, was the knowledge that something he had done had disappointed her. Indeed, her influence on his young life he considered second only to that of his grandfather.[25] His mother's nurturing devotion and the affection lavished on him by his older siblings undoubtedly were major elements in the formation of his personality. So, too, was the stability of his home environment once the family returned to Berea, the constant uprooting of his early years behind them. The order of his grandparents' home, the respect accorded his family, the steadiness of village life allowed him to reach early adulthood with a deep sense of personal security. He did not see the world as a threatening place. He felt no need to be wary of strangers, had no fear they might take advantage of him. From the circumstances of his upbringing, he developed the self-confidence and optimism that prepared him to meet the world on his own terms.

In the summer following his freshman year of college, knowing his mother was in poor health, he returned to Berea. He was there when she died in July, the day before his twentieth birthday. With her passing, his grandparents already gone, and his siblings scattered across the country, he no longer had close relatives in the Kentucky town. When he returned to New Haven, Connecticut, for his second year at Yale, he did not forget his mother's teachings. Yet the deep piety and straitlaced morality that marked her life would not typify his. College introduced him to many of the "temptations" his mother had inveighed against. It also opened to him a world far removed from the frontier outposts of his childhood and the provincial hamlet of his youth.

* * *

Yale determined in large part the trajectory of Embree's life. At the time he began college, much in his life was unsettled, perhaps more than for most young men of his time. Even where he would choose to live was unclear. His two older sisters had married ranchers and remained in the West, one in Wyoming, another in Utah. His third sister was a missionary who had gone to Argentina. Two of his brothers had returned to Wyoming, and another, until his accidental death, had been in Nebraska. Thus, there were family connections and job possibilities in the West as well as in Kentucky. Moreover, his future career was uncertain. In spite of the family's expectation that he would enter the ministry, Edwin himself had shown no great enthusiasm for that prospect. Even so, when he left home for college, theological study still seemed the most likely option. These uncertainties would be largely resolved at Yale. Indeed, their resolution was primarily due to Yale.

When one considers the course of Embree's life, it quickly becomes clear that the Yale experience, both as a student and later as a staff member, was central to his development and prospects. Had he attended a less well-established university, it is hard to imagine how he could have acquired the sophistication that marked his adulthood. Had he not been a Yale graduate, he would not have been considered for the journalistic and administrative positions he would hold there for ten years. It was those administrative positions that allowed him to extend his range of acquaintances, establish a network of important connections, and acquire a sense of ease in dealing with men of impressive wealth, influence, and pedigree. Were it not for those connections, the cachet of his

Yale degrees, and his apparent confidence, it is unlikely the Rockefeller Foundation would have deemed him suitable for its second-highest executive position. And it was through Rockefeller that he came to know Julius Rosenwald, and through his subsequent management of Rosenwald's philanthropy that he would make his mark in the foundation world and on the national stage. Embree's life journey started in Osceola and passed through Berea; his career path began in New Haven.

Embree's decision to attend Yale strikes one at first as a bit surprising. Why would a young man born on the frontier and reared in a peculiar Kentucky village choose to study at one of the nation's most prestigious universities? Why not Oberlin, the school central to Berea College's early years, which the younger institution deliberately sought to imitate? Or why not attend Berea College itself, as four of his siblings had done? Why leave his mother and the only community he had ever known to travel to a distant city in a different part of the country, there to undertake studies he might well have pursued in a more familiar setting? Why Yale indeed?

Two reasons seem to explain Edwin's decision. For one thing, the paternal side of his family was from the Northeast. The American progenitor of the family, the England-born Robert Embree, had been resident in New Haven by 1643, and he had died in the neighboring town of Hamden. Even so, the family connection to Connecticut had long been severed, as Robert Embree's descendants had relocated to New York, New Jersey, and Pennsylvania. Edwin never developed much interest in these forebears, but perhaps the fact that the family roots were traceable to the region made it seem less alien than it otherwise might have. Far more important in his thinking, undoubtedly, was the presence in New Haven of a remarkable number of young men from Berea. Embree was part of a contingent of no fewer than six Bereans in the university town. One of those was his older brother William Dean Embree, who had transferred to Yale as a junior and, after completing his undergraduate degree, would earn both a law degree and a master's degree in Italian language and literature. The fact that his brother was there probably gave Yale a special appeal. Moreover, the fact that the other Bereans at Yale had academic preparation identical to his own undoubtedly encouraged belief that the university would present no unmanageable problems.[26]

Contrary to his expectations, however, the university refused to admit him. He had already moved to New Haven when he took Yale's entrance tests, only to learn a few days later that he had failed every one. Such an outcome would shake the confidence of most young men, but Edwin does not seem to have been unduly affected. Many years later, he confided to a friend that he had not questioned the quality of his secondary schooling, nor did he doubt his own intelligence and ability. The problem, he explained, was that he had never troubled to commit to memory important passages from his textbooks, and it was such memorization that the entrance tests emphasized. Unlike most other applicants, he had not known what to expect and consequently was not prepared for what he encountered.

Now, understanding what was required, Embree set about remedying his deficiencies. Unable to afford a private preparatory school, he enrolled as a senior in New Haven's public high school. His courtly manners and his southern drawl made him stand out among his classmates. Yet, far from feeling insecure about these traits, he seems to have adjusted readily to the school and to have been well liked by other students. After a year at the school, he retook the entrance examinations and was admitted to Yale without difficulty in 1902.[27]

* * *

Yale when Embree entered was not the complex and imposing institution of today. The undergraduate college at the turn of the twentieth century enrolled fewer than 1,300 students, with his own classmates numbering no more than 300. Students in an allied scientific school and the professional schools brought the total university enrollment to about 2,500. The college faculty, about ninety men altogether, were inclined to stress character building as much as scholarship. Apart from professional degrees, graduate work was not emphasized, with only 15 percent earning master's or doctoral degrees. The future direction of the institution, its curriculum, and the relationships among the various units were under active debate. The quadrangle was a bit scruffy, and the classroom buildings and dormitories were not always well maintained. But Yale had tradition, a deep sense of itself, and a consequent spirit that infected its students and impressed visitors.[28]

One such visitor, a decade before Embree's arrival, was George Santayana. Then a young philosophy instructor at Harvard, Santayana was struck by the diverse geographic origins of the student body and concluded that this fact made each student initially a stranger, hence almost forced to make friends to avoid personal isolation. Thus, relations that developed between students were "simple and direct," leading to a "sort of primitive brotherhood, with a ready enthusiasm for every good or bad project, and a contagious good humor." The campus ambience was described by Santayana as marked by "sound, healthy principle[s], but no overscrupulousness, love of life, trust in success, a ready jocoseness, a democratic amiability." Like Santayana, most observers regarded Yale as highly conservative—"traditional in its habits, religious in its spirit, earnest and moral in its atmosphere, conforming in its opinion, old-fashioned in its education."[29]

Reinforcing Yale's traditions, indeed embodying them, was President Arthur Twining Hadley. In his daily chapel addresses, attended by all undergraduates, Hadley preached an enthusiastic moral idealism. Secure in his own deeply held convictions, he emphasized four cardinal attributes of Christian manhood: purposeful activity, loyalty, personal integrity, and intelligence.[30] Emphasis on such attributes was of course not new to Embree, for they had certainly been stressed by Grandfather Fee. But hearing them presented in a different situation, and with an eloquence and force not possible in an intimate family setting, undoubtedly served to embed them even more deeply into the young man's character. Idealism, forthrightness, an expectation of accomplishment, a zest for living, congruence between word and action—such qualities would mark Embree from the Yale years on. At the same time, the small scale of the college, combined with his natural affability, enabled him to establish warm relationships that he would maintain for the rest of his life. Yale became a central element in his personal identity.

* * *

To his New Haven high school classmates, Embree had seemed appropriately mature and confident, but that was not the case as he began his college career. He thought he was several months older than most Yale freshmen, yet in their presence he felt "young, green, and overwhelmed by [their] maturity." Most of the young men he looked up to struck him as "seasoned and world-wise." A virgin until his senior year, he imagined he might be the least sexually experienced member of his class.[31] While some measure of unease is common among beginning college students, for Embree that sense was unusually acute, and it apparently extended well beyond his first few months at Yale.

That Embree felt insecure in the collegiate setting is not surprising. His small town upbringing in Kentucky simply had not prepared him for the sophistication of the northeastern students. What is striking is how well he overcame his sense of social inferiority. In large part, this was due to the efforts of some of his classmates. Perhaps they were drawn to him by some aspect of his character. Or perhaps they simply found him a congenial companion. In any event, several undertook to help him adjust, to introduce him to the pleasures of undergraduate life, and to hone his social skills. They did their work well, for over the next few years Embree became increasingly aware of his own competence and comfortable in settings that had earlier made him ill at ease. His growing confidence notwithstanding, he remained somewhat diffident in the presence of older, prestigious men until well after his graduation.[32]

Embree had arrived in New Haven with a total of fifty cents in his pocket, less than twenty dollars to his name, and no prospect of significant financial help from his family. Thus, it was necessary for the eighteen-year-old to find ways to support himself, even during the year at the high school. Remarkable ingenuity and perseverance were required to meet his expenses. He took a room over a funeral parlor and obtained his meals by waiting tables, first at a boardinghouse, later at an ice cream shop. He served as a gardener for a local doctor, then landed a job tending furnaces. Once enrolled at Yale, he gained his board at the college's dining hall by printing menus on a small printing press he set up in the basement. To meet incidental expenses, he monitored chapel attendance, distributed handbills for a political candidate, assembled toys in a department store. During the summer following his sophomore year, he worked a lonely job as a sheepherder at the Wyoming ranch owned by his eldest sister and her husband. Returning to Yale, he met some of his expenses by keeping books for a tailor, while he also held numerous short-term jobs: selling suits for two-year-olds, wrapping bundles in a dry-goods store, addressing envelopes, serving as a water company inspector, typing other students' papers, taking dictation from an Episcopal priest, occasional tutoring. Beginning to write as a means to supplement his uncertain income, he managed to sell several pieces on college life to New York newspapers and occasionally contributed articles to a local paper. Throughout his undergraduate years, Embree proved resourceful in finding employment, jobs of varying responsibility that enabled him both to earn enough to cover his expenses and to develop new skills. His early success in getting published led him, by his senior year, to decide on a career in journalism.[33] The idea of entering the ministry had been left far behind.

The need to earn his own keep while maintaining a full load of courses meant that Embree had less free time than the typical Yale student. Yet he seems to have been as active in extracurricular affairs as most of his classmates. As a freshman, he joined the banjo and mandolin club, an organization he managed in his senior year. As an upperclassman, he made arrangements for intercollegiate debate competitions and took part in various literary activities. He joined a fraternity and played intramural baseball.[34] A member of the class of 1906, he was able to take advantage of a new undergraduate curriculum that allowed more electives after the freshman year. Under this curriculum, Embree chose a concentration in mental, historical, and social sciences, with emphasis on the last of these.

Embree's choice of major field brought him into the classroom of the renowned sociologist William Graham Sumner. As Yale's first professor of political and social sciences, Sumner had introduced America's first university course in sociology in 1875. The country's foremost Social Darwinian, he had pioneered study of the evolution of human customs and originated the concept of ethnocentrism.[35] Embree found Sumner's lectures interesting and inspiring, but he was most affected by the way the professor opened up for students "the vistas of diverse social systems all over the world. He lured us into balancing the quaint habits of Samoan chiefs and dancing girls against the equally quaint habits of New Haven bankers and debutantes. He sent us scurrying to the libraries to read about the Fijians, the Papuans, and the Hottentots, about

British peers, French raconteurs, and German savants." Moreover, he inspired many of his students to travel to remote parts of the globe to "observe for ourselves the fascinating ways of life which people had built up for themselves."[36] To Sumner's influence, then, can be traced Embree's lifelong thirst for overseas travel, his wide-ranging curiosity, and his fascination with cultural distinctions. The sociologist was nearing retirement by the time Embree entered his classroom, and he probably never imagined how deeply he had influenced the life of this young undergraduate.

Embree was a conscientious student, increasingly so as his academic career progressed. By his junior year, his grades had earned him a "dissertation appointment," the highest of three levels of academic recognition then in effect at Yale. Yet there is no evidence that his life was a grind, or that he lacked social outlets and friends. In an entering class numbering a bit more than 300, he was one of only 6 white students (2 others were black) from below the Mason-Dixon line. His Kentucky background quickly resulted in the nickname "Colonel," a designation his classmates continued to use long after graduation. He seems to have been widely known and liked, and he was best friends with one of the wittiest and most popular members of the class.[37] After graduation, his regular attendance at annual class dinners, even when he lived far from New Haven, reflected a deep and abiding affection for his alma mater.

While study and work claimed most of Embree's waking hours, he still had time for romance. During his year at the New Haven high school, he had met an attractive girl a year his junior, Kate Clarke. Theirs had been no more than a casual acquaintance, with neither paying particular attention to the other. That changed three years later, when Embree began to make his plans for Yale's junior prom. More than a dance, the prom involved a four-day-long weekend, requiring such extravagances as a Prince Albert coat, flowers for one's young lady, and transportation by carriage to various events. If one's date came from out of town, hotel expenses, for which the man was responsible, could easily drive total costs above $200. Such expenditures were well beyond Embree's limited means, though he figured he could manage the flowers and the transportation. The dress coat he finagled from the tailor whose books he kept. Far more important for the future, he avoided the hotel expenses by inviting a local girl, Miss Clarke. The weekend apparently was a great success for both; three years later, Kate Clarke became Mrs. Edwin Embree.[38]

The daughter of a Canada-born realtor and his wife, Kate was an attractive, willowy young woman. Her father's real estate business had been quite successful, and Kate had been reared in comfortable circumstances in New Haven. Yet the family had not been free of difficulty. The two eldest daughters had died of diphtheria while still children, and an infant son had been taken by cholera. An undated family portrait shows Kate, not yet an adolescent, with her parents and a younger brother and sister. All are somber, and about the eyes and mouths of all but the youngest there is an unmistakable air of sadness.[39]

Not long after that picture was taken, Kate's mother became chronically ill. She remained in that state for several years before dying when Kate was in her mid-teens. Subsequently, as the oldest female in the family, it fell to Kate to maintain the household, cook the meals, and care for her younger siblings and their father. Partly as a consequence of these duties, and because higher education was not then customary for young women, Kate never attended college. She was, however, a voracious reader, and she remained one throughout her life. It even seems likely that, at the time of her marriage, she was better read than her college-educated husband. Their marriage took place in 1907, following a year during which Embree commuted regularly on weekends between New Haven and New York.[40]

Receiving his baccalaureate degree in 1906, Embree had immediately moved to Manhattan as a cub reporter for the *New York Sun*. Under the guidance of seasoned reporters, he began to sharpen his writing skills. His initial assignments, covering the Jefferson Market Police Court, brought him into contact with some of the seamier sides of urban life. During a hot political campaign, he wrote several articles against William Randolph Hearst, the facts for which he "raked up in the police court mire."[41] After some months, he was assigned to do pieces on the New York drama scene. Attendance at such performances intensified, if it did not initiate, his lifelong interest in the theater, with his developed tastes ranging from Shakespeare to Broadway musicals.

Embree's employment as a New York reporter lasted only one year. Yet its effect on his development should not be underestimated. The year gave him a chance to enhance his skill with language. His later writing, over a dozen books and more than fifty magazine articles, shows the benefits of this journalistic training. The remarkable clarity of his prose, often written against tight deadlines, owed much to that year's experience. His public addresses, increasingly numerous as his life progressed, and usually given without notes, were no less vivid and forceful. Equally important, his work as a reporter introduced him to the variety of big city life, a variety scarcely imaginable on the western frontier or in a Kentucky village. Urban living captivated him, and the small town setting he knew no longer held any appeal. Throughout the latter half of his life, he resided in the two largest cities in the United States. Before that, however, New Haven claimed him for a decade.

* * *

A year after leaving New Haven, Embree returned as the assistant editor of the *Yale Alumni Weekly,* a publication recently purchased by the New York writer Clarence Day. Having graduated from Yale several years before Embree, Day was from a family with strong connections to the university.[42] His plan, shared by several other Yale men, was to make the *Weekly* an instrument for spreading the best ideas of the university's scholarship and institutional life. Embree's role as assistant editor was to help bring that plan to fruition.

Clarence Day soon became one of the most important figures in Embree's life. They were frequently in touch during Embree's time in New Haven, and when Embree later moved to New York, they attended the theater together, often followed by conversations extending well into the early morning. Still later, after Embree left New York for Chicago, they exchanged long, confidential letters, and whenever Embree returned to Manhattan, he stayed in the Day home. Their correspondence, like their lengthy discussions, ranged over a variety of topics: the greatness of ancient Egypt, the nature of human goodness, the need for beauty in life, the inexorability of time, the proper role of philanthropy. No topic was off-limits, and vigorous disagreement was common. Embree once described their talks as "the best things in my life."[43]

As Day's literary reputation grew, beginning with publication of *This Simian World* in 1920 and followed by the highly popular *Life with Father* fifteen years later, Embree sought his advice about his own writing career. Embree looked up to Day, and not only for the latter's literary success. Their correspondence reveals Day's custom of challenging Embree's thinking, forcing him to clarify and articulate his views. As a consequence, Embree credited the older man for his own intellectual awakening. He enjoyed Day's companionship and admired his general cheerfulness, in spite of crippling arthritis that occasionally made him cranky. He valued as well his friend's warm generosity, typified by Day's offer to assist him financially when the collapse of the stock market plunged Embree deeply into debt. Apart from his grandfather, Day influenced him more profoundly than any other man. He was the closest friend Embree ever had.[44]

In addition to his work at the *Yale Alumni Weekly*, Embree in 1910 was appointed to the newly created university post of director of the Class Secretaries Bureau. As the first person to hold that office, he was instrumental in defining its duties and establishing its policies. He continued with those responsibilities when, a year later, he was named alumni registrar. The latter position brought with it the rank of assistant professor, making Embree the first member of his class to receive such an appointment at Yale, a development he reported with no small pride to his classmates. In 1910, he also began taking courses in education. In light of his new situation, Embree resigned from his editorial work at the *Yale Alumni Weekly*. His interest in the publication remained strong, however, and he continued to submit occasional articles to it and, a decade later, would serve on its three-member management board.[45]

Embree's new professional responsibilities were accompanied by changing responsibilities at home. In 1909, he and Kate had their first child, a son. In recognition of his grandfather's influence in Embree's life, their son was named after him: John Fee Embree. Two years later, a daughter joined the family. The parents probably did not expect to have other children, for Embree believed strongly in family planning and the importance of limiting population growth. With a second son unlikely, therefore, and a daughter who could not be a "junior," there would be no one to carry forward Embree's name. No written record suggests that having a namesake mattered much to Embree, but if that was an issue, it was readily resolved. Their daughter, called "Eddy" throughout her life, was given her father's name with one additional letter: Edwina Rogers Embree.

Embree's duties placed him under the supervision of the secretary of the university, Anson Phelps Stokes. Ten years Embree's senior, Stokes played an influential role in university affairs, and under his direction, Embree took on a variety of responsibilities. He arranged alumni meetings all over the country, planned university events, handled publications, made arrangements for guest speakers, and dealt with public relations generally. Impressed by the younger man's "vigorous and vital personality," Stokes came to regard Embree as the best man in alumni affairs in the country.[46] As Stokes's principal assistant, Embree occasionally substituted for the secretary when he was away from campus for an extended period.[47] During these years, Embree edited an anthology of pieces about life at Yale, and he and a classmate put together a history of their own class.[48] With Stokes as mentor, he learned how to establish administrative procedures and office routines, experience that would prove invaluable in the future. Success in his initial positions led in 1914 to greater responsibilities as the secretary of the Bureau of Appointments. That same year, he completed a master's degree.

The responsibilities of the Bureau of Appointments bridged several areas of college life involving assistance to students. Managing student employment was a major activity, and Embree's own experience of working his way through Yale proved to be valuable preparation for those duties. By his second year in the office, reported student earnings approached a quarter of a million dollars, with a substantial portion secured directly through the bureau. Related to student employment was the university's program of financial aid, and that too became Embree's responsibility. The scholarships and fellowships he administered, many of which were funded by Yale alumni clubs, together with loans had a total value of almost $100,000. Beyond these duties, Embree was responsible for job placement for graduating seniors. In this connection, as the university undertook to improve student guidance, he began to give talks to seniors about possible professions and appropriate preparation. These talks proved so successful, perhaps owing to his growing competence as a public speaker, that a number of underclassmen attended them as well.[49]

Like his work at the *Yale Alumni Weekly* and preparation of the volume on life at Yale, Embree's duties at the Bureau of Appointments brought him into contact with alumni clubs across the country, with individual graduates, and with graduates-to-be. While deepening his ties to the university, these interactions undoubtedly strengthened his confidence in dealing with men of influence, many of whom became part of his personal network. Similarly, he broadened his relationships within the academic world. He was a leading figure in the creation of a national organization of college and university alumni secretaries.[50] Also important was a lecture series that brought to campus university presidents, which gave Embree the opportunity to meet Alexander Meiklejohn of Amherst, A. Lawrence Lowell of Harvard, and George Vincent of Minnesota.[51] Such professional and personal connections, the mentoring of Anson Phelps Stokes, and the generally broadening experience of those years prepared the young man for new responsibilities.

* * *

Late in 1916, Embree was at work in his Yale office when he was summoned to a telephone call from New York City. Thinking the call was a hoax, he was initially inclined to dismiss it. He soon realized his mistake. The person on the other end of the line was in fact John D. Rockefeller Jr. Would Embree come down to discuss a position with the Rockefeller Foundation?

All that underlay that call, who or what first brought Embree to the younger Rockefeller's attention, is not entirely clear. Frederick Gates, the central figure in Rockefeller Sr.'s philanthropies, may have known of the young university administrator through his three sons who graduated from Yale during Embree's tenure there. Or Anson Phelps Stokes, a trustee of the Rockefeller-funded General Education Board (GEB), may have put his name forward. The incoming foundation head, George E. Vincent, who for some years had been acquainted with Embree through an informal group known as the Association of University Handymen, undoubtedly was significantly involved. What is certain is that the post was first offered to Embree's lawyer brother, William Dean Embree, who had impressed Rockefeller Jr. through his work as head of the Voluntary Defenders Committee of New York, a Rockefeller-supported project to provide legal aid to the indigent. Unwilling to leave a promising legal career, the elder Embree declined the offer, but suggested that his brother might be just the man the foundation was looking for.[52]

A few days after the phone call, Embree took the train for New York and the Rockefeller philanthropies' headquarters at 61 Broadway. What impressed his interviewers favorably is not known. Like several Rockefeller executives, he had risen from humble beginnings, and that may have resonated with such self-made men.[53] The fact that he had worked his way through college—and a prestigious institution at that—while earning a creditable academic record was indicative of energy and initiative. His abolitionist ancestry and views on race provided common ground with the younger Rockefeller, as did the deeply pious circumstances of his upbringing. Both men were familiar with mealtime gatherings for Bible reading and prayer, and with repeated admonitions to avoid tobacco and alcohol, dancing and card playing.[54] And though no established model for a successful foundation executive existed at that early date, Embree's experience in university administration fit what was soon to become a pattern of exchange between the academy and organized philanthropy. Whatever considerations came into play, the interview proved highly successful, and the proffered appointment was readily accepted.

Arrangements were made for Embree to begin part-time work at Rockefeller almost immediately, while retaining his duties at Yale until the end of the academic year. The university had been good to him, and the decade and a half in New Haven had left an indelible mark on his personality. His undergraduate experience had quickened his imagination and introduced him to a world far beyond his youthful provincialism. His journalistic and administrative work had honed skills that would serve him the rest of his life. Through Yale, he had made invaluable contacts, and interactions with people of high social standing had deepened his poise. Moreover, he had been steeped in an ethos that stressed enthusiastic living, a profound sense of purpose, and significant professional achievement. He recognized the power, and the presumed responsibilities, of the nation's elites, and he had no doubt that he belonged in that company. Without the foundation laid at Yale, his subsequent career is scarcely imaginable.

On January 1, 1917, Embree assumed the post of secretary of the Rockefeller Foundation. At age thirty-three, he had become the second-highest official of the organization which, with its related boards, constituted the richest philanthropy in the world. Osceola, Nebraska, and Berea, Kentucky, lay far behind him.

TWO

LEARNING PHILANTHROPY: FROM APPRENTICE TO MASTER CRAFTSMAN

At the time Embree arrived at 61 Broadway, the Rockefeller Foundation was very much a work in progress. It shared office space with the General Education Board (GEB), a Rockefeller-endowed trust established to aid education without restrictions of race, sex, or creed. A decade younger than the GEB, the foundation had a far broader purpose: "to promote the well-being of mankind throughout the world." Such a sweeping mandate neither determined direction nor limited possibilities; programs, organizational structure, operating principles, even its relation to other Rockefeller trusts remained to be determined. For some months after its 1913 incorporation, the philanthropy had consisted of no more than a secretary, a clerical worker, and a four-drawer file cabinet. Reorganization in 1916 had created the office of president, thereby downgrading the secretary from the chief executive to the number two position. The subsequent resignation of the first occupant of the secretary's post, Jerome D. Greene, had created the vacancy Embree filled.[1]

In his move to Rockefeller, Embree joined the remarkable group of social reformers who made up the first generation of philanthropy executives. Far more than most Americans, these men (and a few women) were acutely aware of the enormous changes sweeping over the country: distances shrunk by telegraph and rail, waves of unfamiliar immigrants choking coastal cities, industrialization churning ahead, urbanization proceeding apace, international events increasingly affecting domestic affairs. With those changes came daunting problems, placing new and pressing demands on governmental bodies for practical solutions. Yet with congestion in the cities, crime, prostitution, disease, and political corruption obviously on the rise, government at all levels seemed too slow, too unimaginative to provide remedies. A handful of philanthropic trusts—prominent among them the Rockefeller Foundation and the GEB—sought to address these problems and, in the process, to affect public policy. Their efforts placed them squarely within the Progressive movement.

Though not quite a member of that initial generation himself, Embree shared, or soon came to share, their outlooks and values. As an impressionable student and junior administrator at Yale during the heyday of Progressivism, he had inevitably been influenced by it. The movement had begun to lose steam after the Great War, but it was still in evidence in Alfred E. Smith's New York, then home to most of the nation's philanthropies. At the heart of Progressivism lay the conviction that human existence could be elevated, institutions made more effective, and in time, "human nature" improved. The road to such improvement, many Progressives believed, required the systematic study and analysis of society's problems, using particularly the scientific and statistical methods of the developing social sciences. The increasing sophistication of those disciplines seemed to promise the knowledge and tools necessary for social reform. Embree quickly adopted that perspective, and from his new colleagues he learned that the central role of philanthropy was to foster such study, fund projects of experimentation and demonstration, and make available for public adoption the effective innovations thus identified.[2] And, recognizing the magnitude of the problems and the urgent need for relief, Embree, like his public policy–oriented colleagues, was motivated by what has been called "a fierce kind of optimism."[3] Brought face-to-face with such momentous issues and that sense of urgency, he encountered at Rockefeller headquarters a far headier atmosphere than he could have imagined.

* * *

During his first six months at Rockefeller, Embree divided his time between Yale and the foundation, commuting between New Haven and New York, in order to complete the academic year at his university post. Also completing the year at his own institution was George E. Vincent, who assumed the foundation presidency only in midsummer. Consequently, for the first half of 1917, Embree was the de facto chief executive of the foundation. Midway through this time, U.S. entry into World War I began to force the reconsideration of philanthropic priorities. New to the work, and the least experienced man at Rockefeller headquarters, Embree seems to have played a minimal role in those deliberations. Understandably, he was not inclined to be overly forward, and though he had some definite interests, he did not promote any kind of personal agenda.

These initial months inevitably involved some awkwardness and uncertainty. Embree had an impressive title, which in the hands of its previous holder had entailed real authority, but the reorganization had left Embree's attendant responsibilities ill defined. Though forced to act as chief executive, he lacked the background, to say nothing of the stature, of his colleagues on the other Rockefeller boards. As a consequence, he occasionally had trouble finding exactly the right tone in dealing with them. His interoffice correspondence at times fluctuated between somewhat overdrawn respect and what may have struck his associates as officiousness, even presumption.[4] The arrival of Vincent, together with Embree's own obvious good humor, soon served to relieve the situation. Increasingly secure in his position, and with the guidance of the man he called "Chief," Embree settled into his duties.

Many of those duties quickly became routine. He notified corporation members of elections, committee assignments, and meetings. He prepared dockets for the meetings, attended them, and wrote the official minutes. He signed contracts and agreements and co-signed checks. He had custody of the corporate seal and maintained all official records. And he performed general administrative functions under the supervision of the president, which included handling most of the office's correspondence.[5]

As he gained experience in the position, Embree took on additional responsibilities. Interviews with a steady stream of office visitors came to consume a good deal of his time. It fell to him to explain the areas of foundation interest and funding policies, often referring applicants to other Rockefeller-funded agencies, particularly the General Education Board. Though he often found himself discouraging applications to the foundation, when a promising appeal for funding was received, he commonly conducted the initial investigation of the proposed project and the applicant's suitability for support. He also was involved in the activities of two of the foundation's operating boards. He attended meetings and prepared the minutes of the International Health Board (IHB), and for several years he served as secretary of the China Medical Board (CMB).[6] As a consequence of such involvement, after a year and a half of what amounted to an apprenticeship, he began to travel extensively on Rockefeller business.

In mid-1918, with German U-boats still prowling the North Atlantic, Embree crossed the ocean to France. Some months earlier, the government of Georges Clemenceau had asked the IHB to assist in combating the tuberculosis that had spread widely during the war. That board had sent a commission which, in the unoccupied sections of the country, had set up dispensaries, established facilities for training nurses to diagnose the disease, and worked to increase the number of available hospital beds. Embree's assignment was to evaluate this program, review the budget, determine what more needed to be done, and develop recommendations for further funding. Not all of his time was spent in Paris. He traveled toward the front, visiting the Marne and Château-Thierry, crossing "torn and mangled" fields, motoring over roads lined on one side with trucks carrying ammunition forward and, on the other, with ambulances returning the wounded to the rear. After almost three months abroad, he returned to the United States late in September, a few weeks before the end of hostilities.[7]

This was only Embree's second venture outside the United States, coming several years after a tourist visit to London and Paris. But the trip seems to have whetted his appetite for international travel, and that appetite remained voracious throughout his life. Moreover, this initial overseas assignment served as a precedent for much of his activity during his years at Rockefeller. Established to promote human welfare "around the world," the foundation had contacts and projects in many sections of the globe. In the decade following the First World War, activities were concentrated in Europe and East Asia, and Embree went repeatedly to both continents. Indeed, he seemed ready to go whenever overseas work was in the offing, even when the assignment meant months away from home and family. Even his travel within the United States was extensive.

Embree's first domestic travel assignment carried him to Cincinnati, Ohio. There, in 1919, he spent four days visiting an experimental "social unit" in a formerly fashionable neighborhood, then populated by poor German Americans. Embree's job was to assess the effectiveness of this externally funded project, with an eye to possible Rockefeller support. The project involved the intensive, block-by-block organization of some 14,000 people for medical care, health education, and community administration.

In making his assessment, Embree ranged widely, talking with an attorney, a bank cashier, a druggist, a saloon keeper, a librarian, the neighborhood medical council, block workers, volunteers, businesspeople, and the city's health officer. He was favorably impressed with the public health measures, but discovered strong opposition from the city administration. In fact, the mayor accused the project of working against American governmental traditions and charged its officials with "Bolshevism."[8] With this firsthand introduction to some of the problems of social experimentation and having seen a vivid example of the current "Red scare," Embree returned to New York. After concluding that the project was too costly to be successfully replicated elsewhere, and knowing the Rockefeller Foundation's reluctance to arouse controversy, he did not recommend foundation support.

The year 1920 found Embree back in Europe. This trip would last more than three months, requiring the longest separation from his family that Embree had yet experienced. Left at the Brooklyn apartment were Kate, eleven-year-old John, nine-year-old Edwina, and an infant daughter, Catherine, born the previous fall. She would be approaching her first birthday when her father returned from this latest journey abroad.

Late in June, he arrived in Paris to confer again with the administrators of the tuberculosis commission and to explore how Rockefeller could aid in the expansion of nurse training. The larger purpose of his trip, however, was to determine how the foundation could help to improve health care overall, which had been profoundly disrupted throughout the Continent. A related concern was the restoration of medical research and scientific investigation in general. Seeking to grasp the desperate situation, Embree embarked on a journey that took him to major cities and universities in Switzerland, Austria, Czechoslovakia, Hungary, Romania, Bulgaria, and the new Kingdom of Serbs, Croats, and Slovenes. Then he was off to Germany for one week and Poland for two. Part of this time, he was accompanied by members of the commission, Colonel F. F. Russell of the IHB, and representatives of the Red Cross. In Vienna, he was joined by Dr. Simon Flexner of the Rockefeller Institute for Medical Research, who provided valuable counsel as together they inspected various health and research facilities. Back in Paris in mid-September, he then left for London by airplane.[9]

Commercial air travel was still in its infancy and notoriously risky. Indeed, the route Embree flew, from Le Bourget to Hounslow field, was the world's first daily scheduled international flight. His decision to fly, in an open cockpit exposed to wind, cold, and deafening noise, on a route inaugurated only the year before, was indicative of his adventurous spirit. The experience delighted him, and he marveled at the speed of the passage—250 miles in two hours and five minutes. And he was enchanted by the aerial view of the French countryside, the English Channel, and "the rolling, sheep-dotted fields of Southern England."[10] At the end of the month, he sailed for home.

During this journey, Embree continued a pattern, begun during his 1918 trip to France, of carefully maintaining what he called a "family journal." There, he not only listed the places he visited and the people he met, but summarized his observations, impressions, and conclusions about each country. These richly detailed accounts, typed in multiple copies and mailed back to the United States, helped to keep him in touch with relatives and friends while abroad. At the same time, they provided an avenue for self-expression, easing the frustration he felt as a writer limited to preparing inevitably dry reports and recommendations for the home office. Commonly running up to thirty pages, the journals offered information and insights not readily available in that less-traveled time. Embree would write such logs throughout his overseas travels, and as his powers of observation and description deepened, they became increasingly fascinating to read, treasured by those who received them. As a supplement to the formal officer's diary maintained throughout his Rockefeller years, the journals occasionally found their way into files right alongside official documents.

Though Embree's 1920 journal contains much serious commentary, it also reveals that he was able to enjoy himself and even to respond lightheartedly to the vicissitudes of international travel. Faced with a labor stoppage that suspended train service from Vienna to Budapest, he took pleasure in a slow but "beautiful sail" down the Danube. In Cracow, he was charmed by a theatrical performance that included some spoken Japanese. Passing through Polish villages, he was impressed by the zest and harmony with which military troops sang as they marched. In Paris on U.S. Independence Day, he visited the Luxembourg Gardens and the Parc Montsouris and attended mass at Saint-Sulpice, primarily to hear its great organ. Needing a new dress shirt for a formal reception, he summoned the courage to attempt to buy one at a fashionable department store.[11]

Aided by a helpful salesgirl, but hampered by his limited French, he managed to determine the proper size (in centimeters) only after considerable discussion. Then, after selecting a shirt from several proffered, he discovered that, to pay for it, he had to go through an elegantly attired male floorwalker and two equally well-dressed cashiers. The transaction took the greater part of an hour. Reflecting on the inefficiency of the French, but marveling at their ability "to carry art and beauty into their everyday life," he brought the shirt back to his hotel room. Only when he slipped it over his head, and it dangled to his ankles, did he realize he had purchased a nightshirt![12]

Beyond its human appeal, Embree's 1920 journal was of interest for its political and social content. Not only did it concern areas of Europe unfamiliar to most Americans but, written less than two years after the Armistice, it addressed as well how individual countries were recovering from the war's devastation. He found Serbia "invaded" and overrun by pretentious, competing, and ineffective relief agencies, not short of food but needing advice in educational development, agricultural rehabilitation, and public health. Elsewhere in the federated kingdom, as in Hungary and Czechoslovakia, he discovered rapid recovery, and, barring another cataclysm in Central Europe, he considered their futures assured. Poland, on the other hand, then engaged in war with Bolshevik Russia, he believed needed "real and lasting peace" before it could emerge from "its present poverty and woe." Vienna seemed to him "a doomed city."

Travel in Germany—"land of *le Boche*"—made him uncomfortable, and after several days each in Berlin and Leipzig, he regarded that country simply as "an enigma."[13]

The Communist movement also drew Embree's attention. Though he did not go to Russia, he was well aware of insurrectionist groups active in several of the countries he did visit, and the consequent threats to public order. The night he arrived in Budapest, a man was killed in a restaurant by a hunger-mad mob. Elsewhere in Hungary, he recognized the linkage between anti-Communism and anti-Semitism. Oversimplifying perhaps for less knowing readers, he described the Red Terror as "the terror of the Jews against the Gentiles" and the White Terror as the "persecution of the Israelites by their enemies." The term "Bolshevism" he found imprecise and, perhaps remembering its use by the mayor of Cincinnati, identified at least four different meanings current in Europe and the United States. The Bolsheviks in Russia, he believed, had actually gained public support as a consequence of "muddling Allied opposition" typified by the Western blockade and the Polish invasion. How to interpret this revolutionary ferment, and what its outcome might be, remained for him uncertain.[14]

Embree's travels had left him "not entirely pessimistic" about Europe's future, but deeply troubled by the near total breakdown of coal supplies, transportation, and administrative structures in the middle of the Continent. If medical care and public health similarly collapsed, he warned, "All Central Europe will be scourged with plagues of disease that may cause even more suffering than the breakdown in economic and government systems."[15] Prior to leaving the United States, he had expressed interest in extending Rockefeller activities in Europe to include general education and agricultural assistance, and he had explored such possibilities. But two months into his journey, while recognizing the needs in those areas, he concluded that medical education and public health alone represented a larger field than Rockefeller could "ever expect to occupy."[16] Thus, he believed that the foundation's activity should be limited to its traditional areas of interest. Specifically, he favored intervention to reverse the serious deterioration of medical schools in Warsaw, Cracow, Vienna, Budapest, Prague, and Zagreb.

Upon his return to New York, Embree made four recommendations to the Rockefeller Foundation board. British and American scientific journals had been largely absent from Continental universities since the middle of the war, and fluctuating exchange rates had made their renewal difficult. Embree proposed that Rockefeller subsidize the purchase of such publications and distribute them to selected institutions. Similarly, the war had resulted in the confiscation or destruction of large quantities of scientific apparatus. Embree proposed that the foundation underwrite its replacement. He recommended as well extending nurse training from its Paris base to urban centers in other countries. Finally, he recommended a program of fellowships for advanced study in the United States for promising young graduates, with the expectation that recipients would return to their home countries as leaders in innovation. The board approved all of these recommendations, and received as well Embree's preliminary reports on a future medical school in Belgrade and a possible expansion of a scientific bibliographic center in Zurich.[17] As it turned out, trustee approval marked only the beginning of these matters for Embree, for he continued to be engaged in the implementation of the new programs. The extension of nurse training in particular would bring him back to Europe three years later. But well before that occurred, he was called upon to familiarize himself with totally different problems on another continent.

* * *

After success in initiating reform of medical education in the United States, Rockefeller money had been committed to strengthening such training in China. To achieve this purpose, the foundation had established a subsidiary agency, the China Medical Board. The board's plan called for replacing several small, underfunded medical schools operating under missionary auspices with a new, modern facility in the nation's capital, with a second center to be established subsequently in Shanghai. Construction had begun in 1916 on the Peking Union Medical College (PUMC), as the new school was called. The fifty-nine campus buildings had been designed by an American architect but, to symbolize the Rockefeller commitment eventually to place the institution in Chinese hands, they were expensively styled to fit into the Chinese landscape. Thus, the walls were of brick similar to the gray of the Great Wall, the gracefully curving roofs were covered with costly green tile, and the eaves were elaborately decorated by local artisans.[18] It soon became clear, however, that the architect, who doubled as the building contractor, had badly underestimated construction costs. And because his fees for both responsibilities were a percentage of total building expenditures, he had little incentive to keep costs low. The financial picture had been further complicated by World War I, which had sharply increased purchase and shipping costs for all building materials that had to be imported. Changes in exchange rates, which caused Chinese silver currency to double in value, added to the problems.[19]

Annual operating costs also posed difficulties. In anticipation of beginning full operation in 1921, on-site officials submitted a proposed budget of $1.1 million to the Rockefeller board. Effective communication between Peking and New York had not been easy to maintain, especially during the war years, and the trustees had expected a budget less than half that amount. Long-distance negotiations over several months failed to reconcile the differences. With discussions at an impasse, the decision was made to send someone from foundation headquarters to resolve the disagreements. The problems, in both building costs and annual operating expenses, were large, and resolution probably should have been undertaken by a senior figure, such as President Vincent or perhaps Dr. Simon Flexner, head of the Rockefeller Institute for Medical Research and a Rockefeller Foundation trustee in close touch with the activities in China. Neither man was willing to take on the mission. Embree was sent instead.[20]

Embree understood budgets, and as the secretary for the CMB for more than two years, he was somewhat familiar with the situation in Peking. Even so, before sailing he sought to acquaint himself with medical school financing by spending two days in conversation with officials of the Yale Medical School. Those discussions allowed him to carry away a budget framework for the PUMC. Assured of Vincent's confidence that he would be successful in Peking, Embree pledged "to use all [his] abilities" to reduce the budget figures, but not "to press these matters to the point of personal or official rupture." The Rockefeller board had demanded containment of building expenditures and a reduction of 25 percent in the proposed 1921–1922 operating budget. The foundation secretary knew the task before him would not be easy.[21]

After sixteen days aboard ship, a stopover in Japan, and a rough, four-day journey overland through Korea, Embree arrived in Peking on July 25. He spent two days inspecting the new plant and being introduced to key figures. Included in these early activities was a dinner, reminiscent of his time in university administration, which was arranged for him to meet the handful of Yale graduates then resident in the capital. By the third day, he got down to the business at hand. He soon discovered that the building budget had ballooned an additional quarter-million dollars over the estimates of just six months earlier.[22]

Early discussions were not auspicious, for Embree probably struck some of his hosts initially as an uninformed interloper from distant New York, sent to interfere with their institutional dream. His presentation of the board's position caused considerable distress. The acting director of the school, Henry S. Houghton, expressed doubt that the positions of those in Peking and those in New York could be reconciled. His sentiments were echoed by the foundation's director of medical education, R. M. Pearce, who for some months had been involved in the project on the scene. Most resistant was the resident director, Roger S. Greene, an old China hand and brother of the man Embree had succeeded as foundation secretary. These three men, together with the school's original director, Franklin S. McLean, comprised the budget committee with which Embree was to negotiate.[23]

For the next three weeks, arduous discussions consumed day and night. Embree met repeatedly with the budget committee, and with its members individually, to go over program plans and staffing levels. He visited each department, asking questions and soliciting opinions about equipment needs, essential supplies, and other budget items. He consulted with the architectural staff about altering an old hospital for dormitory use instead of erecting an additional structure. He searched for other cost-cutting measures that could be taken in construction of the physical plant. His responsibilities weighed heavily on him, and he lay awake nights worrying about the slow pace of the negotiations. Midway through the process, Roger Greene wrote to President Vincent sharply criticizing both Embree's efforts and his attitude. By that time, the faculty was on the verge of revolt, demanding a clear statement of what Rockefeller headquarters was prepared to do financially for the next five years.[24]

By late August, after a period Embree described as "difficult, unpleasant and taxing," the job was essentially done. To George Vincent, who was soon to embark for Peking, he expressed the hope to "never have so bad a month again." Five buildings had been eliminated from the campus plans, and even after some necessary items had been added, the overall construction budget had been reduced $300,000–400,000. The annual budget also had been adjusted downward, with savings achieved primarily in staffing levels, reductions which Embree expected to be permanent. He had also been able to identify other potential economies.[25]

Reaching agreement on the budget adjustments did much to relieve Embree's anxiety, but he was still not at ease. He continued to feel pressure as final arrangements were made for the formal dedication of the school, with festivities to begin in mid-September. Participating in the planning, he had constantly in mind the impending arrival in Peking of not only President Vincent, his "Chief," but almost all of the foundation's trustees, a group of twelve led by board chair John D. Rockefeller Jr. And these were by no means the only dignitaries expected. The president of the American Medical Association was coming, as was the governor-general of the Philippines. The ambassadors to China of Cuba, Denmark, and Brazil were to be present. Even the president of China, along with the ministers of foreign affairs, interior, and education, were to take part in the formalities. And rounding out the list of distinguished guests were over a hundred medical missionaries drawn from across China and delegations of scientists from Britain and Japan, three continents, and the islands of the Pacific.[26] In describing the occasion, one historian avowed there had never been "another assemblage of intellectual might, of prestige, of diplomatic rank, and of global representation for the dedication of a medical school equal to that which converged on Peking for the week beginning September 15, 1921."[27] In light of the monumental scale of these dedicatory events, Embree's nervousness does not seem out of place.

The activities stretched over eight days. Each morning, there were two-hour clinics, with demonstrations in medicine, obstetrics, pathology, and various surgical specialties, followed by the reading of scientific papers. Afternoons were devoted to inspections of the new facilities, official receptions, and guided tours around Peking. Each evening saw an address on a medical topic of general interest, and on one occasion a recital on the school's newly installed great organ, only the second instrument of its kind in the country. And all the while, there were elegant dinners, formal teas, and luncheons sponsored by Chinese societies. The festivities culminated with the dedication proper, complete with a procession across the campus with PUMC faculty and visitors in academic regalia.[28]

His assignment completed and the ceremonies behind him, Embree immediately took a train through Korea en route to Japan. In Yokohama, he boarded the *Empress of Asia* for the voyage back to the States. Breaking the trip in Hawaii, he had a welcome reunion with his wife and children, who were spending the winter there. He had not seen them for over three months, but sooner than any of them wished, he had to leave for New York and the work awaiting him there. Thus began the third long separation from his young family, a pattern several times repeated during the peripatetic years at Rockefeller.

On the voyage home, Embree wrote a vivid and moving description of PUMC and the dedication ceremonies, expressing his appreciation for that ambitious undertaking.[29] He had good reason to feel personally gratified. True, he had not succeeded in reducing the annual budget as much as the Rockefeller trustees had mandated. But probably more important, he had achieved a compromise that had been accepted by PUMC administrators and faculty, with a final figure approved by the board members when they arrived in Peking. And he had conveyed the unmistakable message that economical management would be required in the future. His task had been fraught with difficulties, requiring of him a delicate balance between negotiating tenacity and openness to rational persuasion. Such circumstances could easily have caused lasting antagonism with the four men with whom he had worked most intensely. Yet that did not happen.

Reporting to Vincent, Embree characterized the role each man had played in achieving the budget adjustments. His comments, and his subsequent relations with each one, testify to the success of his personal interactions. They also reveal a great deal about his temperament and character. The help of Richard Pearce he considered "simply wonderful," and avowed that little could have been accomplished without him. As a continuing Rockefeller official, Pearce proved to be one of Embree's most reliable supporters. Embree described Henry Houghton as "a tower of strength, . . . working like a Trojan, never yielding in principle but ever ready and resourceful" in finding ways to economize. Years later, even after Embree no longer had any official connection with PUMC, Houghton kept him informed about the school's affairs. And when Houghton spent some months in the United States on leave in 1925, he was a welcome guest at the Embree family's vacation home. Roger Greene had presented Embree with the greatest resistance, and Embree thought him bitter, unreconciled to the adjustments. Yet, in his report, Embree charitably attributed Greene's attitude to overwork and tiredness.[30] The two men would remain in contact for some years thereafter and would even collaborate in a national organization a quarter-century later. Franklin McLean became one of Embree's closest friends.

*   *   *

Eight months after leaving, Embree was back in Peking. He no longer served as the secretary of the CMB, but as a knowledgeable foundation official he was sent to help prepare the PUMC budget for 1922–1923. Before leaving for China in May 1922, he received a telegram from George Vincent wishing him bon voyage. Referring to ongoing conflicts between warlords and, ironically, to Embree's earlier struggles, Vincent wrote, "Chinese war settled in advance of your arrival. Do not become involved in renewed hostilities. . . . Hope you will maintain your economical standards at Peking. Do not weaken."[31]

In the negotiations at PUMC, Embree benefited from the good relations established a year earlier with Henry Houghton. Acting on principles adopted then, he and the school's head in two weeks were able to work out with Roger Greene a satisfactory budget. Embree also was pulled into a variety of issues that may have reminded him of his days at Yale as a university "handyman." He had to gather current estimates of construction costs, decide whether to sell land in Shanghai, determine an appropriate stipend for a Chinese doctor to study in the United States, and consider a contract extension for an American in Peking. He participated in the resolution of some kind of scandal, involving bad behavior by a faculty member, which had made American women indignant and caused a male staff member to threaten resignation. Called upon to resolve a burgeoning public relations problem between PUMC and the American community in Peking, Embree delivered a formal address outlining the Rockefeller Foundation's purposes in China and explaining why the medical school had to limit its services to U.S. citizens.[32] Few of these problems had been on his agenda when he left 61 Broadway, but he apparently took them in stride.

This sojourn in Peking proved to be far less stressful than the one a year earlier. Embree was able to visit every family, both Western and Chinese, in the PUMC compounds and to address scores of concerns. He also found time to attend a Chinese opera that so impressed him he wrote four pages of description in his journal. His PUMC tasks completed, he and Houghton embarked on an extensive trip to survey the state of medical practice and scientific education in East Asia, part of Rockefeller efforts to upgrade Asian science by introducing Western methods and equipment. Along the way, Embree identified young researchers to receive fellowships for study in the United States, expecting them to become innovators when they returned home.[33]

Stopping first in Shanghai, the two travelers discussed with officials of several missionary hospitals and colleges the possible establishment there of a Rockefeller-funded medical school similar to PUMC. They then proceeded through east central China, with visits to Nanking, Tsinan, and Tientsin for similar inspections and discussions pointed toward foundation subsidies for equipment. The trip was long and hot, but after a few days' rest in Peking, they were back on the road to Hankow and Changsha, then down the Yangtze to Wuhu and Kuling, and again to Nanking and Shanghai for follow-up discussions. From the coastal city, they sailed to Hong Kong and Canton, with a stop at Manila. Returning to Shanghai, they then took ship for Japan for a week inspecting hospitals there. Well into the journey, Embree reported to Vincent that, though the heat was "excessive," it had not been so debilitating as to prevent them from carrying out their program of "ten or twelve hours a day of meeting dozens of people and walking over miles of hospital and laboratory space, and climbing thousands of stairs."[34] At the conclusion of their travels, he and Houghton put together two dozen recommendations for foundation general policies and specific actions in China and the rest of East Asia.[35]

Traveling around the country had introduced Embree to a variety of missionary activities. He applauded the spread of Western education and science, but overall his observations left him discontent. While recognizing good intentions and admirable service by white missionaries in many instances, he also encountered attitudes of "aloof superiority" and behavior that was deplorably discriminatory. He was struck by the pattern of keeping house servants in segregated quarters, resisting attempts to raise their wages, and even occasionally treating them as "scarcely human." Could such Western Christians be looking forward to some color line in heaven? he wondered. Did they expect that Negro and Chinese and Indian souls would be kept in a subordinate position, serving white souls? A self-described "believer in many aspects of missionary work," he had come to a critical view only after "hours of tormented thinking." Human nature, he knew, was "strange and inconsistent at best," but the contrast between missionary preaching and frequent missionary behavior he regarded as the "most bizarre spectacle" he had seen in Asia.[36]

Embree returned to China in 1926, but his visit was brief. Following a few days of discussions at PUMC, he planned to travel into the interior. The nation's civil war, raging since before Embree's first visit, had intensified, however, and he was held up by troops blocking the river mouth at Tientsin. Unable to proceed, he was forced to return to Peking. Before departing the capital for Japan, he prepared a letter to Roger Greene expressing his dismay at the deterioration of China's political and economic circumstances and his concern about the negative consequences for educational progress. The letter brought an immediate rejoinder from Greene, in the form of a seven-page document agreeing that there were problems, but presenting a list of accomplishments, advancing a number of reasons for optimism, and suggesting Embree was expecting too much too soon. Had he known China before the revolution, and had he had time for a longer visit, Greene wrote, perhaps Embree would not have come to such a gloomy conclusion. In his reply, Embree agreed that time was necessary for education to take hold, but affirmed that what he had seen "compared unfavorably" with his observations in 1921 and 1922.[37]

Embree's 1926 trip to China was all but incidental to a longer visit to Japan. As on his two previous journeys to East Asia, he spent several weeks in the island nation, visiting the cities, exploring the countryside, experiencing the culture. From his first encounter, he had been taken by the Japanese people. He found them "alert, keen, and able, cheerful and vivacious, polite and courteous to a degree unknown in the West." He admired their love of nature, their appreciation of beautiful things, their devotion to family. He noted with approval the deep attachment to their homeland, instilled from youth through school trips around the country. And by his third visit, after observing numerous Japanese at shrines and temples, he considered them "the most devout people" he had ever seen.[38]

With his great interest in Japan, Embree was appalled by American talk in the 1920s of a future war with that country. He recognized that Japan had spent a great deal to strengthen its army and navy, but he found much less militarism there than in the United States. In his own country, he lamented, day in and day out the Hearst press was "screaming at the top of its lungs," and some "unscrupulous businessmen" wished to cripple their chief competitor in the East by any means at hand. Around Honolulu, one was struck on every side by "soldiers and sailors and airplanes and barracks and forts." Among military personnel and others of European descent, he saw the same attitude of racial superiority he had seen in Western missionaries. Militarists in Japan he expected to become less influential, while in the United States bellicosity seemed to be gaining. War in the Pacific would be senseless, a disaster for both nations, and if any such catastrophe occurred in the foreseeable future, he believed America would "certainly have been the aggressor. We are in a sense aggressor now with our increased armaments, our refusal to join any international body to prevent war, our thoughtless jingoism."[39]

Approaching his mid-forties, Embree had already become, as he later described himself, "a student of races." His youthful experiences with Native American playmates and Chinese railroad workers and African American fellow students, together with his college studies in sociology, had acquainted him with racial differences and sensitized him to racist attitudes. Anti-Japanese sentiment, however, seemed something more than conventional American xenophobia. It was rooted, he suspected, in resentment at the Japanese refusal, in word and manner, to concede Western superiority.[40] Whatever superiority the West might claim, Embree had come to understand, was technological and organizational, neither moral nor cultural, hence unlikely to be long lasting.

* * *

Trips to East Asia in these years did not comprise all of Embree's professional travel. After his 1922 visit, he was back in New York only for the fall. The turn of the new year found him in Puerto Rico, where he spent more than three weeks assessing progress in the foundation's program to control hookworm disease. Five months later, accompanied by Kate and Edwina, he sailed for Europe. His wife and daughter were with him for three weeks in England. Then, crossing the Channel, they waited in Paris while Embree spent almost two months in Central Europe and the Balkans.[41]

Embree's itinerary involved retracing many of the steps of his 1920 trip. He traveled again to Warsaw, Cracow, Prague, and Vienna. In Vienna, he was surprised by the city's "striking recovery." Having considered the Austrian capital "doomed" only three years earlier, he now credited its survival to Herbert Hoover. The feeding program organized and administered by the future U.S. president, in Embree's view, exceeded "in magnitude and in result any humanitarian effort in history." That accomplishment notwithstanding, there were still ominous possibilities, notably that the recent collapse of the German currency might "suck down Austria and other Central European states into the great maelstrom." In Germany, there was talk of a revolution "more or less Bolshevik in character," as well as attempts to restore the monarchy.[42] In the latter concern, Embree was not mistaken, for two months later Communist-inspired uprisings occurred in Saxony and Thuringia, soon followed by the abortive, right-wing Beer Hall Putsch in Munich.

From Vienna, Embree traveled south to Croatia and Serbia, Bulgaria and Turkey. Throughout his journey, as he visited urban centers and talked with government and university officials, his purpose was to assess the state of recovery in each country and to determine current problems and needs. Just as in his 1920 tour of the region, he sought situations where Rockefeller interventions could be most helpful, and, as before, he was particularly attentive to needs in medical education, scientific research, and nurse training. Nurse training was also high on his agenda when he returned to France for the final four weeks of his trip. Back in New York in mid-October, after a hundred days in Europe, Embree testified to the Continent's "terrible" need of funds, but also suggested that the war's social upheaval had left the population "open-minded and fertile in new ideas." Outside North America, he believed, Europe represented "the present chief hope of the race, a particularly appealing field" for Rockefeller efforts.[43]

On his way back to France from the Balkans, Embree had stopped for two days in Venice. His only trip to the city gave him "a new picture of beauty. Nothing has ever more immediately bowled me over," he wrote, "than the fantasy of canals, marble palaces, soft air and noiseless streets which make up this ancient seat of the Doges." St. Mark's Piazza struck him as the only place he knew that rivaled Nikko's temple complex in Japan "for concentrated beauty in a single spot."[44] His time in the jewel of the Adriatic was brief but highly rewarding. As always, his international travel involved intense activity, but a demanding schedule, he had learned, should not prevent nourishing the spirit. The ability to combine business with pleasure would characterize his entire life.

* * *

Embree's travels were an unfailing source of pleasure, and they helped to satisfy his adventurous spirit and restless search for novelty. Yet his readiness always to be on the move is suggestive of another basic element of his personality: he never developed a strong sense of place. Before his seventh birthday, his family had moved five times. He then lived for a dozen years in Kentucky, even longer in New Haven, a full decade in metropolitan New York, and twice that long in Chicago. None of these places, however, did he ever consider in any genuine sense his "home." After his mother's death, he returned to Berea only for a few brief visits, and the thought of living there gave him nightmares. In New Haven, he and Kate had owned a house, a wedding gift from her realtor father, and Embree did develop strong attachments, but they were to Yale, not to the town. In New York and Chicago, the family quarters were always rented; an owned residence that might have deepened a connection was never acquired. He and Kate did own some acreage on an Ontario lake, where after a few years a house was erected, but this was a vacation spot inhabited only a few weeks each year, not a place to put down roots. In the usual sense of the term, then, there was no place that Embree would say he was "from."[45]

Owning no permanent residence after New Haven was in some regards liberating. At a mundane level, it meant that Embree never had to contend with a leaking roof or a frozen pipe or lawn maintenance, leaving him free to concentrate on his work and his writing. It meant he could spend extensive time abroad without worrying about the physical circumstances at his domicile. Far more significant, it meant he avoided the incipient provincialism that can accompany strong identification with a specific locality. In a time when most Americans were moving toward isolationism, his overseas travel eliminated any trace of parochialism or narrow nationalism. His "province" was never a city or a state, not even a region, but the entire country and, in time, the whole world. Consequently, his attention tended to be broadly focused, his concern commonly with large questions. Thus his travels gave him an unusually broad perspective, which served to deepen some important personal traits.

The excitement of overseas journeys notwithstanding, by 1923 Embree had become restive, finding too little opportunity in his position at the Rockefeller Foundation for creative activity. He began to lobby Vincent to create a new division within the foundation, one that would parallel the already existent divisions dealing with medical education, international health, and medicine in China. Vincent was amenable to the proposition for, like Embree, he was impatient with programs initially funded by Rockefeller that moved so slowly toward self-sufficiency.[46] Moreover, he was eager to gain space and budget flexibility for new initiatives, to begin to move the organization away from its almost exclusive emphasis on medicine and public health. The possibility of fresh ideas and a new direction also appealed to trustees Raymond Fosdick and Arthur Woods, the junior Rockefeller's personal representatives on the board. With Vincent's encouragement, Embree put together a formal proposal for a new unit. Responding to the proposal late in 1923, the Rockefeller trustees approved the creation of a Division of Studies (DS). Embree vacated the secretary's position to become the director of the new division early the following year.[47]

Though the new division had been approved, the nature of its work was far from clear. The establishing motion specified only that it was "responsible for administration of projects which lie outside the field of the other departmental agencies of the Rockefeller Foundation."[48] Two aspects of this imprecise wording stand out. First is the indication that the division would serve as a kind of catchall, responsible for a miscellany of activities lying outside the jurisdictions of the other divisions. And the Division of Studies did come to serve that function, with Embree engaged in such diverse programs as nurse training in the United States and Europe, pilot testing of medical clinics in New York, and awarding fellowships to natural scientists in Europe, Asia, and Australia. More important, however, was the open-ended quality of the language. Such vagueness was undoubtedly intentional, for it gave Embree and Vincent maximum latitude in determining the activities of the DS.[49] Though much about the new unit remained to be worked out, on one fundamental point the two men were in full agreement: the division would enable them to put their own stamp on the foundation; it would be the vehicle to convey the whole organization into new territory.

At the time the DS was established, neither its director nor the foundation president knew what direction it would take. In the first few weeks of the division's existence, Embree promoted movement into the arts and humanities, areas he had long considered deserving of philanthropic support. Vincent expressed personal interest in those areas, but believed they were more suitable for other Rockefeller boards than for the foundation. Embree did not drop his advocacy of the arts entirely, but he was left to cast around for another emphasis, a central focus that would define his operation.[50]

For weeks, the new director pondered what would be the most promising avenues for his division to take.[51] He expected to continue involvement with nursing education, especially through promoting public health nursing and demonstrating how it differed from bedside care. Embree considered extending the nurse training program from the Northeast to other sections of the country and into the United Kingdom, France, Poland, Yugoslavia, Mexico, and Japan as well. The program held promise, yet it lacked the scope the division needed. The same was true of the experimental medical clinics, an ongoing activity that had generated little enthusiasm at Rockefeller headquarters. Such programs, while potentially valuable, represented neither the eye-catching initiative Vincent hoped for nor the creative challenge Embree sought. Then came a proposal from the Galton Society.

The Galton Society was dedicated to advancing eugenics, a movement rooted in the ideas of British biologist Francis Galton. At its core, the movement was a response to unprecedented population growth and the presumed consequences for human well-being. In the United States, its supporters, drawn almost entirely from the country's elites, viewed with alarm the way improvements in medicine and public welfare programs worked against the operation of natural selection, allowing people they considered physically and/or mentally inferior to survive and propagate. They were concerned that marriages in which one member had an inheritable disposition to one or another disease tended to pass that weakness on to their offspring, thus spreading the problem more widely. Moreover, they worried that people like themselves tended to have much smaller families than their "inferiors," a pattern that threatened in time to severely limit their group's influence in an increasingly democratic society.[52] Left unchecked, these trends would lead inevitably, they feared, to increased mental problems, reduced physical health, deterioration of the world's gene pool, great pressure on natural resources, growing political ferment, increased racial tension, and a general decline in quality of life. The Galton Society and eugenicists generally were committed to preventing such dire outcomes, relying on the more or less scientific study of human populations—individually and collectively, past and present—to discover appropriate preventive measures.

Founded in 1918, the society was headquartered at the American Museum of Natural History in New York. Both its location and its membership gave the organization considerable luster. Its nine charter members included the museum's president, the head of the prestigious Carnegie Institution of Washington, the director of a major eugenics research center, a leading educational psychologist, and distinguished zoologists from Princeton, Columbia, and Berkeley. The twenty-four other members, drawn from Britain, France, and Italy as well as the United States, were similarly prominent in their fields of specialization.[53]

Though its members were highly accomplished, the society as an organization had done little by 1924 to publicize or promote its cause. It now sought funding for a "significant scientific investigation of broad human interest, such as might prove to be of definite and tangible benefit to mankind, both in the immediate future and in the centuries to come." The present and future of "civilized races," the proposal asserted, could be fully appreciated only through comparison with primitive peoples among whom natural selection had not been affected by medical science. The society proposed, therefore, a multidimensional study of the most primitive people known, the aborigines of Australia.[54]

Embree was intrigued by the proposed "Study of the Origin and Evolution of Man." He had long believed that the most difficult problems facing the world centered on population growth and control, even pressing the point on his colleagues by reading excerpts from Malthus's *Essay on the Principle of Population* at an inter-board luncheon.[55] "Careful and deep research" in the "vast field" of population he considered both essential to human progress and fundamental to Rockefeller's purpose. Moreover, he already shared some of the eugenicists' beliefs. He favored clinical research on birth control methods and efforts to educate the broad public. And, like most Americans of his time, he viewed sympathetically governmental action to restrict, if not eliminate, the reproduction of "lower feeble-minded and criminal types."[56] Genetic studies, data gathering on human heredity and longevity, analysis of mental health problems—population-related research in general—were high in his priorities.[57] Within six weeks after arriving at Rockefeller, he had expressed interest in the foundation's expansion into the mental health field. In his interest in eugenics-linked issues, he was far from alone among those at 61 Broadway.[58]

Embree immediately set about exploring the project's possibilities, conferring with his colleague Beardsley Ruml, head of the Laura Spelman Rockefeller Memorial (LSRM), one of the foundation's sister trusts. On a Wednesday, with Ruml in tow, he lunched with Galton Society chair Charles B. Davenport, secretary William K. Gregory, and Mu-

seum of Natural History anthropologist Clark Wissler. The elements of
the study were tentatively identified. Embree told George Vincent about
the conversation the next morning. Wasting no time, he then met with
Ruml that very afternoon, and they quickly concluded that the project
held considerable promise, both for the foundation in its physiological
components and for the LSRM in its social science aspects. A weekend
intervened, but on Monday Embree outlined the proposal to the Rockefeller Institute's Simon Flexner, who expressed great interest, promised
to support the proposal, and indicated that the Institute would probably
assign an immunologist to work with the research team. Two days later,
in New Haven with Ruml to discuss nurse training, the two men used
the occasion to inform Yale president James Angell of the project and to
receive his encouragement. Before the week was out, the excited director
of the Division of Studies had conferred with Raymond Fosdick, who
seemed "delighted" with the project and its backing. Shortly thereafter,
Embree privately briefed Stanford University president Ray Lyman Wilbur, a trustee strongly interested in the foundation's movement into areas
beyond medical education and public health. Buoyed by the support he
had found on every hand, Embree outlined the project to the Rockefeller
board. Only two weeks after the Wednesday luncheon with the Galton
Society representatives, the board approved the project in principle, authorized consultation with scientists in the United States and abroad,
and asked that a more detailed proposal be prepared.[59]

Embree's enthusiasm is not hard to understand. Here was the kind
of breakthrough project he had been seeking. It involved sophisticated
scientific investigation, with the likelihood of important results, which
in turn might open other promising areas for DS support. The prominent
figures engaged as sponsors and researchers would guarantee attention
from the scientific and scholarly communities. Cooperation across the
boundaries of the natural and social sciences was built into the project, a
sort of arrangement uncommon at the time. Also appealing, especially to
Embree, was the international dimension, stemming from both the location and the participants. The fact that he seized on the project without
hesitation is not surprising.

In the months that followed, Embree devoted most of his time and
energy to the aborigine project, in effect taking it over from the Galton

Society and making it a Rockefeller venture.[60] But the significance of the project goes beyond its claims on the attention of the DS director. Working to put it together enabled Embree to look beyond the project itself and to conceive of a program that would become the central effort of the division. That program, under the rubric "human biology," sought to bring together research in physiology, anthropology, psychology, and psychiatry at the points where those disciplines might most productively intersect. The goal was to encourage and fund the kinds of investigations that would illuminate the dark corners of human life, behavior, and interaction. The expectation was that such findings would in time reveal the steps necessary to deal with the myriad problems posed by population growth.

In important ways, human biology was an inspired choice for the division's focus. The field captured Embree's imagination, interesting him more keenly than anything he had undertaken since arriving at Rockefeller. With a firm base in physiology, it was clearly linked to the foundation's traditional emphases, a point Embree stressed to the Rockefeller board. At the same time, it embraced some of the burgeoning social sciences, making possible foundation cooperation with the Laura Spelman Rockefeller Memorial, the kind of coordinated effort among Rockefeller boards that both Vincent and Rockefeller Jr. sought to achieve. And because such cross-disciplinary study could lead to answers to the problems of overpopulation, urban congestion, crime, prostitution, disease, political corruption, racial tension, and related issues, it seemed to fit nicely into the agenda of the progressives who inhabited many philanthropic offices.[61] But its potential and suitability notwithstanding, the field of human biology was not without its difficulties.

One of those difficulties was the field's linkage to eugenics. Embree's Rockefeller associates seem to have made no distinction between the two areas; "human biology" connoted "eugenics." Indeed, Embree himself did not distinguish sharply between the field of study and the movement. And undoubtedly the lines became increasingly blurred as he came to rely heavily on the advice of two Galton Society members, anthropologist Clark Wissler and Princeton zoologist Edwin Conklin.[62]

By the time Embree's Division of Studies got under way, the eugenics movement had reached, if not passed, its peak, though its emphases, and to some extent its ideology, remained squarely in the public eye. By the end of the 1920s, almost 400 colleges, encouraged by a committee of the National Education Association, listed courses with eugenics content, courses enrolling tens of thousands of students. A substantial cohort of natural scientists, however, had come to view eugenics as insufficiently rigorous, inclined to propagandize without sufficient factual backing. Rising doubts about the movement, and the foundation's practice of avoiding potentially controversial matters, may have given some Rockefeller trustees pause.[63]

Another problem stemmed from the novelty of human biology as a cross-disciplinary field. Its components were diffuse, and from the outset Embree was not entirely clear on the field's parameters. He had a visionary's sense of the potential benefits of bringing various disciplinary perspectives to bear on societal issues, but he was unsure how that was to be done. His own university studies, primarily in the social sciences, had not provided a firm grounding in the natural sciences, and his on-the-job training in medical education and public health at Rockefeller had been insufficient remedy. Fully aware of this deficiency, he began to read prodigiously, seeking information about the state of knowledge in a number of disciplines. As the pitfalls of self-education became evident, he toyed with the idea of devoting several months to formal coursework in anthropology.[64] At the same time, he sought guidance through the field's complexities in many quarters.

For months, Embree crisscrossed the continent, conferring with leading university authorities at Johns Hopkins, Chicago, Toronto, Stanford, Yale, Princeton, absorbing their insights and seeking their counsel on how best to proceed. Considerable help came from Princeton's Conklin, arguably the most renowned American zoologist of his generation.[65] Another man extensively consulted, Carnegie Institution head John C. Merriam, warned of difficulties in reaching measurable or immediately applicable results, but affirmed that human biology was then the most important field for foundations to explore. Close relations were established as well with Hopkins biometrician Raymond Pearl, whose views on eugenics and population control were closely akin to Embree's own.[66] With Isaiah Bowman, the director of the American Geographical Society, Embree conferred about the effects of geography on human development. Reproductive biologist Frank Rattray Lillie of the University of Chicago, while emphasizing the importance of population studies, acknowledged their relationship to anthropology and psychology. Connections were maintained as well with Charles B. Davenport of the Galton Society, and Embree visited his research establishment at Cold Spring Harbor. Closer to home, he consulted frequently with the influential Flexner brothers, and from Beardsley Ruml and trustee Ray Lyman Wilbur he received steady counsel and encouragement.[67]

Early in 1925, almost exactly one year after approval of the Australian aborigines project, Embree presented his plan for a varied program in human biology to the Rockefeller trustees. Much to his dismay, the board, finding the proposal vague, expressed willingness to consider individual projects in the future, but declined to sanction the program as a whole. Not rejecting his efforts entirely, however, they did authorize continued exploration of the field.[68] That decision set Embree off, in the months ahead, on extended trips overseas—to New Zealand and Australia, Japan and Hawaii, Germany and England.

Embree's quest took him first to the Pacific. From San Francisco, he sailed with his wife and family in late August 1925 for Honolulu. Kate and the three children would spend most of the year in Hawaii, thus deepening what became a long family connection with those islands. Fourteen-year-old Edwina and six-year-old Catherine were enrolled in local schools. Sixteen-year-old John attended classes as well, but he interrupted his studies to travel with his parents to Japan (while his two sisters stayed with family friends), and then journeyed on his own to France.[69] Though a U.S. territory, Hawaii was different enough from their home in the Northeast to seem almost a foreign country. Thus, from an early age, all three Embree offspring benefited from studying and friendships with children of different cultural backgrounds. That experience, along with later travel abroad with their parents, gave them a strong international orientation that lasted throughout their lives.

Leaving his family behind, Embree took ship for New Zealand, accompanied by Clark Wissler. With the anthropologist at his side, he evaluated the strength of universities in Wellington, Christchurch, and Dunedin. Together, they looked into possibilities for promoting anthropological studies in Oceania. In Auckland, they assessed research progress on the Maori, then moved on to Australia to examine work on aborigines there. In Sydney and Melbourne, Adelaide and Brisbane, they conferred with medical school faculties and social and natural scientists of different stripes, during one seven-day period conducting no fewer than thirty-seven interviews. Having solidified Rockefeller interest in the region, Embree then returned to Honolulu, where Wissler left him.[70]

In Hawaii, Embree linked up with Professor Conklin and his wife, his own wife Kate, and son John, and the party sailed for Japan. There, after appraising the state of health care and basic scientific research, the two men concluded that studies in human biology were especially appropriate and feasible, due to a rapidly growing population and the availability of ample vital statistics in the island nation. Traveling to China by way of Korea, they soon found their way blocked by civil war operations and were forced to return to Japan, then to home. On the return voyage, Embree stopped in Honolulu to confirm arrangements for studies by the Bishop Museum on inter-ethnic marriages. Eleven days after leaving Hawaii, following more than seven exhausting months of inspecting laboratory sites, visiting hospitals, examining museum holdings, making countless acquaintances, and identifying young investigators to receive fellowships, he was back in New York. Though he had just crossed half an ocean and an entire continent, he was eager to get back to work. He went directly to his office, even though it was Sunday.[71]

The punishing pace of Embree's long journey was reminiscent of his intense efforts on behalf of the Peking Union Medical College more than four years earlier. But it is also suggestive of a growing uneasiness about the program in human biology. His long sojourn abroad brought home the magnitude of what he had undertaken, and, recognizing the need for continuing guidance, he discussed with President Vincent the creation of a standing committee of expert advisors. Midway through 1926, his understanding of the field was certainly much deeper; he had read widely, established valuable contacts, and initiated several worthwhile projects. Yet some project proposals had been met with skepticism by the Rockefeller board and, like prominent trustee Simon Flexner, even Vincent had begun to sound cautionary notes.[72]

Confronted with trustees' doubts, the foundation's president had fallen into a pattern of withdrawing proposals from consideration, presumably with an eye to further refinement, rather than attempting to push them through against possible objections. Such withdrawals occurred so often that Embree eventually felt the need to complain that he needed firmer presidential support. Vincent, mentor as well as superior, repeatedly urged his younger associate to clarify his thinking, develop long-term plans, and buttress his proposals by citing supportive opinions of the prestigious authorities he had consulted. Embree in turn made his presentations to the board more extensive, elaborating project descriptions and listing so many illustrious researchers as backers as to seem eager to overwhelm his audience with the sheer weight of their credentials.[73]

But impressive supporters notwithstanding, something was missing. There had been little objection to the individual projects that did win approval: funding a chair in anthropology at the University of Sydney, underwriting an institute to study human longevity and population control at Johns Hopkins, support for Yale's comparative primatologist Robert Yerkes, grants to biological research centers at Woods Hole and Pacific Grove, fellowships for young Japanese scientists. All seemed worthwhile in and of themselves. But viewed together, they seem even now more like discrete projects than a coherent "program." No unifying purpose was evident; no thread tied the various initiatives together. The disparate nature of the field was all too obvious. With the information at hand, a board member might well have doubted that human biology was a field at all.

Seasoned trustees may have recalled the warning of the recently retired Frederick Gates to avoid wasting funds in "scatteration." Wary of that danger, and unsure where Embree's initiatives might lead, the board never gave formal approval to the program. Left with neither discernable program nor clear purpose, the division itself came into question when reorganization of all the Rockefeller boards began to be considered in 1926. As those deliberations proceeded, it soon became evident that most activities of the DS could be subsumed under other foundation units. Hence, no dissent was recorded when the board, acting on the recommendation of its reorganization committee, voted late in 1926 to eliminate the Division of Studies.[74]

* * *

Embree's failure to win approval of his program, and thereby ensure the life of his division, was the result of various factors, some personal, some organizational. Embree blamed himself. Never doubting that understanding human biology was key to social progress, he lamented his inability to persuade the Rockefeller board of its importance. The heart of the problem, he confided to his closest friend, was his own immaturity and slow learning pattern. Though he had "sweat blood" in study and planning, he "did not get the philosophy of the thing for years and years and was therefore unable to formulate a really statesmanlike program." Because his own ideas were sketchy, he was unable to present them convincingly to dubious trustees.[75]

Apparently taking Embree at his word, historian of science Robert E. Kohler concluded that the board's rejection of the human biology program was indeed largely due to Embree himself. His attempt to link scientific research to social service and reform was essentially outdated, according to Kohler, more appropriate for the years before 1917 than for the postwar era. Moreover, Embree "was a man of rather poor judgment and administrative capacity" and was possessed of certain personality traits that irritated others.[76] Yet the entire situation was more complex than Kohler presents it, and Embree was perhaps too hard on himself. Other considerations bore importantly on the outcome.

Seeking to establish the Division of Studies on a firm footing, Embree continually encountered the entrenched interests of other Rockefeller agencies. The division had been established with a vague mandate: to administer a medley of activities and, when undertaking new ventures, to avoid encroachment on the areas of other divisions and boards. But the lack of clear boundaries around those areas complicated matters, and when Embree tried to define his domain, he set off disagreements over territorial limits. With Beardsley Ruml of the LSRM, he shared a deep interest in social science research, and the two friends had little trouble reaching an understanding about a division of labor.[77] That was conspicuously not the case, however, with Wycliffe Rose.

Rose was president of the General Education Board and, at the same time, one of the most influential trustees of the Rockefeller Foundation. In addition to these posts, Rose headed the International Education

Board (IEB), a new Rockefeller-funded agency created at his insistence only months before the Division of Studies. These two new agencies were soon at odds over their programs; they were inevitably competitors for foundation funding. Embree's officer's diaries for these years are replete with accounts of meetings with Rose, sometimes involving Vincent as mediator, to determine the distinct arenas in which their units would operate.[78]

Among numerous other instances, the rivalry took specific form when Rose encouraged officials of London's University College to submit directly to him a proposal for a new building that would house faculty in anatomy, experimental psychology, psychiatry, anthropology, and several biology subdisciplines. Embree had initiated such discussions some time earlier, for the building would facilitate the kind of cross-disciplinary research he favored by bringing together several of the fields central to human biology. Rose's preemptive invitation to the London officials, coupled with his obviously higher rank, served to undercut Embree's already tenuous position.[79] Beyond claiming contested organizational turf, Rose was primarily committed to promoting the physical sciences, had little interest in the social sciences or general education, and distrusted projects that seemed vague or visionary.[80] About Embree's emphasis on applying research findings directly to societal reform, he also had serious misgivings, and his position on the foundation board allowed him to express those doubts where they mattered most. Similarly, other trustees, proud of the advances in medicine and public health made possible by Rockefeller largesse, were reluctant to approve new initiatives that might divert funds from those traditional interests.

Such reluctance was undoubtedly intensified by the overall financial situation of the Rockefeller trusts. Well before the creation of the Division of Studies, President Vincent had begun to consider how resources could be redirected so that new fields could be explored.[81] At the same time, he was well aware of ongoing claims on those resources: the PUMC, the young IEB, the LSRM's escalating expenditures in the social sciences, among others. Thus, in the very months when Embree was preparing his program proposal, Vincent alerted the board that the years ahead would require budgetary caution. The budget for 1925, originally over $3.5 million in deficit, had been brought into balance, he reported, but looking ahead "so far as income is concerned no project of any magnitude . . . can be entered upon before 1928."[82] That limited prospect was surely in the trustees' minds when they were presented with a novel program that lacked the compelling promise of medical education and public health. Their hesitancy to move into new territory is not hard to understand.

Aware of that hesitancy, and believing he had several years to develop a definitive program, Embree had taken the advice of senior colleagues and moved with considerable caution.[83] Following his extensive trip to the Pacific, his recommendations for funding were surprisingly modest.[84] Even the timing of his board presentations was a factor. There were two key occasions when Embree needed all the support he could get. One came in early 1924 when, at a board conference, he presented the case for the new division and a brief outline of its possible activities. At this time, when the vigorous advocacy of the foundation president was crucial, George Vincent was absent due to illness.[85] The board agreed to create the division, but with a limited budget that implied limited commitment. The second occurred at a formal board session when, after months spent in study, consultation, and planning, Embree put forward the more detailed program proposal the board had requested. On this occasion, trustee Ray Lyman Wilbur, president of Stanford University, was unable to be present. Wilbur considered human biology the most interesting foundation endeavor at the time, and Embree had not only kept this eager champion well informed of his thinking, but had lobbied him extensively.[86] As head of a leading university, Wilbur had the standing to be an effective spokesperson for Embree's plans. But above all, as a medical doctor and a recent president of the American Medical Association, he was uniquely positioned to persuade his board colleagues, one-fourth of whom were physicians, of the value of the proposed undertaking. His absence at this critical juncture deprived Embree of support on which he had counted heavily. At Vincent's urging, Wilbur wrote a highly enthusiastic letter, which may have been read to the board, but it inevitably lacked the force of an in-person defense.[87] The board voted funds to allow Embree to continue his explorations, but they declined to endorse a full-fledged program. Later, when Wilbur was again able to play a substantive role, the most propitious time had passed.

But even after the formidable obstacles of institutional structure, bu-reaucratic inertia, and territorial competition are taken into account, Em-bree's accomplishments in the division seem fairly meager. Though not insignificant, they fell far short of his ambitions. Indeed, the "blood" he sweated notwithstanding, it is hard to avoid the conclusion that Embree was not the right person to develop the program he attempted, certainly not at that time. The concept of human biology was novel and ill defined, and when highly influential trustees like Simon Flexner and Raymond Fosdick had difficulty grasping it, he had trouble spelling out its pur-pose and its promise. Without medical or even a natural scientific back-ground, he lacked qualifications undoubtedly important to the trustees of a foundation which had "to all intents and purposes been captured by the doctors."[88] Nor is it trivial that, unlike Vincent and Ruml and Rose, Embree lacked even a Ph.D., a disadvantage he acknowledged privately, if not defensively, to the foundation president.[89] At the time he took over the Division of Studies, Embree had a highly creditable record at the foundation. But in promoting human biology, he was in the position of a layman attempting to lead highly accomplished professionals in new, uncertain directions when he lacked the background and the credentials, hence the credibility, to do so.[90]

In spite of the division's limited achievements, Embree deserves credit for both foresight and initiative. In a time when some Rockefeller trusts were in danger of falling into bureaucratic routine, he was able to envision a new direction and propose some initial steps along the way.[91] Nor did he stint in his efforts to obtain sound advice, crossing two oceans and consulting authorities on four continents. While he never got the picture clear enough in his own mind to convince skeptics, he sensed the fruitful potential of research across the boundaries of the natural and social sciences. And as a cross-disciplinary bridge, he recognized the centrality of biology, a field in the twenties moving forward rapidly and seeming to promise solutions for various social problems. Even after he left Rockefeller, Embree continued to promote human biology, solicit-ing Max Mason, the head of the new Division of Natural Sciences (and Rockefeller Foundation president-to-be), for an opportunity to discuss the field's possibilities.[92] Decades later, much of what he was feeling his way toward would be widely accepted as the field of "social biology."[93]

Moreover, not long after Embree left Rockefeller, the foundation began substantial support for research along lines he had laid out. Three of the newly organized Rockefeller divisions of natural, social, and medical sciences joined in a project to develop "a new science of man," focused on the analysis and control of behavior. In addition, Alan Gregg, head of the Division of Medical Sciences, shared many of Embree's concerns and pursued some of his initiatives.[94] Following World War II, under the urging of John D. Rockefeller III, the foundation returned to serious consideration of the world population issues to which Embree had called attention twenty years earlier. But well before these developments, he had moved to a new situation offering a different set of challenges.

THREE

SOMEONE TO KEEP JULIUS ROSENWALD STRAIGHT

At the beginning of 1927, Edwin Embree's situation at the Rockefeller Foundation bore all the outward marks of success. Under the reorganization then under way, he had returned to the central administration as second only to the foundation's president. After almost a decade with the foundation, he was its longest-serving official. Twice during that period, he had served for several months as acting president, as he would do again before the year was out.[1] Early in his tenure, he had played an important role in the stabilization of the Peking Union Medical College, one of the trust's most challenging enterprises. And on several trips through Europe, Asia, and the Pacific, he had been the face of Rockefeller, assessing progress on projects under way and exploring additional funding possibilities.

The Rockefeller years had also greatly extended the range of Embree's important acquaintances. His alumni work at Yale had brought him into relationships with prominent men in the Northeast and Midwest, but now he interacted with figures of national stature. Twice-yearly meetings of the Rockefeller board brought to headquarters two former nominees for the U.S. presidency, John W. Davis and Charles Evans Hughes. The foundation's involvement in war relief in the early 1920s had put him in touch with future president Herbert Hoover, and occasional contacts were ongoing. Prominent New York bankers Dwight Morrow and Frederick Strauss held board seats, as did current and future heads of major universities Charles William Eliot of Harvard and Ray Lyman Wilbur of Stanford. Also among these molders of opinion was the influential journalist William Allen White of Kansas. The natural sciences were represented on the board by entomologist Vernon Kellogg, secretary of the National Research Council, and the pathologist and future Nobel laureate George H. Whipple. Within the United States and abroad, Embree's extensive contacts included university officials, foundation leaders, seasoned researchers, and promising members of the rising generation. To any outside observer, his title and the circles within which he moved bespoke an executive well established, professionally secure, and amply rewarded.

Yet as he entered his mid-forties, Embree was increasingly restive. Months earlier, he had hinted at his dissatisfaction to GEB trustee Anson Phelps Stokes, his former Yale mentor.[2] His discontent was undoubtedly intensified by the board's refusal to approve his program in human biology. Even more dismaying was a subsequent decision stemming from efforts to eliminate structural problems within and among the several Rockefeller philanthropies. An examination of those efforts, and Embree's relationship to them, offers a window into the internal dynamics of the foundation. At the same time, these interactions help to explain Embree's departure from the organization by the year's end.

*   *   *

By 1925, officials throughout the Rockefeller trusts had recognized that they were not effectively organized. Having been created at different times, often with undifferentiated areas of interest, individual boards and divisions within boards often found themselves pursuing overlapping objectives, even in the same country or region. Not infrequently, as Embree had experienced, conflicts arose as each agency attempted to define its own arena of operations. President Vincent had tried to resolve such disagreements through negotiation and to coordinate matters through weekly luncheon meetings of officers of the various boards. These efforts proved both time-consuming and largely unproductive.

Complicating the situation was the uncertain extent of Vincent's authority, an uncertainty rooted in conflicting understandings of the nature of the Rockefeller Foundation itself. One view considered the foundation to be a kind of holding company, responsible for maintaining financial assets but leaving their expenditure largely in the hands of related organizations functioning almost autonomously. Initiative, in that view, rested primarily with the boards and divisions, with the foundation's president serving primarily as a mediator among them. The contrasting opinion saw the president as a genuine chief executive, holding substantial authority over other Rockefeller trusts, determining initiatives to be submitted to trustees for approval, and making recommendations on the allocation of funds. Lacking clarity on such matters, Vincent had become increasingly frustrated as he tried to control expenditures, limiting budgets for established programs so as to secure funds for new ventures.

To resolve these issues, early in 1926 Vincent persuaded the trustees to establish an inter-board committee to assess the situation and formulate proposals for a more efficient structure. Named to the three-man committee were senior trustees John G. Agar, Simon Flexner, and Raymond B. Fosdick. Fosdick, a member of both the foundation's board and the GEB (and later president of both), was known on occasion to speak for board chair John D. Rockefeller Jr. As the trustee most in the chair's confidence, he played the dominant role on the committee, organizing its work, taking the lead in conducting interviews, and drafting the final report and recommendations.

As the trio proceeded with their work, opinions and ideas were solicited from trustees and officers of the various boards. Embree had long been unhappy with organizational arrangements at Rockefeller headquarters, particularly the lack of clear presidential authority and the pattern of officers of one board serving as trustees of another.[3] In a straightforward memorandum to the committee, he advocated simplification of the structure by eliminating individual boards, concentrating authority in the president and trustees of the foundation, and creating a council of key officers to review and coordinate proposed projects before their submission to the trustees.[4] But beyond his own preferences, Embree made clear in conversations that he would find acceptable any new structure that strengthened the foundation's president and produced quicker decisions and greater efficiency.

The reorganization committee did propose strengthening the office of the president, as Embree hoped. But, as previously noted, another of its recommendations left him deeply dismayed. The Division of Studies had been created less than three years earlier; yet the committee now recommended its elimination altogether. The committee's report gave the division short shrift. Board members perusing the report could readily conclude that the unit was inconsequential when they read, "[F]rom time to time it has taken up a number of miscellaneous activities such as the training of nurses, aid to dispensaries and the human aspects of biology, which are now all grouped together under a so-called Division of Studies."[5] The language was Fosdick's, and it reflected disdain for both the division and the field of human biology. That attitude was expressed more directly in a confidential letter to committee members Agar and Flexner. The biological aspects of Embree's unit, Fosdick stated, should be transferred temporarily to another division "with the understanding that they are to be terminated as soon as possible. I find that they do not amount to anything anyway."[6]

Fosdick's opinion was apparently unchallenged by his committee colleagues. A minor player on the committee, Agar seems to have been content to leave key decisions to Fosdick. Flexner played a more active role, but though he had approved several of Embree's initiatives, he doubted that, taken together, they constituted a real program. If either man chose to respond to Fosdick's conclusion, much less to disagree, no record has been discovered. On November 5, the board approved the committee's recommendations in principle, with final approval to come three months later.[7]

Elimination of the Division of Studies was not the only important recommendation of the Fosdick committee. Also proposed was disbanding the International Health Board and moving its activities into an International Health Division of the Rockefeller Foundation. Similarly, dissolution of the China Medical Board was proposed, with the specification that a separate corporation be established to receive a sizable Rockefeller endowment and then operate independently. The foundation board readily approved both measures, along with one other. To strengthen the central administration, three vice presidencies were created, one for Europe, one for Asia, and one for the home office in New York.[8]

In light of Embree's long experience with the foundation, he clearly had to be considered for one of the vice presidential posts. Immediately after the board's preliminary decision to eliminate his division, Embree talked with three other division heads about his suitability for a vice presidency. One expressed the hope that he would accept the position in the home office, and another later indicated he would approve if Embree took the post.[9] The view of the third, Roger S. Greene, with whom Embree had clashed at least twice over PUMC matters, is not known, but earlier he had warned against new initiatives that could jeopardize current programs, precisely the innovative measures Embree advocated.[10] George Vincent, too, made it clear he would "warmly welcome" his longtime associate back into the central administration but, aware that the younger man was considering a career move, stipulated that Embree himself should be convinced that the work could be made "interesting and important."[11] Simon Flexner voiced similar sentiments, while stating that others at 61 Broadway should also be enthusiastic about such an appointment. The issue was still unresolved when Embree left in mid-November for a three-month stint in Europe.

In making the trip, Embree's purpose was to inform various Rockefeller officials in Europe of the coming reorganization and to advance conversations already under way with several organizations. Earlier, he and Vincent had discussed a broad survey of facilities and research in Great Britain, but that idea was apparently shelved in light of reorganization plans. Vincent also had in mind that Embree should familiarize himself with a number of foundation programs on the Continent, with an eye to a possible future assignment.[12] During Embree's time abroad, however, Raymond Fosdick injected himself into the situation, setting off an alarm bell that, at least temporarily, put Embree on the defensive.

Midway through Embree's trip, Fosdick happened to see a letter Embree had sent to Beardsley Ruml from England. In the letter, Embree commented on a University of Chicago scholar with whom he was traveling, and said he expected they would "dig up a few bones before we get through. England, however, is no easy scratching." He went on to mention briefly "a few good sessions" he had had with a half-dozen anthropologists and "the psychiatric crowd at Kings Square." The entire passage consisted of four short sentences, totaling fewer than forty-five words. Fosdick, however, seems to have read more into it than strikes the current reader. He fired off a confidential memorandum to Vincent, quoting the four sentences and asking, "Are you sure that Embree is not getting into that biological situation in Europe? . . . I confess I do not quite understand what he is doing over there. I though[t] it had to do with nursing education."[13]

Vincent replied immediately that he was "somewhat surprised" by the quotation from Embree's letter. It was his understanding that Embree was to visit a few English institutions with his Chicago companion, to examine nursing programs thoroughly, to familiarize himself with the entire foundation program in Europe, and to "do nothing at all in the biological field on the continent." He closed with the hope that "nothing indiscreet" had been done. He also attached a copy of an earlier letter to Embree, clarifying the purpose of his visits to English universities and advising him "to be careful not to arouse expectations or to cross wires."[14] Embree had responded to that letter promptly, acknowledging that initially he might have misunderstood Vincent, affirming he had told everyone he had met that projects for foundation funding could not even be discussed, and agreeing to curtail his visits to English campuses.[15]

Vincent may have been a bit uneasy about Embree's conversations but was apparently content that his cautionary note would suffice. Fosdick, on the other hand, was unwilling to let the matter rest. Instead, he brought Simon Flexner into the picture, sending him Vincent's letter and Embree's reply, along with a confidential letter of his own summarizing the background. It was "regrettable that Embree went ahead with his study," Fosdick wrote, and he feared it would "only add to the confusion that already exists in the minds of our friends abroad. My impression is that Embree in this whole business is going to be a little difficult to control." He was raising the matter with his colleague, Fosdick explained, "because you and I have a real responsibility in this matter."[16] How Flexner received this information, and what if anything he did about it, is not known. Statements he made in other contexts, however, suggest that he would have regarded this as fundamentally a matter for administrative consideration, not one for trustee intervention.[17]

Indeed, the matter does not seem appropriate for trustee involvement, and the doggedness with which Fosdick pursued it is not initially easy to explain. Historian of science Robert Kohler has apparently taken Fosdick's version of the episode at face value. In an important scholarly article, he presents Embree as driven by ambition but hampered by limited ability, as recklessly promoting a program that was on the verge of extinction. As director of the Division of Studies, Kohler contends, Embree sought to create his own fiefdom within the foundation, thereby becoming a "baron" in the style of Wycliffe Rose and Beardsley Ruml. Implicit in Kohler's portrayal is Fosdick as the conscientious and concerned trustee, acting to ensure that soon-to-be-established policy not be violated in advance.[18] That Embree was ambitious and disappointed at his division's demise cannot be denied, but the full explanation is more complicated than Kohler's presentation.

Fosdick's actions apparently stemmed from an expectation, if not a hope, that Embree would leave Rockefeller as a consequence of the reorganization. Before the new structure had received even tentative approval, he had written confidentially to the other two members of the reorganization committee, "After talking the situation over with Vincent and others, I believe that Embre [sic] could not possibly be the vice president of the Home Office. Nor do I think he could act in any general administrative capacity." Elimination of his division would leave Embree "out on a limb," he acknowledged, but the committee needed to "consider this thing from the standpoint of the good of the Foundation as a whole and not from the standpoint of a particular individual." There would be a place for Embree in the Medical Education Division "as a sort of assistant for the time being," but Fosdick was confident that Embree would not accept such a position.[19] Fosdick's involvement in the affair of Embree's European trip, indeed his creation of the affair, it seems, was intended to discredit the foundation's longest-serving official, to forestall any consideration of Embree for the vice presidency. And suggesting the possibility of only a subordinate position, an obvious demotion, was designed to ensure his departure. Yet Fosdick did not prevail. For some weeks, he continued in private discussions with Vincent to protest against offering Embree the post. The issue was finally resolved only when Vincent traveled to Fosdick's home in a New Jersey suburb, and the two men agreed on "the underlying principles and policy to be pursued."[20]

Having acquiesced on offering the position to Embree, Fosdick then began to remonstrate over the salary Embree was to receive, arguing that it should be lower than the maximum authorized for division heads, despite the fact that all of them would rank below the vice president. Vincent, attentive to the welfare of his protégé of ten years, and no less concerned to block encroachment on presidential prerogatives by even this most powerful trustee, stood his ground. Discounting Fosdick's latest objection, he offered the appointment at a salary he thought appropriate. Embree, who had been pondering a move into banking or a position with Chicago's planned Museum of Science and Industry, accepted the new appointment. Vincent promptly informed Fosdick and Simon Flexner of this outcome. Flexner readily received the news; Fosdick's response is not recorded.[21]

Fosdick's persistent efforts against Embree lead inevitably to speculation about his motives. He professed low regard for Embree's administrative abilities and sought to gain allies by implying to fellow trustees that Vincent shared his view. Yet no evidence suggests that Vincent or Embree's colleagues at the foundation or the other Rockefeller trusts held similarly negative opinions. Moreover, Embree's subsequent success as head of another major philanthropy testifies to his impressive leadership skills, thereby calling into question Fosdick's judgment. The suspicion arises that Fosdick's private assessment of Embree was perhaps less negative than he let on, that an ulterior motive was in play.

Fosdick may well have had in mind Vincent's likely retirement within a couple of years. Whenever the president's office fell vacant, whoever was vice president in New York would inevitably be considered a possible successor. It is not clear that Fosdick himself aspired to the foundation presidency at that time; another decade would pass before the position became his. Even so, it is notable that Fosdick and Embree not only were of the same generation, but were separated in age by less than two months. Moreover, they held remarkably similar views about critical foundation issues—strengthening the president's office, moving into new fields, fostering social reform, avoiding institutional stagnation.[22] True, Embree did not enjoy the younger Rockefeller's confidence to the extent Fosdick did—indeed, no one did. Yet even at this early date, Fosdick seems to have been maneuvering to remove a potential rival.[23]

It would be interesting to know if Embree had any inkling of Fosdick's actions against him. It appears he was either unaware of those machinations or possessed of an unusually forgiving temperament, for the two men continued to have productive discussions as long as Embree remained at the foundation. And a year after leaving Rockefeller, he made a special trip to New York in an effort to persuade Fosdick to take a position on the Rosenwald Fund board, an improbable initiative if their relations were in fact strained. Fosdick declined the Rosenwald trusteeship, but he and Embree continued to correspond occasionally, and their interchanges were always cordial. As Embree later began to turn out a steady stream of books, he routinely sent an autographed copy to Fosdick, who commonly responded with a gracious note of thanks. The latter, no longer troubled by Embree's presence at 61 Broadway, evidently kept his own counsel.

* * *

Embree's return to Rockefeller's central administration gave him an impressive title and continued prestige. With conscientious attention to his responsibilities, he set about deepening his understanding of the foundation's wide-ranging activities. In the spring of 1927, he spent a month in Central America, examining public health issues in five countries. This was his first trip to the region, and it left him with some strong impressions. In a family journal, he recorded his most vivid memories: "Mixed bloods and variegated colors, hookworms and mosquitoes, the United Fruit Company, the Panama Canal, torrid seacoasts with bananas and mosquitoes and cool uplands with coffee and cattle, the activity and ambitions of Salvador, the primitive Indians of Guatemala, universal hatred of the Gringo."[24] Such travel always appealed to his adventurous spirit, and he had begun to plan this trip almost as soon as he took on his new duties. Overall, however, his new position left him unsatisfied.

Embree's growing impatience was due largely to his appraisal of the atmosphere that had developed within the foundation. To his mind, the organization had lost the innovative spirit that had characterized Rockefeller Sr. and the first cohort of foundation leaders, resulting in a tendency to justify the trust's existence on its past accomplishments. While he did not doubt the value of Rockefeller programs and their effectiveness, he believed that important opportunities were being missed. The board's skepticism regarding human biology was, to him, proof that a kind of bureaucratic sclerosis was setting in. In such "an ultra-conventional organization," as he described it to a friend, his creative abilities were unlikely to find the outlet he craved.[25]

One aspect of Embree's creativity that was denied full expression at Rockefeller was his writing. From his undergraduate days, through his year with the *New York Sun* and the next decade in New Haven, Embree thought of himself as a writer. His love of writing is evident in the long, well-crafted journals he maintained during his travels. But these journals, informative and colorful as they were, were intended to reach only a narrow circle of family and friends. To be sure, his foundation trips also involved the preparation of numerous reports, complete with extensive assessments and carefully framed recommendations. Yet these were for internal consumption only, and as he later explained to a Rockefeller board member, writing for publication was not encouraged at the foundation.[26] During more than ten years at Rockefeller, Embree's publications were limited to a handful of articles in the *Yale Alumni Weekly* and three brief pieces in national magazines. With his enjoyment of expression and a growing desire to inform and persuade a broad audience, the lack of opportunity at Rockefeller must have been more than a bit stifling.[27]

Throughout 1927, Embree's frustration continued to mount. On several occasions, he had frank discussions about his career possibilities with George Vincent. The foundation's president was generally supportive, but careful to avoid exerting any kind of pressure, leaving his younger colleague free to make up his own mind. Yet it became increasingly evident, as perhaps Vincent had foreseen, that Embree would not long remain at Rockefeller. It was at this point that the philanthropist Julius Rosenwald, the retired president of Sears, Roebuck, approached him about a new position.

* * *

Embree and Rosenwald had known each other for over a decade. They had met when the older man had joined the Rockefeller board in 1917, only a few weeks after Embree had taken up his foundation duties. During the closing months of the First World War, when both were in Paris, they dined together on several occasions. Early in 1920, following Embree's next trip to Europe, he shared some of his observations with Rosenwald, and then visited him in Chicago for dinner at his home and a tour of the huge Sears plant. On these occasions, they discussed Rosenwald's giving practices, and Embree offered to help in any way that did not conflict with his Rockefeller responsibilities.[28]

As early as 1923, Julius Rosenwald had begun to ponder how his philanthropy could do the greatest good. For ten years, he promoted the building of schools in black communities across the rural South. He provided the initiating spark, seed money, building plans, coordination, and overall leadership, resulting by 1928 in construction of over 4,000 schools. This was a thriving enterprise, with great needs still unmet. But with a growing fortune during the booming twenties, and his profoundly generous impulses undiminished, the merchant prince was open to new ventures. From his friend Abraham Flexner of the GEB, he sought advice about how the Rosenwald Fund should be structured and its efforts focused.

Through his own work, Flexner had been captivated by the pervasive problems of southern blacks and the improvements that could result from philanthropic interventions. He counseled the former Sears president to concentrate his giving on efforts to improve the lives of that oppressed minority, pointing to critical initiatives that could be taken in education, medical care and public health, community centers, and recreation facilities. But, he emphasized, no field for the advancement of African American citizens was more important than education, and the prestige Rosenwald already had in that field "ought not to be wasted and which perhaps no one else will ever again acquire."[29]

Rosenwald needed little persuasion to continue giving to black communities across the South, but many months would pass before he was ready to restructure what was basically a family foundation. By 1927, however, the claims on his time and largesse had become so great that reorganization and professional leadership could no longer be avoided. As he confided to Flexner, he needed "someone to keep me straight . . . the best man I can get to enable me to use my money wisely."[30] After interviewing several candidates who proved unsatisfactory, and perhaps after learning from Vincent of Embree's discontent, the Chicago philanthropist asked Flexner to explore the possibilities with his Rockefeller colleague. Flexner did so, emphasizing to Embree the importance of black advancement and pointing out the immense opportunities for courageous philanthropy in the South.[31] Embree was intrigued.

Following preliminary conversations with Rosenwald in New York, Embree in late November traveled to Chicago for more detailed discussions. The two men came quickly to an understanding. Offered the newly created position of president of the Julius Rosenwald Fund, Embree gave his oral acceptance at once. His decision meant leaving the wealthiest group of trusts in the country for a much smaller philanthropy. It meant distancing himself from the nation's center of power in New York. It meant abandoning the Northeast, where he had lived for a quarter-century, and moving to a city unfamiliar to him and initially unattractive to his wife and family. He had crossed what amounted to a personal Rubicon.[32]

The gravity of his decision did not register with Embree at first. But within hours, he was struck by agonizing second thoughts. Back in his Chicago hotel, he felt "perfectly miserable." He saw himself losing all the prestige of his position at Rockefeller, and he wondered how he could explain his reduced status to his associates and his Yale friends. During that night, he "rolled and tossed in deep dismay." He experienced "a nightmare of terror," then and for several nights following. Though Rosenwald offered him the opportunities and the freedom for which he had yearned for months, there now bubbled up from his subconscious deep-seated, heretofore unrecognized anxiety about his professional status. The respect, even deference, he received as a consequence of his positions at Yale and Rockefeller, he feared, would be irretrievably lost. His connections to major institutions, his relations with important people, his club memberships, the advantages he had come to take for granted now took on unexpected importance, and the prospect of losing all that left him, even in his dreams, "in a cold sweat." This newly discovered attitude in himself, he admitted to Clarence Day, until quite recently he would have considered "unworthy and repugnant."[33]

That doubts should arise immediately after such a momentous career decision is not altogether surprising. Yet most striking is what those doubts reveal about the man himself, about his ambition and his character. Embree was ambitious, but the nature of his ambition was not conventional. He did not aspire to conspicuous wealth or personal power. What he sought was influence, the opportunity and the means to affect popular thinking and, subsequently, social practices and public policy.

To achieve those goals, he needed access to the national media and entrée to persons of wealth and stature. He had come to know some of the nation's elites, and he found movement in such circles highly congenial. Leaving the power centers of the Northeast, he feared, might close off such avenues to him. Moreover, his position at the much smaller, far less well-known Rosenwald Fund, even as its chief executive, held no guarantee of increased influence. Lacking the resources of the Rockefeller or Carnegie philanthropies, the Fund was not likely to undertake the large, showy projects that would attract great attention and enhance the reputation of its president. Rather than increasing his influence, the new position might consign him to a kind of terminal obscurity.

Embree's doubts, marking a profound crisis of confidence, illumine important aspects of his character. It is remarkable that Embree recognized his misgivings for what they were. And far from pushing them aside, he used them as a stimulus for deep personal reflection. Seeking to understand what his reactions revealed about his innermost self, he turned upon himself his searching curiosity. All that he discovered was not personally pleasing, but he did not try to keep the episode entirely to himself. He was secure enough in his own person to describe it to his closest friend. Embarrassing as his feelings might be, he acknowledged them as an authentic expression of his own personality.

As days and weeks passed, and as Embree analyzed his emotions, he gradually came to terms with the consequences of his decision. Moving to the Rosenwald Fund was undoubtedly the most important action of his professional life, but its effects were not limited to his career. Also important was what this episode revealed to Embree about himself. He continued to relish association with people of prominence, and opportunities to address difficult issues continued to attract him. But he was more self-aware, clearer about his own motivations, better prepared to gain respect through his own ideas and accomplishments rather than borrowing it from the institutions he served. He had become, in an authentic sense, his own man.

* * *

Upon returning to New York, Embree immediately informed President Vincent of his decision. Two days later, Vincent, mindful of Embree's long chafing, agreed to release the vice president from his post at the end of the month. On the next business day, Rosenwald had Embree's formal letter of acceptance.[34] Events had moved rapidly. The remaining time at Rockefeller was short.

Those few days were put to good use. Between clearing items on his desk and arranging for his relocation, Embree managed to squeeze out time for another event that proved of unforeseen importance. Back from Chicago, he found his colleague Leonard Outhwaite of the LSRM deep in planning a conference on the problems of black Americans and black-white relations. This was to be a small, racially mixed affair, a rare occurrence in the 1920s, and the arrangements had not gone smoothly. Less than two weeks before the conference was to open, a place for the meeting had not been found. With participants coming primarily from the South and East, Outhwaite had considered Princeton to be the most convenient location, until he was advised that "the atmosphere in Princeton [was] not particularly suitable for this type of meeting," and warned that finding a venue anywhere would be difficult.[35] In desperation, Outhwaite turned to Embree for help. Drawing on his Yale connections, and knowing students would be away on holiday, Embree arranged for accommodations in New Haven, in the house of Zeta Psi, his own fraternity. Information about the location was received by participants only six days before the conference opened. In appreciation, Outhwaite invited Embree to attend as a guest.

Organizational difficulties notwithstanding, the conference turned out to be quite valuable for Embree. Though he was already acquainted with a few of the participants, he was able to renew those connections and to make a number of new ones. His Yale mentor, Anson Phelps Stokes, had to withdraw, but in his place came Thomas Jesse Jones, the education director of the Phelps Stokes Fund, whose decade-old book on black education still generated controversy. Prominent among those in attendance were two men who would become Embree's principal collaborators at the Julius Rosenwald Fund: Will Alexander of the Atlanta-based Commission on Interracial Cooperation and Charles S. Johnson, then director of research for the National Urban League (NUL) and editor of its magazine, *Opportunity*. Also attending were the heads of the NUL and the National Association for the Advancement of Colored People

(NAACP), along with the presidents of four historically black universities. Several church bodies were represented, as were business, labor, medicine, and the YMCA.[36]

For three days, the fourteen black and eight white men met and talked, eating together, living together, relaxing together. In setting up the conference, the LSRM organizers had hoped for consideration of not only current circumstances, but efforts to foresee how race relations might develop over the next decade or two. With an informal atmosphere, a limited structure, and no expectation of any resolution or public pronouncement, the conference lent itself to freewheeling discussion. Morning and afternoon sessions were devoted to economics, education, the black church, legal issues, housing, and travel. On Embree's suggestion, a special evening session was devoted to consideration of culture and the arts. The intense conversations informed and energized Embree, and he left New Haven with a number of initiatives in mind for possible action at Rosenwald. Some of these ideas were by no means new to him, but his thinking was clearer, his resolve greater than it had been even three days earlier.[37]

The New Haven conference ended on Wednesday, December 21. Embree was back in the office the next two days. With Christmas Day occurring on Sunday, a three-day weekend followed, but he was back at his desk on Tuesday. The three days before the New Year's weekend were undoubtedly a slack time, but even with his accumulated vacation time untaken, he was not one to leave Rockefeller business unfinished. Nor did he feel the need for a respite before moving to his new assignment. Julius Rosenwald encouraged him to extend the holiday period, take a few days to prepare for his move, spend some time with his family. But Embree was eager to get started. He would take an overnight train to Chicago on January 2, he wired Rosenwald, and as soon as he could drop his bags off at his hotel in the morning, he would arrive at the fund's headquarters "with sleeves already rolled up."[38] Leaving his family in Brooklyn to complete the school year, he boarded the New York Central for Chicago.

As his train steamed westward, Embree had time to reflect on his years at Rockefeller, to think about what he was leaving behind and what might lie ahead. He was leaving the foundation with some regrets, but

also with reason for considerable satisfaction. Though he had not succeeded in moving the organization as far into new fields as he had hoped,
some progress had been made. With a "dramatic speech" in 1924, he
had initiated consideration of the humanities as an area of Rockefeller
interest, and he had ably seconded the efforts of Abraham Flexner to
push the GEB in that direction.[39] Similarly, he had joined with the flam-
boyant Beardsley Ruml of the LSRM to ensure that the social sciences
received increased attention. The fact that the reorganized Rockefeller
Foundation now had divisions devoted to these two areas of knowledge
was cause for some self-congratulation.

The venture into human biology had not turned out as he had hoped,
but even there his efforts had met with some success. Due to Rockefeller
funding, the field of anthropology was more firmly established in Australia, and research at Honolulu's Bishop Museum was more adequately
supported. In the United States, Raymond Pearl's work on human heredity and Robert Yerkes's study of primates were moving forward. And
as a result of Embree's activity, networks of scientists on four continents
had been formed or strengthened. He had not persuaded most Rockefeller trustees of the viability of the cross-disciplinary research he had
promoted. Yet he remained convinced he had been on the right track, as
unfolding events would make clear.[40] Nor did he doubt that his steady
emphasis on the problems stemming from population growth had been
appropriate. Though several decades might pass before such problems
would begin to preoccupy intellectual and political leaders, he was convinced that the issues would multiply, sooner or later requiring concentrated attention and decisive action.

Embree may well have mused on how, over more than two years, his
dissatisfaction at Rockefeller had risen and how that had affected his associates. Years later, one of them would credit his "restless exploration" of
new fields as the only notable effort to diversify the foundation's interests
before the 1927–1929 reorganization.[41] His continual challenging of established policies and procedures and his suggestions for fresh initiatives
had not always been appreciated. That he knew; yet his conscience was
clear. His questioning had not been free of self-interest, to be sure, but
its purpose extended well beyond his career concerns. It was intended to
combat the deadening bureaucratic routine that so troubled board chair

Rockefeller and future president Fosdick. Against institutional inertia, he had not prevailed, but knowing he had persisted valiantly might have yielded some comfort.

Whatever mark Embree left on the Rockefeller trusts, they left a far larger mark on him. The decade at 61 Broadway, including his wide-ranging travels, had prepared him for his new responsibilities at the Julius Rosenwald Fund. He now knew how to organize a philanthropic office and build a talented staff. He had mastered the arts of evaluating grant proposals and of helping applicants to improve their plans. He recognized the necessity of fieldwork. He understood the importance of shaping a supportive board and how best to keep its members informed and engaged. He had come to know the value of concentrating initiative and authority in the hands of the chief executive. He had gained familiarity with the problems of the American South, problems he realized could be best addressed through education, broadly conceived. Above all, he had learned how to use money to effect change. His apprenticeship in philanthropy completed, his journeyman years behind him, Edwin Embree was ready to prove himself a master of his craft.

* * *

The offices of the Julius Rosenwald Fund were located in a corner of the vast Sears distribution center on the industrial outskirts of Chicago. Arriving at headquarters with his "sleeves already rolled up," as promised, Embree set to work. His challenge in the early months was to move the fund from a family philanthropy to a professionally organized foundation. The staff had to be increased, office procedures refined, policies developed, and, in time, institutional direction and emphases clarified. Central to the task was the reorganization and enlargement of the fund's board of trustees.

At the beginning of 1928, the board consisted only of Julius Rosenwald, his wife Augusta, and their eldest child Lessing. In the reorganization, Augusta Rosenwald left the board, and eight new members (in addition to Embree) were named. Five of the new members were from outside the family, including two men Embree had handpicked. One was his closest associate from 61 Broadway, Beardsley Ruml of the LSRM.[42] The other was Franklin C. McLean, the eminent bone physiologist Embree had first met at the PUMC, who was then in the process of establishing the University of Chicago Medical School. Julius and Lessing continued on the board, and three new family members were added: daughter Adele Rosenwald Levy, and Alfred K. Stern and Edgar B. Stern, the husbands of the Rosenwalds' other two daughters.

Alfred Stern, described as "a charming and handsome fellow," had married the Rosenwalds' daughter Marion in 1921.[43] Recognizing that his new son-in-law had no particular career plan, Julius Rosenwald had placed him on the fund's payroll. Though Stern lacked significant management experience, he was later named director of the fund, marking him as second in command behind the founder. Of all the younger generation of the family, Stern had been most actively involved in, hence most firmly attached to, the philanthropy's customary activities. Relations between Stern and the fund's new president began well enough, but as Embree's different vision of the trust's direction began to take hold, Alfred found himself steadily eased to the sidelines. The creation of additional executive positions carrying the director's title, which hitherto only Stern had held, symbolized his diminished status. He would remain on the payroll until 1935 but, lacking a specific portfolio, he was relegated primarily to routine tasks.[44]

Edgar Stern, husband of the Rosenwalds' daughter Edith, was a prominent New Orleans businessman, with a sizable fortune accrued in cotton trading. With two degrees from Harvard, he shared with Embree an Ivy League background, a circumstance that may have contributed to a good relationship. In any event, after some initial strain caused by an impolitic Embree remark about the South's lack of initiative and resourcefulness, the two men and Stern's strong-willed wife worked together quite well. The Sterns were particularly gratified when Embree helped them select a biographer for Julius Rosenwald, and Embree cultivated the couple assiduously, visiting their palatial home, inviting them to his Canadian retreat, and carrying on an active correspondence. Apart from Lessing Rosenwald, who served on the board throughout the fund's life, Edgar Stern became the most consistently active family trustee.[45]

The founder excepted, members of the Rosenwald family seem to have had some initial uncertainty about Embree's authority and their role on the fund's board. Such uncertainty, perhaps even anxiety, about the family's influence on fund affairs rose after Alfred Stern's departure from the board in 1931 and the death of Julius Rosenwald a year later. A term limit on board membership meant that subsequently there would be no more than three family trustees at any one time, which presaged their declining influence as the board continued to expand. Such a consideration probably underlay the decision, made four months after the founder's death in 1932, to reverse a decision taken just two years earlier, and reduce the number of trustees from thirteen to eleven, thereby increasing the relative weight of the family members.[46]

As board membership changed over the next few years, Embree moved adroitly to build strength and to diversify the perspectives and regions represented. In addition to Ruml and McLean, the early additions were Cincinnati mayor Murray Seasongood, University of Illinois president Harry W. Chase, Commission on Interracial Cooperation president Will W. Alexander, Harold H. Swift of the meatpacking family, and Chicago manufacturer Frank L. Sulzberger. No less notable were others Embree put forward as potential board members: U.S. senator Dwight Morrow (erstwhile ambassador to Mexico and an Embree family friend from New Jersey), Harvard law professor and future U.S. Supreme Court justice Felix Frankfurter, industrialist Henry S. Dennison, and Social Sciences Research Council chair Wesley Clair Mitchell.[47]

Embree's commitment to broaden the experiences and views represented on the board extended into the nation's African American community. An important breakthrough occurred with the election to trusteeship of the first black man to join a philanthropy board: sociologist Charles S. Johnson, whom Embree and Julius Rosenwald had tried unsuccessfully to recruit for the staff years earlier. First chosen in 1934, Johnson would be closely associated with the fund for many years, as Embree's steady confidant and through repeated elections to board membership. Also beneficial was the election in the early 1940s of the eminent Washington lawyer Charles H. Houston, the principal architect of the NAACP's attack on racial segregation and an active trustee for the remaining life of the fund. These Rosenwald Fund precedents notwithstanding, more than two decades would pass before other philanthropic boards would begin to elect black members in significant numbers.

No less innovative was the ethnically mixed composition of the fund's professional staff. Within months of his arrival and with the enthusiastic support of Julius Rosenwald, Embree invited a black Chicago YMCA executive to join the organization. George R. Arthur, probably the first person of African descent to work for any foundation in a professional capacity, remained with the fund for six years, serving primarily with the school-building program. In the mid-thirties, M. O. Bousfield, a physician prominent in the segregated National Medical Association, was appointed director for Negro health. He would continue in that role until called to military service in 1942. In the mid-thirties, a man of Hispanic background, George I. Sanchez, held a full-time research position. In 1943, Charles S. Johnson joined the staff on a part-time basis as co-director of the newly established Division of Race Relations. During the Second World War, in spite of great anti-Japanese sentiment throughout the country, the philanthropy employed on its clerical staff at least three women of Japanese ancestry, one of whom was Embree's own secretary. In making such appointments, Embree made clear that the fund not only opposed workplace discrimination rhetorically, but rejected it conspicuously in practice.

The growth of the board and staff enabled the fund's president to shape the philanthropy with persons likely to ratify his initiatives, and it strengthened his hand in another way as well. With trustees increasingly scattered across the East and South as well as the Midwest, the full board was able to meet only twice a year. As a consequence, decision-making power, apart from major policy matters, came to rest primarily in the board's executive committee. That committee consisted of five persons: the fund's president (who set the agenda and presided), the fund's secretary, and three other board members. And though the three other trustees were customarily drawn from the Chicago area, it was not unusual for one to be absent from the monthly meetings, leaving Embree and the other two trustees to constitute the quorum. Nor was it uncommon for the official membership to be joined by "guests," such as Embree's closest associates on the board, Charles Johnson and Will Alexander, or a member of the staff, persons who could reinforce the president's ideas.[48]

The executive committee had wide-ranging authority. The fund's bylaws authorized the committee to appropriate up to $250,000 between board meetings. Yet that limit could be exceeded with specific approval of the full board or the written consent of two other trustees not members of the executive committee. The committee had the power of resolution, "except in matters of fundamental policy," to broaden or otherwise modify the actions of the full board.[49] Thus, the composition and broad powers of the committee, the president's role within it, and its pattern of operation gave the fund's president great latitude to determine the fund's activities and the distribution of its resources. As a consequence of these arrangements, and Embree's careful preparation, there were few instances when his proposals did not win board approval.

* * *

Because the South had been the domain of the General Education Board, not the Rockefeller Foundation, Embree had little professional reason to travel in that region during his time at 61 Broadway. Consequently, when he moved to Chicago, eight years had passed since he had last visited the area where Rosenwald Fund interest was centered. Keenly aware of the importance of being "in the field," he quickly set about gaining firsthand knowledge. Even before accepting the fund's presidency, he had held a long discussion with the GEB's Leonard Outhwaite about the circumstances of southern blacks. Their conversation ranged over housing, water supply and sewage disposal, education and children's recreation, the training of physicians and nurses, opportunities for entertainment and personal expression.[50] A few weeks after arriving at his new position, Embree embarked, with Outhwaite and S. L. Smith of the fund's Nashville office as guides, on a tour of the southern states.

The men traveled to Richmond and Atlanta, Nashville and Little Rock, Tuskegee and New Orleans, and places in between. They visited historically black colleges and examined some of the Rosenwald-funded rural schools. They talked with educational leaders, state officials, and university presidents. They reviewed in detail the fund's activities in the region and discussed possible new programs. After eight intense days, Embree had a clearer view of the sorts of initiatives that might prove useful.[51]

The southern journey was essential preparation for the first meeting of the Rosenwald Fund's new board, scheduled for late April. Embree planned a three-day conference, a chance for the trustees to get to know each other and to begin thinking about the fund's direction. As part of their orientation, he put together a packet of information about the nation's principal foundations, their histories, assets, and current interests. To supplement the printed materials and provide opportunity for informed dialogue, he invited consultants to meet with the trustees. Most of the consultants were knowledgeable about southern education: Outhwaite of the LSRM; Jackson Davis of the GEB; N. C. Newbold, the North Carolina agent for Negro schools; and Harry W. Chase, former president of the University of North Carolina who was now leading Illinois' principal public university.[52]

During the course of the conference, the trustees were captivated by Julius Rosenwald's announcement that he was adding to the fund's endowment a large block of Sears, Roebuck stock, bringing the fund's capital assets to over $20 million. Though dwarfed by the endowments of the Rockefeller and Carnegie trusts, the Rosenwald Fund nevertheless immediately became the tenth-largest philanthropy in the country and the largest one west of the Hudson.[53] Moreover, the surging economy of the late twenties, epitomized by the Sears empire, promised to raise the endowment's value to even greater heights. But the fund's founder was not through with striking announcements.

Rosenwald had long held firm views about perpetual endowments, and as the former head of the country's largest mercantile enterprise, he knew how easily complex organizations could lose dynamism and fall victim to bureaucratic routine. As early as 1912, even before his first gift for a southern rural school, he had suggested in a public address measures designed to keep philanthropy dynamic.[54] As a trustee of the Rockefeller Foundation, he had aroused the opposition of John D. Rockefeller Jr. when he suggested that the trust should be prepared to spend capital if necessary on a particularly promising venture.[55] Now, placing his own giving on a professional level, he was determined to avoid both obsolescence and stagnation.

The sixty-six-year-old Rosenwald coupled his endowment announcement with two stipulations. The fund was not to be a perpetuity; its capital and accrued interest were to be spent within twenty-five years of his death. In addition, the fund's board was to have a changing membership.

All members were to be elected to three-year terms. Election to a second term was permitted, but apart from the board's chair and the fund's president, service was limited to two consecutive terms, followed by at least a year's absence before becoming eligible for reelection. By prescribing a limited lifespan and regular renewal of its board, the founder intended that the Julius Rosenwald Fund remain innovative and bold.

These provisions of the fund's charter were not entirely novel; at least two other foundations had similar arrangements for the distribution of capital, and two others had comparable arrangements for board turnover.[56] But their specification in connection with such a sizable gift was without precedent. Newspapers across the country seized on the story of this new philanthropic powerhouse in the Midwest. Within days, a half-dozen Chicago papers carried articles or editorials on the fund's new principles. The *Chicago Tribune* praised Rosenwald for his generosity and expressed the hope that other persons of wealth would follow his example. National newspapers, the *New York Times* and the *Christian Science Monitor* among them, picked up on the fund's news release. One commentator wrote that Rosenwald's "discard of the dogma of the inviolacy of principal is a solar plexus blow at the present system of trust endowment and administration."[57]

Such publicity ensured that the ideas of the fund's founder and its new president would get the broad hearing they sought. For their purpose was not just to publicize the fund; they intended also to remove from the public mind some of the mystery shrouding large-scale philanthropy. More important, they sought to stimulate dialogue about how organized giving could be made most effective. They were in fact embarking on a campaign to change the way foundations conducted their business.

* * *

The campaign got under way with an Embree-written essay in the fund's first annual report. There, he described the philanthropy's activities and explained the innovative features of its charter.[58] Such a report would usually find only a limited audience, but a wider public was reached by a *Saturday Evening Post* article by the fund's founder. There, after affirming the importance and difficulty of giving wisely, Rosenwald laid out his views on large benefactions. No chartered philanthropy should be perpetual, he contended. Such endowments in all countries present "a disheartening chronicle of misuse, disuse, and abuse." Because human needs change over time as society progresses, no one could predict accurately what those long-term needs might be. Consequently, philanthropists of one generation should avoid tying up funds devoted to particular purposes, however broad, lest those purposes become obsolete and the funds underused. As a corollary, foundations should be prepared to spend not just interest income but, under certain circumstances, principal as well. A major purpose of the philanthropic enterprise was to encourage social experimentation, and trustees should be legally empowered to change the organization's objectives if necessary to remain useful. Also important were timeliness in giving, operation according to sound business practices, and the use of challenge grants to encourage contributions from others. Concluding the piece, the retired Sears president illustrated how the last of these principles had been applied in his own giving, calling attention to the school-building program, his lead gift for Chicago's Museum of Science and Industry, and his support for Jewish agricultural communities in Ukraine and the Crimea.[59]

Four months later, another article under Rosenwald's name appeared in the *Atlantic Monthly*. Initiative for this piece came from neither Rosenwald nor Embree, but from *Atlantic* editor Ellery Sedgwick. Writing to commend the philanthropist for his opposition to perpetual endowments, Sedgwick asked for a more detailed explanation of Rosenwald's views for publication. Undoubtedly researched by Embree and others, and ghost-written by a Michigan journalist, this piece was aimed at the more sophisticated readership of that magazine. It contained substantial historical information, dealing particularly with the unhappy results of some English philanthropy. Its points were more fully developed, but essentially it elaborated the themes of the earlier essay, sounding them more strongly. Perpetuities could not only become useless, as changing conditions nullified their purposes; they even could do harm by undergirding discredited institutions such as orphanages. Equally grievous was the tendency of trustees to insist on keeping a trust's principal intact, rather than distributing a portion to respond to a pressing need or to take advantage of a promising, perhaps fleeting, opportunity. Perpetual endowments encouraged an attitude of timidity, rather than imaginative and productive use of the funds for more significant societal benefit. By limiting the range of decisions trustees could make, donors were to some degree implying a lack of confidence in their judgment. Instead of devoting their wealth to narrowly defined, long-term charities, the article concluded, makers of large gifts should be confident that future generations would be no less wise and generous than they, and equally prepared to respond to the social needs of their own time.[60]

A rejoinder to Rosenwald soon appeared. Its author was Henry S. Pritchett, president of the Carnegie Foundation for the Advancement of Teaching. Rosenwald's name appeared in the article only once, but there can be no doubt that the Chicago philanthropist was in mind when Pritchett wrote that "some of the most generous givers" were urging that all large gifts should provide for principal and interest to be disbursed at the discretion of the trustees. Acknowledging that the English experience of charitable trusts had involved both obsolescence and abuse, Pritchett nevertheless avowed that such problems were "far from being universal" and largely a thing of the past. Determining whether an organization promoting intellectual or moral causes was being successful was not easy, he pointed out. Moreover, such bodies as governments, universities, churches, and school systems could not be scrapped and reconstituted every quarter-century. They were by nature continuous and, like permanent charitable trusts, remained useful so long as society continued to adapt its structures to address changing needs. Perpetuities, far from implying a lack of confidence in their trustees, were "an act of faith in mankind itself." Both permanent endowments and gifts to be expended within a specified period had their place, but the problem of determining the best use of such philanthropy would not be solved "by surrendering the capital of a great trust to the real, or imaginary, demands of the present moment."[61]

With Pritchett's response, the debate was well under way, and the *Atlantic* decided that public interest was sufficiently aroused to justify yet another article on the subject. Published like the earlier one, under Rosenwald's name, "The Trend Away from Perpetuities" was apparently Embree's idea and written by Embree himself. In fact, he had done much to generate public interest by distributing 50,000 copies of the first *Atlantic* piece to libraries, newspapers, law firms, and numerous individuals.[62] Accompanying the copies to many recipients was a letter requesting responses to Rosenwald's ideas. The replies, numbering in the hundreds, came from captains of industry; bank board chairs; the presidents of Harvard, Yale, and Princeton; the heads of the two largest Rockefeller trusts; and the likes of Thomas Cochran of J. P. Morgan and Lou Henry (Mrs. Herbert) Hoover. Almost without exception supportive of Rosenwald's position, the replies were extensively quoted in this new "Rosenwald/Embree" piece.[63]

Beyond citing positive responses, the author presented evidence suggesting movement away from perpetual benefactions. Authorization from their founders for the Rockefeller boards and the Commonwealth Fund to spend from their endowments was commended. Two new foundations, each capitalized at $10 million, had been established in Pennsylvania and Michigan with the provision that all assets should be spent within a generation. Perpetuities had long ago demonstrated their futility, the article contended, as evidenced by their failure among ancient Egyptians, Greeks, Chaldeans, and Romans. Nor did more recent experience indicate a need for perpetual endowments, for the great seats of learning in Europe and America had prospered not as a consequence of their initial endowments, but because their obvious usefulness had generated additional gifts. Real endowments were ideas, not money, and so long as an idea met a significant public need, society's support was assured.[64]

In the meantime, Frederick P. Keppel, president of the Carnegie Corporation of New York, had entered the debate. His opportunity came when he delivered the University of Virginia's Page-Barbour Lecture, which was published in 1930 under the title *The Foundation: Its Place in American Life*. Having selected the topic partially in response to the discussions triggered by Rosenwald, Keppel undertook to treat it comprehensively and to present a "body of foundation doctrine" heretofore lacking. Reviewing the range of contemporary foundation practices, he pointed to the attractiveness of sizable gifts that addressed large concerns, yet suggested that focused small grants could also be useful. He endorsed the value of conditional grants, but cautioned that they could lead recipients into financial commitments they could not sustain. On the contentious question of perpetuities, he sided with his Carnegie Fund counterpart Pritchett, avowing that both permanent endowments and foundations which disbursed both capital and interest had their place. Maintaining a measured approach throughout, Keppel emphasized the importance of full public disclosure of every foundation's finances and activities. At the same time, in what may have been a subtle reproof of the Rosenwald/Embree initiative, he inveighed against foundation efforts to influence public opinion.[65]

Even as Keppel was preparing his lectures, Embree was at work penning his own overt contribution to the discussion. That contribution took the form of an article in *Harper's*, published within weeks of Keppel's lecture. With the verve that characterized all his writing, Embree provided ample information, telling examples, and a farsighted perspective. The problem facing American foundations, he emphasized, was deciding how to secure maximum social benefit from the unprecedented largesse of the country's most prosperous businessmen. He called attention to instances of unwise generosity (including the now well-worn example of endowing orphan asylums) and to bizarre appeals that envisioned the creation of a "Negro navy" or a foundation to eliminate crossed eyes ("The Cross-Eyed Foundation," Embree jocularly labeled it). But the article focused on examples of intelligent and productive giving, stemming from the work of the Rockefeller, Carnegie, and Rosenwald philanthropies.[66]

Drawing on his insider's knowledge of the Rockefeller trusts, Embree described in detail the success of the General Education Board in reforming medical education, the Sanitary Commission in fighting hookworm, the Rockefeller Institute in medical research, and the Laura Spelman Rockefeller Memorial in promoting the social sciences. The Carnegie Institution of Washington, alone among the Carnegie foundations, received several paragraphs describing various initiatives in basic scientific investigation. In regard to the Rosenwald Fund, Embree hinted at pending ventures in health insurance, the "mental sciences," and the fine arts, but his emphasis was on its signature program of school building for rural black communities. More significant than the schools themselves, he suggested, was the fact that, as a result of Rosenwald cooperation with state agencies in the construction effort, the South had come to recognize its obligation to provide education for all its citizens. Thus, the method of giving—using challenge grants and involving other public agencies and citizens group—enabled the fund to achieve larger purposes than originally envisioned.

The piece did not stop with this historical recounting of philanthropic achievements. Embree went much further, presenting the views expressed in the article ghost-written for Julius Rosenwald, but here spelled out more fully under his own name. The "new philanthropy," he declared, did not need perpetual endowments. By making a public need evident and demonstrating through a funded project how to meet it, a foundation could render valuable and sufficient public service, and be confident that society would assume responsibility in the future. The purpose of organized giving was to generate new knowledge and show how it could benefit society; the goal should not be to satisfy current "social appetites" but to create new ones. A trust could slide into perfunctory performance, he warned, if its leaders became timid or lacked vision. The real danger was not, as some political figures feared, that large foundations would subvert democracy, but that they would "fritter away their potential power in small and insignificant enterprises." Grant makers should always insist on excellence, avoiding mediocrity, "the curse of democracies." Moreover, public-spirited donors should avoid establishing private agencies to perform what should be public services, the province of the state. And, perhaps recalling his undergraduate study of J. S. Mill's essay *On Liberty*, Embree pointed out that even giving to worthy persons could be dangerous, for "it is sinful to do for any individual what that individual can do for himself." Modern philanthropy, he concluded, should seek to initiate, then stand aside, "to give as little as possible for as short a time as possible."[67]

Of all the pieces on organized giving published during this time, Embree's was decidedly the most informative and farsighted, entertaining and persuasive. Its style, its appearance in a high-toned magazine, and the interest generated by earlier articles meant that it was probably widely read. What gave it a particular point, however, was the fact that Embree and his fellow commentators were providing information and viewpoints unfamiliar even to the educated public. To be sure, Henry Pritchett, long and deeply involved with the Carnegie trusts, had turned out a small volume on philanthropy a few years earlier. Frederick Keppel had published an address on "Opportunities and Dangers of Educational

Foundations," in which he had aptly described the foundation as "a social instrument still in the experimental stage."[68] Yet both these works lacked Embree's illustrative detail, and neither can be considered comprehensive. And if these two spokesmen for Carnegie philanthropy made only limited contributions to public understanding, representatives of the Rockefeller trusts made even less. From the heyday of Frederick Gates, it had been well-established policy to avoid publicity whenever possible, partly to protect the privacy of the Rockefeller family, partly to avoid arousing uneasiness about the philanthropies' power. Thus, during his time at the foundation, Embree, like his colleagues on related Rockefeller boards, had been strongly discouraged, if not prohibited, from writing about their philanthropic work.

Having arrived at Rosenwald, however, he was able to give his love of writing free rein. Even as he was orchestrating the campaign against perpetuities and timid foundation leaders, he was working on other publications. Beyond the important *Harper's* piece, he published five articles in this period, all designed to inform different audiences about national needs and philanthropic efforts to address them. An April 1928 piece described the inadequate health care available to black Americans and emphasized, as Embree would do for the rest of his life, that what disadvantaged citizens of color harmed the majority population as well.[69] The following month, an educational journal carried his account of the Rosenwald school-building program, complete with pictures of finished buildings and the nine different designs used in construction. Two months later appeared an article calling for improved training for nurses.[70] August 1929 saw the publication of "What Is Organized Medicine?" a summary of advances in medical education and public health, and a call for new arrangements to enable the middle class to pay for medical care.[71] Based on an earlier presentation to the American Hospital Association, this piece foreshadowed Rosenwald-funded projects demonstrating the feasibility of prepaid health insurance. The benefits of such an approach were subsequently promoted in an extensive *New York Times* piece and in a popularly written article, which included descriptions of health-related initiatives taken by various foundations.[72] The Milbank Memorial Fund, the Duke Endowment, and the Commonwealth Fund received attention, but pride of place went to Rockefeller philanthropy. "No influence in world history," Embree affirmed, "has been greater in advancing medicine and in reducing preventable sickness than that of the boards set up by Mr. Rockefeller."[73]

The Rosenwald/Embree effort to change national thinking about organized philanthropy attracted considerable public attention, but its long-range consequences are not entirely clear. Certainly, perpetual trusts continued to be created, and many already in existence were careful to preserve most of their capital. Yet the campaign was not without effect. After a daylong visit from Julius Rosenwald, who arrived with supportive letters from prominent citizens in hand, George Eastman of the giant photography firm Eastman Kodak decided to require his new foundation to spend all principal and interest during his lifetime.[74] Similarly, a fund-raising collaborative of American colleges in the Middle East, on Rosenwald's insistence, agreed that some proceeds of a current campaign would not be held in perpetuity. Michigan senator James Couzens, in establishing his $10 million fund for child welfare in 1929, exceeded the Rosenwald example by stipulating that its life be no longer than twenty-five years. J. P. Morgan's Thomas Cochran, calling the first *Atlantic* piece "one of the most constructive contributions to the subject I have read," wrote Rosenwald that the article had changed his thinking about a substantial gift he was planning to make.[75] Cordage magnate Robert Brookings, whose endowed institution was only four years old, considered Rosenwald's ideas even more valuable than his large donations, and expressed an intention to look into his own gifts with an eye to relaxing stipulations about perpetuity. Portions of a scholarly book published during this time echoed Rosenwald's strictures on perpetuities. And in 1931, six months after the second *Atlantic* piece appeared, R. T. Crane, a Chicago manufacturer of plumbing supplies, donated his first $1 million to the Institute of Current World Affairs, with stipulations that trustees were to have limited terms and be empowered to spend the capital.[76] That same year, participants in a conference on philanthropy heard a paper that went beyond the Rosenwald position, arguing that "endowment . . . is not in the public interest and should not be solicited or permitted in any form."[77]

Whatever successes Embree and Rosenwald achieved in their campaign was due to their combined strengths. The fund's president knew how to manage the undertaking and articulate its key elements; the founder, with unparalleled experience in merchandising, brought to their efforts the name recognition that ensured their ideas would get an extensive hearing. But the significance of this initial effort to shape opinion is not limited to its demonstration of effective collaboration between the two men.

Their campaign reflected as well a keen awareness of how ample publicity could advance their goals. More important, it served as a precedent for what would become a distinctive thrust of the Julius Rosenwald Fund a few years later. In addition, Embree's extraordinary publishing activity during these months, viewed in context, reveals much about the man himself. The number and variety of his publications convey an impression of pent-up creativity, which had just been waiting for an opportunity to burst forth. Freed from the strictures of the Rockefeller Foundation, he was now able to exercise his talent, to describe programs he knew, and to present convictions he held. And even as he was gathering information and constructing paragraphs, he was also adjusting to a new setting, selecting a staff, reorganizing an office, weighing new directions for the organization, traveling the country, deepening relations with Julius Rosenwald, and establishing himself with family trustees somewhat skeptical of the new man. That he was able to write so much while successfully carrying out the varied responsibilities of a new position is indicative of remarkable flexibility, well-honed personal skills, and no small energy.

* * *

Embree's uncommon energy continued to be manifest, as it had been at Rockefeller, in unending travels and the diverse issues he was able to address in an inevitably crowded schedule. In 1928, a month after leaving for Chicago, he was back in New York. In a busy week, he devoted a full day to discussion of education in Liberia, followed by three days soliciting suggestions for Rosenwald staff appointments and holding job interviews. On Sunday, he met with National Research Council head Vernon Kellogg and Secretary of Commerce Herbert Hoover to consider ways to facilitate land acquisition by black tenant farmers in the South. Twelve days later, he embarked on his week-long tour of six southern states discussed earlier. By the end of March, he was back in Manhattan for another round of interviews and discussions. Most of May and early June found him in Mexico, surveying the school situation and exploring possible Rosenwald-funded projects there. During this same period, he was also familiarizing himself with education in Nicaragua. Before the year was out, he would return twice to the South and three times to New York.[78]

Embree's trips to New York were unusually frequent in 1928, for his family remained there for some months, but even after their relocation his duties required two or three trips there each year. The most persistent reason was the concentration of foundations in the city and the need to maintain contact particularly with the GEB and other Rockefeller trusts with which the fund cooperated. Occasional conferences with NAACP and NUL officials brought him back. So, too, did regular meetings of the New York Colonization Society, an organization interested in the educational and economic advancement of Liberia, on whose board Embree served for many years. Whenever he was in New York, he relished going to the theater, often attending with his closest friend, Clarence Day. The Rosenwald president would reside in America's midwestern metropolis for over twenty years. But the Northeast and, especially, the nation's largest city never lost their appeal.

FOUR

SOUTHERN INITIATIVES, ASSET COLLAPSE, TRANSFORMATION

Sixteen months after arriving in Chicago, Embree could exult that he was having "the time of my life."[1] As president of the Julius Rosenwald Fund, he for the first time was fully responsible for an organization, its shape, direction, and accomplishments. He had from the founder a broad mandate to move the fund forward, and he was assured of Julius Rosenwald's commitment to bold use of its assets. Those assets, consisting entirely of Sears stock, had grown spectacularly from their $20 million book value soon after Embree arrived. During his second midwestern autumn, they were valued at almost $35 million, apparently guaranteeing the funds necessary for large and promising ventures.[2] The opportunity was at hand to exercise his imagination, to undertake the kind of innovative projects he had found lacking at Rockefeller. Moreover, he was free of the restrictions on his writing that had frustrated him in the former position. Highly energized by his new situation, he was confident about his ability to deal with the future he saw ahead. Yet only a few more months would pass before he was confronted by unforeseen problems, difficulties so severe as to threaten the very life of the Rosenwald Fund.

* * *

Embree in mid-1929 had good reason to be enthusiastic. From its original preoccupation with building rural schoolhouses in the South, the fund had moved far in a short time. Aid was now being extended to high schools and colleges, hospitals and health agencies that served black communities. Money had been allocated for pilot projects aimed at expanding county library services in the South. Planning was well under way for demonstrations of ways to make medical services more afford-able for persons of modest income. And in keeping with a firm Embree commitment, a program of fellowships had been established to enable talented African Americans to advance their careers.

Embree's interest in the South and in the nation's African American citizenry inevitably became more intense with his move to Rosenwald. But it certainly did not originate then. His rearing in a racially integrated community and his understanding of the uniqueness of that social envi-ronment had sensitized him from an early age to black-white relations. Two decades in the Northeast had demonstrated that racial discrimina-tion, while more pronounced in the South, was not limited to that region and its heavily agricultural population. Early in his foundation work, he recognized the pressing need for improved health care for urban blacks, and how such improvement would benefit the white population as well. With that in mind, he had strongly supported a Rockefeller-funded dispensary demonstration project in New York's predominantly black neighborhoods. Though his work at Rockefeller had centered on national and international projects of research and training, he had maintained southern connections. Throughout the 1920s he, along with his brother Will, had been an active trustee of an industrial boarding school for Mis-sissippi blacks, whose founder and principal had been a Berea College classmate of their sister Hallie.[3] And he remained in occasional contact with some of his Berea classmates.

Highly conscious of racial discrimination as a national problem, Embree nevertheless continued the fund's concentration on the South and its large minority population. Even with several fresh initiatives under way by 1929, he continued to cast around for other ideas for phil-anthropic investment. Toward that end, he consulted widely—with Howard University president Mordecai Johnson, the "dean of south-ern liberals" Will Alexander, National Urban League executive Charles S. Johnson, Phelps Stokes Fund official Thomas Jesse Jones. His Yale mentor, Anson Phelps Stokes, now dean of the National Cathedral in Washington, frequently passed on advice and suggestions. Throughout the Rockefeller years, Embree had benefited from the tutelage of the GEB's Abraham Flexner, and he now called repeatedly on the older man's fertile mind. Flexner's long-standing friendship with Julius Rosen-wald, together with his knowledge of the South, made him an unusually valuable consultant.[4]

Yet even with a regional focus clearly in view, Embree did not quickly rule out fund efforts of broader scope. Long fascinated by the fine arts, he continued to consider initiatives in that area, particularly in the rap-idly developing field of film, which he considered the popular expression of the fine arts of his time. How to advance human development still intrigued him, and he pondered possibilities for the kind of eugenics-related research he had promoted at Rockefeller.[5] From his Rockefeller experience, reinforced by conversations with Flexner, he also had ideas for projects in general education, involving experimentation and demon-strations along progressive lines at the elementary and secondary levels. The broad field of mental hygiene continued to hold his interest, and to stimulate board discussion, he suggested such possibilities as devel-oping a major research center at the University of Chicago, clinics for marital counseling, and studies of child development. Promotion of the social sciences, an interest deeply shared with new trustee Beardsley Ruml, seemed promising. Building up two or three private universities in the South, in the expectation that they would serve to raise standards throughout the region, as the University of Chicago had done in the Midwest, was yet another option.[6] Embree allowed his imagination to roam freely, but the breadth of his interests, his awareness of societal needs, and the latitude of his mandate did not make choices easy. With so many tempting possibilities to consider, he had to constantly remind himself, and his associates, of the need to focus their efforts on a few areas, to avoid "scatteration."[7] One idea that occurred to him early on, however, he pursued vigorously to fruition.

In the late 1920s, there were in the South a hundred or so institutions claiming to offer college-level work to black students. Yet few had either the academic standards or the resources to justify their claim to collegiate status. Embree, like other foundation officers and such astute observers as W. E. B. DuBois, was convinced that educational progress could be best achieved by concentrating philanthropic support on a small handful of those schools, encouraging some to consolidate and allowing others to languish until they disappeared altogether. Howard University in

Washington, D.C., and Fisk University and Meharry Medical College in Nashville had the obvious promise to merit such support, as did several Atlanta institutions moving toward federation. Yet in the area between Alabama and eastern Texas, home to many black Americans, there was no comparable private institution. Embree had been struck by that fact on his initial foray into the South as the fund's president.[8]

Soon after returning from his southern trip, Embree wrote to the secretaries of the education boards of the Methodist Episcopal Church and the Congregational Church's American Missionary Association. In New Orleans, the American Missionary Association operated for the local black population small, underfunded Straight College, while the Methodist Episcopal Church controlled the similarly struggling New Orleans University and a nurse-training facility. Embree's letter invited the two men to meet with him to discuss the possible merger of the three institutions.[9] As the cultural center of that region, and as the southern city with the largest black population, New Orleans seemed the obvious place to create a strong university.

Under Embree's impetus, the initial meeting with the two church officials was quickly followed by others. The GEB, already involved in support of Howard, Fisk and Meharry, and the Atlanta group, soon joined the discussions. Six months after his initial letter, discussions of the merger strategy had become sufficiently advanced for Embree to broach the subject to New Orleans businessman and Rosenwald Fund trustee Edgar Stern. Conferences continued into 1929, at the end of which the four organizations agreed to combine the two collegiate institutions to establish Dillard University and to create the hundred-bed Flint-Goodridge Hospital. Under the agreement, the two church boards each agreed to provide a start-up payment of a half-million dollars and an annual operating subsidy for the next ten years. The Rosenwald Fund and the GEB contributed a total of $1 million for land and buildings. A fund-raising campaign centered on New Orleans was then mounted, and construction on the new site was soon under way. In September 1935, the university celebrated its formal opening.[10]

Dillard University came into being largely as a result of Embree's initiative and drive, and it remained for many years closely linked to the Rosenwald Fund. From the beginning, its board was chaired by Edgar

Stern, who played a critical role in building support and raising money within the city's white community. Its first president was Will Alexander, a key member of the Rosenwald board, who agreed, only at Embree's urging, to accept the position.[11] Alexander, who would be the university's only white president, was succeeded after a few years by A. W. Dent, appointed earlier as administrator of the Flint-Goodridge Hospital. Dent, like Horace Mann Bond, the university's first dean, and several founding department heads had been recipients of Rosenwald Fund fellowships. The fellowship program, established primarily to foster development of black leadership through awards for graduate study and creative activity, benefited numerous institutions, but probably none more than Dillard.[12]

Nor were the links between Dillard and the fund limited to individuals. Beyond its initial contribution for land and buildings, Rosenwald continued to make grants for operating expenses and temporary endowment. Indeed, the fund's gifts to Dillard exceeded those given to any other institution, more than triple those made to Howard, almost double those to the Atlanta schools, one and a half times the amount received by Fisk. Dozens of other historically black colleges and universities received relatively small grants from time to time, but all of those together do not approach what went to Dillard. By the time the fund closed in 1948, it had awarded that institution more than $1 million, almost 5 percent of Rosenwald's total expenditures over a thirty-one-year period.[13] Having taken the lead in creating a new center for black education, Embree and the Rosenwald board sought through continuing subsidies to ensure its success.

As the fund moved energetically into support for black higher education, it began to move away from its signature school-building program. By the time Embree joined Rosenwald, the effort to build elementary schools in rural black communities had been sustained for a decade and a half. From the program's beginning, the erection of a school had been a cooperative undertaking, involving seed money and guidance from the fund, contributions in cash and in kind from the local black community, donations from white citizens, sizable infusions of tax money, and a commitment from school officials to take responsibility for the building when it was completed. This arrangement had been spectacularly successful, in both vastly increasing elementary schools for black youngsters and, indirectly, encouraging improvement in facilities for white youth.[14]

Yet Embree, Julius Rosenwald, and the fund's board became concerned that school boards might become overly dependent on external aid, thereby failing to take full responsibility for properly educating their youth. In the fund's view, the primary purpose of the program was not to put up buildings, important as that was, but to dramatize educational needs and to establish understanding throughout the South that education of all its young citizens was a public duty, to be funded through taxation.[15] Thus, within his first year, Embree began planning to close the program, not because the educational needs of black communities had been fairly met, but because its fundamental purpose had been achieved. The decision was consistent with the fund's approach of "giving as little as possible for as short a time as possible," that is, calling attention to a societal problem, funding demonstrations to show how it could be met, and then leaving full implementation of the solution to the public at large.[16]

The phasing out of the program began with eliminating support for one-teacher schools in 1930, eliminating support for two-teacher schools in 1931, and steadily reducing the number of multi-teacher structures to which the fund committed. In 1932, when the program formally ended, there stood across the fifteen southern and border states 4,977 Rosenwald elementary schools, supplemented by 217 teachers' homes and 163 shops also erected under the fund's initiative. Attending those schools (and a few Rosenwald-aided secondary schools) were more than 650,000 students. The buildings provided sufficient space to accommodate more than 40 percent of the African American students enrolled in rural schools throughout the region.[17]

The fund's educational assistance to black communities was not limited to putting up buildings. With entrée to school districts well established, Rosenwald officials promoted, with limited but notable success, increased pay for teachers. Concerned that schools were sometimes open for blacks only four or five months a year, the fund used start-up subsidies to induce over 200 counties to extend the school year toward a standard eight or nine months. When school consolidation got under way, Rosenwald moneys were used to defray the initial costs of bus service.[18] Such efforts continued even after the school-building program came to an end.

Its demise coincided generally with the close of a much shorter-lived venture in the construction of secondary schools.

By the 1920s, technological changes in southern agriculture were driving thousands of farmers off the land, with the displaced workers flocking to the nation's cities. With its attention focused south of the Mason-Dixon line, the fund was particularly concerned that the younger generation of new town-dwellers be educated beyond the elementary level and be able subsequently to obtain satisfactory jobs.[19] In light of the slow but steady industrialization of the South, with the accompanying demand for skilled labor, many of the region's youth, black and white, needed opportunities to prepare for such jobs. Terms such as *vocational education, manual training, trades preparation,* and *industrial high school* moved rapidly into the popular lexicon.

Closely attuned to societal trends, Embree was fully aware of the need to diversify the educational options available to young men and women. The case for shifting some educational funds from classical studies to industrial training for black youth had been made most comprehensively in 1917 by Thomas Jesse Jones of the Phelps Stokes Fund in his two-volume *Negro Education.* Like others concerned about the nature and quality of black education, Embree was undoubtedly familiar with the book, and the controversy it engendered.[20] Sharp disagreements notwithstanding, when he arrived at Rosenwald, he did not oppose a recent initiative by Alfred K. Stern to support the construction of industrial training facilities. The new president's intention was to provide financial assistance to a few such projects and to study them closely to assess their effectiveness.[21]

As Embree made clear to his trustees, support for industrial training was intended to supplement, not supplant, traditional academic education. It was important to keep the two distinct, he emphasized, lest the latter be watered down by including it in a manual training facility, thereby "glorifying" such training. Academic preparation ("general education," in Embree's parlance) should take place in regular grammar and secondary schools, while vocational preparation should resemble an apprenticeship, requiring six to eighteen months at most. But Embree did not consider such training appropriate for all African American youth. He recognized the importance of the "talented tenth" and insisted that students with professional aspirations have an academic curriculum available throughout their secondary schooling. Even so, it was clear that the number of students continuing through to graduation was small. Academic study should not be neglected, in his view, but enabling young black adults to obtain satisfactory jobs seemed "the greater need" at the time. The necessity of good industrial training became even more pressing in the early Depression years, as black craftspeople began to lose construction jobs to more skilled white workers moving from the North.[22]

During a four-year period ending in 1932, the fund contributed to the construction of industrial facilities at five high schools—in Little Rock, Arkansas; Columbus, Georgia; Maysville, Kentucky; Winston-Salem, North Carolina; and Greenville, South Carolina.[23] As in the elementary school–building program, the fund contributed only a portion of the cost of construction and equipment—one-fifth for an addition to an existing comprehensive school, one-third for a totally new school—with the remainder provided by local money. At these schools boys could learn such trades as carpentry, bricklaying, plastering, and auto mechanics, while girls could study tailoring, millinery, and other branches of home economics. It did not take long for Embree to become dubious about the experiment.

Eighteen months after authorizing the first grants for industrial high schools, the Rosenwald board voted to restrict such aid to projects already approved or currently under consideration. Six months later, Embree reported that vocational education in general was "a very questionable movement," and its results were unsatisfactory. Though millions of dollars were being spent on such training, there was "astonishingly little evidence of careful, realistic study and demonstration of feasible methods to achieve the desired ends."[24] To conduct such a study, he spent months trying to find just the right person. When that search proved fruitless, and with the fund's assets and the Depression itself at their nadir, Embree recommended and the board approved terminating support for industrial education facilities.[25]

* * *

Even as the fund moved away from defraying the costs of school buildings and equipment, it continued a program of providing learning materials. Aware of the dearth of reading materials readily available to rural children in the South, Embree established a system to provide a basic collection for elementary school libraries. Experimentation with various sets of books revealed which titles were appropriate for the various reading levels present in a typical school. By purchasing those titles in bulk, the fund was able to reduce costs by half. Sets of up to fifty books were then offered to schools, with the fund covering one-third of the reduced cost and the community and the state's board of education paying the rest. Offered initially only to black schools, the program was subsequently extended to white schools, though they typically received no fund subsidy. These small library sets were often the only books available for use outside of school and, in some instances, for in-school use as well. During the twenty-year life of the program, over 12,000 sets—more than a half-million books—were distributed.[26]

With the effectiveness of the elementary school approach established, the library program was extended to higher levels. Sets of fourteen books were made available to secondary schools of both races on a shared-cost basis. Clearly intended to broaden students' cultural horizons, the set included such titles as *Young Mexico, All-American, Happy Times in Norway, Here Is Africa,* and *Men Are Brothers.* During its first six years, over 1,700 schools benefited from this component of the program. From the high schools, the fund moved to improve the libraries of historically black colleges. Forty-three institutions received matching grants for book purchases, on the conditions that suitable space, shelving, and furniture be provided, and that at least one trained librarian be on staff. The Rosenwald initiative sparked interest in further library development, with the result that these institutions spent over $2 million for that purpose during the six years the college program was in effect.[27]

Nor were the reading needs of those outside the formal educational setting ignored. In 1928, over 70 percent of the southern population had no access to public library facilities. Service for whites was not well developed, and that for blacks was considerably worse. To address this problem, the fund mounted almost a dozen demonstration projects involving central libraries in county seats, branch stations in other public facilities across the county, and book trucks providing service to residents on the back roads. As in other Rosenwald programs, receiving a grant entailed conditions. Counties had to agree to provide adequate facilities, trained library staff, and equal treatment to all county residents—and to continue equivalent service when the fund's subsidy expired after five years.[28] These projects served not only to demonstrate a rising demand for reading materials and ways to increase access, but also to require nondiscriminatory service for all citizens regardless of race or place of residence. And, as in school building, giving as little as possible for as short a time as possible provided leverage for social reforms.

The promotion of libraries began in Embree's first year at Rosenwald and continued throughout the two decades he headed the philanthropy. Direct beneficiaries of the fund's investment numbered in the hundreds of thousands, and when the stimulus given to public support for library development is considered, the program's overall benefit becomes incalculable. This was one of only two programs sustained throughout Embree's tenure at Rosenwald. The other program was arguably even more far-reaching in its impact. Certainly, it was the single undertaking to which, year in and year out, Embree devoted the most time and energy and the one in which he took the greatest pride.[29]

* * *

The idea of a fellowship program was very much in Embree's mind when he arrived in Chicago. From his Rockefeller experience of awarding fellowships, he knew how effectively such grants could contribute to the careers of young researchers. And he was well aware of programs already under way, notably those for black teachers of education and liberal arts subjects sponsored by the GEB and the Social Sciences Research Council. While still in New York, he had been influenced by conversations with James Weldon Johnson of the National Association for the Advancement of Colored People about a grant program for talented African Americans.[30] As soon as he and the new fund board had settled into their roles, he sought consideration of that promising initiative.

Seven months after the board's organizational meeting, when it came together for only the second time, Embree presented a statement explaining how even small sums could produce impressive results if awarded to "individuals of exceptional promise." Any foundation would have been proud, he pointed out, if in the previous century it had supported the work of Louis Pasteur, Robert Koch, or Charles Darwin. Identifying persons of the greatest potential benefit to society would not be easy, but the possible outcomes should be worth "a few experiments." The trustees expressed interest in the idea, but Embree, proceeding cautiously with a group he still did not know well, did not propose a program. He did, however, recommend a substantial grant to Howard University to support the work of the brilliant African American marine biologist E. E. Just. The board, knowing that Julius Rosenwald had aided Just's research with personal contributions for several years, readily approved the appropriation. In a related matter, a one-year appropriation was made for scholarships for black students at northern universities.[31]

When the board next convened, Embree, now more certain of his ground and with two precedents established, proposed an ongoing program of fellowships and scholarships. In his earlier presentation, he had suggested that the fund should not restrict itself "to any race or nation or subject matter." What he now recommended, however, was a two-pronged program for blacks alone. To avoid duplicating the GEB's efforts, he explained, a division of responsibility had been negotiated, under which Rosenwald would limit its awards to practicing professionals and "individuals of unusual promise who desire to study in Northern colleges or abroad."[32]

To supplement this more general aspect, Embree recommended a second prong aimed at what he labeled "creative workers," primarily those in the arts but not limited to those fields. Achievements in singing, acting, painting, and literature, he pointed out, had brought recognition not only to individuals but to "the Negro race as a whole." Artistic expression had probably done more than anything else to demonstrate that the group was "capable of contributions equal to those of the members of any other race."[33] Such accomplishments seemed most likely to win the respect of the majority population. In stressing this point, Embree touched on the underlying goal of the entire program.

In establishing the fellowships, the fund's president had more than one purpose. He obviously wanted to give promising individuals a chance to develop their abilities, to move closer to their full potential, during a year of concentrated work. In the process of completing a set of canvases or writing a novel or earning an advanced degree, they would enhance their professional standing and career possibilities. For those who used the fellowship for graduate study, as several hundred with plans to become college teachers and researchers did, the additional preparation would benefit their students as well as themselves, while strengthening the institutions they served. In addition, the accomplishments of recipients would serve as inspiration to the next generation, sparking imagination and fueling dreams. The program promised to have the kind of multiplier effect that Embree, and perhaps his more perceptive trustees, envisioned.

But from a larger perspective, the fellowship program can be seen as a great demonstration project, functioning like other such projects but with the possibility of far greater impact. It was intended to show that, in spite of handicaps imposed by racism, given a reasonable chance African Americans could produce and achieve as well as those of European ancestry. Its fundamental purpose, in short, was to make evident that there was nothing inferior about black people, except the opportunities available to them. Establishing that point in the minds of the white majority, Embree realized, would take years, and might never be universally successful, but he saw the fellowships as a highly effective step toward that end.

With board approval, the program got under way immediately, with the first award going to James Weldon Johnson.[34] During the early years, most fellowships went to persons already active in their fields—doctors, nurses, librarians, teachers of applied and vocational subjects—to enable them to get additional training. Sixty-five grants were given in 1929, with the number of new ones rising to eighty-five the following year. But when the full force of the Depression hit, with devastating effects on fund assets, only eight awards were made in 1932, and the numbers were even smaller in the next three years.[35] Yet, even in these most stringent times, as Embree struggled to enable the philanthropy to meet its commitments, he determined to keep this program alive.

Though the number of awards went down, grants did go to several fellows, still at crucial points in their preparation, whose careers were strikingly successful. A twenty-seven-year-old Ralph Bunche, the first black man to earn a Ph.D. in political science at Harvard and a future undersecretary-general of the United Nations and winner of the Nobel Peace Prize, used his fellowship for dissertation research in Africa, his first trip outside the United States. The contralto Marian Anderson, who was unable to get significant engagements at home due to her race, spent her Rosenwald year studying and performing in Germany, where she was so enthusiastically received that, when she returned to the States, her career blossomed. A penniless Charles Drew, on the verge of dropping out of medical school, received a fellowship that allowed him to complete his degree, graduating second in his class at McGill University. Later making the incomparable discovery of how to preserve blood plasma, he created the first American Red Cross blood bank. Horace Mann Bond, a child prodigy who entered high school at age nine, used his Rosenwald fellowship to pursue graduate study at the University of Chicago. Before his thirtieth birthday, he had established himself as a leading authority on the history of education and was on his way to becoming a prominent champion of civil rights. These would have been exceptional achievers under any circumstances, but the grants were obviously critical to their career advancement.[36]

When the fortunes of the fund began to improve in the mid-thirties, the fellowship program, established as a separate division and energized by a full-time director, took on new vigor. The selection committee usually consisted of four voting members: Edwin Embree, Charles S. Johnson, Will Alexander, and, initially, Henry Allen Moe of the Guggenheim Foundation.[37] The criteria for selection, however, became quite different. Earlier, when most of the awards had gone to professionals seeking advanced training, the selection process had not stressed intellectual prowess or creative promise. Beginning in 1936, however, these became the committee's principal considerations. As a consequence, grants soon clustered around Howard, Fisk, and the Atlanta schools, the leading black institutions.[38]

Embree, supported by his committee colleagues, insisted that recipients be "first-rate." There were many deserving persons of above-average ability, he knew, but Rosenwald fellowships were not for them. With the fundamental purpose of demonstrating African Americans' talent as an opening wedge to break down racial prejudice, the program could accommodate only the most promising candidates, those most likely to achieve at the highest level. Undergirding that consideration was Embree's basic elitism. There was nothing snobbish about the Rosenwald president; few members of his generation were more eloquent spokespeople for democracy. But influenced by Arnold Toynbee's notion of the "creative minority," he understood that societal progress usually resulted from the efforts of persons of uncommon intelligence, imagination, and dedication. His elitist outlook was akin to Thomas Jefferson's "aristocracy of talent," and its essence is captured by DuBois's term the "talented tenth." Allocating funds to those who fit that category, he was convinced, would most rapidly undermine racist structures.[39]

The reinvigoration of the program was accompanied by expansion. In 1937, a category of fellowships was established for white southerners.[40] Like the fellowships for blacks, these were directed toward improving race relations, but in a more direct and open fashion. Applicants were not restricted by occupation, but their careers were expected to be pursued in the South. Moreover, they were to use the fellowship for work on "some problem distinctive to southern life."[41] Embree believed that good race relations could be best assured by improved southern leadership and "more intelligent attacks" on the region's problems. Thus, the fellowships were open not only to social scientists, but to molders of southern opinion: creative writers, artists, teachers, journalists, university presidents, preachers, prospective holders of public office.[42]

During the dozen years that fellowships were awarded to white southerners, recipients included a future governor of Georgia, the South's most influential newspaper editor, several educational leaders, and other figures of notable stature. Yet, as a group, the white fellows lacked the luster of the black, and few individuals could claim achievements comparable to the most illustrious of the African American recipients. Certainly, none matched painter Jacob Lawrence or dancer Katherine Dunham, photographer/movie maker Gordon Parks or novelist Ralph Ellison, sculptor Augusta Savage or composer William Grant Still; none was a Bunche or a DuBois or a Marian Anderson. The assembled talent of the black recipients was the result of a continuous, energetic effort, drawing on a widening network of contacts across the country, to identify promising individuals and encourage their application. Every applicant was interviewed by at least one member of the committee, and successful applicants often by several. Similar time and effort did not go into the program for white southerners.[43] Nor were the fellowships apparently as critical for the development of the white recipients as they were for the black.

The fellowship program came to an end only when the Rosenwald Fund itself closed its doors in 1948. Of all the fund had undertaken, the demise of the black fellowships seems to have caused Embree the greatest regret, and prompted the hope that some other foundation would adopt the program and continue it. During its lifetime, the number of applicants had peaked at 700 in a single year, from whom fewer than 75 were chosen. World War II brought a sharp decrease in the applicant pool, but a substantial rise in women's applications and awards. Over a twenty-year span, almost 1,000 grants were made to 587 African American men and women.[44] Those numbers undoubtedly would have been much higher had it not been for the war and, perhaps more significant, the Great Depression.

* * *

By the fall of 1929, the capital assets of the Julius Rosenwald Fund were approaching $35 million, representing an increase of 75 percent in a mere twenty-one months. Completely undiversified, those assets consisted entirely of stock in the Sears, Roebuck Company which, like other retail enterprises, had benefited enormously from the decade's economic boom. The Rosenwald board met in the middle of November 1929, three weeks after the U.S. stock market began its precipitous decline. Economic questions were probably uppermost in members' minds, but no one seemed to doubt the strength of the fund itself. "The Julius Rosenwald Fund has large resources," Embree confidently proclaimed. "[T]hey are likely to enlarge rather than shrink in the years ahead."[45] Neither Julius Rosenwald nor his son Lessing, the most economically astute members of the board, offered any contrary opinion, probably because such a ringing affirmation had been cleared in advance with the founder.[46]

Thus assured, the board proceeded to make appropriations for a variety of projects recommended by Embree. A half-million dollars was voted to support the experimental honors program at Swarthmore College. The sum of $180,000 was approved for a campaign to fight illiteracy.

The International City Management Association received $30,000 for studies aimed at improving municipal government. Consideration was given to supporting the establishment of a native medical school at the University of Johannesburg, but it was not funded. By the end of the day, no fewer than twenty projects received funding, to be paid over several years, with appropriations totaling $1,437,500.[47] The moneys voted so confidently at that meeting would represent, a scant thirty months later, almost half of the entire value of the fund's capital.

By mid-1932, Sears stock had lost almost all its 1929 value. A share that, just before the crash, had sold for about $190 now brought only $10. Most distressing, this 95 percent decline in the fund's only asset meant that the value of its holdings was less than its financial commitments. Technically, the philanthropy was bankrupt. Months of scrambling to keep the Rosenwald Fund afloat had proved insufficient.[48]

As early as mid-1930, Embree, his sanguine outlook of six months earlier now abandoned, had begun to adjust to the fund's diminishing capital. To the trustees, he emphasized the need to limit appropriations lest all fund assets be expended in two or three years. The appropriations budget proposed for 1930–1931 was smaller by almost 50 percent than those of the two previous years. Even that proved too optimistic; four months later, the budget actually approved involved a reduction of two-thirds from the previous year. Phasing down the school-building program, limiting grants to colleges outside the four major centers, and curtailment of support to most of the hospitals serving blacks were proposed.[49] Conditional grants, when the receiving institution had been unable to raise matching funds, were allowed to lapse. In other instances, multiyear contributions were deferred or stretched out, or payments of interest rather than principal were negotiated, thus reducing the annual demand on the fund's resources. Non-essential office staff were eliminated. To avoid having to sell Sears stock when it was severely undervalued, a sizable bank loan was negotiated, using the stock as collateral. Embree even explored the imaginative, but improbable, idea of merging with two other philanthropies with similar interests, the Falk Fund of Pittsburgh and the Spelman Fund of New York.[50]

Stringent measures notwithstanding, as the Depression entered its third year, the fund's situation was desperate. Until the "intensely acute emergency" passed, Embree wrote to a staff member, "it is now a matter of hanging on by our teeth for dear life."[51] Help from Julius Rosenwald could not be expected; after months of intermittent illness, the founder had died early in 1932. Lessing Rosenwald succeeded his father as chair of the board, and with him Embree discussed reducing new appropriations to not more than $150,000 a year and a 10 percent reduction in all staff salaries. Both men were keenly aware of the ramifications if the fund were forced to default on its obligations. Considerable embarrassment for the Rosenwald family and for the fund's officials would be one result. Far more serious, numerous southern institutions, already under great strain, might suffer irreparable harm if anticipated contributions were not received.[52]

Eager to meet the fund's commitments, but lacking the liquidity to do so, Embree took the unprecedented step of appealing for help to more richly endowed, financially secure philanthropies. The Rockefeller Foundation, the Rockefeller-endowed GEB, and the Carnegie Corporation of New York were approached. Their responses were strikingly different. The GEB had much in common with the Rosenwald Fund, sharing a primary interest in the South and, in fact, supporting a number of the same institutions. Of all the nation's philanthropies, the GEB seemed best suited to respond with financial assistance, even up to the half-million dollars the Rosenwald Fund needed. Rockefeller's legal counsel ruled, however, that one philanthropy could not legally make a contribution to another. After two Embree trips to 61 Broadway and several weeks of discussion among Rockefeller officials, arrangements were made for the GEB to make emergency grants directly to Rosenwald-supported institutions and agencies, rather than to the fund itself. The arrangements involved complicated, indeed embarrassing, provisions. One required Embree personally to inform each of the recipients that the fund could not meet its financial obligations. Institutions, on the other hand, had to agree that, if and when Rosenwald was able to fulfill its pledge, the GEB would be reimbursed. The GEB subscription, which benefited eight institutions and agencies, was initially $200,000, but a second appeal on behalf of forty-five Rosenwald schools raised the total to a bit more than $250,000. The Rockefeller Foundation provided no assistance at all.[53]

The Carnegie Corporation was more forthcoming. Though chartered in the same state, headquartered in the same city, and subject to
the same laws as the Rockefeller trusts, Carnegie saw no legal problem
in making a direct contribution to the Rosenwald Fund. It promptly appropriated $200,000, equaling the GEB's initial subscription. Nor did it
impose elaborate procedures or payback arrangements. The money was
used to meet Rosenwald's commitments to its library service program,
an undertaking to which Carnegie also was committed.[54]

Financial assistance from the GEB and Carnegie, though grudg-
ingly given in the one instance, enabled the fund to meet its most pressing obligations in its most trying time. The value of the projects and the
dire consequences if they collapsed were key considerations in untying
the purse strings of both organizations. Also not to be overlooked is
Embree's willingness, on behalf of causes he deemed vital, to endure
personal embarrassment at the hands of his former associates. He was
prepared to have his professional reputation diminished if the fund
and its receiving organizations could escape the financial shortfall un-
harmed. That shortfall he expected to be temporary. Indeed, in less than
eighteen months, when stock values had begun to recover, he was able
to begin paying off the pledges to the institutions that had received GEB
funds, and they in turn reimbursed the GEB. By 1937, the GEB was fully
reimbursed, except for payments for Rosenwald schools, for which re-
imbursement was not required.[55]

As the value of Sears stock continued its slow rise in the mid-thirties,
the fund was again able to meet all its obligations from its own resources.
Yet the stock never came close to its worth in 1928, to say nothing of the
heady days just prior to the crash. As a consequence, the fund never
again had at its disposal the moneys available during Embree's first two
years. Such straitened circumstances posed formidable questions about
the fund's future. Should it continue with its customary activities, rapidly exhaust its remaining capital, and go out of business? Alternatively,
should it suspend operations, disperse its carefully selected but no longer
needed staff, and resume significant activity only when the market recov-
ered sometime in the indefinite future? Or was there some other option,
some way to avoid disappearing or fading into irrelevance and obscurity?
The issues were painful and pressing, and a resolution could not be long

delayed. The response, when it came in 1933, was imaginative and bold, reflecting Embree's temperament, his capacity for strategic thinking, and his journalistic background. The result was a sharply different orientation for the fund and a type of activity new to the world of organized philanthropy. The Rosenwald Fund itself was transformed.

*   *   *

On Embree's recommendation, the fund changed its self-conception and its mode of operation. The board voted to regard the fund no longer "as a disbursing agency but as an institution exerting direct influence through our own operations and our own staff activities."[56] Income and capital would continue to be spent, of course, as its charter required, but the focus of giving would be narrowed, some programs consolidated, others abandoned altogether. The fund would conserve its shrunken resources, thereby avoiding a premature end to its life. There would be no more expensive, showy projects, no large grants to help universities acquire land and erect buildings, no contributions to institutional endowments. Instead, the emphasis would be on stimulating fresh thought aimed at innovative action. The fund would become less a source of money and more a source of ideas.[57] Implicit in this orientation was increased attention to public policy.

Besides Rosenwald, there were at the time few foundations significantly engaged in public policy issues: the Commonwealth and Twentieth Century Funds, the Russell Sage Foundation, various Rockefeller trusts, the Carnegie Corporation—not even a dozen all told.[58] For such organizations, the acceptable mechanisms for affecting policies were experimentation, demonstrations, and published reports. The common procedure was to provide grants to other agencies or individuals, enabling them to conduct research or mount demonstration projects. This approach minimized the likelihood of negative publicity for the grant-making body in the event the project aroused opposition or its conclusions proved controversial. Eager to maintain the image of nonpartisan, disinterested public citizens, these philanthropies were not inclined to play the advocate's role or otherwise call undue attention to themselves. The fund's decision "to exert direct influence," to become more an intellectual than a financial resource, marked a break with conventional foundation behavior.

That behavior involved relatively slow processes, while the severity of the economic crisis seemed to demand rapid adjustments in social structures and patterns. Moreover, the fund no longer had the financial strength to follow that accustomed path far into the future. The new "direct action" called for Rosenwald staff to initiate studies themselves, explore issues independently, and arrive promptly at their own conclusions. Even more important, those conclusions would not be merely reported in technical documents unlikely to be widely read. Instead, outcomes and recommendations would be actively, even energetically promoted, using methods and media that could reach a broad audience. In order to affect public policy, the fund would concentrate on the antecedent step, presenting fresh ideas to the educated citizenry and to policy makers, working to create the climate of opinion in which useful change could occur.

Effective policies, Embree knew, rested ultimately on popular beliefs and customs, and he had no doubt that, under suitable conditions, these could be changed. He had not forgotten how Grandfather Fee, in their rides around the Kentucky countryside, had pointed out individual examples of changed outlooks among former slaveholders. And since public opinion was in some sense personal outlooks writ large, then public opinion could be shaped.[59] At the same time, he recognized that generating ideas was one thing; getting them accepted by a sufficiently large or influential segment of the public was another. Unless the ideas were persuasively presented, their formulation would be no more than a sterile exercise. If the fund was to avoid such futility, it had to move, deliberately and forthrightly, into uncharted terrain.

Embree was well aware that he was entering new territory, in fact reversing a direction he had taken earlier. At his very first board meeting, he had advised the trustees:

> Attempts directly to influence popular thinking through propaganda or through any other means than the indirect results of research and demonstrations have been avoided and explicitly denounced by practically all of the foundations. The public is very sensitive on this subject. While, especially in a democracy, public opinion and the actions which result from it are of the greatest importance, there are self-evident difficulties and embarrassments in the undertaking of any direct propaganda by a private group which has the power of large funds.[60]

Now, without referring to his earlier caveat, he pointed out that, in moving from "a disbursing policy to one of direct effort through staff activities, we are breaking with the usual policy of foundations." Philanthropies commonly avoided direct responsibility for societal innovation, he reminded his board, preferring to work through separate agencies whose activities they subsidized. But having already established "precedents of direct action" in regard to African American welfare and medical economics, the Rosenwald Fund, in a time of "imminent and transforming change in American life," had "an opportunity and obligation to 'do our part' in informing and guiding social action in these and in related fields." A program of publication in particular, he suggested, might enable the fund to exert considerable influence on public opinion and social change without incurring large expenses.[61]

Examples of "direct effort through staff activities" were already in evidence. In the first months of the Franklin Roosevelt administration, Embree had taken steps to ensure that the concerns of black citizens were not overlooked by the federal government. From fellow Chicagoan Harold Ickes, now in charge of the Department of the Interior, he had secured agreement for a person to serve at that agency, at the fund's expense, as a high-level advocate for the nation's black citizens. A young Rosenwald staff member, Georgian Clark Foreman, was first to assume that role. Foreman soon moved on to another government post and was succeeded by an African American Ph.D. economist, Robert C. Weaver. Weaver's appointment was subsequently replicated with the appointment of other black professionals to prominent positions in Washington agencies. With Rosenwald funds, Embree continued to underwrite such appointments, thereby breaking the color barrier for federal executives and creating the nucleus of what came to be called Roosevelt's "black cabinet."[62]

The presence of Foreman at the Department of the Interior had served to facilitate another important instance of Embree's direct effort. Using the facilities of that department as meeting space, the fund's president sponsored a national Conference on the Economic Situation of the Negro. The meeting brought together for three days of discussion in the nation's capital scores of influential participants: heads of black institutions, federal officials, university economists, race relations authorities, industrial employers. The event was very much a Rosenwald Fund affair. Not only did the fund organize and finance the conference, it also drew heavily on people linked in some fashion to the philanthropy. Of the conference's seven sessions, one was presided over by Alfred K. Stern and five others by heads of historically black institutions supported by the fund. Of the twenty-five presenters and commentators, eight were either past or future Rosenwald fellows. Embree's two most valuable associates at Rosenwald were prominent: Will Alexander presented a paper, and Charles S. Johnson chaired the five-person committee charged to prepare the official report. Embree himself gave the final address.[63]

This mid-1933 conference is illustrative of the important connections Embree had established with current and future leaders, both black and white. It also serves as an example of a special power of foundations—the power to convene, to assemble knowledgeable people for deliberation on significant issues, and to call attention to such matters through published reports and press releases. Embree was not the first to recognize the potency of this method but, taking advantage of the fund's reputation as well as its money, he used it again and again as a means to broadcast information and influence thinking.[64] His success in this regard, as in other instances of direct action, was heavily dependent on access to the media.

*   *   *

Benefiting from his own journalistic experience, Embree constantly worked the daily press, bombarding editors with news releases—describing staff appointments, projects initiated, grants made, board meetings, conferences sponsored, books published. In contrast to the decade before his arrival at the fund, when apparently only three news items were given to the press, Embree issued seven press releases in his first four months on the job. While such announcements continued apace, a news story or a guest editorial occasionally appeared in a New York or Chicago paper under an Embree byline.[65] Instances of racial injustice often resulted in a letter to the editor decrying the offense and its underlying attitude. Ever alert to the power of the press, he added to the Rosenwald board Mark Ethridge, the liberal editor of the *Louisville*

Courier-Journal, and *Chicago Sun* publisher Marshall Field. Other editors and journalists were cultivated with invitations to social events he hosted.[66]

Embree's efforts to shape public opinion were not limited to the daily press. He regarded statements and publications by the fund's officers as an increasingly important element in the total program. He wanted the organization to be a "direct intellectual force," functioning on a level "as high as that of a university."[67] And the output was impressive. From the early thirties until the Rosenwald Fund closed down in 1948, the philanthropy was responsible for an imposing list of publications addressing social issues. Eight officers of the fund authored or co-authored thirty-three books, most of them examining some aspect of race relations. More than twenty other books came into print with Rosenwald subsidies. Over eighty articles written by fund officers appeared in a variety of journals and magazines, ranging from the *New England Journal of Medicine,* through *Asia,* to the *Atlantic Monthly.* Extending its outreach still further, the fund issued over two dozen pamphlets and even more article reprints, distributing copies in the hundreds of thousands to libraries, schools, social service agencies, the military, government offices, nonprofit organizations, and selected individuals. Two years after initiating the fund's direct effort, Embree considered such publications to be one of the fund's "important means of lasting influence."[68]

The most prolific writer of all was the fund's president himself. Beginning with the pieces on philanthropy done with Julius Rosenwald and continuing well into the thirties, it was a rare year when Embree did not publish at least three articles. Subsequently, even as his time and energy went increasingly into civic activities and the writing of books, pieces continued to appear in periodicals, though less frequently. The subjects commonly mirrored the fund's activities. In the early thirties, a half-dozen pieces dealt with health in the black community and the lives of individual African Americans. The library development projects were described in *School and Society* and *Library Journal.* When the fund's attention centered on rural education and teacher training, Embree devoted no fewer than seven articles to those subjects. He published on other topics as well, including accounts following trips abroad of life in Samoa and Russia and on the importance of preserving indigenous cultures. But even the last of these fit into Rosenwald's central purpose, for they were intended to introduce American readers to diverse cultures, to open minds to other societal patterns, and to lay the groundwork for increased racial understanding.

During his twenty years at the Rosenwald Fund, Embree published in twenty-two different periodicals, intending by such variety to inform and persuade a wide reading public. Some essays were directed at specialized audiences, such as the Chicago Institute for Psychoanalysis, the 1936 graduating class of the University of Hawaii, and readers of the National Urban League's *Opportunity*. Several appeared in magazines for the well-educated general reader: *Harper's, American Scholar, Atlantic Monthly, American Mercury, Saturday Review of Literature*. Six pieces were scholarly in nature, half of them addressing sociological topics. A like number were carried by professional journals dealing with public health, librarianship, and education.[69]

Embree did not limit his writings to the general media, but also used to advantage the fund's biennial reviews.[70] Published in booklet form, these official reports summarized the philanthropy's recent activities, the grants made, and the agencies assisted. This detailed information was always preceded by an Embree-authored essay—twelve or so pages long, bearing a catchy title—that addressed some fund interest. The 1929 essay, for example, dealt with organized giving and was entitled "The New Philanthropy." The next year, Embree played off the title of Erich Maria Remarque's just-published *All Quiet on the Western Front* with a piece labeled "The Negro Front." Following his studies of education in Samoa and the Dutch East Indies, he discussed cultural diversity and racial adjustments in "A World of Interesting Peoples." By the 1940s, the common theme was ending racial injustice and extending America's democratic promise to all its citizens, concerns addressed in "Three Ramparts We Watch," "Race Relations Balance Sheet," and "Human Relations in America." Containing current information and the author's assessment of trends, these essays were, above all, instruments of advocacy. They presented in direct and challenging language both Embree's personal views and the Rosenwald Fund's primary commitments. Printed in runs of 12,000–15,000 copies, the reviews were sent to libraries, journals, other philanthropies, and "representative individuals."[71]

While Embree's essays were inevitably somewhat ephemeral, that was not true of his books. Seven he wrote alone and four others he co-authored during the Rosenwald years.[72] Considered together, they present an unusual range of subject matter and intended audience, indicating Embree's broad interests and his talent and flexibility as a writer. Issues of racial discrimination, and the individual and group accomplishments of African Americans, were addressed in four of the volumes. Another work analyzed the 1930s crisis in southern agriculture and contributed significantly to the passage of national legislation. The rich variety found in Native American cultures was depicted in one volume, while another described colonial education in the Dutch East Indies, ending with a resounding condemnation of Western imperialism. Yet another introduced teenage readers to the diversity of the world's peoples and urged an attitude of tolerance and accommodation.[73] At the end of the Second World War, he contributed to a book that analyzed the international situation and outlined a strategy for maintaining peace. His final work told, from the inside, the story of the Julius Rosenwald Fund itself.

What links all these longer publications is Embree's perennial interest in a single question: How can diverse peoples manage to live together in harmony and prosperity in a rapidly shrinking world? That vexing question preoccupied him throughout his mature years. Time and time again in his public addresses, he raised this issue, for he considered it the most important, and complicated, facing humankind.[74] By stating the matter in dramatic terms, he undoubtedly intended to prod his audience into serious thinking. At the same time, he was expressing his sociological sensibility and his own deep conviction. In a country where various ethnic groups were increasingly rubbing against each other, in a world where interactions among nations would increasingly generate tensions, he knew that this question—lying at the heart of both domestic race relations and international affairs—could be ignored only at great peril. In the United States, that peril involved at its core the country's largest minority.

That minority was described sympathetically in Embree's most groundbreaking book. *Brown America: The Story of a New Race* appeared in 1931, when Jim Crow was solidly entrenched in the South, and suspicion and unyielding discrimination met black migrants in the North.[75] Embree had worked hard on the manuscript, gathering extensive information, reading widely, and seeking help from prominent African American intellectuals. James Weldon Johnson had encouraged him to do the volume, and Embree in turn peppered Johnson with questions about black artistic achievement, requests for reading suggestions, and, before submission to the publisher, an invitation to critique the book's organization, content, and language. Similarly, he sought comments on two chapters from W. E. B. DuBois, deciding subsequently to rewrite entire sections. He was glad to see the book go to press, for as he confided to his closest friend, writing it had been "a terrible task," causing "great sweat and deep gloom" although it was also "a good deal of fun."[76]

Addressing the great ignorance about Americans of African ancestry and the misconceptions and stereotypes such ignorance spawned, the book attracted a surprisingly large readership. The first printing sold out in three weeks. Within three months, two additional printings were run, and continuing sales resulted in a total of five printings in the first two years. Late in the decade, when a special edition was printed for study groups, 2,500 copies sold in the first three months. Widely acclaimed in the African American press, it received largely favorable reviews in mainstream newspapers and scholarly periodicals.[77] A decade later, it was described as "perhaps the definitive study of the Negro's contribution to American culture" and "a standard reference book on the Negro people."[78] Still later, it was credited with "having done much to forge new links of understanding between American Negroes and the nonwhite peoples of the earth."[79] Three-quarters of a century after its initial publication, with reissues in 1936 and 1940, almost 600 copies could still be found in libraries across the country.[80]

The book's principal theme was that the 10 million Americans categorized as "Negro" actually represented a new people, an amalgam of African, European, and Native American stock. Expanding on this idea, the book traced the emergence of the group from the arrival of the first Africans in Virginia, through the mingling of the races during slavery and the vicissitudes following emancipation, to the changing circumstances of the two most recent generations. The work concentrated, however, on the current situation of "brown Americans." Embree's approach was factual and direct, but he did not mince words: "There is no use pretending that Negroes are better than they are," he wrote, "for in the mass they are still poor, uneducated, subject to more than their fair share of disease and crime."[81] But his concern was less to describe than to explain, to highlight the difficult circumstances of black life as consequences of unremitting racial prejudice, and to analyze the economic and psychological factors among whites that underlay such attitudes.

With a tone reasonable and balanced, Embree emphasized a point that characterized much of his subsequent writing and speaking: what worked against its black citizenry was of great harm to the nation as a whole. Yet about the future of African Americans and their relations with the majority population, he affirmed his deep optimism, an outlook rooted in the impressive progress that had been achieved in the two generations since emancipation. Indicative of such progress were the lives of a handful of historical and contemporary persons profiled at the end of the work, sketches that illustrated as well the human diversity within the African American population.[82]

Embree dedicated *Brown America* to "John G. Fee, my abolitionist grandfather, and to Julius Rosenwald, great-hearted friend of the Negro." Beyond the dedication, Embree devoted an entire chapter to his grandfather, describing his upbringing in a slaveholding family, his conversion to abolitionist activism, and his actions against racial injustice for the rest of his life. That part of the book aroused great interest among reviewers, who gave it more attention than any other section. Embree was particularly gratified when a leading magazine agreed to publish the chapter uncut.[83]

* * *

Of all Embree's books, *Brown America* did the most to increase knowledge about the country's largest minority, but the most politically important was a far briefer work, written in collaboration with Rosenwald colleagues Charles S. Johnson and Will Alexander. Published in 1935, *The Collapse of Cotton Tenancy* presented conclusions from a two-year study of southern agriculture and offered recommendations for moving from crisis to prosperity.[84] Embree had long been interested in the plight of southern tenant farmers, and in the late twenties had met with then

Secretary of Commerce Herbert Hoover to consider how the federal government might help tenants to acquire land of their own.[85] As the Depression deepened, he and his two collaborators became convinced that enabling poor farmers to gain possession of land was essential to southern economic progress. Work on the book was divided among the three friends, with Johnson assigned data collection, Alexander tasked with building support through personal contacts in the South, and Embree taking overall responsibility for the project and writing most of the prose. Yet their efforts were not limited to the study and the publication of their findings.

The three friends mounted a substantial lobbying campaign that reached to the highest levels of government. In a suite at the Hay-Adams Hotel, they entertained with cocktails and dinner Secretary of Agriculture Henry Wallace and Rexford Tugwell, then plied them with information about the problems of the cotton tenant farmer. Tugwell, then head of the farm resettlement program, was particularly taken by the issue. On the day *Collapse* appeared, a copy was placed in his hands as he entered his office. He immediately opened it, took a seat, and did not put it down until he had read it all the way through. There followed a long afternoon of conversation with the three authors. From that conversation, Tugwell went directly to the White House to discuss the matter with President Roosevelt. The book also came directly to the president's attention when his wife, undoubtedly encouraged by the authors, placed a copy on his bedside table and urged him to read it. Subsequently, Will Alexander himself had a chance to confer with the president about the problem and proposed solutions. Senator John H. Bankhead II of Alabama became the trio's next target. Once informed, he agreed to sponsor a bill to include cotton tenants in the farm resettlement program. Embree and Alexander then worked with Department of Agriculture officials to craft the legislation.[86]

Not content with lobbying Washington officials, the triumvirate continued to build public and political support for broadening farm ownership. They persuaded prominent philanthropist George Foster Peabody to call a national conference on the problem at the Brookings Institution. At the conference, Embree was chosen to lead a citizens committee to publicize the issue and to promote Bankhead's bill. As part of that effort, the Rosenwald president prepared for a wider audience a magazine article describing the problem, summarizing the detailed contents of the study, and presenting its recommendations.[87]

The article, like the book, pointed out how cultural holdovers from slavery, declining soil productivity due to single-crop cultivation, loss of world markets, and limited access to capital had come together to reduce many southern tenant farmers to a state of peonage. While the hardships fell disproportionately on black farmers, in fact there were twice as many white farmers in such desperate straits. Both groups were subject to control by frequently unscrupulous and abusive landlords. The solution proposed was federal acquisition of large tracts of land, its distribution in twenty- to forty-acre plots to tenants under favorable loans or long-term leases, and the creation of a system of service agencies to provide scientific advice and initial funding for seed, fertilizer, and supplies for the new homesteaders.

The two publications did much to galvanize support for federal action. As persuasive as the prose, perhaps, was an editorial cartoon that appeared in the book. It portrayed a fat, whip-carrying plantation owner, pockets bulging with cash, walking away from a dilapidated shack, counting money just taken from some black tenant farmers. The farm family—man, woman, small child, baby, all in rags—is totally disconsolate. The shack is precariously propped up by splintering boards labeled "acreage control" and "government control." Stalking in the background is a gaunt figure—"Starvation." The cartoon was reproduced widely in the African American press, and it appeared as well in mainstream newspapers in Detroit, Indianapolis, Cleveland, Chicago, San Antonio, St. Louis, Cincinnati, and Philadelphia.[88]

While the cartoon effectively dramatized the plight of the tenant farmer, the study itself received mixed responses. A Louisiana reviewer opined that the problems of tenancy had "probably never been set forth any more clearly and forcibly," while from Virginia came the accusation that the authors had presented "an embittered and distorted picture," a portrayal of conditions "prejudiced, one-sided, and manifestly unfair."[89] An African American sociologist observed that the solution proposed was reminiscent of the unfulfilled promises made to emancipated slaves. Seventy years too late, the reviewer insisted, the authors' program would

only create rural slums, would serve primarily to rescue large white land-
owners and mortgage holders, and was intended to build support for a
bill making its way through the U.S. Congress.[90]

In connecting the book with pending legislation, this most negative
reviewer was not far off the mark, though he evidently inverted cause and
effect. Instead of the study supporting the bill, it would have been more
accurate to see the bill as an outgrowth of the study. When passed in 1937,
the Bankhead-Jones Farm Tenant Act embodied the book's principal
recommendations. The legislation also authorized the creation of a new
federal agency, the Farm Security Administration, to oversee the program. Soon to head the organization was one of the book's co-authors,
Will Alexander.[91]

* * *

Embree's work on behalf of southern farmers was of a piece with his efforts to reform rural education in the region. The need for such reform
had been revealed by a study of educational effectiveness that the fund
had conducted even as it began to phase down the school-building program. That analysis had produced a dismal picture. Instruction commonly consisted of dull, routinized drills, a pattern resulting from other
obvious deficiencies. Teaching materials were not only in short supply,
but ill adapted to the region and the life circumstances of the pupils.
Equipment and furnishings, especially in black schools, were woefully
inadequate. Most important, many teachers were seriously underpre-
pared to meet their responsibilities. Significant reform, therefore, inevitably had to begin with teacher education.

Embree had been interested in ways to improve education in the
South ever since his arrival in Chicago.[92] But while education of African
American youth remained the fund's central concern in this regard, he
believed that concentration on one segment of the population would not
be wise. In America's complex racial situation, real harm, the arousal of
racial animosities in particular, might be done "if a great foundation attempted to force progress much beyond its natural course" or singled out
"any minority group for exclusive aid."[93] Just as federal support for land
acquisition was intended to benefit both white and black farmers, and
the library program had included white patrons, so educational reform

needed to target both races. Thus, when experiments in teacher education got under way, both black and white institutions were involved.

From the mid-thirties until U.S. entry into the Second World War,
the improvement of rural elementary education was the central program
of the Rosenwald Fund. The program operated only in the South, with
most activity in the deep southern states of Georgia, Alabama, Mississippi, and Louisiana. To assist in guiding and planning the program,
Embree established a Council on Rural Education, drawing from the
South, Northeast, and Midwest professional educators, sociologists and
anthropologists, foundation officers, and representatives of state education agencies. Convinced that the fund was "running with the tide" of
educational reform, Embree embarked on the venture with high hopes,
describing it with characteristic exuberance as "the best project we have
ever tackled."[94]

For over five years, Embree reported on the program in a variety of
periodicals: *Educational Record, Atlantic Monthly, Journal of Negro Education, Yearbook of Agriculture, Survey Graphic, Social Forces, American
Scholar,* as well as the biennial reports of the Julius Rosenwald Fund.[95]
These accounts, and the public addresses on which several were based,
paid particular but not exclusive attention to the education of rural black
youth. Embree considered such an emphasis necessary, in part because
he expected most southern blacks, migration to urban centers notwithstanding, to remain on the land for the indefinite future. In addition,
he wanted to drive home the enormous discrepancies in the funding of
black and white schools. Though the pieces coming from his pen were
numerous, not all were original. Several developed the same points, often
using identical language for extensive sections.

Common to these articles was the observation that most curricula,
developed in the North for an urban population, had been adopted by
southern districts in spite of their unsuitability for rural students. Moreover, many teachers, often ill educated themselves and overwhelmed by
too many students and too many subjects to teach, were forced to rely
heavily on mere rote learning. Consequently, even in the crucial elementary grades, student curiosity was frequently dimmed and interest in
learning extinguished. To be effective, teachers had to understand thoroughly the circumstances of rural life and the importance of the school

as a center for community activity. Only then could they focus on the kind of preparation children needed for rural living. That preparation, Embree came to believe, consisted of five elements: competence with written language, some skill in using numbers, knowledge of farming and the underlying biological processes, manual dexterity and familiarity with simple mechanics, and understanding of personal health. Above all, he stressed reading as "the fundamental tool of knowledge."[96]

Embree also addressed other considerations not confined to education for rural living. He inveighed against the widespread emphasis on memorization, pointing to the limited value of "intimate acquaintance with . . . lists of the Kings of England, or other traditional tricks of the schoolmaster's trade." The purpose of formal education, especially in the early grades, was not "to cram knowledge into the child but . . . to find ways to stimulate his interest, to help him get started in the most effective way on the road of learning." Even at the college level, the fundamental goal should be "the development of the personality, especially the stimulation of [the student's] ability to think and thus to make use of his learning."[97] When it was successful, education enabled the individual to arrive at fully developed personhood and lead a happy and useful life.

Such success, Embree continually lamented, seldom attended the education of black youth, and the consequences were enormously damaging to them, to the South, and to the entire nation. The case for radical improvement in African American education he presented most forcefully in a 1936 address to a group of educators meeting in St. Louis.[98] Black Americans had made remarkable progress since emancipation, he proclaimed, in spite of forbidding hurdles and great discrepancies in educational opportunity—expressed in shabby buildings, hand-me-down furniture, tattered textbooks, poorly trained and even worse-paid teachers, and school terms far too short to be effective. Basic democracy and humanity alone argued for equality in education, but his plea for change was based on "nothing more ethereal than the good old-fashioned principle of enlightened selfishness." In an interdependent society, what affected one group affected all. Improved health in the black community would benefit whites, because disease germs recognized no color line. Better living conditions for blacks would reduce crime and disorder, an advantage for all groups. Raised incomes would give blacks more buying power, the surest way to move the entire South toward prosperity, and education was the surest pathway to higher pay. Moreover, eliminating the mistreatment of African American citizens would remove a source of moral evil in the majority population, for the hatred and injustice of the race issue had "corrupted the whole Christian Church. . . . The surest way for the white South to make its own progress on the continuing road of civilization, and the only way for it to save its own soul, was to remedy this disparity in educational opportunity." To those who said that better schools for blacks could not be afforded, Embree rejoined, "We cannot afford not to provide education for all the people."[99] Only on the principle of free and universal education, he concluded, could the nation's democratic public school system stand. Embree's words were hard-hitting, bound to arouse disagreement even outside the segregated South. Such public statements and numerous articles brought him and the philanthropy he headed increasingly into the public eye. And the more attention he attracted, the more disagreement he encountered.

By the late thirties, the fund's efforts to improve rural education had expanded beyond the college-level training of teachers to graduate school preparation for county supervisors. In Georgia, the state where reform efforts had been most extensive, those activities precipitated a raging controversy.

At the University of Georgia's School of Education and at three other state-supported colleges, the fund had underwritten several experiments in teacher preparation. In 1941, forces led by race-baiting Governor Eugene Talmadge raised the charge that the reforms were in fact an attack on racial segregation. As proof that their real aim was integration of the public schools, the governor emphasized the funding from Rosenwald. The controversy centered on the dean of the School of Education, Walter D. Cocking, an Iowan appointed with a mandate for change. As the leader of the reform effort, he was depicted by Talmadge and others as an opponent of the state's long-standing policies on race.[100]

When the university's Board of Regents met to consider charges against the dean, the "evidence" presented against him included portions of Embree's *Brown America,* read aloud by one board member to his colleagues. Unconvinced, a narrow majority of the board voted to uphold the dean. Angered by this outcome, Talmadge assigned a state official to seek additional information against Cocking. In the course of this investigation, Cocking's house servant was reportedly kidnapped, threatened with a pistol, and then offered a bribe to steal Cocking's briefcase. When this "investigation" failed to uncover information that could be used against the dean, the governor replaced three of the dissenting regents with more submissive members, and then demanded a new hearing.

This second hearing, with the governor present to press his case and numerous state police officers ominously standing guard, was "tumultuous . . . marked by heated verbal exchanges, boos, and applause from packed galleries."[101] In a predictable outcome, the reconstituted board voted to oust the education dean, along with the president of one of the state colleges cooperating with Rosenwald. These actions immediately deepened and broadened the controversy. Alarmed by such blatant political interference in academic affairs, the regional accrediting body subsequently withdrew accreditation not only from the state's flagship university but from the nine other state-supported white colleges as well. Embree had hoped for such an official condemnation, believing it would force Governor Talmadge to back down.[102]

Reporting to his trustees, the fund's president pointed out that the hearing had focused on the race question, "the only issue that seemed to arouse popular interest." The Georgia situation, he averred, did not "approach the Huey Long dictatorship in Louisiana," nor was it as "crass" as earlier actions by Mississippi's Senator Theodore Bilbo or South Carolina's Cole Blease. "But it is bad enough, for it again shows how strong a weapon for political power can be forged—in this country as well as in Europe—by stirring up race hate." He had no doubt that the fund's policy was sound, but even so, he declared, the "Georgia business leaves a bitter taste in my mouth."[103]

The university crisis remained a hot political issue the following year, when the arch-segregationist governor campaigned for reelection. During the course of the campaign, constantly appealing to racist sentiment and stressing the dangers posed by "furriners" like Cocking and other "Northern agitators," Talmadge quoted passages from *Brown America* in his stump speeches. On at least one occasion, according to news accounts, copies of the Embree book were publicly burned. As it turned out, Talmadge lost the election, a fact Embree noted with quiet satisfaction. Even four years later, when Talmadge again sought the governorship, it was a rare issue of his newspaper that did not attack the Rosenwald Fund.[104] Talmadge's reelection in 1945 Embree considered "a tragedy," one that would set back the fund's educational work and have negative effects throughout the country.[105]

The "Cocking affair" plunged Embree deeply into political controversy in the South. But it was neither the first nor the only time he encountered disagreement in the region. In an address to Tennessee educators a decade earlier, he had stated baldly that the South was in "a sorry plight," lagging behind the rest of the nation in all aspects that typify a civilized state. At the root of the problem, he asserted, was the region's limited effort to cultivate intelligence, to develop young minds. To reverse that situation, he challenged his audience to create in the region a university of the highest quality, one that would help raise the standards of other institutions and thereby staunch the brain drain to more progressive sections of the country.[106]

Three years later, in an address titled "Marks of the Educated Man: How to Tell a College Graduate from the Birds and the Fishes," Embree affirmed the same point to another group of southern educators. "[T]he greatest single lack of the South as a region," he proclaimed, "is one university of scholarly eminence comparable to Harvard or Yale or Columbia or Chicago or any one of a score of institutions of the North and West." Such a statement was sufficient to raise southern hackles, but Embree was only beginning. Borrowing a picturesque phrase from the region's past, he described the ideal man as "a scholar, a gentleman, and a judge of good whiskey." In elaborating on this trilogy, he attacked anti-intellectualism and emphasized the development of character and moral leadership. Being a "judge of good whiskey" was a metaphor for good taste in general, a well-honed capacity to exercise judgment and to enjoy life. The South's failure to produce more such men he traced in part to organized religion, particularly a narrow-minded Puritanism. Yet in criticizing the church, he emphasized, he was in no way showing disrespect for the founder of Christianity, for he considered Jesus of Nazareth "the ideal embodiment" of the traits he espoused.[107] Such remarks, delivered only two years after the end of Prohibition, in the still largely dry Bible Belt, quickly aroused strenuous opposition.

One influential southern newspaper extended the dispute by over two months, first publishing Embree's complete address, accompanied by an almost equally long rejoinder from a southern college president, and then soliciting responses from college and university presidents around the country. Over a dozen responses, some quite lengthy and a few obviously self-serving, were published in the weeks that followed. Most were from the South, and most took issue with Embree on one or more points. Embree himself received uncounted complaints, inquiries, and requests from university presidents, professors, parents, and students. With his choice of subject matter and colorful language, and the obvious intention to stimulate thought, he probably was not displeased with the uproar he had caused.[108]

*   *   *

Embree's insistence on the South's need for a first-rate university kept the pot of controversy bubbling. Around the time of the "Educated Man" speech, former Governor Huey Long of Louisiana, perhaps having misunderstood an Embree comment, began to claim that the fund's president had conferred such high status on that state's flagship campus. Embree, who had earlier gone so far as to link Long's politics with those of Mussolini and Hitler, at first ignored the claim but, faced with the repeated distortion, felt compelled to issue a public disclaimer.[109] In that statement, he had presumed to list the country's twelve greatest universities. Subsequently, as he described the situation, a "storm at once broke about my temerarious head."[110] His response to the wave of criticism was to conduct, and publish in a national magazine, one of the earliest attempts to arrive systematically at a ranking of America's leading institutions of higher education.

At the outset of this essay, Embree made clear he was considering university scholarship, not college life. At issue was the relative eminence of institutions dedicated to "the higher reaches of scholarship," those engaged in both transmitting known truth and working to expand the boundaries of knowledge. To the extent that universities succeeded in those twin endeavors, they were great. To the extent they fell short in those regards, no matter the beauty of the buildings, the success of the football team, or the pleasures of campus life, they were to be deemed inferior. In arriving at his assessment, Embree used three measures: peer evaluations of academic departments, tabulations of the concentrations of the most eminent scientists, and consultations with individual scholars and national committees. The number of highly regarded departments in each institution was then used to determine its overall scholarly eminence, hence its national ranking.[111] Embree eventually ranked only eleven universities, explaining that no others approached the overall quality of those listed and that one space was left open for several institutions that might properly claim membership in the top dozen. Of the eleven named, six were in the East, four in the Midwest, one on the West Coast. And consistent with his repeated admonitions, none was located south of the Mason-Dixon line. Nor were any southern colleges or universities included in the brief descriptions of other institutions that might soon ascend to the highest rank. Indeed, of more than 200 academic departments across the country considered to be distinguished, only one was located in the region. Seven southern institutions—three public, four private—were listed as potentially great, but he believed they were unlikely to fulfill that potential without money from elsewhere in the country. "A great university in the South," the author emphasized, "is the insistent need in American scholarship today."[112]

In his repeated calls for building up a great southern university, Embree had in mind the decisive influence of the University of Chicago in raising academic standards across the Midwest. He never wavered in his belief that similar benefits would follow in the South if a comparable institution could be developed there. At the same time, he was concerned that the intellectual strength already present in the region was dispersed among too many institutions, rather than being concentrated in a limited number of significant centers. Thus, just as Rosenwald and the GEB had built up four academic centers for African Americans, which had involved mergers in Atlanta and New Orleans, so Embree attempted to forge bonds of cooperation among white institutions in northern Georgia. Under his prompting, deliberations toward that end were initiated in the late thirties among three Atlanta schools—Emory University, Agnes Scott College, and the Georgia Institute of Technology—and subsequently expanded to include Columbia Theological Seminary and the University of Georgia.[113] Engendering significant cooperation among so many schools, so varied in size and purpose, seems an insuperable undertaking, as in fact it proved to be. Yet the effort serves to illustrate Embree's ability to think imaginatively and to move vigorously in the hope of advancing southern prospects.

The abortive effort in northern Georgia marked Embree's last notable initiative in formal education in the South. The fund's educational efforts in the region continued in the 1940s, but both the direction and the tone were different. From his youth, the fund's president had been opposed to racial segregation, but throughout the thirties he believed that race relations could be most readily improved, and black citizens benefited, by avoiding overt challenges to southern laws and practices. But new circumstances, largely brought on by war, made a new strategy both possible and necessary. Without forsaking the linked goals of fostering new leadership, changing the racial climate, and blunting the sharp edges of discrimination, the Rosenwald leader in the 1940s mounted a direct, decade-long assault on legally enforced segregation itself. Having long recognized, however, that racial tensions were not confined to the country's poorest region, he was also attentive to such problems in the section where the fund had its headquarters. His interest in the South remained undiminished, but Chicago and the Midwest also laid claim to his time, energy, and expertise.

FIVE

CHARACTER TO COPE WITH DISAGREEMENT

Chicago in the summer of 1933 had much to arouse public enthusiasm. The end of May had seen the opening of the world's fair, titled "A Century of Progress Exposition," celebrating the city's hundredth birthday. The opening had generated great excitement, and emotions were even higher by Independence Day. On July 6, the first major league baseball All-Star Game was played in Comiskey Park. In the third inning, with a man on base, Babe Ruth hit the first home run in an All-Star Game, giving the American League the margin needed to win by a final score of 4–2. Four days later, Illinois became the tenth state to ratify the Twenty-First Amendment to the U.S. Constitution, presaging its final approval and implementation before the year's end. For Chicagoans, the abolition of Prohibition was a promising development, for it could help reduce the crime and violence that had long plagued the city.

Two months earlier and 800 miles to the east, a new president had moved into the White House. Franklin Roosevelt had promised decisive actions in his first 100 days, and the period for delivering on those promises had just ended. How those dramatic initiatives and all that followed would play out, and whether they would in fact begin to pull the country out of the Depression remained to be seen, but they had given rise to a sense of hope, of expectation. And as a consequence of Chicago's centrality in the nation's economy, they were bound to affect Carl Sandburg's "tool maker, stacker of wheat, . . . nation's freight handler."

Edwin Embree was mightily impressed by the new president. He knew and admired Herbert Hoover, had worked with Hoover's war relief representatives in Europe, and had not hesitated to vote for him in 1928.

Most of Embree's associates at Rockefeller, from whom he took many cues as a young man, had been staunch Republicans, and Julius Rosenwald had been among Hoover's most prominent supporters. Within Hoover's cabinet, Embree knew well Secretary of the Interior Ray Lyman Wilbur, and he had met on several occasions with Secretary of State Henry Stimson and Secretary of Commerce Robert P. Lamont. Such considerations notwithstanding, the dire state of the economy and the strains on the nation's social fabric had caused him to switch allegiances. He had voted the Democratic ticket in 1932, and, like many Americans, he looked for great things from the smiling patrician at 1600 Pennsylvania Avenue.[1]

Three and a half years after Black Monday, the Rosenwald Fund continued to suffer from the economic collapse. Desperate steps had prevented a declaration of bankruptcy, but the value of the fund's assets remained severely depressed. Stringent budgetary measures adopted months earlier remained in effect. Support staff was still minimal. The time frames for paying grant appropriations had been extended wherever possible. New initiatives had been largely postponed. These essential adjustments had been painful, yet office morale remained high. The good feeling was due in part to the excitement of new quarters.

No longer housed in a corner of the vast Sears plant on the edge of the city, the fund had moved to a more convenient setting in the fashionable Kenwood section, just outside Hyde Park. Unable to sell his elaborate mansion in the depressed market, Julius Rosenwald, not long before his death, had acted on an Embree suggestion and arranged for the building and grounds to pass to the fund. The house was spacious and well appointed, easily converted to office use. Moreover, its proximity to the University of Chicago, where the fund's officers maintained numerous contacts, made 4901 S. Ellis Avenue a practical location.

A mile east of the fund's new headquarters was the site of the Chicago World's Fair. Stretching for almost thirty blocks along the lakeshore, the fair acclaimed both the city's and the country's steady technological advances. For the inspection and enchantment of tens of thousands of visitors, it brought together the latest locomotives, furniture designs, agricultural machinery, automobiles, and home appliances. In the depths of the most severe economic downturn in the nation's history, it presented a picture of prosperity and comfort, convenience and pleasure. It held out the promise of a better life yet to come. Its slogan appeared on countless souvenirs: posters, ashtrays, keys, sewing kits, toy cars, men's caps, medallions, small lamps, salt and pepper shakers, tin boxes. Throughout the city, "A Century of Progress" was seen at almost every turn.

Arriving at the office on the last day of July, Embree encountered a surprise. Stretched across the room was a large, handmade banner. "A HALF CENTURY *OFF* PROGRESS," it shouted. It was Embree's fiftieth birthday, and his staff had decided to recognize the occasion with a clever word play on the fair's title. Suggesting that his half-century of life had been unproductive, they knew, would appeal to his ironic sense of humor. When the general laughter subsided and the good-natured ribbing was at an end, refreshments and appropriate festivities followed.

Embree was delighted. He was glad his associates were comfortable enough with him to make jokes at his expense, and loving language, he could not have been more pleased with their wit. He laughed heartily at the time, and the memory gave him many a good chuckle long thereafter. The episode passed into family lore, continuing to amuse his children three-quarters of a century later.[2] The staff's decision to celebrate his birthday in such fashion is indicative of their affection for the fund's president. Moreover, the occasion and Embree's response to it provide insight into his personality. Who was this fifty-year-old? What did people see when they looked at him? What did they discern when they interacted with him? What was distinctive about his character, his disposition, his enthusiasms, the patterns of his life? How did he generate commitment and loyalty from those with whom he worked?

As he began the sixth decade of his life, Embree stood five feet, nine inches tall. His weight hovered around 170 pounds, a mere 15 pounds more than when he graduated from college. His body was sturdy, free of the thickening often characteristic of middle age, despite the fact that he played neither golf nor tennis, and his only regular exercise consisted of vigorous walking. He moved with an obvious sense of purpose, as if eager to get to his destination and the business awaiting there. One longtime friend said that Embree could get out of a chair faster than anyone he had ever known.[3] His hair was brown, beginning to gray at the temples, parted on the right. With regular features and eyes of light blue, he had a pleasant face; many considered him handsome. Contemporary photographs present a man open and direct. He looks squarely into the camera, confident and alert, serious but not unduly so. About his face there seems to flicker a hint of bemusement, a capacity to see the world as it is, to grasp the complexities of the human condition without being daunted by them. More than a decade later, when in his mid-sixties, Embree would be described as "ever-youthful."[4] And, as countless commentators attest, he was able to enjoy life to the full.

Edwin Embree was an affirmer of life. One of his favorite expressions was "zest," a term he used often and one that applied directly to his own approach to living. Living well he regarded as a fine art and "the very root of any true culture."[5] He was fond of ceremony and ritual, including those he had experienced among the island peoples of the Pacific. His experience with different cultures had revealed the satisfactions of life in less technologically advanced societies, so different from the perpetual hustle and bustle encountered in New York and Chicago. Yet he loved the vibrancy of those cities and the sense of power and purpose they radiated. And while he was very much a part of the urban scene and thoroughly dedicated to his work, he was never a driven man. He knew how to relax and have fun.

Even at work, he knew how to encourage pleasure and camaraderie. After the Rosenwald Fund moved into its own building, a coffee break in mid-morning brought everyone together. Each day, lunch was served in the dining room to the entire staff and to any notable visitor passing through Chicago whom Embree could entice to join them.[6] Good conversation about the visitor's pursuits and ideas served to inform and stimulate those at the table. Such discussions were largely intended to maintain the intellectual vigor of the fund's officers, to ensure their ability to function at a level "comparable to a university."[7] The fact that support staff participated along with the professionals is indicative of Embree's democratic approach, his rejection of needless differentiations.

On days when no guest was present, another activity took place. At some point, the game of bridge was introduced into the workplace, and after some initial scoffing at such frivolity in the middle of the day,

Embree was taken by the game. Soon, there were two tables, with Embree and the three most adept players at one, and those a bit less skilled at the other. The games routinely occupied thirty minutes after lunch, though occasionally, when the competition was especially keen, play was allowed to continue beyond the normal time. Years later, long after the fund had closed, former staff members recalled with pleasure the luncheons and bridge games, and the good spirit and high morale they engendered. The office atmosphere seems to have reflected Embree's own spirit, his enthusiasm, his joie de vivre.[8]

As much as Embree enjoyed those bridge games, they did not interfere with his work habits. One of his Yale associates remembered him as "wonderfully energetic."[9] His energy had also impressed his Rockefeller contemporaries, though some believed that, like others at the foundation, he overworked. Following his exhausting 1921 stint in East Asia, an older colleague chided him for not taking some time off for sight-seeing in Japan and China, asking facetiously if he were "blessed (or cursed) with an exaggerated New England conscience?"[10] As a young man at Rockefeller, Embree certainly encountered the advice of the fiery Frederick Gates: "Never allow the least relaxation of the nervous tension in yourself, in your friends, or in the public until the work is done.... Bring every ounce of vital energy, every moment of waking time to bear. Regard every suggestion involving delay as *treason* and *death*."[11] Although Embree greatly admired Gates, he was not inclined to follow that particular admonition, but he did display a similar expectation of accomplishment. Even when approaching middle age, he was said to have "the spirit of ebullient youth to which nothing seems impossible."[12]

Embree's personal warmth, his ebullience, was fully evident in his personal life. After working hours, he and Kate enjoyed entertaining. Living in an apartment or a residential hotel, they lacked the space to accommodate large numbers of people, but they delighted in going for drinks and dinner at Chicago restaurants. They entertained smaller groups at home. Guests at their table were local friends, colleagues from the East passing through town, or persons associated in some way with the Rosenwald Fund. Many of those invited had national reputations: singer-actor Paul Robeson, dancer Katherine Dunham, best-selling author Lillian Smith, poet and NAACP official James Weldon Johnson,

Miss America 1945 Bess Myerson, the dethroned heavyweight boxing champion Joe Louis.[13] The first racially mixed occasion, however, brought a surprising problem.

While Edwin and Kate Embree were completely at ease with African Americans, their perspective was not shared by the family retainer who prepared their meals. Reared in the South, this middle-aged black woman (fondly remembered only as "Estoria") considered it improper for people of different races to eat together. Soon after coming to work for the family, she prepared dinner for several people Embree had invited home. But when the food was ready, and the family and guests already seated, she bridled. Coming into the dining room and seeing several dark faces around the table, she would not serve the meal. Retreating to the kitchen, she remained ensconced there, refusing to bring in the hot dishes. When Kate went to look into the delay, she found herself confronting a full-fledged protest. Her efforts to resolve the matter quietly were of no avail. Finally, Embree, undoubtedly chagrined, had to go into the kitchen and override the cook's objections. What he said and how he said it are not known. Nor have the responses of the guests, whether irritation, bemusement, or some combination, been retained in the Embree family's memory. What is known is that the meal was eventually served, and that the woman remained for many years as a deeply loved member of the household, with a room of her own in the Embree home. In time, she came to take pride in serving the distinguished African American guests who came to dinner.[14] As for Embree himself, it seems safe to assume that this particular exercise in overcoming deeply entrenched racial attitudes was not expected, nor enjoyed.

At times, Embree's entertainment combined fund purposes with his personal interests. On a business trip to New York, for example, he indulged his passion for the theater with attendance at the play *The Green Pastures*. So taken was he with the play that, a few nights later, he arranged through NAACP friends James Weldon Johnson and Walter White to host the entire all-black cast at dinner at his hotel.[15] Back home in Chicago, Embree's entertaining routinely brought whites and blacks together on a footing of equality. Typical was a "lively" party at the fund's office to honor several African American writers—W. E. B. DuBois, Richard Wright, Arna Bontemps, and Langston Hughes—all of whom had earlier received Rosenwald fellowships. On another occasion, when former fellow Katherine Dunham was in town, Embree held an afternoon reception for her and some other guests. The next day, he led a two-car caravan of fund trustees and friends to attend a performance of *The Ballad of Dorie Miller*, a play written by one Rosenwald fellow, Owen Dodson, and staged by another, Charles Sebree.[16] Calling attention in this way to the fellows' accomplishments served to demonstrate the intelligence and creativity within the black community, a key goal of the fellowship program. At the same time, Embree's entertaining expressed his own festive spirit, his deep-rooted optimism.[17]

Embree's behavior, whether at work or leisure, displayed not only high physical energy, but comparable intellectual energy. Unfailingly curious, he was always eager to learn new things, experience a new section of the globe, consider a novel idea. He read widely, but much of his learning came from searching conversations with authorities in various fields or with individuals engaged in important ventures. From his extensive travels, he developed a capacity for keen observation and vivid description. His international travel, like his activities in the United States, brought him into contact with diverse patterns of thought and behavior, serving to stimulate and sustain his lively imagination.[18]

Along with physical and intellectual energy went a certain boldness, a kind of courage that might strike a more cautious observer as occasionally bordering on the foolhardy. Beginning with his experience with a skittish horse as a three-year-old, he was inclined to take risks, to avoid the conventional and safe, to seek the daring adventure. This disposition was on display when, at age ten, he determined to explore the Chicago World's Fair on his own. It was evident when he crossed an Atlantic not yet free of German submarines, and again when he climbed into an open cockpit for a flight over twenty miles of open water when commercial air travel was a new and dubious proposition. From his grandfather, he had learned something about maverick behavior, and he was similarly disposed to speak and act on his convictions, without undue worry about the immediate public response. Indeed, his commitment to taking action, to moving forward, was one of his salient characteristics.[19] It was that eagerness to explore new paths that had caused his mounting frustration at Rockefeller, and he brought to Chicago a firm intent to avoid similar constraints. Physical and moral courage, nonconformist tendencies, insistent activism—that combination of traits goes far to explain why Embree was often steeped in controversy.

Embree was not by temperament combative, and apart from a dubious charge that he had publicly opposed Prohibition, there had been no contentious public incidents during the Rockefeller years.[20] That situation changed early in his career at Rosenwald, when his commitment to change aroused opposition in various quarters. In his first year at the fund, he tried to bring about a merger of the National Association for the Advancement of Colored People and the National Urban League. Though he promoted such a union for several years, his efforts were systematically resisted by officials of both organizations. With similar lack of success, he urged Carter G. Woodson to affiliate his Association for the Study of Negro Life and History with Howard University. Rosenwald involvement in efforts to increase hospital facilities in Harlem brought a protest that racial segregation would be strengthened as a result. When the fund experimented with pay clinics, vigorous complaints from a group of Chicago doctors ensued. By the mid-thirties, Embree's criticism of Christian hypocrisy and the misguided efforts of missionaries in Asia brought additional disapproval. And his outspoken opposition to legally enforced racial segregation in the forties embroiled him in further strife. During his twenty years at Rosenwald, one of his supporters declared, Embree was "without any lingering doubt, the most controversial figure in the field of Negro education, culture and race relations."[21]

That such controversy should rage around Embree's head, once he entered the tangled thicket of race relations, was to some degree inevitable. Relations between blacks and whites, more than any other issue in the nation's life, were inordinately subject to disagreement, and anyone who dared to venture into that highly emotional area was bound to encounter not only opposition, but hostility.[22] Yet it seems that, in his most productive years, Embree deliberately courted controversy. It is as if he had concluded that, since disputation could not be avoided, he might as well plunge fully into the fray and speak forthrightly the message he believed needed to be heard. Well rooted in his psyche was a large measure of the spirit of Grandfather Fee.

Embree's tendency to arouse disagreement was but one of the behaviors learned from his grandfather. More fundamental and powerful was his outlook on race relations. His grandfather's fervent belief that black Americans deserved full equality and every opportunity routinely available to whites was a lesson Embree readily absorbed. That belief, for Reverend Fee, was rooted in what he saw as the plain truth of Scripture, particularly the doctrine of the kinship of all peoples. His grandson, however, by his adult years based that conviction on more than personal piety. His upbringing in a racially integrated town, his schooling and play with African American classmates, led early on to the conclusion that this was the natural pattern of social arrangements. His travels in Europe, Asia, and the Pacific quickened his appreciation for distinctive cultures and deepened his commitment to their preservation. In maturity, he regarded racial discrimination in all its forms as contrary to reason, a violation of the most basic principles of a just society. His understanding of social justice, to be sure, owed much to Fee's emphasis on brotherly love but, without rejecting that teaching, Embree came in time to a more nuanced, largely secular justification.

The enduring influence of his grandfather was evident in other ways. Embree never forgot the mealtime devotionals around the dining room table, and throughout his life he often used scriptural passages or biblical language to drive home a point. As a boy, he had been baptized by total immersion, the only form of that ritual the strong-willed Reverend Fee considered valid. Like his grandfather hostile to religious divisiveness, Embree became dubious about organized religion in general. Religion for him was not about doctrine or formal worship, metaphysics or a life after death, but about ethical behavior.[23]

In his mid-forties, Embree was taken by the concept of a "new religion," a fellowship composed of those who rejected religious institutions and formal creeds while remaining committed to ideals rooted in Hebrew and Christian scripture, but reaching beyond biblical formulations. Such a fellowship, as he described it, might in time include "not only all nations but also all creeds, [and] embrace all sincere seekers after truth, all persons who try to live the good life." Such idealists were concerned not with an anthropomorphic God and subordination to some kind of divine will, but with "human personality and its slow growth toward truth and full development." Imbued with the scientific spirit, they saw truth as the slowly accumulated result of constant search and discovery, not as an act of divine revelation.[24]

When Embree spoke or wrote about Christianity, the tone was commonly that of an outsider, and he was reputed to be "contemptuous of the Christian churches."[25] The basis for that characterization appears in various pronouncements, but is nowhere more forcefully expressed than in a passage from a book he co-authored on colonial education:

> Brotherly love without regard to race or caste, the Golden Rule, pacifism, humility, communal sharing of goods and services, the abrogation of worldly wealth—these which were the cardinal teachings of Jesus are directly opposed to just those things which the Western nations have founded their power upon: capitalism, armaments, individualism, disregard, even scorn, of one's neighbor if he be of a different race or color, the accumulation of material wealth. It is one of the ironies of history that Christianity by a series of accidents should have become the professed religion of just those nations which by all their dearest practices are furthest from its teachings. The principles of Jesus . . . have never been accepted by the West and are not today a part of Western civilization.[26]

Though some of Embree's books won praise for their balance and reasonable tone, *Island India Goes to School* was intentionally provocative. After receiving a copy of the book, a college president wrote to express the hope to read someday one of Embree's works that omitted "a certain condescension toward the preacher and toward organized religion."[27] Prompted to explain his views, Embree replied that his complaints were not about religion itself, but about interpretations of Jesus' teachings that he regarded as unjustified. Those teachings were "beautiful and humane," unlike the doctrines and practices of the churches which call themselves Christian. He was "not at all opposed to the teachings of Christianity—in fact, sometimes I think I am the only person living who believes in them."[28] What he took exception to was the false interpretation that he called "Puritanism," and its emphasis on self-denial. Puritanism in combination with industrialism had an especially deadening effect on the enjoyment and richness of daily life, he proclaimed. The emphasis on a heavenly afterlife and a disdain for life on earth had made enjoyment "almost synonymous with sin." Taking pleasure in art and expression, the enjoyment of living, had come to "seem the shirking of a great life duty, the abandonment of the march toward heaven and success." The result tended to make life "routinized, dull, and barren."[29]

What particularly offended Embree was the racist behavior of many who professed the faith. The contradiction between the stated beliefs of Christians and their actions had been brought home to him most forcefully during his China travels, and what he saw there profoundly affected his views on religion. Missionaries were often motivated by altruism, pious zeal, and commitment to the welfare of native peoples, he acknowledged, but their cultural arrogance blinded them to the value of indigenous beliefs and practices. Hence, their schools, hospitals, and churches tended to destroy native traditions in an effort to create "Little Westerners" who could fit into a Western economic system, albeit at a subservient level.[30] Christians of European ancestry affirmed the fundamental principle of universal brotherly love, he observed, but persisted in treating unfairly, often disdainfully, persons of color. Similarly, in the United States, Christians of African descent were victims of unremitting discrimination by their white coreligionists. Native Americans were likewise discriminated against. Many had joined churches, but they had difficulty appreciating the teachings of Jesus "when they see what Christians do, when they meet so little brotherly love in the white men who profess the gospel."[31]

Embree's rejection of Christian hypocrisy undoubtedly reflected the influence of his maternal grandfather. He knew well how John Fee's views on slavery had estranged him from parents and siblings, and how his preaching had subjected him to persecution, multiple beatings, and death threats. With that example of unswerving adherence to principle before him as a youth, it is no wonder that, as an adult, Embree had so little respect for the behavior of lesser men. Nor is it surprising that, when buffeted by the winds of opposition, he neither changed course nor trimmed his sails. The public response to his ideas and activities did not overly concern him, but he was not altogether indifferent, for he was not lacking in ambition.

Embree had ambition, but it was not of a conventional sort. He never aspired to great wealth. At one point in his life, he thought about going into banking, but business never attracted him strongly. In middle age, he became active in Illinois politics, yet remained content to support persons and causes he favored, not choosing to stand for public office himself. Though his experience and connections qualified him for a university presidency, he never pursued such a position. Never seriously considering any of those avenues, he sought not personal power but a sturdy platform from which to broadcast his ideas and influence opinion.[32] Exerting such influence required constant use of the media and cultivating an extensive network of important contacts.

Embree enjoyed being associated with persons of prominence. His desire for such associations probably originated at Yale. There he had encountered fellow students of impressive pedigree and substantial wealth, assets that he obviously could not claim. There, too, he was enveloped in an ethos that assumed personal and professional success, achievements that he, without family backing, would have to manage on his own. At Rockefeller, he came into contact with intellectual leaders, captains of industry, and towering public figures, including two nominees for the U.S. presidency.[33] In light of his own modest background and admitted insecurity as a young adult, he undoubtedly found such involvements initially intimidating. In such a rarefied atmosphere, it is only natural that he would want to develop a sense of comfort and to have the outward indicators of belonging. It was the fear of losing those symbols and losing access to those circles of power that explains his crisis of confidence when leaving Rockefeller and New York for Rosenwald and Chicago.

One element in Embree's ambition was the success of his children, and he saw education and its opportunities for networking as the essential key, as it had proved for him. When the private Lincoln School opened in uptown Manhattan, he had enrolled son John, even though attendance required a complicated journey each day by public transportation from the family's Brooklyn home. Embree considered the benefits worth the inconvenience, for the school's Progressive philosophy matched his own educational views, and he liked the fact that John would be associating with the offspring of other foundation officers, including four sons of John D. Rockefeller Jr.[34] After the move to Chicago, his and Kate's youngest child, Catherine, also attended private school, continuing through the Depression even when the family's finances were straitened. Much to Embree's regret, when John was ready for college, his own overseas travel interfered with efforts to get his son admitted to Yale. And though relatively few young women then sought college degrees, he insisted that both his daughters attend institutions where they would be challenged to achieve, perhaps beyond their own expectations.[35]

Because his duties frequently took him out of town (and, especially during the Rockefeller years, out of the country), he was away from home for extended periods. Hence, the several weeks each summer that the family spent at their Canadian retreat were particularly treasured. The day-to-day responsibilities of rearing the children fell largely to Kate, yet Embree worked hard at staying in touch, via the family journals describing his activities and the warm letters that his daughters remembered with great pleasure even late in life. Those letters reveal a parent offering sound fatherly advice to his son at various stages of growth and a doting father's easy relations with his daughters. They contain as well a hint of protectiveness and paternalism, reflecting perhaps a sense that the father had been less deeply involved in their upbringing than he would have liked.[36]

As each of the children left home for college, the exchange of letters was not interrupted, and Embree's travels occasionally allowed him to visit them on their campuses. Later, when the first marriages of the two elder children failed, he was disappointed, but with their subsequent marriages he was highly pleased. By the time all three children had reached full maturity, Embree's pride in them was unmistakable. To the extent that his own ambition was predicated on their accomplishments, that element of his aspirations was well satisfied.[37]

Embree had a gift for friendship, and he had many friends. Those who knew him well appreciated his ironic humor, valued his generosity of spirit, and enjoyed his positive outlook on life. But admirable traits aside, he was not flawless. As a young man of modest background, he did not display the equanimity of his seasoned, better-established associates. Given responsibilities and opportunities beyond his years, he may at times have seemed brash. Even in full maturity, he tended to be impatient with dull people, and fools he did not suffer gladly. Pomposity and pretension irritated him, and when he encountered those qualities, he could be quick with a cutting remark. During the early thirties, when under unusual strain as he struggled to keep the fund afloat, he was not above adopting a harshly pedantic tone with a young staffer. On uncounted public occasions, he was deliberately provocative, knowing he would likely offend some of his listeners. Even at his most provocative, however, his words were usually intended in some sense to be educational. His goal was to jolt his listeners out of lazy, unexamined attitudes, to encourage them to think anew, to envision heretofore unimagined possibilities.[38]

Apart from his provocative moments, Embree's statements were commonly nuanced, reflecting his even temper. Such attributes were not shared in equal measure by Kate Embree. An avid reader, she formed strong opinions, which she was not reluctant to express. Like her husband, she enjoyed conversation, but was more likely to dominate it. Given an opportunity to tell a story, she presented it with considerable dramatic flair. She was known to raise her voice on occasion. Yet a niece who lived in the Embree home for two years while attending school with daughter Catherine recalled a calm household, free of any element of tension or turmoil.[39] As in most marriages, the two partners had different personalities. Yet those differences seem to have caused no unusual problems. For forty-three years, through frequent, sometimes long separations, their union lasted. Its longevity indicates how well Kate understood, and shared, her husband's ambitions and her acceptance of the conditions his work imposed.

* * *

Embree's professional aspirations, his capacity for unconventional thinking and bold action, and his convictions about philanthropy's responsibility for societal progress plunged him repeatedly into controversy. Yet one such occurrence, in his third year at Rosenwald, cannot be attributed to those personal qualities. Stemming from the fund's multifaceted effort to improve the health of the nation's largest minority, the episode illustrates how well-intentioned initiatives could become entangled in local issues.

During the 1930s, the fund's efforts on behalf of African American health took several directions. Demonstration projects on the control of venereal disease and tuberculosis were funded, and measures to improve maternal and infant welfare were tested. A half-dozen southern states received subsidies to encourage the employment of black public health officers. Fellowships were awarded to numerous doctors and nurses of African ancestry to promote their professional development. Contributions were made to the building and equipment funds of a score of hospitals serving black communities, almost all in the South. Outside the South, the fund urged teaching hospitals to allow black physicians-in-training to have access to up-to-date procedures and equipment by expanding opportunities for internships and residencies. Chicago's Provident Hospital received more than a half-million dollars to demonstrate how upgraded facilities and practices could improve health care for the city's residents of color.[40]

At the beginning of the decade, however, the fund's approach to the whole matter of black health came under fire. With its commitment to improvement well known, the fund was invited by a group of Harlem doctors to take part in a survey of New York City hospitals to determine whether additional hospital beds were needed for the city's black community. Immediately, some members of the Manhattan Medical Society objected that singling out a minority population for such study would contribute to racial segregation. The fund subsequently agreed to assign a member of its medical staff to examine the situation, while making clear it had no plans to help build a new hospital in Harlem or anywhere else in the city. Yet the agreement triggered a public statement by a political appointee in the city's Department of Hospitals. No new hospital was needed, he claimed, for doctors and patients were fully served without discrimination. Not only was the survey unnecessary, but private philanthropy in such matters was "of doubtful value in a democracy."[41]

One of the city's black community newspapers immediately took issue with the official and his supporters. Fundamentally, the *Amsterdam News* intimated, their outcry was no more than a salvo in an ongoing battle on the part of the Tammany Hall–dominated city government to maintain control of health care. An editorial, running over fifty column inches, disputed many points raised by the protesters and pointed out that, contrary to their assertions, black physicians were denied privileges at most hospitals outside Harlem, black interns were to be found only in Harlem Hospital, and black patients were segregated in some city institutions. Moreover, the column continued, the survey was opposed by only part of the Manhattan Medical Society, itself a primarily political organization established by the secretary of the Harlem Hospital Board. Applying general medical statistics to Harlem's population indicated that this section of the city alone needed more than half again as many hospital beds as were currently available. Philanthropic support was essential to most private hospitals, the editorial concluded, and the proposed survey could help to direct such support where it was most needed.[42]

With the lines sharply drawn, the NAACP entered the fray with a statement, crafted by W. E. B. DuBois, opposing segregated hospital facilities. As the controversy continued to bubble for some weeks, Embree found it necessary to offer a public explanation of the fund's policy regarding hospitals. In an address at the dedication of new medical facilities in Philadelphia, to which Rosenwald had contributed, he affirmed that the fund did not advocate the segregation of any racial group, but the immediate concern was improving health in the African American community. In that regard, a central consideration was ensuring that black physicians and nurses had opportunities to gain experience with the best equipment and under modern conditions. Yet, across the country, there were no more than ten "really first class" hospitals where such opportunities were available. Even in the North, he pointed out, professional staffs were almost always exclusively white. Thus, unless the training of African American practitioners was to be sacrificed, along with the care of their patients, it was necessary to increase the number of hospitals providing access to state-of-the-art facilities and practices. The issue was the same as that faced by other discriminated-against groups—female and Jewish physicians—which had been addressed by the establishment of women's and Jewish hospitals. It was important for black doctors to be in active association with their white colleagues; since germs do not follow segregation patterns, whatever measures improved health in the black community benefited both races. Though there had been positive developments, health conditions among blacks were "such as no civilized country can afford to permit," with tuberculosis three times more prevalent than for whites and mortality rates 62 percent higher than for whites.[43]

Embree's doughty address received wide and favorable comment in the black press, but it did not silence the New York opposition. Instead, they responded with a fifteen-page open letter to the fund's president, charging that Rosenwald hospitals were "Jim Crow in spirit and Jim Crow in fact." Special arrangements for black physicians and patients served to perpetuate racial segregation, the letter asserted, while fostering a sense of inferiority on the part of blacks and a sense of superiority on the part of whites. Such Jim Crow projects, under a misguided sense of philanthropy, did not benefit African Americans but did them "irreparable harm." The Rosenwald Fund had "stimulated and advanced tremendously the separation of the Negroes from all other races." All that was needed by black Americans was simple justice, but Embree, as a southerner, could not be expected to act fairly.[44]

Embree informed his board of the attack and his response, but did not give the matter undue weight. The survey proposal was allowed to lapse, and the furor died down, with no significant harm to the fund's reputation. Yet this was not Embree's first conflict with part of the medical profession. Months before the Harlem Hospital issue arose, opposition to another Rosenwald initiative developed within the Chicago Medical Society. The contention centered on demonstration projects involving pay medical clinics, a key element in the fund's program in the new field of medical economics.

* * *

Medical economics concentrated not on medical research, a province already occupied by various philanthropies, but on discovering ways to reduce treatment costs in order to make them more affordable to middle-class patients. That portion of the population was of particular concern because, unlike the wealthy, they commonly lacked the means to meet private medical and hospital costs and, unlike the poor, they had no access to free clinics operating as charities. During Embree's time at Rockefeller, the foundation, in association with Cornell University, had experimented with a clinic in which patients paid for care, but at costs notably less than those charged by private physicians. Medical econom-

ics was not a major interest of Rockefeller or any other foundation, however. Thus, when the Rosenwald Fund entered the field in 1928, Embree
was able to recruit Michael M. Davis, director of the Cornell operation
and the country's foremost authority on pay clinics, to head the new
program. Named as Davis's assistant director was economist and ac-
countant C. Rufus Rorem.[45]

Under Davis's leadership, the fund completed the nation's first comprehensive assessment of the costs of medical care. It then conducted
a variety of studies, stimulated experimentation, provided consulting
services, and underwrote the expenses of several demonstration projects. One such project in Iowa, for example, tested the efficacy of pay
clinics in an agricultural region, while a Chicago project made similar
assessments in an urban setting. Chicago also saw experimentation with
dental pay clinics and the employment of nurses on an hourly fee basis.
Of particular importance also for middle-class patients was the fund's interest in prepaid insurance for hospitalization, which was promoted most
energetically by Rorem. By the mid-thirties, Rosenwald headquarters
had become the country's principal center for information on voluntary
medical and hospital insurance.[46]

With so much of the fund's activity centered in Chicago, it is not
surprising that loud opposition to the clinic initiative arose there. Before
embarking on the program, Embree had wisely conferred with Dr. M. L.
Harris, president of the American Medical Association (AMA), and Mor-
ris Fishbein, editor of the association's influential *Journal,* and received
their support and suggestions.[47] Yet approval at that high level was no
guarantee of acceptance by local physicians. Even before any new facility was opened, a branch of the Chicago Medical Society protested that,
because pay clinics would advertise their services, they would violate
professional ethics. Moreover, the organization claimed, clinics would
harm private physicians financially by depriving them of patients. Thus,
it warned, at a forthcoming meeting its members would consider a resolution affirming that the clinics represented "a tendency toward the socialization of medicine, pauperization of the public, and a lowering of
medical standards."[48]

Controversy over the Rosenwald clinic program soon merged into a
long-standing dispute between the Chicago Medical Society and a local

public health institute, a clinic offering treatment of venereal disease. The dispute had been simmering for over seven years, but the announcement that the fund would sponsor the institute gave the issue fresh intensity. That intensity grew when the city's leading newspaper reported that the fund's sponsorship was the "first step" in plans to provide low-cost medical care for "people of moderate means." That development, the paper suggested, could be expected to lead to "events of great importance in medical history." Soon thereafter, a noted surgeon connected to the institute was expelled from the society, ostensibly because the institute advertised its services. His expulsion propelled the matter onto the front pages of Chicago newspapers.[49]

Embree responded to the growing row in several ways. In an address to the American Hospital Association meeting in Atlantic City in the spring of 1929, he defended pay clinics in principle and Rosenwald's experimentation in particular. Back in Chicago, he met with several prominent laypeople and physicians in an effort to negotiate their differences, but the issue of advertising proved irresolvable. At the same time, he and Michael Davis put together an advisory panel of seven area doctors and dentists, inviting both the president of the Chicago Medical Society and the president of the AMA to join as well. Though neither man accepted the invitation, the members of the panel were sufficiently distinguished to receive favorable comment in the press.[50]

But these steps did not end the matter. Early in 1930, the *Bulletin of the Chicago Medical Society* devoted nine closely printed pages to the issue of pay clinics, quoting at great length Embree's description of the program in the fund's 1929 report, and then presenting an almost equally long rejoinder in the form of an open letter to the Rosenwald president from the society's secretary. Received by thousands of Chicago physicians, the article expressed hostility to pay clinics, praised the medical profession, and proclaimed that "one of the most constructive things" the fund could do would be to educate 120 million Americans "to the fact that all medical services must be paid for no matter what the financial status of those receiving them or the type of service received."[51]

Far from being deterred by such disapproval, Embree pushed on. On his recommendation, the Rosenwald board authorized the executive committee to appropriate up to $100,000 in the next eight months for the project, an unusually large amount for such a short period. Though some board members may have had reservations, the experiment continued with the strong support of Julius Rosenwald himself. As the attacks in the Chicago Medical Society's *Bulletin* continued, he brought his personal prestige to bear. In an address to the annual convention of the American Hospital Association late in 1930, the philanthropist emphasized that hospital operations should follow sound business practices, and he called attention to the success of Chicago clinics operating with fee schedules suitable for persons of limited income.[52]

The following year, the announcement of a fund experiment to offer dental services at cost brought the Chicago Dental Society into the dispute. The issues for these practitioners were essentially the same as for the physicians: the inability to compete with low-cost clinics, a fear of losing clientele, the violation of ethics by advertising. Yet the introduction of pay clinics was not without defenders. The dean of Northwestern University's College of Dentistry suggested to his colleagues that such clinics were inevitable and that the profession should lead the way on humanitarian grounds. Though the majority of the dental society's members subsequently voted to oppose the Rosenwald plan, that outcome was reached only after "more than three hours of heated debate."[53]

While criticism by Chicago doctors and dentists mounted, Embree encountered dissent within his own board over another clinic venture. Convinced that the "shockingly rapid growth" of population was "the most pressing problem in the whole world," he had begun meeting with Margaret Sanger while still at Rockefeller.[54] Discussions with the family planning advocate and Michael Davis were renewed after the move to Chicago. Subsequently, the fund's executive committee approved a grant to establish a birth control clinic in the "Negro district of Harlem." When the committee's minutes came before the full board for approval, however, considerable discussion ensued. How the public would respond to foundation activity in that controversial area was not known, for no philanthropy had ever made an appropriation for that particular cause. Embree focused his defense of the grant not on birth control education per se, but on the fund's commitment to improve the health and well-being of the African American population. An unconvinced

Lessing Rosenwald, son of the founder and his presumed successor as chair of the board, was adamantly opposed. Indeed, he insisted that his vote against the grant—the only negative of the eleven cast—be formally recorded. Such strong opposition to an Embree recommendation had not previously occurred, and the outcome is indicative both of his support within the board and his disposition to push his own agenda in spite of disagreement. Even so, he later declined a funding request from the Chicago Birth Control League.[55]

The fund's direct involvement in medical economics came to an end in 1936. By that time, as Embree informed the trustees, the fund had assumed "some measure of leadership in this subject before the country," but had aroused opposition not only from individual doctors, but from the county, state, and national medical associations.[56] Yet withdrawal from the field was the result not of this opposition, but of the need at that point to narrow the fund's focus. By then, much had been accomplished. The American Nursing Association at its annual meeting had called attention to the burden of medical costs on the middle class. Many doctors had become more open to clinical arrangements for delivering service. At the University of Chicago, Davis had initiated the nation's first graduate-level course in hospital administration. Rorem had published a volume prescribing uniform accounting and statistical systems for hospitals, which proved so influential that it reached a fourth edition in 1949. The benefits of prepaid hospitalization insurance, championed by both men, had been emphasized at a national conference held under fund auspices, and enrollment in such plans had increased tenfold in just a few years. The American Hospital Association, assisted by the fund's data and experience and a sizable grant, had created a standing committee to provide information and advice to hospitals and groups considering such insurance. Chaired by Rorem, this committee in time became the Blue Cross Commission, a national leader in hospitalization insurance and counterpart to medical insurer Blue Shield.[57]

Davis and Rorem remained key figures in medical economics after leaving the fund, and they continued for some time to benefit from Rosenwald financing. Even as it was vacating the field, the fund contributed $100,000 to Rorem's committee, and it granted $165,000 over a five-year period to a fledging Committee on Research in Medical Economics, to function under Davis's leadership. Both men, like Embree, had good reason to feel gratified by the results of the work they had pioneered. Controversy aside, the program was among the fund's most far-reaching successes. Indeed, it could be seen as a textbook example of how a philanthropy could best serve—by recognizing a societal problem, demonstrating how it could be effectively addressed, and then leaving full implementation of the solution to society at large.

* * *

Ever ambitious to extend the fund's reach, and his own influence, Embree attempted in 1933 to push his trustees even further into direct action. Less than a year after the board adopted that policy, he proposed another major step intended to give the new approach great force. Like the earlier decision, his proposal was imaginative—indeed, unlike anything any other philanthropy had attempted. And like that decision, it exemplified his capacity for bold thinking and his willingness to undertake ventures that most foundation executives would not even have considered.

At the same meeting at which direct action had been approved, Embree informed the board that he had been asked by the Institute of Pacific Relations to lead a survey of native education in the Dutch East Indies. The survey was expected to take more than three months, and though the fund would need to underwrite most of the cost, moneys already budgeted were more than sufficient to meet the expense. The study, as he conceived it, would be akin to the abortive work in Mexico and a sequel to an examination of schools in Samoa he had completed a few months earlier, all part of a contemplated series of fund reports on education in nonindustrialized countries.[58] Unlike those earlier activities, he warned, this one was likely to arouse dissent. Short notice and questionable conditions notwithstanding, the board approved the undertaking. Six weeks later, Embree sailed for Java, accompanied by the fund's secretary, Margaret Sargent Simon; her husband, James; and W. Bryant Mumford, the superintendent of education for Tanganyika Territory, British East Africa.[59]

On the way to Java, while stopped over in Kyoto, Embree sketched out plans for a monthly magazine he hoped the fund would undertake to publish. Tentatively entitled the *Aristocrat,* it was to be a publication "not for the masses," but "high hat and proud of it." In keeping with its beautiful format, it would carry the forbidding price of a dollar per issue. As he ruminated about people who might join him in such an undertaking, Viking Press head Marshall Best and author Sherwood Anderson came to mind.[60]

As he continued to turn over the prospect in his mind, perhaps he thought of some of his own acquaintances—creative writers Thornton Wilder, John Dos Passos, James Weldon Johnson, Archibald MacLeish; and sociologist Robert Staughton Lynd—as possible contributors. The magazine might also fulfill his long-standing interest in boosting the arts by publicizing the work of painters like his friend Grant Wood or sculptors like Rosenwald fellows Augusta Savage and Richmond Barthé. Indeed, the publication could advance the fellowship program's underlying purpose by showcasing the talents of other Rosenwald fellows— economist Abram Harris, novelist Zora Neale Hurston, poet Langston Hughes—just as the Urban League's *Opportunity* had done for Harlem Renaissance figures a few years earlier. Months later, as his ideas matured, he acknowledged he had become "pretty keen on this magazine business," for he had gained more enjoyment, "even thrill," from the two books and the articles he had published than from anything else he had ever done.[61]

Embree's thinking was well advanced when, months later, the inimitable editor of the *American Mercury,* H. L. Mencken, let it be known that he planned to retire at the end of 1933. That magazine, after considerable literary and financial success in the late twenties, had seen its circulation fall by half during the early Depression, with an even more serious decline in advertising revenue. Following several years when the magazine barely broke even, and facing the need to find a new editor, publisher Alfred Knopf decided to sell it. Learning upon his return from Java that the magazine was available for purchase, Embree sprang into action.[62]

Working hurriedly, the Rosenwald president set about gathering information and advice about the fund's direct entry into the publishing business. He consulted key figures in the periodical world, not only Knopf and Mencken, but Henry Luce of *Time* and *Fortune,* Arthur and

Paul Kellogg of *Survey* and *Survey Graphic*, and *Atlantic* editor Ellery Sedgwick. He contacted established authors Sherwood Anderson, Christopher Morley, and his friend Clarence Day. He called on a half-dozen key figures at the University of Chicago and approached eminent social scientists at other institutions to determine their availability as contributors. In the fall, he was ready to make his thinking known to the fund's trustees.

At a special meeting of the Rosenwald board called for that purpose, Embree presented a carefully reasoned, twelve-page proposal that the fund establish in Chicago a general monthly magazine. As he described it, the magazine would focus on "discussion of social and economic questions by the editors and by highest authorities" and would cover "in its general scope biography, literary interpretation, fiction, poetry, and the fine arts." Rather than starting a new enterprise and adding another entrant to an already competitive field, he suggested taking over the subscription list and advertising goodwill of an already established publication. The availability for purchase of the *American Mercury* was fortuitous, for nothing of comparable quality was likely to come on the market in the foreseeable future.

Proposing that the magazine venture start with the new year, only three months distant, Embree pointed out the need to take advantage of a business upswing apparently under way. Other factors made the time propitious, he suggested, for much social experimentation was taking place as a consequence of the Depression, and outlooks were changing, marking "a rich era" for a magazine featuring interpretation of social movements. In addition, because the World's Fair had focused national interest on the Chicago area, it was "the natural time for an important new influence to be created here."

Embree's outline of the magazine made it clear he was thinking in large terms. It was to be "distinguished, dignified, and beautiful [in] format and typography." Pictures and art would be featured as well as text. Included would be a new type of book section, containing reviews, brief comments on "all important books," and occasional reading lists of the best books on a topic. Contributions would be solicited from experts in various fields and from established or unusually promising creative writers. Rather than the standard 5,000-word limitation, articles might run up to 20,000 words if necessary to present a subject fully. Attracting the best manuscripts would require a larger budget for contributors than was "customary among the present quality magazines." An expenditure of $350,000, he projected, would enable the magazine to become self-supporting after three years.

Taking responsibility for such a publication, Embree emphasized, would be "a spectacular venture: brilliant if successful, a doleful experience if it failed or lagged on a mediocre level." The magazine could add to the intellectual resources of Chicago and the Midwest in general, while providing a platform for discussion of topics in which the fund was interested but could not take up directly. The list of examples was long: birth control and population problems, cultural clashes between East and West, African American art and literature, improvement in governmental procedures, art as a necessary element in civilization, implications for education of recent findings in psychology. Yet there were risks. A national magazine that originated outside the New York area might not succeed. The vitality of monthly magazines was in question, as daily and weekly newspapers, film, and radio cut into their readership. The periodical could easily lose touch with its public, and a conflict could develop between the "reformist" orientation of a foundation and a journal devoted to expression and ideas.

Embree's proposal was undoubtedly debated at length, but fund records do not reveal details of the discussion. The outcome, however, is clear; the proposal to acquire and publish a magazine was rejected. What led the majority of trustees to this conclusion is subject to speculation. Perhaps the undertaking seemed too risky with the fund's resources already badly stretched. The time frame for deciding, much less putting together the first issue, may have seemed too short. Those who knew Embree well may have considered the list of suggested topics too obvious an expression of his personal interests. To some, the very idea may have seemed dubious, a potential diversion from more immediately promising activities. Publishing a magazine, after all, was not something philanthropies did, not even a pioneering organization like Rosenwald.

Embree's enthusiasm for the project is beyond question, though he had not shied away from revealing contrary considerations. Unaccus-

tomed to having his ideas rejected by the board, he undoubtedly was
disappointed by the decision. Even so, he came away from the episode
with an affirmation of the trustees' desire to "continue and enlarge the
scope and influence of their general activities in publicity and publication."[63]

*   *   *

Among the people Embree had consulted about the publishing venture
was University of Chicago president Robert Maynard Hutchins. Though
Hutchins was Embree's junior by half a generation, their lives had connected at several points. Both held undergraduate and graduate degrees
from Yale. Both had served in Yale's administration; indeed, years after
Embree had moved to Rockefeller, Hutchins became head of the office
where Embree had learned administration. Hutchins's father, the president of Berea College, was a man Embree greatly admired, corresponded
with, and visited whenever he was in Kentucky. And in 1929, when the
University of Chicago was seeking a new president, Hutchins had been
dropped from consideration until a highly enthusiastic letter from Embree served to revive his candidacy.[64]

Hutchins's appointment had served to strengthen still further an
already strong relationship between the university and the fund. Long
before the 1928 reorganization of his philanthropy, Julius Rosenwald
had been one of the institution's major benefactors, and Embree's arrival did nothing to impair the good rapport. The university's president
and the fund's president met often to discuss areas of mutual interest:
professorial appointments, joint projects, college football, fine arts in
the university, even faculty morale. In numbers exceeding those for any
other institution, Rosenwald fellows chose Chicago for their graduate
study. Embree and his fund colleagues were in steady contact with various members of the university faculty, and with several he developed
enduring friendships. Beardsley Ruml, head of the Social Sciences Division in the early thirties, and Franklin McLean were Embree's friends
long before they came to Chicago. Their election to the fund's board
in Embree's first year served to deepen the professional and personal
connections between them. The same thing happened when Hutchins
became a trustee a few years later.[65]

Embree's close relationships with Hutchins and other university presidents are indicative of how he, like other foundation leaders, bridged academic officialdom and the world of philanthropy. Virtually alone among his counterparts, however, Embree was also solidly established as an author and well regarded by researchers, particularly in the social sciences. In addition to the three volumes edited at Yale, he could by the mid-thirties claim primary responsibility for two collaborative books, the sole authorship of two others, and the publication of almost two dozen articles.[66]

Embree never claimed to be a professional scholar, but he attained a quite respectable standing among those who were. In 1932, he was chosen to give the annual Moody Lecture at the University of Chicago, which placed him in the prestigious company of other speakers in the series: Kingsley Amis, E. E. Cummings, Wallace Stevens, John Dos Passos. In 1934, when four of the principal social science groups held their national meetings together in Chicago, he was chosen to chair the formal opening session. The following year in New York, he led a panel on "The Education of Minority Group Members" at the annual meeting of the American Sociological Society. His authority on race matters was further recognized when the *Encyclopedia Britannica,* after rejecting successive drafts of W. E. B. DuBois's essay on American blacks, passed that assignment to Embree. His first piece in the encyclopedia appeared in the fourteenth edition, with other articles published subsequently. Editors of scholarly journals, recognizing his wide-ranging expertise, asked him repeatedly to contribute book reviews. In 1936, the University of Hawaii awarded him his first honorary degree.[67]

Thus, after a few years at Rosenwald, Embree's growing prominence rested on more than his imaginative performance as a foundation executive. Increasingly, recognition came not from his philanthropic activity alone, but from the articulation of his ideas and commitments, his knowledge and professional connections. Earlier—at Yale and Rockefeller—his stature had depended largely on the organizations he served. Now, that circumstance was moving toward reversal; the fund gained luster from the accomplishments of its president. Thus, his situation at the philanthropy was firm when he encountered significant opposition from within his board.

* * *

The year 1936 was a critical time for the Rosenwald Fund. Sears stock
had regained part of its 1929 value, and though the philanthropy's assets
would never approach the level of the pre-Depression days, they were
again substantial. It was no longer necessary to function with a sharply
reduced staff or, as Embree had lamented earlier, "hang on by our teeth
for dear life." There were now moneys to be allocated, proposals to be
considered, promising demonstrations to be mounted. The question before Embree and the Rosenwald board was: What kind of agenda should
be pursued? While continuing to mold opinion for societal change, toward what ends should those efforts be directed? How could resources
be concentrated for best effect? And since concentration was unavoid-
able, what areas of interest should now be abandoned? This was the central issue for the board's spring meeting.

Embree prepared an extensive statement of the fund's activities and
prospects, which was circulated in advance of that meeting. But before
the board met, Alfred K. Stern submitted to his fellow trustees a twenty-
five-page memorandum taking issue not only with Embree's document,
but with the whole direction the fund had taken. The program lacked integration, he claimed. There had been "a tendency to lose sight of the objective," and if the proposed program were adopted, the result would be
"if anything, more extensive and diffuse than in the past." Of particular
concern were the attempts to mold public opinion, which he dismissed as
a "propaganda policy." Moving on to other topics, he was sharply critical
of the plans for rural education, which had been developed by a group
he referred to, with no small sarcasm, as the "Commission of Three"
(Embree, Will Alexander, Charles Johnson). That group he faulted for
collecting virtually useless information, being overly ambitious in its
planning, and "quixotic" in its emphasis on stabilization of the southern
economy as a prerequisite for education reform. Attempting to combine general education with technical agricultural training was similarly
wrongheaded and would lead to failure in both areas. Concluding his
tirade, Stern recommended the termination of fund efforts in medical
services, race relations, rural education, and the economic advancement
of blacks. Attention should be concentrated on the repair and beautifica-
tion of Rosenwald schools, the continued strengthening of Provident

Hospital in Chicago, and conditional grants to two or three of the best historically black colleges.[68]

Stern's position was essentially that the fund should return to the original program of the erstwhile family foundation. But his sharp language betokened not just programmatic disagreement, but personal animus against Embree. The longest-serving fund officer and, until Embree's arrival, titular second in command, Stern had been marginalized and now lacked any genuine influence.[69] His challenge was direct and forceful; the fund's president had to respond in kind.

With the point that the fund had spread its efforts too widely, Embree agreed; he had warned of that danger several times since 1928. As he explained to the board, however, it was essential to avoid the stagnation that could come from unwavering devotion to a narrow set of interests. Instead of following "the easy road of a routine program," the fund had pursued a policy of "enlightened opportunism, attacking first here and then there as opportunity offered or as allies richer than we [e.g., Rockefeller] could be persuaded to furnish the greater part of the sinews of war." But while opportunistic, the program had not been haphazard, for it had always been directed by "the single intensive purpose of doing the most we could, momentarily and continuously, for the advancement of the Negro and the promotion of better race relations."[70]

With improved financial standing, Embree continued, the period of "treading water to stay afloat" was at an end. It was now time to focus energy and resources more sharply, to give greater definition to the fund's efforts. Thus, while continuing work to mold opinion through direct action, he was recommending that half of the current fifteen programs be dropped and the remainder consolidated under three main heads. The fields of general education and general social studies were to be vacated altogether, library activities curtailed, and all involvement in construction of African American schools and colleges terminated. The three major categories of effort proposed were black welfare and race relations (including fellowships, university centers, health, and "other activities"), rural education (addressing the education of whites as well as blacks), and medical services.[71]

The virulence of Stern's attack and the broad sweep of his criticisms were unprecedented. Had they come from another quarter, they might have had a significant effect. But Stern's opinions did not carry great weight with the rest of the board, and Embree readily overcame his objections. Yet that did not end Embree's problems. He soon faced a far more formidable challenge from his friend Robert M. Hutchins.

The University of Chicago president was then deeply engaged in efforts to change the curriculum of his own institution to emphasize the "great books." Related to that initiative, he proposed that the Rosenwald Fund devote all its resources toward a similar end, forsaking its historic fields of interest. Embree vigorously resisted Hutchins's proposal but, as he acknowledged in a candid letter, it would have gotten little attention from his practical-minded board "had it not come from so distinguished a source and been presented so clearly and impressively." When the matter finally came down to a vote, Embree's view prevailed 7–2.[72]

Debate over the fund's direction was bruising, and it did not end with the rejections of Alfred Stern's view and the Hutchins proposal. In June, when Embree sailed for Hawaii to deliver a commencement address and receive an honorary degree, he believed the trustees' "insurrection" had been defeated. Even so, he realized further discord could arise. He and Kate returned to the mainland after a month, and for most of the next year board matters remained relatively calm. In the summer of 1937, however, Embree cut short his vacation at the family's Canadian cabin and returned to Chicago to "keep a firm hand on the controls of the office."[73] A meeting of a board committee in August "left a pretty sour taste" in his mouth. A month later, there were still "some rumblings within the [Rosenwald] family group."[74]

The long period of contention within the board left Embree uneasy, uncertain about his future and that of the Rosenwald Fund. He had even begun to consider whether he should resign, and had initiated steps to ensure that he "could not be damaged too greatly by any possible future disputes."[75] Numerous writing projects continued to beckon, and perhaps disappointment over his failed magazine proposal and the possibility of an *Atlantic* editorship were still in his mind. Yet, as the fractiousness wore on toward its conclusion, he found assurance in the reelection to trusteeship of the steady Will Alexander. Similarly, he believed that Edgar Stern's return to the board would relieve Rosenwald family discontent. And knowing that the great majority of the trustees were at ease with the fund's direction, he was not inclined to worry unduly about the complaints of "two or three members, at least two of whom are actuated by peculiar motives." He expected the board to become again an "almost wholly constructive group," particularly with the addition of at least two "wise southerners." Knowing the myriad problems of the South, and ever optimistic, he hoped that, as the board addressed the educational and economic problems in the region, it would become a "sort of board of strategy for southern growth."[76]

* * *

As the year 1937 waned, Embree was completing his tenth year at the Rosenwald Fund, almost as much time as he had spent at the Rocke-feller Foundation. He had brought the philanthropy through what was technically a bankruptcy, without defaulting on any of its obligations. Confronted by a devastating shrinkage of financial resources, he had envisioned a new dimension for the foundation's activity—molding opin-ion through direct action—and had demonstrated its potential for influ-encing public policy. Through experimentation and demonstration, the fund had decisively called attention to methods for making health care affordable for the middle class. He had established himself not only as an imaginative foundation leader, but as an authority on race relations and a writer of consequence. Mastering significant dissension within his governing board, he had set the fund on a course consistent with its past and promising for the future. Those accomplishments, and that season-ing, would serve him well in the coming decade.

Grandfather John G. Fee, approximately a year before his death in 1901. Embree called him the "great inspiration of my life." *Courtesy Devereux-Embree Family Papers.*

The Fee family home, where Embree lived with his mother and three brothers from age seven until he left for New Haven in 1901. *Courtesy Devereux-Embree Family Papers.*

Embree's mother, Laura Fee Embree, ca. 1866. Embree as a boy felt that his greatest punishment was knowing that his behavior somehow had disappointed her. *Courtesy Devereux-Embree Family Papers.*

The Embree Family Quartet, ca. 1898. *Left to right:* Edwin and brothers Howard, Raymond, and Will. *Courtesy Devereux-Embree Family Papers.*

Embree's Yale graduation picture, 1906. *Courtesy Devereux-Embree Family Papers.*

Embree and his brother Will in Paris, 1910. This first trip outside the United States whetted Embree's appetite for overseas journeys. In his lifetime, he traveled to no fewer than forty-five countries, a remarkable number for that time. On all of these trips, he wrote for his family and friends detailed accounts of his observations and experiences. *Courtesy Devereux-Embree Family Papers.*

Cracow, Poland, September 1920, during Embree's three-month trip to determine how the Rockefeller Foundation could help to restore public health and medical research in Central Europe. With him, left to right, are an unidentified Polish officer, Dr. Frederick F. Russell of Rockefeller's International Health Board, Colonel F. F. Langley of the Rockefeller-funded Tuberculosis Commission, and Colonel Henry A. Shaw of the Red Cross. *Courtesy Rockefeller Archive Center.*

(*facing page, above*) At the dedication of the Peking Union Medical College, September 1921. *Left to right:* Embree; Dr. Edward Hume, dean of the Yale-in-China Program, Hunan; Dr. William H. Welch of Johns Hopkins, a medical educator and Rockefeller trustee; George E. Vincent, president of the Rockefeller Foundation. *Courtesy Devereux-Embree Family Papers.*

(*facing page, below*) Embree and anthropologist Clark Wissler of the American Museum of Natural History posed for this picture in Australia during their 1925 evaluation of research on that country's aborigines and on the Maori of New Zealand. *Courtesy Rockefeller Archive Center.*

In Tokyo, during Embree's 1926 assessment of public health records and scientific research in Japan. *Left to right, back row:* Embree; son John; Princeton professor of zoology Edwin Conklin; Dr. Kinnosuke Miura, member of a medical commission that toured U.S. medical schools under Rockefeller auspices; one of the Miuras' sons. *Front row:* Kate Embree, another Miura son, Mrs. Miura, Mrs. Conklin. *Courtesy Devereux-Embree Family Papers.*

En route to Panama City in 1927 as Embree explored public health issues in Central America. Traveling with him was Dr. Victor G. Heiser of the International Health Board, an authority on tropical diseases. *Courtesy Rockefeller Archive Center.*

Embree in late December 1927, a few days before he left the Rockefeller Foundation to head the Julius Rosenwald Fund. *Courtesy Devereux-Embree Family Papers.*

Mount Olive School, Rankin County, Mississippi, which was financed in part by the Rosenwald Fund. With W. C. Strahan (*wearing hat*), the superintendent of the district's black schools, Embree visited the site during his spring 1928 trip to assess funding possibilities in the South. *Courtesy Rockefeller Archive Center.*

The deplorable condition in which cotton tenant farming and share-cropping has fallen in the south has thousands of Black Belt farmers chained to the land under conditions little better than serfdom. The situation is graphically shown in the book "The Collapse of Cotton Tenancy" by Charles S. Johnson, Will W. Alexander and Edwin R. Embree, after an exhaustive survey by a large corps of investigators. The University of North Carolina Press published the volume. (ANP).

Editorial cartoon attacking the evils of tenant farming. Carried by newspapers across the country, it helped to mobilize support for the 1937 Bankhead-Jones Tenant Farm Act, which established the Farm Security Administration under the New Deal. *Courtesy Fisk University, Franklin Library, Special Collections.*

Embree in his Rosenwald office examining Native American artifacts in 1938, while gathering information for *Indians of the Americas: Historical Pageant*. Of all his published works, this book probably required the most extensive research and consultation with authorities. *Courtesy Devereux-Embree Family Papers.*

Taken in the mid-1940s, this picture is suggestive of Embree's engagement with global issues and his efforts to prepare the public for the new world order he expected to emerge after the Second World War. *Courtesy Devereux-Embree Family Papers.*

Embree talking informally with a mixed group at the 1946 Race Relations Institute at Fisk University. Though his keynote address did not spark the hostile public response to his remarks that had erupted the previous year, he again emphasized the pressing need for greater racial tolerance at home and abroad. *Courtesy Fisk University, Franklin Library, Special Collections.*

Charles S. Johnson, November 8, 1948, on the occasion of his inauguration as president of Fisk University. Drawing on their close collaboration and long friendship, Johnson asked Embree to arrange speakers for several inauguration events and to edit the addresses for publication. *Courtesy Fisk University, Franklin Library, Special Collections.*

At a Waldorf-Astoria dinner, May 4, 1949, honoring the undersecretary-general of the United Nations and former Rosenwald fellow Ralph Bunche, Embree was a principal speaker. To his right is former First Lady and Rosenwald trustee Eleanor Roosevelt. *Courtesy Devereux-Embree Family Papers.*

SIX

TOWARD
"FULL DEMOCRACY"

From the difficult mid-thirties discussions within the board, the Rosenwald Fund emerged with a focus narrowed to three main areas: rural education, African American welfare and race relations, and medical services. Embree had recommended these areas of interest early in 1936, but before the year was out medical services was dropped as a fund activity. That decision left only two fields of concentration, and even they were not distinct. Rural education, with its concern for schooling of both blacks and whites, obviously overlapped with considerations central to African American welfare.[1] And though there was genuine concern to improve educational effectiveness for both groups, the minority community received the lion's share of attention.

This narrowing of the fund's interests did not entail any overall reduction in effort. In fact, the opposite occurred, for the improved financial situation made increased activity possible. At the same time, closure of the fund's Nashville office in 1937 meant that management of all programs in the South shifted to the Chicago headquarters. As a consequence, the claims on Embree's time and energy apparently increased. The changed situation is reflected in the pattern of his writing. Though his pen remained active, the number of pieces that found their way into print declined markedly.[2]

Throughout the late 1930s, as he concentrated on rural education in the South and the day-to-day activities of the fund, Embree kept a wary eye on the gathering clouds of war in Europe. His outlook was heavily conditioned by the First World War and its aftermath. His experiences in France during the last months of that conflict and in subsequent visits had been happy and informative, and he continued to view that nation sympathetically. Revolutionary Russia fascinated him, and throughout the thirties he was inclined to withhold judgment, waiting to see how events in that vast country would unfold. Toward Germany, on the other hand, he was decidedly antipathetic in the 1920s, and the advent of Hitler certainly deepened those feelings. To a lesser but still significant degree, Italian fascism aroused his ire. Ever optimistic, however, he refused to believe such authoritarian regimes presaged the world's future.

Embree's optimism, even in darkening times, was expressed in an unpublished piece he drafted early in 1940. At the dawn of a new decade, with international aggression seemingly ascendant around the world and Europe newly plunged into war, he decried the pessimistic outlooks of most of his friends. To be sure, he wrote, religious liberty had been "stamped out" in Russia and Germany; Jews were subject to persecution in Central Europe; Ethiopia, Albania, Czechoslovakia, Poland, and China were victims of ruthless conquest. In the United States, blacks were segregated in Chicago as well as in Alabama, and religious and racial hate abounded. But the point missed by the pessimists, he emphasized, was the emergence of "a striking change of attitude,... a new order of liberalism and tolerance," which was growing steadily in extent and effectiveness. Recent brutalities were not the prevailing trend but "the last dying gasps of outworn customs."[3]

The territorial conquests of the previous five years were deplorable, Embree agreed, but the new factor was not conquest, but the "reaction of the world's conscience" against it. Developments in the world were always a moral mix; choices were seldom posed between good and evil, "but between good and better, between evil and something not quite so bad." Yet "this mixture of muddy grays in human affairs" should not be cause for discouragement, for progress was always made by "small and faltering steps." And in human relations, progress stemmed not only from altruism, but from "the solid earth of enlightened selfishness." In a world tightly linked by travel and trade, plans and practices in one land could affect liberty and security in every other. In such a world, it was increasingly clear that "cooperation and free exchange benefit all groups more than conquest and exploitation can benefit any group." Good neighborliness and the Golden Rule were "not only good religion but good business, not only desirable private ethics but sound public policy." The coming century would see "the further working out of the difficult, fascinating, all-important problems of how diverse peoples may live together happily and successfully in this rapidly shrinking world." In his understanding and embrace of the movement that a half-century later would be called "globalization," Embree was well in advance of most of his contemporaries. But in the near term, he had no doubt that international aggression had to be resisted.

In June 1940, the day after the last Allied troops evacuated from Dunkirk crossed the Channel, and as German forces began their final push toward Paris, he addressed letters to the entire Illinois congressional delegation and to the Senate Committee on Foreign Relations. Identifying himself as an outspoken member of the Committee to Defend America by Aiding the Allies, he urged those elected officials to support the Lend-Lease bill then under consideration. Three days later, he wired President Roosevelt to "urge immediate sale of planes and other war materials to allies who are fighting in defense of our own principles." Before two weeks passed, he telegraphed former presidential candidate Alfred M. Landon, then at the Republican Convention in Philadelphia, to "strongly urge" rejection of any platform plank that would favor "our isolation from the struggle for democracy. Tragedies of other hopefully isolationist nations make ostrich attitude criminally stupid."[4]

By the following spring, he was convinced that supplying the British with destroyers and war materiel was insufficient; the United States should enter the conflict directly. In letters to the senators of all twelve midwestern states, he urged repeal of the neutrality acts. "We are struggling against a terrible menace," he wrote. "It is absurd to pretend that we are neutral, and it is stupid to handicap in any way our aid to those who are fighting the same foe." Exactly one month before Japanese planes appeared in the sky over Hawaii, his telegram to nine senators implored them to "Repeal neutrality acts. Lets [sic] stop the enemy while we can."[5]

Importuning elected officials was not all that Embree did in the months before Pearl Harbor. He sought as well to persuade friends and associates of the necessity to enter the war directly. One manifestation of that effort was a highly personal, six-page statement written in March

1941. The occasion of his writing, if not the motivation for it, was the publication of Anne Morrow Lindbergh's *The Wave of the Future*. The author was a well-known personage, and Embree was concerned that the book's argument against U.S. participation in any war-related activities could well prove influential. Lindbergh acknowledged that evil forces were rampaging around the world, but she hoped that two oceans would keep them far from American shores.[6]

Expressing disappointment in the book, Embree claimed that Lindbergh not only failed to identify the "wave of the future," but did not explain how a better world could be built without going to war. He admitted to some uncertainty about the right course of action, both because he knew war would bring "serious losses [to] the democratic way of life" and because he recognized more than most the problems needing attention at home. Even so, he saw no reason to believe that those problems would be addressed just by remaining formally out of the conflict. Moreover, the nation would lose more "in moral sense and moral fiber by standing by" while the war raged than by taking on a combatant role. Failure to resist the present evils, he contended, would lead to an "inevitable" moral collapse. Sending arms to one's neighbor while refusing to fight beside him seemed to show "confusion of mind as well as pusillanimity of spirit." He had come reluctantly to favor "joining the war right now" and bringing the full strength of the United States to bear.[7]

Yet even in the midst of war, he insisted, "sane people all over the world, and specifically the United States Government," should immediately begin planning for peace. That planning should be based on the world's growing interdependence, the need for international law and order, and the removal of nationalistic trade barriers that interfered with prosperity and opportunity around the globe. The wave of the future, he concluded, had to do with the happy and successful coexistence of diverse peoples.[8]

Embree's views on U.S. policy put him at odds with many of his fellow midwesterners. In September 1940, the same month that Congress voted the first peacetime draft law, opponents of any U.S. involvement in the war established the America First Committee in Chicago. The organization spread quickly, particularly in the Midwest, and Illinois had more chapters than any other state. The most important of the isolationist groups, America First owed much of its growth to the popularity of its foremost spokesperson, aviator Charles A. Lindbergh, the husband of Anne Morrow Lindbergh. President of the organization was Sears board chair Robert E. Wood, one of the thirteen trustees of the Rosenwald Fund until he withdrew from the philanthropy in 1941 after serving only a single term.

The America First Committee and similar organizations dissolved immediately after Pearl Harbor. The attack caught all Americans by surprise, and Embree may have been more surprised than most. From his very first visit to Japan twenty years earlier, he had been taken by the island nation—its natural beauty, its cultural charm, the cheerfulness and vivacity of its people, the strength of the family structure there. Subsequent trips had served to deepen his appreciation, as did encounters with Americans of Japanese descent he met in Hawaii. Throughout the 1920s, he had been troubled to hear Americans speak of a future war with Japan, convinced such an outcome would be ruinous for both countries. Though aware of increases in the Japanese army and navy, he had considered them far less menacing than similar activity in the United States. American militarism, whipped up by the Hearst press and other media, he regarded as the more serious threat to peace, and he was convinced that if war did come, the United States would be the aggressor. Anti-Japanese sentiment went beyond conventional American racism, he came to believe, drawing strength from the fact that the Japanese refused, in word and manner, to concede Western superiority.[9]

Embree clearly favored U.S. entry into the war, but he soon observed some of the dire domestic consequences he had feared.[10] He happened to be in northern California early in 1942, when the relocation of persons of Japanese ancestry from the coast to the interior began. He saw families being transferred from their homes to assembly points, in circumstances much like the rounding up of Jews in Nazi-controlled Europe. This experience left Embree with searing, unforgettable memories, the most poignant, perhaps, the sight of a two-year-old anxiously clutching fresh flowers as he left his home behind. Like many Americans then and since, he was greatly troubled by such treatment, which was eventually imposed on some 110,000 people, most of whom were U.S. citizens.[11] The evacuations he regarded as "one of the most terrible crimes America has ever committed against her own citizens and against democracy."[12] His views soon came to be shared—indeed, exceeded—by daughter Catherine, a recent graduate of Swarthmore College. At age twenty-two, Catherine Embree began service at an unfinished "relocation camp" for Japanese Americans on a desolate Indian reservation in Arizona.

Under stringent conditions—extreme heat and cold, choking dust storms, minimal housing, rattlesnakes, lack of instructional materials— Catherine Embree taught school and performed other duties during 1942 and 1943. Soon after her arrival, she began to inform her parents of the harsh conditions and to enlist them in support of some of the evacuees. When it became possible for those of college age to enroll in institutions in the Midwest and East, a number on the way to college had to change trains in Chicago, which often involved waits of hours or even of over- night duration. Alerted by Catherine to their arrival, Embree or Kate met the trains, offered food and temporary lodging, assisted with train schedules, and otherwise provided comfort and encouragement to the weary travelers. On at least one occasion, her parents allowed a young woman who lacked an adequate wardrobe to rummage through Cath- erine's closet and take whatever she needed. Another young woman, released from an internment camp to attend college, lived with John Embree and his wife, Ella, during the latter war years.[13]

Throughout the war, Embree considered the forced relocation of Jap- anese Americans a particularly egregious example of racial intolerance. Working to combat such attitudes, in 1943 he joined with over sixty aca- demics, ministers, journalists, union leaders, and corporation heads to sponsor the Japanese American Citizens League. Devoted to protecting civil rights and opposing discriminatory treatment, the league protested against the internment policy, while emphasizing the fundamental pa- triotism of citizens of Japanese ancestry. In the league's Chicago chapter, its largest and most active, Embree played a prominent role during the war and afterwards, attending events, chairing formal dinners, introduc- ing speakers, lending his name as patron of the annual fund-raising ball. And in 1944, with Guam, Saipan, and the Philippines still in Japanese hands and anti-Japanese sentiment in the United States at a peak, he braved great unpopularity to call publicly for the return of the internees to their homes.[14]

Embree's concern for these victims of discrimination found expression even in his hiring practices. Knowing how difficult it was for Japanese Americans to find jobs, he provided rare employment opportunities. During the latter years of the war, his secretary was of Japanese descent, as were at least two other women on the fund's support staff. As the founding chair of a new municipal commission in Chicago, he established policies that led to agency jobs for no fewer than five Japanese American women. During 1945–1946, two graduate students of Japanese ancestry were commissioned to conduct research for the fund.[15]

*   *   *

Even as the problems of the internees awaited solution, racial tensions were rising throughout the country. Mobilization of the economy for war brought to the cities of the North, Midwest, and West Coast large numbers of migrants, both black and white, for work in war-related industries. In part, this phenomenon was an extension of the Great Migration of African Americans from the farms of the South, but at a greatly accelerated pace. An acute shortage of housing quickly developed. Families often were able to find living space only in sheds, boxcars, converted chicken coops, and cramped apartments, while single male shift workers each morning turned over their beds to men coming off the night shift. The growing problem was only partially relieved by the sprawling developments of hastily constructed buildings that soon sprang up in and around urban centers. New arrivals, many from rural settings, found themselves crowded together in narrow quarters, bereft of relatives and friends, far from familiar surroundings and customary life patterns. Often adding to their discomfort were neighbors whose speech, skin color, diet, and behavior differed sharply from their own. In such often desperate circumstances, encounters between blacks and whites became increasingly tense. In the summer of 1943, the tensions boiled over, and major race riots erupted in four cities. The most devastating of these was in Detroit, where in mid-June thirty-four people were killed and thousands of troops were required to restore order.[16]

Mayor James Kelly of Chicago recognized that conditions in his city were similar to those in Detroit. Like the Motor City, Chicago had a large and rapidly growing working class and a highly diverse mix of ethnic groups. The African American population alone had grown from 44,000 in 1910 to an estimated 350,000 by 1943, with some 70,000 arriving in just the first two years of the war.[17] Earlier than municipal officials anywhere else, Kelly moved to forestall racial outbreaks in the city's neighborhoods. In July, he appointed a committee of prominent citizens to examine the problems that underlay racial tensions and to recommend measures to alleviate them.

Chicago was the first American city to recognize an official responsibility for the opportunities and relationships of its citizens, and the Mayor's Committee on Race Relations was the first organization of its kind. (The committee was soon renamed the Mayor's Commission on Human Relations.) At its initial meeting, a month after the Detroit riot, Edwin Embree was elected the commission's chair, an office he would hold for five years, as long as he remained a citizen of Chicago.[18] His performance in that role led to greater prominence within the city and the region and, in time, to efforts to extend the Chicago pattern across the country. It also served to enhance his national reputation.

The commission consisted initially of fourteen persons of different racial backgrounds. Ten of these, drawn from business, labor, and the professions, were appointed by the mayor. But in three of the other four positions, presumably filled by the commission's chair, the influence of Embree was evident. His fund colleague Charles S. Johnson was named the commission's consultant. Johnson was well chosen, for he was not only Embree's trusted friend, but a leading authority on race relations and the principal author of the report on the Chicago race riot of 1919. The commission's first executive director was Robert C. Weaver, a young Harvard economics Ph.D. specializing in housing issues, who had served on the small Rosenwald fellowship selection committee. One of the assistant directors was Harry J. Walker, a Johnson protégé and Rosenwald fellow, who was then completing a sociology doctorate at the University of Chicago. From the very beginning, Embree and these associates, unlike members chosen primarily to lend their prestige to the effort, did the critical work of the commission.[19]

The Commission on Human Relations began its work without specification of its duties by any city ordinance. From the outset, it acknowledged responsibility for all the citizens of Chicago, including small but growing populations of Mexican Americans and Japanese Americans. Yet it stated forthrightly that its major concern was the city's largest minority and the improvement of black-white relations. Feeling its way under Embree's leadership, it investigated various problems: discriminatory housing restrictions, employment opportunities, the quality of police protection, racial clashes in the public schools, violations of civil rights, limitations on access to health and recreation services. At the heart of the city's problems, the commission concluded, was the persistence of insufficient and squalid housing, which led to overcrowded schools, conflicts when blacks began to move into previously all-white neighborhoods, and hostile interactions when groups competed for access to parks and playgrounds. In each of these areas, the commission received complaints, worked to resolve differences, and counseled municipal agencies on how best to address the issues. On several occasions, it helped defuse volatile situations that could have erupted into disastrous riots.[20]

A major aspect of the commission's work was public information, acquainting the citizenry with the nature and severity of race problems. In 1944, it arranged a conference, held in the City Council's chambers, to allow municipal officials, civic leaders, and several hundred guests to hear presentations on Chicago's racial situation. The success of this meeting led the following year to a citywide "Conference on Home Front Unity," with sessions on three afternoons in the spring and two further sessions in the fall. Those in attendance heard the city's ethnic composition described by University of Chicago sociologist Louis Wirth and an explanation of prejudice by Northwestern University anthropologist Melville Herskovits, along with a variety of panel colloquies and open discussions. From the conference emerged a number of volunteer working groups, resolutions to provide direction for their efforts, and a decision to continue similar meetings in the years ahead.[21]

In these proceedings, Embree played a central role. With his professional contacts and his experience in organizing groups for productive endeavor, he recruited speakers and arranged much of the agendas. As the commission's chair, he presided at each of the sessions. There, his responsibilities went well beyond moderating and keeping the meetings on track. Particularly important were his opening remarks, succinctly providing background, outlining purposes, and setting a context both local and national. At the conferences' end, he presented summaries of the proceedings, accompanied by statements of the next steps to be taken. In these circumstances, his understanding of social tensions, his knowledge of ethnic diversity and accommodation, and his management skills were fully on display. No less evident was his unfailing belief in human relations progress, which he expressed with his customary eloquence. Yet, even as he celebrated the city's advances in race relations, he pointed out in vivid detail the deep-rooted problems still to be overcome. Throughout, he kept the conference discussions on a high level and with a positive tone.

The proceedings of the conferences, held throughout the late forties, were printed and widely circulated throughout the city, part of a steady stream of information that flowed from the commission's offices to the public through newspapers and radio. The commission issued annual reports of its activities and a variety of educational booklets. The illustrated pamphlet "The Negro in Chicago," for example, was printed in 100,000 copies and distributed to schools, elected and appointed officials, labor unions, libraries, and churches. City employees were provided guidance in dealing with cultural differences in publications typified by "Recreation for All: A Manual for Supervisors and Workers in Recreation." Chicago police officers received in-service training in human relations, supplemented by appropriate printed materials. City teachers were included in the commission's outreach with publication of the curriculum unit "Negro History," which was soon required in elementary schools.[22]

The commission's emphasis on the publication and dissemination of such materials clearly reflected its chair's understanding of how to inform and mold public opinion. There is no difference between the commission's pattern in this regard and that followed by Embree and the Rosenwald Fund for more than a decade. In several instances, the fund paid the commission's publication costs and, on occasion, the underlying research expenses. (Though the commission had a small budget from the city, it was insufficient for meeting all such costs.) When the "Primer on Negroes in Chicago" came out in 1945, for instance, Rosenwald paid for 75,000 copies, while the commission paid for only 25,000. The fund at times also paid other commission expenses, including salaries, luncheons, and travel.[23]

Efforts to inform and energize the public were not limited to the
print medium. Radio, film, and theater were also brought into the mix,
and Embree used special events and prominent people to generate publicity for the cause. The commission's annual awards to local individuals,
businesses, and organizations that had made important contributions
to human relations provided a ready-made occasion to call attention to
its work. When a workshop on cultural patterns was arranged for school
principals and selected teachers, Embree chose his friend anthropologist
Margaret Mead to deliver the keynote address. An even more notewor-
thy endeavor involved the 1946 visit of Bess Myerson, the reigning Miss
America and the first Jewish woman to hold that title. In Chicago for
five days to speak on ethnic discrimination, she appeared before various
groups, addressed school assemblies, did radio broadcasts, and attended
a pageant in her honor at a racially mixed housing complex.[24]

The work of Embree's group soon came to the attention of officials
in other cities who were concerned about rising racial tensions. From
across the country, requests for information and advice poured in, both
to commission headquarters and the Rosenwald Fund's offices. Mayors
and governors, civic and religious groups set up local and statewide organizations to address race relations issues. Less than a year after Embree assumed the commission's leadership, over 130 similar groups had
sprung up in the North and West, most of them based on the Chicago
model. Recognizing the significance of this grassroots movement, Embree pondered how it could be extended and strengthened by a national
organization, and what role the fund might play.[25]

Human relations work in Chicago Embree considered fully in line
with Rosenwald purposes. His leadership of the commission and his
willingness to underwrite part of its expenses could readily be seen as a
fund contribution to Chicago as a corporate citizen. But there was also
a significant personal dimension, for his role as the chairman allowed
Embree to bring conspicuously to bear his knowledge, organizational
skills, public relations sense, and wide-ranging contacts. With his long-
standing desire for influence, he undoubtedly welcomed the chance to
perform on that well-lighted stage. Indeed, his work with the commission is suggestive of a growing fusion of the corporate and the personal.
By the 1940s, well into Embree's second decade as the fund's president,

his own interests and commitments could not be easily distinguished from those of the philanthropy he led. No longer just the face and brain of the Rosenwald Fund, he had become its heart and soul as well. That merging of the personal and philanthropic was manifested in the creation of a new Chicago educational institution.

* * *

The new institution came into being as another one died. In the spring of 1945, the Central YMCA College in Chicago enrolled about 4,000 full- and part-time students. The student body was remarkably diverse: 25 percent black, 4 percent Asian, 35 percent Jewish, 20 percent Catholic. Concerned about what they saw as disproportionate minority enrollment and conscious of the YMCA's specifically Christian orientation, the college's board of directors undertook to restrict the enrollment of some categories of students. Their decision was opposed by the president, E. James Sparling, and his refusal to agree caused the board to demand his resignation. The resignation was kept secret for two months, but when it was announced in mid-April, the college faculty voted no-confidence in the board. Over two-thirds of the faculty and administration then submitted their own resignations, effectively requiring the college to close.[26]

Even as these events were unfolding, steps were under way to ensure that minority Chicagoans would continue to have access to higher education. With his resignation submitted but still unannounced, Sparling, seeking both public support and financing, first had approached *Chicago Sun* publisher and philanthropist Marshall Field III; then he went to Embree. In a matter of days, the three men agreed to collaborate in founding a new college, which would be open to all without regard to race or creed. The new college, chartered on the day after the announcement of Sparling's resignation from the YMCA school, was originally scheduled to bear the name of Thomas Jefferson, but the death of Franklin Roosevelt five days earlier resulted in a change. Established as a memorial to the just-deceased president, the new institution was named Roosevelt College. The teachers who had resigned from the YMCA College comprised the core of the faculty. Sparling at once assumed the presidency. The chair of the institution's board was Edwin Embree.[27]

Embree had spent almost his entire life in close association with higher education. Reared in a college town, in the home of the institution's principal founder, he moved for his undergraduate preparation to a university whose presence was the dominating feature of its city. For a formative decade, he served in a university office, with steadily expanding responsibilities and a broadening national network, being mentored by a key administrator. His years at Rockefeller, filled with incessant travel, put him in touch with university administrators, scholars, and scientists in Asia, Australia, Britain, and much of the Continent. And his move to the Rosenwald Fund, far from diminishing his engagement with the academy, gave him extensive contact with historically black institutions, and many white ones, throughout the South.

For more than a decade, Embree had been widely recognized on college campuses, and academic audiences had found him an appealing speaker. His remarks on those occasions were typically provocative, seldom inconsequential. Following an address at the University of Kentucky, the university president wrote that Embree had caused students to think, creating more campus comment "than we have had for a long time."[28] In a commencement speech at the University of Hawaii, he emphasized that the West owed its current dominance to its mechanical and intellectual tools, not its culture, and pointed hopefully to the emergence of a "new civilization" combining the productive strengths of the Western world with the communal sharing, creative leisure, and graceful living of the East. Presciently, he warned the graduating class at the University of Iowa, a year before the Manhattan Project got under way, that the physical sciences had been overemphasized, and "if we are not to destroy ourselves with our own inventions we must gain much more understanding of ourselves as individuals and as a society." After a Swarthmore College lecture on "The Place of the American Negro in Democracy Today," in which he pointed out that no black person had ever attended the college, students and faculty in response formed a committee that lobbied successfully for the admission, three years later, of students of color. He had been the featured speaker at more academic meetings and institutions than can be readily counted.[29]

By the early forties, Embree had received two honorary degrees, spurned others, been strongly recommended for at least two university presidencies, and flirted with the idea of accepting such a position. He had repeatedly turned down invitations to join institutional governing boards before consenting in 1944 to join that of Sarah Lawrence College, an experimental school for women outside New York City. Thus, his experience and his reputation gave him impressive preparation for the responsibilities at Roosevelt. Even so, in light of his other heavy obligations, he accepted the new challenge "reluctantly."[30]

Embree chaired the Roosevelt College board for its first three years, as long as he remained in Chicago. Due to the unusual circumstances of the college's founding, the demands on the chair's time and energy were enormous.[31] In the first few months, the full board met almost weekly, and even when it moved to monthly meetings, its executive committee got together on a biweekly basis. Beyond planning for and chairing these sessions, Embree undertook numerous tasks not usually required of a board chair. He negotiated with the defunct YMCA College to acquire its furniture and 26,000-volume library. He led a small committee that drew up Roosevelt College's bylaws. With his numerous contacts in academe, he actively participated in the recruitment and selection of key administrators. He seems to have given some advice on curricular matters. Alone, he arranged for the rented space in which the college opened. And when rapidly expanding enrollment made that space too small, he became deeply involved in the frantic search for adequate quarters, a search that ended with the purchase of the landmark Chicago Auditorium Building.[32] The acquisition and remodeling of that impressive structure, together with the spectacular growth of the student body, put great strains on the college's limited finances. Consequently, Embree was required not only to sustain the institution with Rosenwald money, but to take the lead in major fund-raising. His network of acquaintances repeatedly came into play, as he sought public attention by associating the college with prominent people: Hollywood stars Orson Welles and Bette Davis, author Thomas Mann, Secretary of Commerce Harold Ickes, and the former First Lady, Eleanor Roosevelt.[33]

Embree and President Sparling, working closely together, ensured that the school would embody the democratic convictions that underlay its founding. From the outset, the faculty, like the student body, was racially mixed and religiously diverse. The same was true of the college's board which, in addition to the customary representatives of business, industry, and education, included members drawn from organized labor and the college's own faculty. When the first classes were offered in September 1945—a short five months after the charter was issued—1,200 students were enrolled. By the following fall, after regional accreditation had been won, enrollment more than tripled. And by 1948, the student body, bolstered by veterans enrolled under the GI Bill, had climbed past 6,000, with an additional 2,000 people taking non-credit courses. After only five years, Roosevelt's president could boast that the institution had become the second-largest private college in the country.[34]

Such phenomenal growth could not have occurred without the sizable and assured support of the Rosenwald Fund. The fund's commitment to the college first became evident when, only four days after issuance of the charter, the Rosenwald board approved a grant of up to $100,000 for its first year, with three-quarters of the money to go to operating expenses. Subsequent appropriations, paid in annual increments and extending even a year beyond the fund's closing, brought the total support from Rosenwald to $190,000, an amount granted to only a handful of other educational institutions.[35]

The magnitude of this financial support, more than double Sparling's initial expectations, is testimony to Embree's commitment as the philanthropy president and as the board's chair to the success of the fledgling college.[36] Indicative of the way he viewed the institution, the fund budgeted its appropriations not as educational expenditures, but under the broad category of race relations. For Embree and for others instrumental in its founding, Roosevelt was to be a living example of racial integration and equal opportunity. Unique among the projects supported by Rosenwald, Embree regarded funding the college as a "remarkable opportunity to demonstrate true democracy in education" and as the culmination of the philanthropy's work "in enlarging opportunities for disadvantaged groups."[37]

* * *

As his correspondence with elected federal officials, his public support for U.S. entry into World War II, and his advocacy on behalf of Japanese Americans all attest, Embree by 1940 was increasingly engaged in political activity. Though prominent as a social critic and reformer, and long comfortable in the public eye, he had heretofore been overtly political only on the tenant farming issue. Yet the reasons for the change are not hard to imagine. The proliferation of authoritarian regimes weighed heavily on his mind, and he did not underestimate the threat posed by Hitler's advance across the Continent. A deeply committed internationalist, he had no doubt that American isolationism had to be overcome, and he saw the reelection of Franklin Roosevelt as critical in that regard. Roosevelt's domestic policies had also won his approval, and he did not want to see them end with the president's second term. And it may well be that Eleanor Roosevelt's consent in 1940 to join the Rosenwald board, with its implied promise of giving Embree access to the White House, emboldened him to move more deliberately into the political arena.[38]

Beginning in 1932, Embree consistently had voted for the Democratic presidential ticket, yet he became an active member of an ostensibly nonpartisan organization, the Independent Voters of Illinois (IVI). Late in the 1940 campaign, that group gave birth to an offspring, Independent Voters for Roosevelt, which then proceeded to ring doorbells, send get-out-the-vote sound trucks throughout the state, and stage a mass rally for 25,000 with New York mayor Fiorello LaGuardia as the featured speaker. Embree helped plan the group's activities and solicited contributions from his friends, and, when a panel discussion on the radio was held on the Sunday morning before the Tuesday election, he served as its moderator.

The program was scheduled at the traditional time of church services, and the moderator welcomed the audience by announcing they would hear a discussion of "matters so fraught with human values as to be essentially religious." For an hour, the panel—philosophy professor and Illinois congressman-at-large T. V. Smith, lifelong Republican and former Chicago city attorney William Saltiel, and economist Paul Douglas—discussed national issues and the presidential campaign. At the end, in "a word of conclusion and benediction," Embree offered three reasons that Roosevelt should be reelected: his commitment to make "democracy strong at home, a bulwark against aggression abroad," his "steadfast" stand against creedal and racial discrimination, and his "first and deepest attention to human values."[39]

Embree's activism did not end with Roosevelt's election to a third term, and much of his activity reflected his sensitivity to international race relations. Six weeks after Pearl Harbor, his name topped a list of eighteen signers of a telegram to the president. The cable praised the Allied unity symbolized by Roosevelt's meetings with British prime minister Winston Churchill. But noting that the Axis powers were calling their conferences evidence of Anglo-Saxon aspiration to global domination, it encouraged similar proof of concord with all the Allied nations, especially China. Pointing out that the war in the Pacific was being portrayed as between "white and yellow races," the signers called for "a spectacular demonstration that this is Armageddon of free peoples regardless of race or color." They urged Roosevelt to arrange a "dramatic conference or manifesto with Chiang Kai-shek and other leaders of yellow, brown and black millions throughout the world." In a personal letter to Mrs. Roosevelt, Embree explained that no statement was being made to the press lest it cause embarrassment to the president. Even so, he and his co-signers believed that every effort should be made "to bring home to the peoples of the world that this war is a struggle for liberality and democracy by freedom-loving peoples regardless of race, creed, or color."[40]

Nor was Embree's lobbying limited to international concerns. During these years, he wrote multiple letters on domestic affairs to members of Congress. One letter sent to all Illinois representatives encouraged eliminating funding for the House Un-American Activities Committee. The committee was not only a confusing duplication of the role of the FBI, he charged; its practices also lowered public morale and interfered with "the vigorous prosecution of victory and world order." Any dollar appropriated to this committee was "a gross waste of public funds and an attack on national solidarity."[41] In this letter, as in many of his public statements, Embree was not inclined to temper his language. When civil liberties were in jeopardy, he believed that opposition should be continuous, direct, and blunt.

After the war, a similar commitment to protect civil liberties led Embree to join with almost three dozen others in a letter to Seth W. Richardson, chair of the federal employees' Loyalty Review Board. The co-signers expressed their concern that the "present wholesale check-up on the loyalty of federal employees" provided insufficient safeguards against injustice. Among other objections, they voiced opposition to such ill-defined terms in the presidential order as "subversive, totalitarian, and sympathetic association." They called specifically for a clear statement of charges, representation by counsel at all hearings, the right to subpoena witnesses and documents, complete documentation of proceedings, a written decision, and sufficient time to prepare an appeal. Moreover, they contended, those same safeguards should be provided to the governmental units exempted from the order: the Departments of War, State, the Navy, and Atomic Energy. In signing the letter, just months before Senator Joseph McCarthy launched his notorious campaign, Embree aligned himself with other prominent citizens in opposition to the anti-Red hysteria and in defense of civil liberties and due process.[42]

Embree's attempts to influence governmental action were accompanied by efforts to change the membership of the Illinois delegation to Congress. In 1940, he became actively engaged in the successful campaign to elect liberal Raymond S. McKeogh as the Illinois congressman-at-large. McKeogh's election encouraged Embree to think more broadly. Hoping to create a bipartisan effort to send other progressives to the House in 1942, he sought advice on strategy from two fellow Chicagoans, Secretary of Interior Harold Ickes, a Democrat, and Secretary of the Navy Frank Knox, a Republican.[43]

In addition to seeking to mobilize independent-minded voters for a common purpose, Embree promoted University of Chicago economist Paul Douglas for the U.S. Senate. Replacing the incumbent, conservative Charles W. Brooks, with an astute progressive thinker seemed to Embree "a cause of national significance." Thus, when no one else could be found to take the responsibility, he agreed "temporarily" to take over the chair of the Douglas electoral committee. In that role, he probably drew up the necessary petition and orchestrated the initial campaign efforts. But before the election, Douglas, though fifty years old and beyond military draft age, decided to enlist in the marines.[44]

The year 1944 brought another presidential election, and Embree joined a national political action committee formed to elect Franklin Roosevelt to yet another term. Admiring the president, and undoubtedly valuing his White House access, he had good reason to join in the reelection effort. The formation of the committee, however, triggered a harsh attack from Republican congressman Fred Busbey, who was dismayed at the prospect of a fourth Democratic victory. The political action committee, the Illinois congressman claimed, was "just the same group of commies, left wingers, and a few reputable boys thrown in as a front to fool the public."

Busbey's charges received full play in the *Chicago Tribune*. Of the eighty-four persons who were then members of the committee, nine were Chicagoans. The *Tribune* published a picture of each one, together with a paragraph providing further information. Embree was among the nine, as was his colleague Robert C. Weaver. Both were identified as key figures on the Mayor's Commission on Human Relations. The paper went on to mention several "alleged communist sympathizers," including *New Republic* editor Bruce Bliven, soon to be a member of an Embree-initiated committee working against racial segregation in Washington, D.C. No response from any of Busbey's targets was printed, nor was any statement that might contradict, or even question, the charges.[45]

Four months later, on the Saturday preceding the Tuesday election, the *Tribune* carried on its front page a follow-up article. Its central theme was that the House Un-American Activities Committee had revealed that 82 members of the Roosevelt-reelection political action committee (now up to 141 members nationwide) belonged to organizations officially labeled by U.S. attorney general Francis Biddle as subversive. The organizations were not specified, but all the individuals were. One was Chicagoan Willard Townsend, a national labor official and vice chair of the Mayor's Commission on Human Relations. Others were Rosenwald fellowship recipients: sociologists E. Franklin Frazier and Ira DeA. Reid, authors Langston Hughes and Lillian Smith. From the Rosenwald Fund itself, Embree was listed, along with two former division heads, Michael M. Davis and Clark Foreman. Also included were theologian Reinhold Niebuhr, Pulitzer Prize–winning poet William Rose Benet, Howard University Law School dean William Hastie, Bethune-Cookman College president Mary McLeod Bethune, and former Pennsylvania governor and U.S. secretary of interior Gifford Pinchot.[46]

The *Tribune*'s charges were not repeated by other Chicago newspapers, and immediately after the election the political squall passed.

The *Tribune* itself dropped the subject, never carrying a relevant state-ment from any of those named. Embree's response to the episode cannot be readily determined; no comment in fund materials or personal cor-respondence has been discovered. But no stranger to controversy—at times, even seeming to court it—he probably was content, even gratified, to be associated with the other notables thus singled out.

By the mid-forties, Embree had become one of three co-chairs of the state's independent voters group, and he would remain on its board until he left Illinois in 1948. He also accepted membership on the executive council of the National Citizens Political Action Committee, an orga-nization he hoped to bring into cooperation with the IVI in getting out the progressive vote in the 1946 congressional election. Two years later, when it appeared the state's liberals might divide their vote between two candidates, he wired Carl Sandburg, urging the Lincoln biographer not to run. Factionalism was the curse of liberals, he wrote, and for the first time in his memory Illinois had a chance for "splendid progressive rep-resentation in Adlai Stevenson [as governor] and Paul Douglas [as U.S. senator]. To compete against them [was] to insure election of Dwight Green and Curly Brooks, two [of the] worst reactionaries."[47] As it turned out, the liberal vote was not divided, and both Stevenson and Douglas were elected.

Unswerving in his commitment to liberal reform in the state and across the nation, Embree in 1947 joined with seven others to organize the Illinois chapter of the Americans for Democratic Action (ADA). The establishment of that chapter, less than two months after the founding of the national organization, was soon followed by efforts to expand the organization throughout the Midwest. Its first regional conference brought to Chicago mayors and members of the U.S. Congress, labor union officials and heads of volunteer organizations, and politically en-gaged citizens from nine states. Embree was chosen to chair the meeting and preside at the formal dinner.[48]

Embree's presiding duties put his urbanity and wit on full display, as he warmed up the audience for the principal address by the youthful mayor of Minneapolis, Hubert Humphrey.[49] Taking full advantage of the occasion, he sounded some of his favorite themes, even using some expressions not customary in his public statements. "Americans have always been radicals," he told the audience. All the national heroes "from Washington, Jefferson, Jackson, to Lincoln, Wilson, Roosevelt, were radicals. Whatever reforms we launch; however sweeping and basic . . . however sweeping the change, it is in the finest American tradition." Yet, there were "super patriots, isolationists and standpatters" who tended to label liberal advocates of change "Communists." On the other hand, there were others who decried everything in the American record as "bad, reactionary, backward"; their favorite term was "fascist." Both of those positions, he said, were "absurd."[50]

Some things America had done "supremely well," Embree continued, and as the ADA advocated further progress, it was important to "realize thoroughly and self-consciously the great good that this country under democracy has already accomplished." Among the nation's most striking achievements were the enormous productivity of farm and factory; education for all the people; impressive advances in public health; establishment of the principles of equal rights, equal opportunity, and civil liberties. The task before the country now was to build on its rich heritage. And, he proclaimed, anyone who would throw over that American heritage was "either a fool or a traitor or probably both." The last remark was greeted with applause, but Embree had one more point to make.

Part of the ADA's building had to be "toward a world community and peace," allowing other peoples to pursue their own intentions and desires with the confidence that they were "as interested in peace and progress as we." The ADA had to be involved in "building toward one world, diverse in race and cultures but united for the well-being of mankind." With such uplifting words, uttered during the early months of the Cold War, Embree affirmed his own unflagging optimism about the long-term future of international and human relations. Those offended by talk of "one world," on the other hand, could only be antagonized by such language and such a vision.

* * *

Embree's use of the word *radical* at the Chicago ADA conference was, for him, unusual, and its application to a panoply of national heroes was undoubtedly for rhetorical effect. Far more common in his parlance of advocacy was "full democracy," an expression heard with increasing frequency in his public statements during the Second World War and its aftermath. What did he mean by that term? How did his understanding of democracy relate to his embrace of Arnold Toynbee's concept of the creative minority? How, in his mind, could full democracy be squared with his own elitist disposition?

Evident in the ADA remarks was Embree's rejection of any notion of economic egalitarianism. Individual enterprise had proved too successful in the West, and attempts elsewhere at redistribution too disruptive and coercive, for that view to have appeal. Moreover, it was the giant fortunes generated under free enterprise that made the great foundations possible, and he had no doubt that scientific philanthropy could be a major force, perhaps the most important force, for human progress. Nor did his concept of democracy entail some rosy view of the equality of human potential. He did not underestimate the great differences in individual intelligence, talent, and motivation. At its most basic level, democracy had to do with neither equality in the world's goods nor equality in personal promise.

For Embree, the central element of democracy was equality of opportunity, which meant particularly the opportunity for an education appropriate to one's capacity and aspirations. Equality of opportunity also meant full access to tax-funded recreation facilities, to places of public accommodation, to employment and health care and decent housing. It also necessarily entailed equality before the law, civil liberties, fair treatment in personal relationships, an end to legally sanctioned discrimination. Such emphases were most conspicuous in his leadership of the Chicago mayor's commission, but they were fundamental throughout his professional life.

Embree's understanding of democracy centered on individuals and groups, but it exceeded those parameters. It extended as well to regions of the United States. His concentration of Rosenwald efforts on the South, especially in education and economics, was intended to reduce inequalities within the region, and between the nation's least-advanced section and the rest of the country. Full democracy in this context involved enabling the South to catch up with the rest of the nation, ensuring that opportunity there was no less than that available anywhere else. Democracy also had an international dimension. When he inveighed against

Western imperialism, Embree was arguing for greater equality among the world's peoples, an end to the exploitation of people of color by those of lighter skin. For those under colonial domination, achieving such democracy required political liberation, untrammeled self-determination, and increased influence in world affairs. Linked to that objective was a notion of cultural democracy. To Embree, there was nothing intrinsically superior about Western ways when compared to, say, the practices of the Japanese or the customs of the Samoans. Thus, full democracy would involve a change in consciousness, a recognition of the equivalent value of cultures, an appreciation of the rich diversity among the globe's population.

Yet, advancing democracy, Embree fully understood, required appealing to the nation's most influential citizens. Adoption of the policy of direct action was a deliberate attempt to affect public opinion, particularly the opinions of those in a position to change the views of others. Embree's books and articles and those of other Rosenwald officials were a primary expression of that effort. So, too, were the regional and national conferences the fund sponsored and underwrote. Similarly, Embree's unrealized plan for the fund to publish a magazine "high hat and proud of it" had the obvious purpose of attracting the attention and support of the country's intellectual and cultural leaders. The fellowships for white southerners are also best seen as part of this larger effort, for they were intended to create a cadre to spearhead the assault on racial discrimination. Embree knew well that the road to full democracy led directly through the land of the elites. Modifying their perceptions and outlooks was prerequisite to changing the thinking of the majority, and only through the changing of minds could changes in practice and policy be expected to occur.

Though he never articulated the point, Embree seems to have understood that politics and large-scale philanthropy had much in common. Both were basically processes of education, the former involving persuasion and consent, the latter, demonstration and adoption. Most philanthropy executives distinguished sharply between the two enterprises, carefully avoiding overtly political issues lest their organizations lose their vaunted aura of disinterest. Embree at Rosenwald took a different course, for the policy of direct action inevitably tended to blur any line of demarcation. As that line became increasingly indistinct, maintaining the posture of objectivity favored by most foundations proved increasingly difficult.

Several of Embree's books, including his most popular ones, won praise for their balance, and no doubt he labored to make them informative and credible. Yet the factual material, though measured in tone, carried with it an unmistakable message, an appeal to the consciences of readers to recognize, and oppose, the injustices visited upon the disadvantaged. The fundamental purpose of his most important works was persuasion, their hoped-for effect, agreement, the prelude to action. In a profound sense, they were political documents, as were many of the journal articles Embree published after the early thirties. This aspect of his writing was, of course, in keeping with his growing political activism in those years. In light of his commitment to societal reform, it probably could have been no other way. Redirecting rural education, ending the peonage of southern tenant farmers, and eliminating the disabilities imposed by racism were goals unreachable apart from politics. They did not lend themselves to the detached stance favored by most foundation leaders. Unlike his counterparts, by the time he reached his fifties, the purposeful activities of philanthropy and politics had come together in Embree's mind.

* * *

Embree's prominence in political affairs in the forties was accompanied by his increased participation in civic committees and volunteer groups. During the 1930s, his activity in the Chicago area had been largely limited to service on the regional selection committee for Rhodes scholars. But as the new decade got under way and his public involvement increased, he joined Friends of the Land, a forward-looking organization devoted to conservation of the nation's soil and water. Closer to home, he served as vice chair of the International Relations Center of Chicago, and he chaired the local branch of the Institute of Pacific Relations. In keeping with his interest in theater, he was one of several sponsors of Stage for Action, a group presenting plays throughout the city. When the local school board had six vacancies to fill, the City Club of Chicago listed Embree as one of twelve citizens well qualified for appointment. Requests for public addresses became so numerous that he had to turn down 90 percent of them. Beyond these commitments and the demands of the fund, the mayor's commission, Roosevelt College, several national trusteeships, and his writing, somehow in this period he found time to chair the board of the Todd School, an academy for boys headed by his cousin.[51]

Political and civic activity enabled Embree to broaden still further an already extraordinary professional and personal network. Beyond the obvious fields of philanthropy and race relations, his acquaintances and friendships extended into the worlds of publishing, entertainment, academia, health care, politics, and international affairs. Those different worlds often came together when he and Kate entertained. On such occasions, Embree served as a kind of connecting link, bringing into contact and relationship people who otherwise might never have encountered one another.

Early in the 1930s, the Embrees' entertainment pattern was fairly modest, tending toward intimate dinners in their apartment or evenings out with another couple or two at a local restaurant or club. By the 1940s, however, the fund president's practices had become more elaborate and, occasionally, lavish. In 1941, he hosted two dozen guests at a performance of *Cabin in the Sky,* followed by a dinner honoring the stars, Ethel Waters and former Rosenwald fellow Katherine Dunham. A few months later, he arranged for important films from the library of New York's Museum of Modern Art to be shown at the fund's office on a succession of Friday afternoons. Invited to attend with their spouses were members of the fund's board and staff, along with fellowship recipients Horace Cayton and Allison Davis, prominent Chicago architect Ernest Grunsfeld, Senator-to-be Paul Douglas, and historian Wilbur K. Jordan, soon to leave for Harvard and the presidency of Radcliffe College. The spring of 1943 saw many of these same people at a reception honoring Lillian Smith and Paula Snelling, co-editors of *South Today.* The guest list on that occasion also included semanticist S. I. Hayakawa, University of Chicago president Robert Maynard Hutchins, and future federal department head Robert C. Weaver.[52]

Encouraged by the popularity of his first theater party, Embree planned a sequel in the fall of 1942, when *Porgy and Bess* came to town. On this occasion, arrangements were made for the Rosenwald trustees and all the fund's staff—forty-seven people altogether—to attend. Following the performance, the group adjourned to the tony Tavern Club, high atop a downtown skyscraper, where they were joined for drinks and supper by the show's cast, the director and producers, the theater manager, twenty-one journalists, drama critics, and their spouses. Most guests attended in formal dress, as the affair was scheduled to run from 11:30 in the evening until the small hours of the morning. As a member of the club, Embree knew it could accommodate a group of that size. But he knew as well that it was unaccustomed to serving such a racially mixed assemblage, a third of whom were black. Consequently, he was pleased that the club accepted his reservation without demur. That fact, and the general success of the event he saw as an important precedent for the club, and perhaps for the city itself.[53]

Perhaps none of Embree's parties attracted more attention than an afternoon "lawn social" held in the spacious garden behind the fund's building. The honored guests that time were the cast members of the play *Anna Lucasta*. As before, those in attendance constituted a racially mixed group. Prominent among the 200 guests were Howard University philosopher Alain Locke, publisher Marshall Field, and the 1945 Miss America, Bess Myerson. Also included were people with whom Embree was associated through his civic activities, including members of the mayor's commission, trustees and senior staff of Roosevelt College, and the board of Rosenwald-supported Provident Hospital. Fund trustees and staff and several newspaper editors rounded out the guest list.[54]

Embree's entertainment practices reveal his love for the stage and film, and his eagerness to share his pleasure with others similarly inclined. At the same time, they show his imagination in using such occasions to strengthen relationships with persons of influence and to extend connections that could prove useful in his philanthropic and civic work. No less imaginative was the way he promoted social interactions across racial lines. His more elaborate parties also indicate a capacity to think on a grand scale and a willingness to use Rosenwald money in unconventional ways to promote the fund's purposes. Such unconventionality was evident in another of his initiatives in the 1940s. Coincident with his racially integrated entertainment, but bolder and more far-reaching, was a plan to undercut racial segregation in higher education.

* * *

In 1940, college and university faculties, historically black institutions excepted, were rigidly segregated. No predominantly white school was known to have a person of African descent on its permanent teaching staff. This situation Embree thought lamentable in and of itself, but as he considered the growing number of highly competent African American Rosenwald fellows completing doctoral degrees, he became increasingly troubled. Their race, no matter their brilliance or commitment, would allow them to obtain teaching positions only at black institutions, most of which were badly underfunded. As a consequence, their teaching loads were likely to be crushingly heavy, library and laboratory resources severely limited, research opportunities scant, and interactions with other scholars beyond their home campus almost nonexistent. In almost every case, professional growth would be stunted, teaching vitality drained, scholarly promise unfulfilled. Improvement could be fostered, to be sure, by foundation grants to struggling institutions, as Rosenwald and other philanthropies had done for almost a quarter-century. Yet the needs were too great for more than a handful of institutions to receive significant assistance. Ultimately more useful, Embree came to believe, would be eliminating the barriers that stood between black intellectuals and appointments to all-white faculties. The essential first steps in that direction would involve, in characteristic foundation fashion, several convincing demonstration projects. It was necessary to show that African American scholars, scientists, and artists could be effective teachers of white youth, valuable colleagues, and significant contributors to institutional eminence. The success of such a demonstration required the most careful selection of the person who would first cross the racial bar.

When the president of the Brooklyn Dodgers decided in the mid-forties that the time had come to break the color barrier in major league baseball, he took great pains to find the man who, by talent and temperament, was best qualified to put on the field. Embree, a half-decade earlier, was no less meticulous in making his own selection. The person he put forward had to have impressive academic preparation, conspicuous success in prestigious institutions, an obvious capacity for significant achievement, and the self-confidence necessary to withstand the inevitable pressures. For there would be pressure to perform at the highest level, and pressure to conform to the professional and personal patterns of white-dominated academia. Such impeccable credentials would be necessary, Embree knew, when he undertook to persuade a university president to make such an unprecedented appointment. Moreover, the institution itself would have to be carefully considered, lest the candidate prove a bad fit for its needs.

Embree's choice for the first, highly critical appointment was one of his favorite Rosenwald fellows. W. Allison Davis had been valedictorian of his graduating class at one of the country's most selective institutions, Williams College. He held master's degrees in English and anthropology, both earned at Harvard. For a year, he had studied at the London School of Economics under famed anthropologist Bronislaw Malinowski. At Yale's Institute of Human Relations, he had held a research appointment, and he had directed a study for the American Council on Education. In addition to the Rosenwald grant, he had received a fellowship from the Social Sciences Research Council. He was co-author of two ground-breaking books, published in 1940 and 1941. Approaching age forty in 1942, he was completing his Ph.D. at the University of Chicago.[55]

With his impressively credentialed candidate in hand, Embree turned to the Midwest's leading private university. A private institution, he knew, would be less subject to the political considerations likely to arise at a public one. The University of Chicago he knew unusually well, and the relevant departments had firsthand knowledge of Davis. Moreover, President Robert Hutchins was not only a longtime Embree friend, but for six years had been a fund trustee, an important consideration when dubious members of both the university and the fund's board had to be convinced. The match between individual and institution seemed as good as Embree could have hoped. Even so, he proceeded cautiously.

Early in 1941, more than a year before submitting a formal proposal to the fund's trustees, Embree presented for discussion the general question of helping black professors to win appointments to national research universities. He mentioned Davis as one of several scholars—all Rosenwald fellows—well positioned to lead the way through the discriminatory gate. He called attention to the reluctance of any university to tackle this "thorny problem," for taking such a lead could arouse controversy, even bitterness. That reluctance was increased by budgetary constraints during wartime but, he suggested, the offer of a salary subsidy for a few years might be sufficient inducement for "one or more institutions" to make the step. He did not push the matter at that point, but continued conversations with University of Chicago officials and faculty.[56]

At its next meeting, the board was informed that the university's Department of Education and Division of Social Sciences expected to recommend Davis for an assistant professorship, with teaching duties in education and anthropology. Because the university was operating on a tight budget, however, the appointment was contingent on a fund subsidy, amounting to two-thirds of Davis's salary for three years. The board chair, Lessing Rosenwald, doubted that such a subsidy was necessary, in light of all the other family contributions to the university. Later, another family trustee, who opposed the project altogether, insisted that the whole matter be acted on by the entire board, not just its executive committee. In promoting his plan, Embree stressed the advantages of the demonstration project, pointing out that Davis would be teaching both southern and northern students and would be in contact with "probably the most important group" of black graduate students anywhere in the country. The appointment would put him in the best possible setting for teaching and research and, as "the most conspicuous academic post held by a Negro in any American university," would raise the ceiling of opportunity for black intellectuals across the country. Finally, at the third meeting when the issue was considered, the board approved the project with the provisions Embree had negotiated with President Hutchins.[57]

The demonstration worked out as Embree had hoped. There were some embarrassing episodes with other faculty members, but nothing that called Davis's professional competence into question. His initial appointment was renewed for a second three-year term, this time without a specific fund subsidy. At the end of the second contract, he and a later-hired professor were granted tenure, the first two African Americans to receive such appointments in any American research university. The following year, Davis was promoted to full professor.[58]

With the color bar successfully breached in one faculty and a crucial precedent established at Rosenwald, Embree moved on to other institutions in the mid-forties. He tried to use his trustee's position at

Sarah Lawrence to get artist Hale Woodruff, another Rosenwald fellow, named to that faculty. When that arrangement proved unworkable, he negotiated an appointment for Woodruff in the School of Education of New York University, with the fund providing almost half his salary over a three-year period. At Michigan's Olivet College, arrangements were made for a couple, philosopher Cornelius and librarian Catherine Golightly, both former fellows, to join the staff, again with the fund initially providing part of their salaries. Extending the demonstrations into the South, Embree underwrote the salaries of four teachers for the summer term at North Carolina's experimental Black Mountain College. Two of the four, biologist Percy Baker and musician Mark Fax, had held Rosenwald fellowships; another was the distinguished baritone Roland Hayes.[59]

Building on these individual breakthroughs, the fund undertook a systematic effort to get black intellectuals appointed to all-white faculties. A list of some 125 names, virtually all Rosenwald fellowship recipients with completed or pending doctoral degrees, was mailed, along with brief descriptions of each person's individual qualifications, to every college and university president in the United States. The mailing was followed up in a number of instances with additional correspondence and personal conversations with deans and presidents. By mid-1946, Embree could report to the board that the yearlong effort seemed to be bearing fruit. In the last twelve months, he announced, more than forty African Americans had obtained positions at northern institutions for a quarter or more, and over half of these were long-term appointments. A year later, the number of such appointments—at forty-three institutions with formerly all-white faculties—had risen to more than seventy-five.[60]

In the gradual opening of all-white faculties to black professors, the Rosenwald Fund was "a leading force."[61] But scarcely less innovative was Embree's work on the Chicago Commission on Human Relations and his central role in the establishment of Roosevelt College. Those initiatives, like his efforts on behalf of displaced Japanese Americans, were all parts of the same whole, an expression of his deepest convictions. His activities took on a more pronounced direction in the 1940s, but not because those convictions had changed or because his consciousness somehow had shifted. What had changed was his analysis of the

national and world situations, his assessment of what had become possible, indeed urgent. Around the country, as around the globe, the war
had accelerated changes in race relations that made return to the status
quo ante impossible. Consequently, it was no longer sufficient to call attention to the universally harmful irrationality of racial discrimination
while broadening the avenues of advancement for people of color. Focus-
ing energy and capital on the South and the Midwest was no longer good
enough. It had become necessary to campaign for justice, to pursue full
democracy on the national level.

SEVEN

ON THE
NATIONAL STAGE

The global conflict of the 1940s propelled Embree more directly into the national political arena. He had foreseen, at least dimly, some of the societal consequences of the war, particularly the perils and possibilities it posed for relations between white citizens and the nation's minorities. Increased migration of rural blacks from the South to the cities of the North and West would inevitably multiply their interactions with whites, increasing racial tensions. Moreover, the greater opportunities discovered outside the South, coupled with wartime rhetoric about the defense of freedom and democracy, would raise expectations within the black community that would not be satisfied with palliative measures within traditional constraints. Thus, what many had mistakenly regarded as a problem peculiar to one region would become a pressing national issue. Nor were racial antagonism and heightened expectations confined to the United States. As Embree understood, those same factors were clearly evident among peoples restive under imperial domination around the globe.

His response to these volatile circumstances was twofold. Continuing efforts to increase interracial understanding, he now mounted a direct attack on racial segregation. At the same time, he promoted recognition of a new world order, involving political independence and greater international influence for people of color. Sweeping changes, he believed, were inevitable and close at hand. Early in 1942, he postulated, "We are at the opening of another era not only in America, but in world affairs." The new era might be no better, and probably would be worse, "[b]ut at any rate, a great many of the traditions and norms of history are being shattered and there is an opportunity now for some quite new things and for organization on a world basis."[1]

* * *

On the day after the attack on Pearl Harbor, Embree wired President Roosevelt, offering his knowledge of Asia to help in the national crisis. Two months later, he followed up with a specific suggestion in a letter and three-page statement, "Race and Color in the Present World Struggle." A serious weakness in the United States and among its allies, he wrote, centered on the low morale of persons of color, to whom the Axis powers presented the war as a new stage in Western and white efforts to dominate the globe. The problem was becoming acute among not only African Americans, but the peoples of China, the Philippines, Malaya, and the East Indies as well. To address it, he recommended that the president appoint a national commission composed of distinguished citizens to clarify issues in race relations, raise morale, and identify measures to make democracy more effective at home and abroad. Special attention should be directed to those populations under imperial domination, to give them hope for a more dignified status and, perhaps, independence. If, at the end of the war, he warned, peace "in the new world order" was established on the old imperialistic pattern, the result could be an even more terrible war pitting Asians and Africans (aided perhaps by Latin Americans and Russians) against the West. To illustrate the kind of person who might participate in such a commission, Embree offered a list of two dozen names and volunteered to help put together a representative membership if the president wished.[2]

Roosevelt's response came more than a month later. He had the morale of peoples of color around the world under continuous consideration, he replied, and several federal agencies were at work on the problems. A time would come when such a commission could be valuable in planning for peace and reconstruction, but right now such long-range planning might distract from the war effort. The creation of such a commission seemed premature but, the president assured Embree, when the time was ripe, he would be in touch with him again.[3]

Embree was undoubtedly disappointed by the president's response, but not disheartened. Convinced that the war would intensify racial problems, he proposed the following month that the Rosenwald Fund create a new unit, one devoted exclusively to race relations. The fund had always been involved in black-white relations in some fashion, but Embree's proposal signaled a determination to give that fundamental purpose even sharper focus, now that wartime conditions had begun to interfere with other programs. The reform of rural education, the fund's principal concern for the last five years, was being eclipsed by more immediate problems. The military draft was draining the pool of promising male fellowship applicants. Moreover, within the board and staff, discussions had already begun about when the exhaustion of its capital would force the fund to close. Embree's proposal to concentrate on this central purpose, however, promised continued vitality as long as moneys were available. Alert to the economic and demographic changes under way and pleased with the increased emphasis, the board approved the new Division of Race Relations with enthusiasm.[4]

Indicative of the new division's centrality was the selection of those to lead it. Veterans in black-white cooperation, active in the fund for more than a dozen years, Will Alexander and Charles Johnson were the obvious choices. Embree met with the two co-directors of the new division, his closest colleagues, early in the summer of 1942. For several days, the three friends shared opinions about critical issues and discussed how the fund could best pursue its narrowed agenda. From those sessions came a far-reaching conclusion: the time had come to mobilize opposition to laws mandating the separation of the races.[5] Their decision reflected not a change of heart, but an awareness of rapidly changing circumstances.

Embree had never been a defender of racial segregation. His upbringing, his extensive experience in Asia and the Pacific, and his friendships across racial lines had firmly established in his mind that such separation was neither natural nor moral. While he recognized some limited advantages for the black community in voluntary separation, in his personal behavior he had resisted such patterns all his life.[6] In his writings and public statements, in the funding grants he recommended, in his private life, he had sought to promote the material well-being of the country's largest minority and to further interracial understanding. Fundamental to those efforts were the elevation of educational levels in the country's black citizenry, the development of effective leadership, facilitating accomplishment in varied fields, and calling attention to those accomplishments as evidence of intelligence, talent, and creativity. Such advances he considered prerequisite to overcoming even voluntary white separatism outside the South; the legally mandated segregation prevalent in the southern and border states was far more formidable. Such laws he regarded as offensive and unjust, but throughout the thirties he had believed they could not be openly combated without severe damage to the fund's efforts to improve the health, education, and prospects of the country's black population. He considered such improvements of paramount importance, and he knew that progress along those lines could be thwarted by the aroused opposition of the South's entrenched leaders. He probed the boundaries of societal change, but was realistic enough to know there were limits beyond which change could not be effectively pushed. The clarity and strength of his own views notwithstanding, and however galling the current circumstances, he recognized the need for both careful preparation and watchful impatience.[7]

Also necessary was the support of the Rosenwald trustees, not all of whom were initially prepared to confront such deeply embedded patterns. Consequently, from early 1943 through 1945, Embree exposed them to a steady stream of information, position papers, and searching discussions of racial separation, all aimed at moving the fund to the forefront of anti-segregation activity.[8] Once the board was persuaded of the unprecedented opportunity and urgency brought by the war, Embree was able to move forward forthrightly. For the last years of the fund's life, he was unswerving in his efforts to combat enforced segregation, and that struggle claimed a steadily increasing portion of the fund's expenditures. Always working closely with Johnson and Alexander, he ensured that the Division of Race Relations had first call on the philanthropy's dwindling resources. None of the claims on those resources was as unusual as one that had been received even before the United States entered the conflict.

* * *

After approving the country's first peacetime draft in September 1940, Congress a few months later ordered the U.S. Army Air Corps to create an all-black combat unit. The Pentagon seemed reluctant to implement this mandate, for many believed that African American men lacked the skill, intelligence, and discipline to handle complicated machinery like an airplane. Even so, the project proceeded with the selection of Alabama's historic Tuskegee Institute as the training site. But a problem immediately arose. The institute had no airfield and no land on which to build one, and the War Department showed little inclination to address the need. At that point, Tuskegee president Frederick Patterson turned for help to Embree and the Rosenwald Fund.

Julius Rosenwald had been a major Tuskegee benefactor and had long served on its board. Relations between the institute and the Rosenwald Fund stretched back almost a quarter-century. Yet, well before 1941, the fund had ceased making grants for physical additions to black colleges and universities. Subsidizing the construction of an airfield—an unprecedented philanthropic undertaking in itself—would not only violate the fund's policy, but would surely unleash dozens of requests from other institutions for assistance with campus improvements. The fund's trustees, mindful of that unappealing prospect and aware of their steadily diminishing capital, were unwilling to make a gift. However, the potential importance of training black airmen, a significant step toward equal opportunity in the armed forces, did not escape the fund's president. Ever eager to support promising demonstration projects, and never hesitant to expand the limits of philanthropy, Embree came up with an imaginative compromise. The fund would not *give* the money to build the airfield but, setting aside misgivings and the lack of precedent, it would provide a loan to make the construction possible.

The loan was made. The first class began training in July 1941. At the graduation exercises eight months later, Embree addressed the first five African American men to earn pilot's wings. In the months that followed, class after class enrolled, until by the war's end the number of pilots trained at Tuskegee was approaching a thousand.[9] In North Africa and the European theater, the Tuskegee airmen, four squadrons comprising the 332nd Fighter Group, distinguished themselves in numerous combat missions.

In July 1943, exactly two years after the first cadets began training, President Patterson submitted to the fund the last payment on the loan. Noting the good account the pilots were giving of themselves, he affirmed that were it not for "the wisdom and generosity of the Rosenwald Fund, in its willingness to make an exception to its stated policy, this favorable accomplishment probably would not be a matter of record today." The Rosenwald action had encouraged the Tuskegee board to devote the majority of the institute's free funds to developing the program. Now, with a total investment of $350,000, Patterson wrote, aviation had become a permanent part of Tuskegee's activities, opening new employment possibilities for graduates in the postwar world.[10]

President Patterson was gratified by the results of this uncommon form of philanthropic cooperation, as was the fund's president. From Embree's perspective, the loan had been essential to getting the training under way, the project had worked out "perfectly from a financial standpoint," and it represented "a notable service to America and to education."[11] But beyond the immediate circumstances, this "demonstration" had far-reaching consequences. The Tuskegee airmen gave the lie to the racist contention that African American men could not be competent pilots or otherwise handle complex equipment. At the same time, their performance in combat made clear that they were in no way inferior to their white counterparts. Their success, in spite of continued slurs and slights, helped to pave the way for the U.S. Air Force to begin planning racial integration by 1947.[12] A year later, President Harry Truman issued Executive Order 9981, mandating equal treatment and equal opportunity for all members of the armed forces. Without the Tuskegee airmen's example, the integration of the U.S. military undoubtedly would not have occurred when it did. As a source of great and enduring pride for African Americans, few match the exploits of these aviators. Similarly rare are the philanthropic ventures that can claim a comparable multiplier effect. Embree had good reason to be pleased with the outcome of this unparalleled project.

*   *   *

Even as a long stride toward equal opportunity was being taken in Tuskegee, steps in the same direction elsewhere were raising racial tensions to the boiling point. At the Mobile shipyards, 200 miles southwest of Tuskegee, the promotion of twelve black men to the ranks of skilled labor led to violent protest by white workers. In the next few weeks, the racial

violence spread to Beaumont, Texas; Los Angeles and Detroit; Philadelphia and New York.[13] An increasingly concerned Franklin Roosevelt
turned to the Rosenwald Fund's head.

Though a year earlier the president had rejected Embree's plea for the
appointment of a national committee to address black-white tensions,
he now sought authoritative information on the state of race relations
across the country. Embree immediately asked Charles S. Johnson and
his Fisk researchers to gather current material. The rapidly developed
report, twelve typewritten pages long, so impressed FDR and the presidential staff that additional copies were requested. It quickly became
evident that such information, regularly developed and widely distributed, would be welcomed by other governmental departments as well
as the White House. The response of Embree and Johnson was to create
the *Monthly Summary of Events and Trends in Race Relations,* a unique
publication prepared by Johnson's Division of Social Sciences at Fisk
and underwritten by the Rosenwald Fund. In deciding to support this
periodical, the Rosenwald executive committee deemed it "of prime importance," an initiative that might prove to be "one of the fund's distinctive contributions."[14]

The *Monthly Summary* was first issued in August 1943, only two
months after the June riots. It contained items gleaned from roughly 800
incidents reported each month in more than 400 daily newspapers and
other publications. Additional information was gathered by some forty
reporters spread around the country, each of whom regularly received a
stipend from the fund. The *Monthly Summary*'s material dealt primarily
with relations between the majority population and the nation's largest
minority but, reflecting Embree's own interests, also included sections
devoted to those of Hispanic, Native American, and Asian ancestry.
Chronicling instances of both racial injustice and racial progress, the
report was soon being mailed to over 8,000 subscribers: federal agencies, congressional representatives, state and local officials, military and
religious leaders. It was read in Mexico and as far afield as the Chinese
governmental headquarters in Chungking. During its five years of life,
the *Monthly Summary* served as the nation's chief source of information
on developments in race relations, with a subscription list at its peak
exceeding 15,000.[15] Publication ceased in 1948, when Charles Johnson

assumed the presidency of Fisk University and the Rosenwald Fund closed its doors.[16]

Even as the *Monthly Summary* was getting under way, Embree moved to accelerate the positive trends the periodical reported. In an event that he and Will Alexander probably orchestrated, Eleanor Roosevelt late in 1943 called together a group to talk over the race situation. More attuned to such concerns than her husband, the First Lady arranged a White House dinner for a handful of race relations authorities to consider what useful steps might be taken to reduce tensions.[17] Possibly as a consequence of that occasion, Embree came to the conclusion that a "new force" needed to enter the racial arena, one with a wider scope than the National Urban League, the NAACP, and other existing groups. Such an organization, as he envisioned it, would concentrate on grand strategy and "command considerable prestige." To discuss establishing such a national body, he and Rosenwald trustees Charles Johnson and Marshall Field invited some 130 leaders of various constituencies around the country to come to Chicago in the spring of 1944.[18]

The Chicago conference drew some seventy-five participants and proved to be a disorganized disappointment. Embree described it to a friend as marked by the "usual bickering and jockeying," with "about 75 different points of view, special ambitions and bitter jealousies."[19] Disputation notwithstanding, he believed that the meeting pointed up the need for a new force and that the conferees recognized that need. Consequently, a second, smaller meeting was held two months later. With only twenty-two participants, these sessions went more smoothly, and though there were frank disagreements over policies and procedures, most were apparently resolved. The attendees decided to form the new organization, with themselves as its initial board. Embree, Johnson, and Field immediately took steps to incorporate the American Council on Race Relations (ACRR).[20]

* * *

From the outset, the ACRR was closely linked to the Rosenwald Fund. The first meeting of the new organization's board of directors was held at the fund's headquarters. At that time, the organization was assured of an annual Rosenwald subsidy of $25,000 for the next three years. When this grant, matched by the Marshall Field Foundation, proved insufficient to meet operating expenses, the fund made supplementary appropriations. Moreover, the organization's bylaws drawn up by board member Leonard Rieser, who had long handled Rosenwald legal matters, mirrored those of the fund.[21]

The close relationship was evident as well in the overlapping personnel, as many of the participants were connected to Embree through either the Rosenwald Fund or the Mayor's Commission on Human Relations. The ACRR had two vice presidents: the eminent civil rights lawyer Charles Hamilton Houston, a member of the Rosenwald board; the other was Will Alexander. The secretary and assistant treasurer was Mary-Jane Grunsfeld, who moved to the council from her post as special assistant to Embree and Johnson at the mayor's commission. Like Grunsfeld, Robert C. Weaver left his position as executive director of the mayor's commission to take charge of housing matters for the council.[22]

Essentially Embree's brainchild, the ACRR embodied many of the organizational features he had sketched out in a Kyoto hotel room more than a decade earlier. Its stated purpose was "to bring about full democracy in race relations." Its activities were expected to center on conducting research, developing materials for use in schools, increasing public knowledge of racial groups through the media, and helping communities to organize to address race-related problems. It served largely as a clearinghouse for information, which was shared with over 400 organizations across the country. In addition, the council, like other Embree-linked groups, was deeply involved in publishing, producing almost four dozen fact sheets, pamphlets, and reprints, and distributing copies of them in the tens of thousands.[23] Though it did sponsor some research, it was more inclined to subsidize projects for other agencies to conduct.

Reflective of Embree's perspective, the ACRR showed unusual sensitivity to the plight of Japanese Americans. Through correspondence and personal contacts, it lobbied energetically for prompt federal action on indemnity claims and the resettlement of those interned three years earlier. In cooperation with the Japanese American Citizens League, it worked to energize civic groups on the West Coast and to promote racial harmony. In the ACRR's Chicago headquarters, perhaps one-fifth of the office staff were of Japanese extraction, people who otherwise would have had trouble finding employment during the war.[24]

In addition, the council sought, through two publications, to convey accurate information about the nation's citizens of Japanese heritage. "Facts about Japanese-Americans," for example, pointed out the valuable assistance of volunteers of Japanese ancestry during the attack on Pearl Harbor and the Nisei's (second generation) contribution to the war effort in intelligence and propaganda activities. Above all, it called attention to the thousands of Japanese Americans in the U.S. Army and especially to the all-Nisei 100th Battalion's heroism in the Italian campaign. These proved to be, probably to the disappointment if not surprise of Embree and his colleagues, the least popular of all its published pieces.[25]

While Japanese Americans and, to a lesser extent, Hispanic Americans claimed some of the council's attention, most of its efforts were directed toward African Americans and their relations with the majority population. Along with bad housing, overcrowded schools, employment discrimination, and the lack of basic civil rights, three other issues were addressed. Training police to deal with diverse populations, a major emphasis of Embree and the Chicago mayor's commission, received extensive attention. Drawing on the commission's experience, the ACRR developed educational materials for law enforcement officers, produced several training films, and hired a former municipal police chief to promote their use around the country. A second problem involved men returning from military service after 1945. A committee led by Charles Houston monitored the circumstances of African American veterans, working to ensure that they received the benefits they deserved and seeking to eliminate segregation in military hospitals and rehabilitation facilities. Meanwhile, placing America's racial problems in the global context, the council urged President Truman and Secretary of State Edward R. Stettinius Jr. at the organizational meeting of the United Nations to adopt a more forthcoming position regarding the eventual independence of peoples still under colonial domination.[26]

The American Council on Race Relations dealt with genuine concerns and had an auspicious beginning, yet it never fulfilled its promise. Early on, Embree became concerned that the organization was preoccupied with less important matters, rather than with the development of the grand strategy he considered its reason for existence. By the third year, serious difficulties—involving purpose, finance, and leadership—began to appear. Within the board, disagreements arose about the proper balance between research and activism, between generating and disseminating knowledge, on the one hand, and direct engagement in political affairs, on the other. Embree favored limiting the group's activities to providing reliable information and shaping public opinion, but when repeated attempts to resolve the matter proved unsuccessful, several African American directors, most notably the NAACP's Walter White, began to distance themselves from the organization.[27]

The dispute over the ACRR's purpose seems to have affected its funding. Both Rosenwald and the Field Foundation continued generous grants, but their core support was insufficient to meet rising budgetary needs, and efforts to attract additional donors languished. The council had begun with an impressive board, including such figures as the secretary-treasurer of the Congress of Industrial Organizations (CIO); a vice president of the Carnegie Corporation; two of the named principals in the prestigious New York law firm of Paul, Weiss, Wharton, and Garrison; the executive secretary of the American Friends Service Committee; and a good balance of prominent business executives, influential editors, and eminent scholars, both black and white. Yet the luster of their names and positions never translated into significant contributions. Substantial funding sources undoubtedly were accessible to the board collectively but, as the council slipped into disarray, its members apparently did not exert themselves to sustain it. Embree in late 1946 had to admit to the Rosenwald board that the council was not operating effectively. Some of the difficulties, he acknowledged, stemmed from a lack of competent leadership.[28]

The leadership problem was addressed in 1947 with a thorough reorganization, involving affiliation with the University of Chicago. The university created the Committee on Education, Training, and Research in Race Relations, housed in the Division of Social Sciences, with which the ACRR was to be associated. The council was to remain an independent agency, however, raising its own funds, continuing its own functions, and the university committee would not be responsible for its actions. The council, in turn, agreed to provide initial funding to stimulate the university's efforts in research on race relations, and the redefined office of president was entrusted to Chicago sociologist Louis Wirth.[29]

The sweeping changes proved of little avail. The council limped along for another three years, but nothing occurred to relieve the organization's fundamental difficulties. At the urging of other directors, Walter White and other African American members returned to board meetings, but they continued to inveigh against "substituting research for action." Financial support was provided to a newly formed National Association of Intergroup Relations Officials, which began to assume some of the council's functions. But with the demise of the Rosenwald Fund in mid-1948, one of the ACRR's two essential supports disappeared. While the Field Foundation might have continued its contributions, realism dictated that, if the council teetered with two financial pillars, it could not stand with only one. On September 15, 1950, the American Council on Race Relations came to an end.[30]

As the ACRR deteriorated, Embree had done what he could to stave off its demise. For more than a decade, he had dreamed of such an organization. He was convinced it could meet a national need, and its continuing problems caused him considerable dismay. He served continuously on its board, but for most of its life he declined an office or membership on any standing committee, perhaps in hopes that other leadership would emerge, perhaps to avoid making the council's connection with the fund even more obvious. Even so, he remained highly active, never missing a meeting of the full board in the first four years and routinely attending sessions of the executive committee, even when he was not officially a member. With seasoned advice, useful suggestions, and essential funding reliably delivered, he had tried to stabilize the tottering structure.[31]

Valiant efforts notwithstanding, the council was never able to clarify its purpose, attract sufficient financial support, or generate a substantial national following. Its failure inevitably raises the question of whether Embree misjudged the moment. Was the momentum for improved relations between the country's minorities and the white population weaker in 1944 than he thought? Did his unwavering optimism about steady advances in democratic living cause him to exaggerate the possibilities for change? Had he somehow misread the signs?

The severe disabilities under which America's citizens of color labored is beyond question. Indeed, their severity was matched only by their vexing nature. Nor can there be doubt that the war had accelerated fundamental changes in the outlooks and expectations of the nation's black citizenry. Though responses to those changes varied widely, the increased militancy itself was evident to all but the most obtuse observers. Embree must be credited for recognizing, far sooner than almost all his contemporaries, the connection between the aspirations of African Americans and peoples in Africa and Asia struggling toward independence. He was not wrong to emphasize the twin aspects of a worldwide movement.

If he erred, the error had multiple dimensions. He may have believed too strongly in the capacity of scholarly research, basically an appeal to human reason, to affect the deeply rooted prejudices of the nation's whites. Similarly, he may have overestimated the power of the media to shape public opinion. The limited advances in race matters possibly led him to underrate the nation's conservatism, the strength of the counterforce brought forward when the racial caste system was challenged. Above all, he may have been temperamentally unable to understand how the United States, though weary of war and preoccupied with the promises of peace, could continue to avoid addressing its most enduring social problem, turning its back on 10 percent of its population. Or, he may have fully comprehended all these things and decided to push on, whatever the obstacles. Such a decision would not have been alien to his character. And it would have been highly reminiscent of Grandfather Fee.

* * *

Though the ACRR never fulfilled the promise Embree had foreseen, he did not place all his hopes and energies in that body alone. An organization that spun off from the ACRR, the Bureau for Intercultural Education, proved more successful. Located in New York, it concentrated on developing materials on intercultural relations for classroom use and, in cooperation with New York University, offered teacher-training institutes and workshops. Though Embree referred to the bureau as a "stepchild," it was handsomely supported, like the ACRR, by both the Rosenwald Fund and the Field Foundation. In addition, it benefited from the fund-raising ability of one of the Rosenwalds' daughters, Adele Levy, who was a member of its board. By 1946, it had become more financially secure and effectively administered than the ACRR.[32]

During this period, the fund also channeled moneys to established organizations as they began to give attention to the nation's racial problems. Churches and labor unions became beneficiaries of Rosenwald largesse. Long critical of Christian groups for their failure to confront racism directly, Embree was gratified when that pattern began to change in the mid-forties. In support of such change, sizable grants for studies and programs went to the Federal Council of Churches' Commission on the Church and Minority Peoples; the United Council of Church Women's Committee on Social, Industrial, and Race Relations; and the Catholic Labor Alliance. Similarly, when the CIO and other elements of the labor movement began to eliminate racially discriminatory membership policies, Embree came to regard them as useful allies in improving race relations. In the South, particularly, he thought that "democratic" education and the development of new leadership could make the labor movement an instrument to combat segregation. Consequently, the Georgia Workers Education Service and other southern labor bodies, as well as the American Labor Education Service, which had programs in the East and Midwest, received grants. Even the National Urban League, whose requests for help with operating expenses Embree had denied for years, received $50,000 for its Department of Industrial Relations.[33]

Of particular note is the Legal Defense and Educational Fund of the NAACP. Throughout the thirties, after NAACP leadership passed from James Weldon Johnson to Walter White, relations between the civil rights group and the Rosenwald Fund had been no more than lukewarm. But while Embree did not respond favorably to requested subsidies for operating expenses, the NAACP was too important to ignore altogether. Embree remained in contact with its executives, and in 1943, when changed circumstances brought a fresh appeal, Embree responded differently.

The NAACP's request was for help with its costs for legal defense. Embree recognized that the burden of fighting racial discrimination through the courts fell most heavily on that organization. As he pointed out to the Rosenwald board, "The defense of constitutional rights is apt to be of increasing importance during the war and post-war emergency."[34] Consequently, the group's legal arm needed to be strengthened, particularly by the addition of a highly competent lawyer as associate secretary or general counsel. He recommended, and the board approved, an annual grant for three years, to begin immediately. This initial appropriation was followed by others, with the result that, in the years leading up to the Supreme Court's 1954 decision in *Brown v. Board of Education,* the Rosenwald Fund was the largest single contributor to the Legal Defense and Educational Fund.[35]

To the effort to eliminate segregation, Embree brought not only his organizational abilities, his nationwide contacts, and the resources of the fund; he employed his voice as well. Known to be a well-informed and engaging speaker, he was in constant demand by various program planners. From women's groups and civic organizations, universities and churches, local PTAs and school boards, national professional associations and international relations councils, invitations for speaking engagements poured in. He tried to be accommodating, but by the 1940s he was able to accept at most one invitation out of ten.[36] Concerned to spread his message of racial reconciliation as widely as possible, he increasingly limited his commitments to those situations in which his words were likely to have the greatest impact. One of those situations was the annual Race Relations Institute held at Fisk University in Nashville.

* * *

The purpose of the Race Relations Institute was to prepare a cadre to lead in reducing interracial tensions and working for social justice. Established by Charles S. Johnson and sponsored by the American Missionary Association, the institute brought together for three weeks in July 100–150 participants from across the country. Attracting a mixed group of blacks and whites, along with an occasional Asian American or Latino, the institute was the first effort of its kind in the South. Through lectures and discussions, attendees learned about racial theory, social problems, human relations, and methods of combating racism. Sessions were led by a distinguished assemblage of sociologists, historians, anthropologists, psychologists, and civil rights figures. Among this group, Embree during the first three years was arguably the most prominent.[37] Certainly, he was the most outspoken.

When the first institute opened on the Fisk campus in 1944, Embree was a featured speaker. He used the occasion to highlight the connection between elevated racial tension in the United States and the restiveness of subordinated peoples around the globe. Just as the United States needed to end racial discrimination at home, he proclaimed, the populations of Asia had to be treated as equals lest they "swiftly rise in a world rebellion and throw off the yoke of the western white men." More than a year before the Japanese surrender, he cautioned against a U.S. occupation of the conquered country based on vengeance, rather than one that would allow the Japanese people to divest themselves of their military rulers and become a force for world peace. Maintaining good relations with China and Japan was critical, for those two nations would join the United States, the Soviet Union, and the British empire as the great powers emerging from the war. The war would bring about a shift in the center of world politics, he predicted, from Europe and the Atlantic to Asia and the Pacific.[38] Embree's bold words were reported in the Nashville press, but they seem to have aroused little concern.

That was not the case the following year. At the 1945 institute, Embree again asserted his conviction that the world was entering a new era. World War I had marked the beginning of the suicide of Western civilization, he said, and World War II, which was now moving to its close, would complete that process. Great civilizations had risen and fallen throughout history and, the current myth of white superiority notwithstanding, the ascent of the West had nothing to do with race or racially related mental capacity. Looking ahead, he foresaw further acceleration in travel and communication, resulting in the eventual disappearance of nationalism, a wider distribution of the world's goods, and a global diffusion of knowledge and mechanical skills that would give "pigmented peoples" opportunity for power. In these new circumstances, if white men understood and would "permit themselves to recognize the rights and capacities of all peoples," they could continue to contribute to world progress. But if they persisted in claiming their own superiority and right to dominate, they were "likely to find themselves without even a position of equality." This global problem, he continued, could be seen in microcosm in the United States, but if it could be worked out here, the solution could become a model for the whole world.[39]

Embree had deliberately, conspicuously challenged the South's racial mores, and the response was "sharp, emotional and bitterly defensive."[40] The *Nashville Banner* editorialized that the Rosenwald Fund had been "misdirected into channels of 'New Order' thinking with its breeding of abnormal hostilities and hysterics." The "problems" Embree described could not be solved by "outside interference and agitation," but only by southerners, using "the means they have labored to perfect."[41] The *Nashville Tennessean*, a more moderate paper, opined that the philanthropy president's speech was "provocative . . . , in bad taste," and not "calculated to help the cause" for which the Rosenwald Fund had been established. Though his words might have pleased his audience at the Race Relations Institute, "elsewhere the reaction was not pleasant." Accused of stirring up racial strife, Embree was warned not to return to the South.[42]

In the months that followed, the owner of the *Banner* and other Nashville leaders pressured Fisk's president to discontinue the institute, emphasizing their objections to Embree's remarks. Defending both his friend and the institute to his president, Charles Johnson insisted that Embree had "spoken a truth," and the eminent sociologist threatened to resign and take his staff with him unless left free to run the program as he saw fit. In this confrontation, Johnson prevailed, and when the 1946 institute convened, the Rosenwald president was again scheduled for several panels and two lectures. In striking defiance of the critics, one of Embree's lectures was the high-profile opening address.[43]

Neither intimidated by the earlier warning nor dismayed by the opposition he had aroused, Embree again spoke of the end of Western domination, the rise of the world's colored majority, and the "absurdity" of notions of white superiority. He went on to predict that the new order would have a single world government, "arrived at either by agreement in a framework of federation or by conquest in one more war." Repeating a point he had made the previous year, he affirmed that plenty and power would be more equitably distributed around the globe. Yet those currently in privileged positions need not worry, he affirmed, for there would be "abundance for all if we . . . distribute it intelligently." Furthermore, the United States was fortunate in having two "neglected but fundamental principles" on which to build: "the Christian principle of brotherhood and the democratic principle of equal rights."[44] In the *Banner*, Embree's remarks were forthrightly reported, and this time neither that paper nor the competing *Tennessean* saw fit to take issue editorially. Perhaps concluding that such comment would only serve to raise the segregation issue even higher in public consciousness, they desisted. The storm of the previous year was allowed to subside.

*   *   *

As Embree's public statements during the forties attest, heightened racial tensions at home and rising expectations among colonized peoples abroad gave him a profound sense of urgency. Believing that the world stood squarely on a hinge of history, he insisted that the door swing wide, opening new avenues of promise. As the war forced some curtailment of the fund's activities, he was left with more time to express that urgency through his pen, returning to the prolific rate of publication that had characterized his first years at Rosenwald. During the war years, he turned out three books and some fifteen articles. The articles lack the range of subject matter of the earlier period, reflecting instead an almost single-minded focus on the race question. The titles are indicative of the depth of his concern: "The Status of Minorities as a Test of Democracy"; "Half Slave, Half Democrat"; "It's Friendship with Colored Peoples or Chaos"; "Education for One World"; "For Whose Freedom?" As in that earlier time, he sought a diverse audience by writing for a variety of opinion-forming publications: *American Mercury, Asia, Opportunity, Atlantic Monthly, Survey Graphic, Nation's Schools*.[45]

Embree's more substantial works during this period of course do not deliver so loud a call for immediate action. Yet they too sought to improve interracial understanding by providing accurate, accessible information about minority Americans. In 1939, Houghton Mifflin published *Indians of the Americas: Historical Pageant*, which was designed to tell high school and older readers of the richly varied cultures that predated the arrival of white people. While emphasizing the traditions, beliefs, art forms, and practices of the indigenous peoples, Embree lamented the efforts of "white conquerors" to eradicate such distinctive features and, acting out of ignorance and arrogance, to impose their own values and patterns in the name of "civilization."[46]

For a book aimed at an unsophisticated audience, *Indians* received a surprising amount of attention from the press. Reviews were carried in the *New York Times* and the *Saturday Review of Literature,* as well as in such scholarly journals as *Social Forces, American Antiquity, Social Studies, American Journal of Sociology,* and *Hispanic American Historical Review.*[47] Though some specialists questioned the book's accuracy, their doubts apparently did not discourage the reading public. The volume of sales a year after publication justified a second edition, with a bibliography added. Two years later, some 5,000 copies had been sold. And in 1970, when the second edition was reissued, Embree won the praise of Native American activist Vine Deloria Jr.[48]

The commercial success of *Indians* encouraged Embree to write *American Negroes: A Handbook,* published in 1942. A slim volume planned for a mass readership, it contained little new information, nor did Embree claim that it did. But the book was intended to have an impact. Few readers could have passed lightly over the closing paragraphs. There, Embree declared that, even while the power of the United States was fully engaged in the international defense of democracy, the anti-democratic pattern of segregation sapped national strength:

> The greatest weakness of our democracy is our treatment of Negroes. Our attitude toward this race is a threat to the whole theory and practice of democracy. . . . We cannot have a healthy nation with one-tenth of the people ill-nourished, sick, harboring germs of disease which recognize no color line, obey no Jim Crow laws. We cannot have a nation orderly and sound with one group so ground down and thwarted that it is almost forced into unsocial attitudes and crime. We cannot come to our full vigor in the arts unless we give scope to the talents of that race which has proved itself most creative in all forms of art and expression. We cannot be a truly Christian people so long as we flaunt the central teachings of Jesus: brotherly love and the Golden Rule. We cannot come to full prosperity with one great group so ill-trained that it cannot work skillfully, so poor that it cannot buy goods.

Justice and freedom for America's black citizenry was not just a matter of humanity or charity. For the majority population, he insisted, ending such ill treatment was a matter of "enlightened selfishness . . . a question of the total health and strength of the nation."[49]

American Negroes was still in bookstores when Embree's next book came off the press. *Brown Americans: The Story of a Tenth of the Nation* recycled some of the material, and even some of the prose, from the earlier *Brown America: The Story of a New Race.* The historical sections were largely unchanged, but facts and figures were updated, and the text emphasized the striking changes that had occurred since the 1931 volume. No longer were black Americans humbly accepting second-class status, Embree reported; they now were demanding their rights as citizens. One-fourth of their number now resided in the cities of the North and West, almost 50,000 were seeking college degrees, and their presence and influence were growing in the press, the labor movement, and political life. Their confidence and assertiveness were bolstered by "the rising power of hundreds of millions of colored people" in Asia, Africa, and the Pacific and by a growing cohort of scholars, artists, athletes, and writers who had achieved national and international recognition.[50] As in *Brown America,* Embree illustrated the falseness of racial stereotypes with a handful of fresh biographical sketches, including one featuring the highly talented and highly controversial scholar-athlete-singer-actor Paul Robeson.

Reviewers had praise for both the book and the author. According to one, *Brown Americans* was "perhaps the best general introduction for the layman to the Negro Problem in existence." Another described it as "the ideal primer" for the study of African American life. A third commentator considered Embree "qualified probably better than any other white American to discuss the Negro question as it obtains in America today." The editor of the *Kansas City Call* commended the author for avoiding the extremes of portraying blacks as either better than they are or as "savages impossible of culture. . . . We Negroes have need to hear you," he wrote, for with war upsetting the status quo, many expected to gain "full equality in one great leap. They expect too much."[51]

Brown Americans also evoked an interesting array of responses from readers. Rockefeller Foundation president Raymond Fosdick read it from cover to cover with "the greatest interest and delight." Robert C. Weaver affirmed that reading *Brown America* and *Brown Americans* simultaneously had impressed him with the changes in the previous twelve years and "with the fact that we are still not dealing with the fundamentals in the field." Professor of English Margaret Just Wormley, a onetime recipient of a Rosenwald fellowship, praised the book for its "excellence, timeliness, and challenging quality," and reported that fourteen of her students had purchased it. A navy ensign responsible for black seamen, finding both officers and sailors grievously ignorant in racial matters, had been lending his copy to his shipmates, who were "anxious to have it." A reader in Haiti praised the book as "a sublime epic . . . for my soul and [for] my ideals just a tonic."[52]

Brown Americans helped prepare the way for Embree's next book, which appeared as planned on Lincoln's birthday in 1944. *Thirteen against the Odds* presented the life stories of a baker's dozen of African Americans who had risen to national prominence. The book was essentially a collection of success stories, some of them the up-by-the-bootstraps variety long admired by the American public. What gave these accounts particular pointedness, however, was that the individuals had triumphed over the obstacles and indignities routinely faced by members of their race. Embree did not belabor this point, but by making "the odds" clear in each case, he dramatized the significance of his subjects' accomplishments. More substantial than the profiles in *Brown America* and *Brown Americans,* these biographies, like those sketches, were intended to counteract stereotypes by portraying the varied talents of unique individuals. Embree had been particularly concerned to present credible portraits, "human figures, not plaster saints."[53]

Embree's thirteen subjects ranged from boxing champion Joe Louis through contralto Marian Anderson and union leader A. Philip Randolph to distinguished scholar W. E. B. DuBois. All of them he had met before beginning the project, and some he knew quite well. Even so, he had not selected them himself, having left that difficult task to some 200 respondents, both black and white, to whom he submitted a list of 83 names drawn from all walks of life. He invited additions to the list, and then asked for the twelve most distinguished to be selected.[54]

Thirteen against the Odds was an instant success. Four months after its publication, Embree noted that the book "had stirred up more interest and comment" than any of his earlier works. Its popular approach to the "Negro question," he believed, had attracted the attention of many people "who would not bother with a sociological treatise."[55] The publisher described the book as "very well liked," with sales at that point of about 7,500 copies. A new printing was done the following year, with a cheaper edition considered for the year after. The fund itself distributed to interested persons and agencies 400 copies of the initial printing and 500 of the second. The Board of Home Missions of the Congregational Christian Churches used 800 copies as graduation presents in its high schools and colleges.[56]

The book's commercial success was matched by critical acclaim. One scholar described it as a "first-class collection of American success stories, . . . an inspirational book [that] should be read and used as such." DuBois, not given to unqualified praise, but perhaps softened by his own treatment in the book, enthused that it was "easily the most human and living group of biographies I have seen." A member of the editorial board of the Book-of-the-Month Club wrote that Embree's reputation for "poise, fair-mindedness, and intellectual integrity" guaranteed the accuracy of the portraits, but what could not have been predicted was the "lively animation, the picturesque detail, the vitality and power and sense of proportion." Vice President Henry Wallace considered *Thirteen* a "swell book" and affirmed that the capacity of African Americans to develop when given the opportunity was a strong reason for optimism about the country's future.[57]

Even less-enthusiastic commentators acknowledged the book's strengths. One considered the writing "eloquent and occasionally full of pathos," but faulted the author for failing, in spite of his great knowledge of black leaders, to meet fully his promise to reveal his subjects' weaknesses. A mildly negative opinion was expressed by Harlem pastor and U.S. congressman-to-be Adam Clayton Powell. His "only beef" was that, in light of the church's influence in African American society, no minister had been selected. Nevertheless, he regarded *Thirteen* as the best book Embree had published. And what Embree undoubtedly regarded as a backhanded compliment came from a U.S. senator from Mississippi. The white supremacist Theodore Bilbo wrote to the publisher for permission to quote two lines and twenty-one sections from the book in his forthcoming *Take Your Choice: Segregation or Mongrelization*.[58]

* * *

Embree's extensive publications in the forties were expressions of his unwavering commitment to keep the problems of race, and the need for solutions, before the American public. In light of all the means he used—press releases, news articles, guest editorials, pamphlets, essays, magazine pieces, books—his efforts must be considered nothing short of prodigious. His commitment carried him far beyond the constrained, less contentious ground frequented by most foundation executives, and the fund's heavy concentration on advancing the welfare of minorities set it apart from other philanthropic trusts. Embree's continuous publicizing of the fund's activities and his own prominence in racial matters were fully in keeping with the views of the fund's late founder, for Julius Rosenwald had obviously built his commercial empire by keeping his company's goods constantly in the public eye. Unlike the Rockefeller insistence on near anonymity for its officers and influence only through appropriations, Rosenwald had wanted his philanthropy to affect social policy through direct appeals as well as through financial contributions. Yet the fund's emphasis on publicity was not just an echo of Sears advertising. More important, it was a manifestation of Embree's recognition of the importance of public opinion and his understanding of how to influence it.

In his writings, Embree combined a time-honored stratagem of the journalist with the vision of the reformer. His approach went beyond reporting on events to anticipating them. Concerned through the thirties that racial issues had not been high on the nation's agenda, by 1940 he believed such consideration could not be long avoided. By providing a steady flow of information about the nation's African American population, while stressing the value of cultural diversity, he sought both to speed up such discussion and to condition the ground on which it would be conducted.

Shaping public attitudes, Embree understood, required persistence allied to patience, reliable information joined to a promising prospect. Much of the knowledge necessary for improved race relations he expected to come from social scientific research, and he knew it would take time for such findings to penetrate deeply into the public consciousness. Thus, his message was insistent, but his words were seldom scolding or shrill. Without minimizing the severity of the problems, Embree consistently affirmed the progress already made and empha- sized the need for large additional steps toward a healthier, more just and prosperous, less racially tense society. Confident about the future, sanguine about humans' ability to improve the conditions of life, he embodied the outlook of the Progressive movement, the bedrock of his own personality.[59]

In his use of the media, the Rosenwald president was playing to his own strengths. Though his journalistic career had been brief and long abandoned, he remained unusually adept at the written word, arguably more than any other foundation leader of his generation. Indeed, the opportunity to employ that gift, and thereby to influence public policy, had been a major attraction of the Rosenwald Fund in the first place. But beyond his personal ambition, Embree clearly saw his publications as part of the overall fund program. While negotiating with the publisher of *American Negroes,* for example, he offered to forgo all royalties so that those moneys could go into promotional expenses, thereby increasing the number of readers. He wrote such books, he explained, "not as a pro- fessional writer, but as a part of the general effort to create understanding and good relations among the various races."[60]

Embree's forte was the written word, but he was not slow to capital- ize on other forms of communication, moving some of the fund's re- sources from the print medium into other means of persuasion. Franklin Roosevelt's fireside chats had demonstrated the effectiveness of radio in molding opinion, and Embree had no trouble seeing its potential for advancing fund purposes. When the U.S. Office of Education planned a series of radio broadcasts on the contributions of blacks to American life, Rosenwald underwrote the production costs. Along with disseminating information, the programs aimed "to develop a sense of the unity of our democratic goals; to instill an appreciation of the values of democracy; and to inspire a determination to defend and enhance those values."[61] Eight half-hour broadcasts were envisioned, along with about eighteen fifteen-minute transcriptions to be made available to schools, colleges, radio stations, and interested groups. To extend the programs' influence even further, the radio scripts were to be revised for use as lesson units and study guides.

Embree was no less alert to the advantages offered by motion pictures. A longtime movie buff, he never missed a Marlene Dietrich film, and he often spent Saturday afternoons with his younger daughter at a Chicago theater viewing a double feature. He considered film "the fine arts of the present generation," and his keen interest in the medium led him to organize a Friday afternoon subscription series to enable friends to view reels from New York's Museum of Modern Art.[62] In light of his fascination with cinema, it is not surprising that he recognized its value as a weapon against racial intolerance.

Soon after U.S. entry into the Second World War, concern arose in some quarters about the morale of black troops and about the loyalty of African Americans in general.[63] Embree understood that such concerns were rooted in white ignorance about black citizens, resulting largely from negative stereotypes portrayed in the media. Learning that a film was to be made about New York's Stage Door Canteen for members of the armed forces, he wrote to producer Sol Lesser of RKO Pathé Studios to urge a realistic portrayal of the way the canteen actually functioned.

In that racially integrated setting, Embree emphasized, blacks and whites had "fraternized for months" with "no unpleasantness." Such instances of positive interracial contacts were seldom presented in films, and far from promoting racial understanding, too many movies portrayed African Americans as "comic characters, domestic workers, and night-club devotees. Only rarely does a picture have a Negro character in whom the race may take pride and who can be identified by white people as having the same ideals and ambitions and sorrows" as their own. Because movies could be such a powerful instrument for good, producers should do whatever they could to combat discrimination and intolerance by "sympathetic and understanding presentations of peoples of all races, creeds, and colors." Such a presentation in Stage Door Canteen would "go a long way toward improving Negro morale in this time of crisis." Embree was highly pleased when Lesser quickly replied that the film would address the points he had raised.[64]

A few months after his exchange with Lesser, Embree traveled to the West Coast, where his activities included a daylong visit to the Disney studios in Hollywood. Back in Chicago, he reported to his host that he had found the film capital "one of the really exciting spots in America," that he had been "swept off my feet by the enthusiasm and imagination that seemed to be bubbling everywhere." Film was likely to become "the great university of the future," he suggested, with a "student body" numbering not a few thousand but the "ninety millions of the movie audience."[65]

With such enthusiasm for the potential of film, Embree was highly receptive when in 1944 the American Film Center sought funding for a mass education project to produce five films stressing African American morale and development. Two of the films were planned for release in the 600 black commercial theaters, one for the white public, and two for mixed groups, with a total audience projected at 20 million. Quality would be assured, Embree believed, through the efforts of a nine-person advisory committee that would collect information and evaluate material. The request to Rosenwald, for $12,000 over two years, was to meet the expenses of gathering the material; the large sums needed for the actual production and distribution were to be met by the motion picture studios. The fund's executive committee speedily voted to honor this first request, with subsequent appropriations eventually bringing Rosenwald's support for the American Film Center to a total of $42,000.[66]

Embree's enthusiasm and Rosenwald's patronage notwithstanding, the project turned out to be a debacle. The expectations proved to be unrealistic; rivalries developed among the committee members; funds were misappropriated. Not one film was produced. Faced with problems that seemed insurmountable, the enterprise folded, and the unspent portion of the grant was returned to the fund. This embarrassing failure notwithstanding, Embree continued to believe in the educational value of film.[67]

In another use of the medium, Embree arranged for the production of a training film on race relations for municipal police departments. Intended to alleviate tensions between law enforcement agencies and the black community, the film was produced, with Rosenwald funding, under the auspices of the Chicago Commission on Human Relations. Apparently the first effort of its kind, the film was used initially for city police officials, then for experienced officers, and later in the basic training of all police recruits. Having been thus tested, the film was made available to law enforcement agencies across the country. Yet this project, too, proved disappointing, for few police departments expressed interest. Embree later admitted ruefully, but not accurately, that his record at Rosenwald in both movies and radio was "zero."[68]

In spite of limited success with film as an educational tool, Embree never lost faith in its potential. The same could well be said for a movement in which he invested considerable time and effort. As public statements and his correspondence with President Roosevelt attest, even before the United States entered the war Embree had begun to ponder the changes the conflict would bring to the world order. Not surprising for a person with his international experience and reformist bent, he gave thought to how the postwar world could be best shaped for a promising future. Such considerations led him into early membership and a key role in a new national organization.

* * *

The World Citizens Association (WCA) was founded in Chicago in 1939, with the initiative and funding of the International Harvester heiress Anita McCormick Blaine. Inspired by the ideas of Salvador de Madariaga, Blaine and her co-founders had in mind the creation of an American division of the World Federation. Though committed to no particular pattern of government, they sought to provide reliable information to the public, encourage thinking about a world community, and foster the objective study of international issues.[69] The emphases on the dispassionate analysis of issues and on efforts to mold opinion were completely in line with Embree's approach to improving race relations. His belief in the efficacy of such strategies and his concern about global issues produced an immediately positive response when he was asked to join.

Embree cannot properly be considered a founder of the WCA, for there had been a handful of organizational meetings before he was invited to become a member. Even so, he became the fifth member of the group's five-person executive committee, joining Blaine, Chicago attorney Edwin H. Cassels, international relations authority Quincy Wright, and Roger S. Greene. Greene and Embree had known each other since their mutual involvement with the Peking Union Medical College in the early 1920s, and Greene had been the Rockefeller vice president for Asia when Embree had held that rank in the New York office. The two men shared an interest in Pacific affairs, and Greene undoubtedly seconded the suggestion when Stanford University president Ray Lyman Wilbur proposed Embree for membership.[70]

The WCA was designed as a mass membership organization, with policy set by a central committee of fifteen and implementation resting with the small executive committee in Chicago. At his first executive committee meeting, Embree, along with association secretary Quincy Wright, was assigned to identify additional persons deemed suitable for the central committee. The two men set their sights high, aiming to add individuals who would bring both experience and luster to the association. By 1941, the central committee, which Wilbur chaired, included among its members Institute for Advanced Study director Frank Aydelotte, veteran diplomat Joseph E. Davies, *Survey* editor Paul U. Kellogg, and future Illinois governor and U.S. presidential nominee Adlai Stevenson. All of these men, save Davies, were long-standing Embree friends. As in other instances, Embree's personal connections across the country were of considerable benefit to the WCA.[71]

Beyond his extensive contacts, the WCA profited from other Embree strengths. He was involved in framing the organization's bylaws. He helped write the association's "Platform for World Citizenship." Not burdened like other executive committee members with a specific office, he was free to take on a variety of other duties. For several years, he seems to have served on every ad hoc committee created: nominating, conference planning, publication development, purpose and policy. Nor did his efforts stop with routine committee work. Worried about the organization's effectiveness a year after joining, he met informally with Wright and Wilbur to consider what could be done to bolster its efforts. Later in 1940, he held a follow-up conversation in California with Wilbur.[72] The outcome of these two extraordinary meetings is not mentioned in WCA records, but Embree apparently was not discouraged. A few months later, his energies were channeled into planning an international conference.

The conference, convened to consider what kind of world order should emerge after the war, was held over three days in the spring of 1941 at the Onwentsia Conference Center outside Chicago. Embree was centrally involved in drawing up the list of persons to be invited, many of them Europeans then finding refuge in the United States. His ability to assemble a diversely talented group and his propensity for attracting persons who could both contribute ideas and attract media attention were much in evidence. Among the invited participants were former German chancellor Heinrich Bruening, erstwhile Czechoslovakian president Edvard Beneš, philosopher Jacques Maritain, novelists Thomas Mann and André Maurois, concert pianist and biographer Eve Curie, historian Arnold Toynbee. Nor did the list of U.S. citizens lack leading lights: businessman Owen D. Young, Harvard president James B. Conant, poet Archibald MacLeish, theologian Reinhold Niebuhr, syndicated columnist Walter Lippmann. But those who attended were far from representative of the world's population. Only weeks before the conference, the almost-completed list of participants included eighteen from Europe, a like number invited from North America, and a dozen members of the central committee. No one from Africa was expected to come, and from China, India, and all of Latin America, only four were expected.[73]

In wartime, the paucity of representatives from countries representing well over half the world's population is not hard to understand, but the composition of the group undoubtedly affected its deliberations. The discussions and the operating assumptions of most of the participants were a source of frustration for Embree. At the heart of his dissatisfaction was the conferees' failure to consider seriously the claims of non-Western peoples. Writing to the association's executive director months after the conference, a scant five weeks before Pearl Harbor, he acknowledged that his insistence at Onwentsia on the rights and interests of such peoples had been "a disturbance." But, he explained, most of the members had been preoccupied with European settlements and the spread of Western industrialism. He, on the other hand, had been shocked by the tendency of almost everyone to think of the postwar world in terms of "(a) which European-American powers should dominate it, (b) how the European boundaries could be satisfactorily arranged, and (c) how the 'natural resources' of the rest of the world could be made available to European industrialism.... [I]f India, East Asia, the East Indies, Africa, and to some extent Latin America are to be considered chiefly from the standpoint of how a Western hegemony can most effectively keep them at peace while it exploits their natural resources," he warned, "we are not going to have a 'good' world."[74]

Such concerns were not new for Embree. A year earlier, he had lamented to a WCA colleague that British leaders seemed to be thinking
of a world "only slightly different from that we have known," whereas
he expected far more sweeping changes in the world's governments,
no matter the victor in Europe.[75] Looking toward a second conference,
Embree recognized that it probably would have to focus on political and
economic questions from a Western perspective. But if that did prove to
be the case, he urged that a third conference then be planned. That one,
in his judgment, should concentrate on the interests and demands of
peoples whose views had been inadequately considered at Onwentsia.

The second conference, to say nothing of a third, never took place.[76]
Restrictions on travel and the general wartime disruption of domestic
routines surely interfered. In addition, the organization itself seemed to
be running out of steam. Wilbur resigned as head of the executive committee. Key members were called away to other assignments—secretary
Wright to the State Department, director Henri Bonnet to the French
Committee on National Liberation. The intended mass membership
base never materialized. The original plan had envisioned the establishment of chapters across the country, but as it turned out, Chicago alone
spawned a local chapter, and even its relation to the central committee was somewhat tenuous. Though the association drew leadership, as
well as individual members, from both coasts, it remained essentially
a midwestern organization. Before it faded into obscurity, however, it
made one additional consequential effort. Embree's skills as a writer
were again called into play.[77]

As the war moved toward its conclusion, delegates of the soon-to-be-
victorious nations met in San Francisco to organize the United Nations
late in April 1945. The surrender of Germany soon followed, and the end
of war in the Pacific came into view. In these circumstances, leaders of
the WCA, eager to take advantage of the public attention focused on the
new international body, rushed into print a 160-page booklet, *World at
the Crossroads*. The text, drafted in May and June, was a collaborative
effort of executive committee members Blaine, Cassels, Embree, and
Wright, joined by *Des Moines Register and Tribune* editor W. W. Waymark. Wright wrote most of the prose, with Embree and Waymark con-
tributing sections, Blaine offering ideas (and financing), and Cassels

and Waymark responsible for editing. Embree's voice was most evident in an opening section titled "One World," where he tersely summarized the prehistoric emergence of diverse cultures and governments, the development of a sense of group exclusiveness leading to conflicts, and the contemporary growing awareness of interdependence among the world's peoples. Apparently calling up a childhood memory of the credo of the college founded by his grandfather, he ended with the affirmation from Acts 17:26: "God hath made of one blood all nations of men."[78]

Following the Wright-composed text, which was an almost breathless exhortation to greater global consciousness, came an array of pertinent documents. Included were various statements related to U.S. participation in the war: the Atlantic Charter of 1941, the 1942 Declaration by United Nations, press releases from Allied conferences at Moscow, Teheran, and Crimea. These were followed by documents pointing toward the peaceful resolution of international disagreements, most notably the Dumbarton Oaks proposals, the charter of the United Nations, and the statute of the International Court of Justice. Appended to these documents was the statement of the aims and organization of the World Citizens Association and the "Platform for World Citizenship" that Embree had helped to craft a half-dozen years earlier.

Like other promotional materials with which Embree was involved, *World at the Crossroads* was widely circulated. Copies were distributed to diplomats, public libraries, higher education institutions, newspaper editors, radio stations, labor groups, members of Congress, government agencies. Some 60,000 copies went to labor organizations alone. Lions and Rotary clubs received 27,000 copies, while over 29,000 were sent to dentists, presumably for placement in their waiting rooms. Though the original plan had been to print only 15,000 copies, by mid-1948 the total number in circulation was approaching 190,000.[79]

The booklet's broad distribution notwithstanding, its influence on public opinion is impossible to determine. Certainly, many citizens had an opportunity to see it. And it did attract some, though limited, attention from reviewers. Most of these, however, seem to have been taken more by the documents than by the text. Having those available in one place, several commented, was of considerable value.[80] Yet, having ready access to such documents did not sit well with all Americans. The perspectives represented by the WCA, like the creation of the United Nations itself, aroused opposition in conservative circles, and Embree's prominence in the organization did not escape their notice. His internationalist convictions, trumpeted in numerous pronouncements, served as the backdrop for another controversy in which he was soon embroiled.

* * *

As chair of the board of Roosevelt College, Embree was inevitably involved when the postwar Red scare shone a spotlight on that institution. The college's president was idealistic and unusually outspoken, and from the beginning the school had manifested a liberal, pro-labor character. Even before the college had reached its second birthday, its leftist orientation took on exaggerated form. In the student government elections of 1946, a well-organized group, whose membership constituted less than 4 percent of total enrollment, managed to win two-thirds of the positions. The election was a victory for the local chapter of American Youth for Democracy (AYD), a national body that had been labeled a Communist front organization by the U.S. Justice Department. Subsequently banned on many campuses, the group was nevertheless active and highly visible at Roosevelt. Thus, in circumstances foreshadowing the McCarthy era, the college came to be labeled Chicago's "little red schoolhouse."[81]

Angered by the 1946 electoral outcome, rival students mobilized opposition for the 1947 election, with the result that the AYD lost seventeen of its twenty-seven offices and was reduced to minority status. A relieved President Sparling regarded the episode as a useful exercise in political education, a judgment with which Embree almost certainly concurred. Red-baiters within the state were not satisfied, however, and the Illinois legislature established a commission to investigate "subversive" influences at Roosevelt and at the University of Chicago.

The investigation dragged on for a year. Defense of the college's reputation was an inescapable duty of the board chair, though in any event Embree was not inclined to dodge a conflict over important principles. By the time the issue was settled, however, the board chair had passed to former Secretary of the Interior Harold Ickes, and Embree had left Chicago for New York. In his new office in Rockefeller Center, he received word from President Sparling that the state commission had found "next to nothing" to incriminate either institution. Adding to Embree's pleasure at this news was the role played by Marshall Field's *Chicago Sun-Times*. The paper, Sparling reported, had been instrumental in "driving the commission to cover."[82]

Well before the "little red schoolhouse" episode had run its course, Embree embarked on another contentious project. In October 1946, he convened a group of some thirty race relations figures in Washington to consider how problems in that city might be ameliorated. From that meeting emerged the National Committee on Segregation in the Nation's Capital (NCSNC), a body organized to conduct a study of the racial situation, call attention to the glaring inequities, and seek to eliminate the national embarrassment they entailed. In taking this initiative, Embree, while obviously concerned about racial problems in Washington, was looking beyond the local situation. Attacking segregation in the District of Columbia, he believed, could establish precedents that might be applicable throughout the country. His hopes for progress were strengthened several weeks later when President Harry Truman announced the formation of a Committee on Civil Rights, which was mandated to address national issues of discrimination against minorities. Though the NCSNC was to focus only on Washington, it was clear that its efforts would dovetail with those of the president's committee.

The NCSNC's eighty-nine members were drawn primarily from the Northeast, Midwest, and West Coast, with a handful of representatives from the South. A number were much in the public eye: Minneapolis mayor Hubert Humphrey; former First Lady Eleanor Roosevelt; actress Helen Hayes; Ellen Borden Stevenson, the wife of Illinois governor Adlai Stevenson; Charles P. Taft and Illinois congresswoman Emily Taft Douglas of the Ohio political dynasty; eminent preacher Harry Emerson Fosdick; future Supreme Court justice Abe Fortas. Naturally, the committee included race relations stalwarts like Will Alexander, Charles H. Houston, Charles S. Johnson, Howard Odum, Channing Tobias, and Walter White. Four of its members were also named to the fifteen-person president's committee.[83]

In populating the NCSNC, Embree undoubtedly played a key role. Though the full extent of his activity cannot be documented, it is notable

that fully one-fourth of the members were associated with the Rosenwald Fund or one of the race relations organizations that Embree had
initiated. All members of the committee's eight-person research subcommittee, the active core of the organization, had such a relationship.[84]
Numerous other committee members were personal friends or professional acquaintances that the fund's president probably had a hand in
recruiting.

Embree's role did not end with the establishment of the blue-ribbon
panel. Sociologist Joseph D. Lohman, newly appointed to the fund's staff,
was detailed to serve as the NCSNC's executive director. The fund covered not only Lohman's salary, but that of an associate director, several
field-workers, and an office staff. The Washington office was established
with a budget for the first six months of $32,000, and though funding
from other sources was sought, Rosenwald provided most of the financing throughout the committee's life. Indeed, even after the fund had
closed its doors, the organization was sustained for many months by
Rosenwald money, which eventually totaled almost $100,000. The link-
age between the fund and the NCSNC was symbolized by the fact that
the committee established its headquarters in the Chicago mansion that
housed the Rosenwald offices.[85]

The NCSNC's report to the nation, written by Kennesaw M. Landis
II, was published late in 1948. *Segregation in Washington* ran to ninety-
one pages of text, statistical information, and photographs. It presented
in telling detail the extent of racial discrimination in housing, education, recreation, employment, health, and public accommodations. So-
ber in tone, the report probed beneath the surface of what was evident
to even the casual observer of the capital scene. It was featured on the
front page of the *Washington Post* and received commentary in national
magazines such as *Atlantic Monthly* and the *Nation*. One commentator,
calling attention to the hypocrisy of statements by government officials
and church leaders, noted that the report had "laid the groundwork for
change. The facts were already known," she wrote, "but here they are
presented graphically and completely."[86]

Laying the groundwork for change was precisely what Embree had
in mind. Well before the committee's report was completed, he had begun to prepare the public for its release. Taking advantage of the public-

ity accorded to the appointment of the president's committee the month before, Embree and Lohman in January 1947 published a *Survey Graphic* article highlighting the race-based problems in the federal district. The NCSNC's findings, when issued almost two years later, bore all the marks of a carefully researched, objective study. The Embree-Lohman piece, by contrast, was an instance of hard-hitting journalistic advocacy.

"If race prejudice and segregated citizenship are incompatible with democracy," the article began, "then Washington, the city is unworthy of Washington, the capital of the United States." The federal district had to be listed "among the most race-prejudiced and undemocratic large cities in the country. It is a grave political weakness as well, and compromises our cause in the court of world opinion."[87] From this arresting opening, the authors went on to summarize the disabilities that racial segregation visited on the capital's African American citizens in virtually every area of their lives: overcrowded and underfunded schools, employment discrimination, woefully inadequate housing, restricted access to medical services. Typical of Embree's style, a dramatic anecdote or illustration was used to drive home the poignancy of each issue.

Contrary to common expression, the article continued, Washington was not really a "Southern city," but a kind of "never-never land," situated between two border states and a southern state. It had its own unique history, but it was "bedeviled by [the] unreconciled regional, ethnic, and economic pressures" found elsewhere in the country. Some advances in race relations had been made during the Roosevelt administration, but progress was frequently stymied by the disproportionate influence of reactionary southern legislators, who dominated the city's domestic affairs, coupled with the continued disfranchisement of its residents. Efforts to perpetuate the patterns of segregation had led to numerous anomalies and frequent complications involving foreign diplomats and other officials of color. Because non-Western peoples would grow in international influence as they threw off Western domination, and because their struggle was linked to the growing militancy of African Americans, the authors concluded, "Washington is not yet the symbol we must make it."[88]

Later, when the formal report had been prepared and the full committee met to give its approval, Embree was unable to attend. Nevertheless, he was surely gratified that, even before the report was published, its research had been put to use. Immediate consequences included the elimination of discriminatory practices at Washington National Airport and the initiation of a campaign to integrate local restaurants. Some information found its way into litigation regarding restrictive housing covenants cases then pending before the U.S. Supreme Court. Most important was the researchers' discovery of laws, passed in 1872 and 1873, that guaranteed blacks equal rights in all the district's places of public accommodation. Never repealed, but secretly removed from the D.C. code around 1900, these laws were judged, after a contested journey that ended in the Supreme Court, to be still valid. Other findings were used by the President's Committee on Civil Rights, whose 1947 report, "To Secure These Rights," called special attention to the lamentable situation in the district, calling it "a graphic illustration of a failure of democracy." Pleased with that report, Embree, as the principal force behind the NCSNC, could feel confident that the organization had done valuable—indeed, essential—work. Anticipating further progress, he agreed to serve on a smaller group to continue monitoring the situation.[89]

* * *

As the NCSNC was moving toward its final report, Edwin Embree reached his sixty-fifth birthday. Yet many who knew him, deceived by his vibrant demeanor, thought him much younger. His energetic pursuit of full democracy and his organizational initiatives toward that end belied the chronological fact. Similarly, his speaking schedule, rate of publication, plans for international travel, and extensive civic activities gave no hint of slowing down. Nevertheless, the age of the philanthropy he had led for over two decades and the approaching end of its lifespan could not be denied. By early 1948, the Julius Rosenwald Fund was but a few months away from closing its doors.

EIGHT

CELEBRATIONS, PROCLAMATIONS, TRIBUTES

In accordance with the founder's specification, the Rosenwald Fund was required to expend all its assets and go out of business no later than 1957, twenty-five years after Julius Rosenwald's death. The great damage done to those assets by the Depression, however, was never fully repaired. Shares worth almost $200 early in 1929, after falling to under $10 in 1932, still commanded only $72 in 1936. Consequently, a decade after the crash, the anticipated annual income from stock dividends and small savings accounts was no more than $150,000.[1] A few years later, when Sears stock split four-for-one, each share carried a price slightly above $42, but by then much of the stock had already been sold to meet the fund's commitments and, in light of postwar inflation, the split was of limited benefit. In light of the dwindling resources, plans for the fund's dissolution were far advanced long before the 1957 deadline.[2]

As early as the spring of 1940, the board had begun to consider the fund's closing, difficult discussions motivated in part by uncertainties stemming from the outbreak of war in Europe. A committee of four, consisting of Embree and three other trustees, was appointed to ponder the matter and report to the full board at the next meeting. When the committee reported in the fall, three members favored a terminal date for the fund, with Embree alone arguing against a specific time. With only eleven of the thirteen trustees present, a vote of 7–4 carried a resolution that the fund "declare its intention to come to an end on or about December 31, 1945, and that its further actions be guided by this intention."[3]

Yet, during the next thirty months, a combination of circumstances —rising black-white tensions, the clarity of purpose represented by the

Division of Race Relations, Embree's persuasiveness, and, perhaps, the perspectives of new board members—caused most trustees to change their minds. In April 1943, the 1940 resolution was rescinded, with only the chair of the board, Lessing Rosenwald, dissenting. As deliberations continued, the board, after reviewing a comprehensive financial plan and resolutions prepared by Embree, concluded that the fund should disburse all its assets and close "not earlier than June 30, 1947, and not later than June 30, 1949."[4] In fact, a time halfway between those two dates— June 30, 1948—was later set for the fund's demise. In the meantime, the remaining resources were concentrated on the fellowship program and race relations.

Even with a time frame for the fund's termination established and with capital assets of no more than $1.4 million, Embree was still able to support promising causes. Acting within the broad authority accorded to the executive committee, he continued to propose and win approval of significant grants. Late 1943, for example, saw $25,000 awarded to the fledgling United Negro College Fund (UNCF). Similarly, when the Southern Regional Council (SRC) was organized in 1944, Rosenwald moneys supported its first-year operation with a $10,000 grant, and additional appropriations were approved later. The fund's shrinking resources restricted, but did not eliminate, Embree's initiatives. Even so, the philanthropy moved inexorably toward its close.[5]

As the end came into sight, the board at its last working meetings appropriated its remaining funds. The UNCF was given a final grant of $15,000, and the Urban League's Department of Industrial Relations received the last of several awards of $7,500. Continuing a pattern begun several years earlier, an appropriation of $7,500 was made for the NAACP's legal defense efforts. Four southern universities long favored by the fund—Atlanta, Fisk, Dillard, and North Carolina—each received $25,000. Will Alexander was granted $35,000 for unspecified "race relations work in the South." Of the other six expenditures authorized at this time, all involved the leadership of Embree, Charles S. Johnson, or both. The SRC, whose executive committee Johnson had chaired, was given a two-year grant of $50,000. The Johnson-edited *Monthly Summary of Events and Trends in Race Relations,* which was totally dependent on Rosenwald funding from the outset, was granted $20,000 for operating costs. Johnson had just been named president of Fisk University, and the office of the president received $15,000 for "transitional expenses." Chicago's Roosevelt College, the board of which Embree had led since the college's inception, benefited from $50,000 for buildings and working capital. The American Council on Race Relations, which owed its existence to Embree, Johnson, and Marshall Field, received the largest appropriation of all, $75,000, to be expended over two years. Finally, the National Committee on Segregation in the Nation's Capital, whose creation Embree had spearheaded, received financial support amounting to $40,000, with a promise of more if needed.[6] Each of these organizations had been heavily subsidized, if not sponsored outright, by the fund, and the board undoubtedly deemed it appropriate that the last resources go to them. Apparently, no question of any conflict of interest arose, even though the beneficiaries were organizations headed by trustees Alexander and Johnson.

With its assets virtually depleted, the fund might well have faded quietly into history. But that was not Embree's way. Clear as ever about the value of publicity, he used the impending closure as an opportunity to showcase the fund's accomplishments and to trumpet the need for further progress. A day of celebration was scheduled in Chicago. Robert C. Weaver, Embree's friend and associate on the Rosenwald fellowship committee, the Mayor's Commission on Human Relations, and the American Council on Race Relations, led the committee planning the occasion. But the hand of the fund's president was evident throughout, for the activities reflected Embree's unshakeable optimism, his love of entertaining, and, above all, his sense of style.

Space for the festivities was secured at Chicago's Stevens Hotel, and hundreds were invited to participate: leaders of nonprofit organizations, all former Rosenwald fellows, public officials, heads of agencies that had benefited from fund support, current and former trustees, race relations figures, representatives of other philanthropies, university executives. Timed to coincide with the board's final—largely perfunctory—meeting, the gala occasion was held on May 28, 1948. When the event got under way, some 600 people filled the hotel ballroom.[7]

The celebration began with a pair of afternoon seminars, keynoted by renowned scholar-activist W. E. B. DuBois and the Swedish socioeconomist Gunnar Myrdal. DuBois's association with Embree and the fund was of long standing. The Rosenwald fellowship received in 1931 and renewed in 1933 and 1934 had enabled DuBois to produce what he considered his most important scholarly work, *Black Reconstruction.* Over the years, DuBois and Embree had corresponded from time to time, and the fund's president held the prolific writer in highest esteem. For his part, DuBois had considerable respect for Embree.[8] Myrdal, whose monumental *An American Dilemma* had appeared just four years earlier, crossed the Atlantic specifically for the occasion. As the author of the most comprehensive work on the subject, he, like DuBois, was a natural choice to offer thoughts on U.S. race relations. Moreover, he had a special reason to appreciate the fund's work; of the twenty-four black social scientists who contributed to his massive study, twenty-one had prepared themselves through graduate study or other research projects with Rosenwald fellowships.[9]

Prominent in the activities were other fellowship recipients, representatives of America's intelligentsia of color. The printed program for the day was designed by painter Jacob Lawrence. The writer Arna Bontemps and Haverford College sociologist Ira DeA. Reid chaired the seminar sessions. In the evening, author Langston Hughes and literary critic Sterling A. Brown presented brief humorous pieces. Additional entertainment was provided by vocalist Pauline Phelps and concert pianist Natalie Hinderas, whose conspicuous talent had won her admission as a special student to Oberlin Conservatory at age eight. The dancer Pearl Primus also gave a stunning performance. Turned down earlier for a fellowship, she now received renewed attention. After reconsideration by the fellowship selection committee a few days later, she received the last of the Rosenwald awards.[10]

The festivities concluded with an elaborate dinner in the hotel ballroom. As the evening reached its high point, Embree received appropriate tribute. Board chair Lessing Rosenwald presented him with a gold watch and expressed thanks "from the sons and daughters of Julius Rosenwald as a token of their respect and appreciation for his services as president of the Julius Rosenwald Fund for twenty years during which time he charted its course with ability, resourcefulness and dignity, and brought [it] to its conclusion wholly within the spirit and purpose of the founder." The testimonial of the former Rosenwald fellows, offered by Charles S. Johnson and probably written by him, was more laudatory and more personal:

> We salute a social statesman of rich wisdom, a student and administrator of rare insight and courageous honesty, a generator of moving ideas, a writer of force and grace, an inspirator [sic] of youth, a prophet of the democratic ideal and practitioner of the art of democratic living, a gentleman of charm, a civilized American. At this moment of history, marked by this day's close of his brilliant administration of the Julius Rosenwald Fund, we offer our tribute of gratitude, respect and affection.

Available records do not indicate, but it would be surprising if such testimony was not followed by a prolonged standing ovation.

The final words were left for the fund's president. Embree was both reflective and upbeat. America had made magnificent achievements in wealth, health, and education, he declared, far more than the nation's forefathers could have imagined. But such triumphs notwithstanding, the country had still failed to reach "the one goal we have talked about most: free and equal opportunity for all the people." He raised this point not in cynicism, he said, but in a spirit of rejoicing at the gains already made and in the belief that the "same combination of brains, courage, and hard work" that underlay earlier successes would produce "the fullness of democracy which more than anything else is the Promise of America." For thirty-one years, the Julius Rosenwald Fund had been involved in that march toward full democracy. There had been discouragements and many failures, he acknowledged, but "[w]e view progress by the Negro tenth of the American people and general progress toward true democracy greater even than our optimistic founder may have dreamed." The torch the fund had carried for a generation was now passed to others, with the rallying cry of faith that "'America is Promises.' Let the promises already fulfilled," he exhorted, "stir our faith and our efforts to realize the greatest of our promises: opportunities rich and equal for all the people."

The event received adequate but not extensive coverage in the Chicago press, and apparently attracted little notice outside the Midwest. Yet it did receive acknowledgment from the president of the NAACP, who offered copious praise of the fund. Relations between the nation's oldest civil rights organization and the Rosenwald Fund had not always been warm in the Embree years, but Walter White's words in his syndicated column were appreciative and gracious. The closing of the fund "would leave a void in the American scene which it will be hard to fill." The $22 million it had expended had produced "an enormous enrichment of American life, and in particular on the raising of education, health and civil rights standards for American Negroes." Like all institutions run by mortals, the fund had made mistakes, but it had been wise enough to abandon initiatives when they proved untenable. Its most lasting contribution, he suggested, might prove to be the fellowships that had been awarded to talented blacks and white southerners to equip them to attack the various problems of their region. "The entire United States," White declared, "owes a greater debt to Edwin Embree, President of the Julius Rosenwald Fund, and Dr. Will Alexander, Vice President, than it will ever be able to repay."[11]

* * *

At the time of the fund's final celebration, Embree had over thirty years' experience in foundation work, more than virtually all his counterparts in other philanthropies. Yet, in spite of his seniority and the impressive achievements to his credit, he did not quite qualify for the mantle of elder statesman. His impatience with injustice, the boldness of his pronouncements, his imaginative use of funds, and his distance from the Manhattan center of foundation activity—all had served to separate him from his more conventional colleagues. His maverick streak, like his deep engagement in the controversial field of race relations, set him apart. Even so, when he chose to state his views on the philanthropic enterprise, he was not easy to ignore. That was particularly true when those views, expressed with his customary verve, appeared in one of the country's most influential magazines.

In the spring of 1949, *Harper's Magazine* carried one of Embree's most widely read articles. "Timid Billions: Are the Foundations Doing Their Job?" presented his thinking about the role of organized philanthropy, distilled from his work in three sections of the United States and dozens of countries on four continents.[12] The article began with a litany of foundation accomplishments early in the century: the Rockefeller victories against hookworm, malaria, and yellow fever; the Carnegie library program; the upgrading of higher education in the Midwest through massive funding of the University of Chicago; the development of musical and artistic talents through the Juilliard and Guggenheim foundations. But these impressive examples were essentially a foil, a backdrop for Embree's fundamental point—that foundations, no longer attacking major social problems, had lapsed into conventionality and conservatism. Almost half of every philanthropic dollar was devoted to medicine and public health, he reported, while education claimed a third, and most of the rest went to local agencies and natural scientific research. Once areas of critical need, these endeavors were now adequately supported by government and private individuals, and no longer required foundation subsidies. But philanthropic trusts, instead of moving on to attack new societal challenges, had fallen into "the great foundation sin, . . . sprinkling of little grants over a multiplicity of causes and institutions." Such a piecemeal approach inevitably fell far short of "that social pioneering that is the essential business of foundations."[13] Philanthropies' failure to conquer new territory, Embree suggested, was almost built into their organizational structure. Large foundations had become overly compartmentalized, making it difficult for creative projects that cut across categories to get a fair hearing. Long-serving foundation officers tended to become comfortable in their customary bailiwicks and hesitant to consider risky ventures. Similar hesitancy commonly characterized trustees who, concerned to perpetuate their organizations, hoarded capital in the name of fiscal prudence and approved only those projects that seemed "sound investments." That behavioral pattern could be traced to the homogeneity of foundation boards, composed largely of bankers, lawyers, and friends of the founders, people of substantial standing and conservative leaning. Such boards routinely lacked active scholars and scientists, representatives of labor, and, unlike the Rosenwald Fund, persons of color. Yet, while lamenting their meek traditionalism, Embree rejected the criticism that such boards sought to use their foundations' power to buttress the status quo and resist changes, just as he rejected the "recent diatribes of the *Chicago Tribune*" that foundations fostered "the red menace." The justified criticism was not that foundations are "vicious, but that they [are] inert."[14]

Embree went on to call attention to the problem of family trusts established to evade taxes, and to the need for the public disclosure of assets and expenditures by all philanthropies. But he devoted the entire latter half of the article to a listing of fields no longer needing foundation support and those that should have it. In the former category were research in the physical sciences, medicine and public health, social agencies and local charities, schools and colleges not engaged in experimentation and innovation. Beyond those fields, however, there were urgent needs, calling for "the very kind of initiative and enterprise that foundations are created to give." Embree suggested a half-dozen fields in need of "foundation stimulus" and offered a fairly detailed justification for each: improved preparation for teachers, "heroic development" of human studies, human relations, the arts, a great university in the South, and world peace and prosperity. Identified in the article as separate fields for foundation attention, in Embree's mind they converged, even overlapped. Accomplishment in one area would inevitably have positive effects on the others, but, he believed, significant progress depended heavily on philanthropic leadership. Social advances were always the work of a creative few, and foundations he considered "especially fitted to be the creative minority to spur society on."[15]

"Timid Billions," with its mixture of praise and criticism, thoughtful analysis and rousing challenge, undoubtedly evoked varied responses from foundation executives. Few in the philanthropic community would have been greatly surprised, however, for Embree had been making similarly provocative statements for many years. But for typical *Harper's* readers, the informed public to whom the piece was primarily addressed, the piece was an eye-opener. Most probably had not previously encountered such a comprehensive, fact-filled, vividly written treatment of the subject. Scores of responses were sent, not only to the magazine but to the writer himself.[16] These comments were overwhelmingly favorable, and even those from the world of philanthropy found elements to commend.

Some of the views in Embree's last significant article reflected his experience at the Rockefeller Foundation. He had learned there that organized giving needed to set its sights high, to address major social concerns. He had taken to heart the insistence of Frederick Gates that truly successful philanthropy had to be "wholesale," not "retail," directed at the causes of distress rather than the symptoms. He was equally clear on the need for grants to be limited in time, sufficient to bring a project to a conclusion or to mount a fruitful demonstration, but not enough to create dependence on the part of the recipient.[17] He knew that, at their best, foundation executives were part of the country's intellectual elite. Abe Flexner had counseled him to follow a regimen of steady reading and disciplined learning, lest administrative routine dull his imagination and blunt his creativity. He had taken that advice to heart, had followed it conscientiously in his personal behavior, and had encouraged such behavior in his Rosenwald colleagues.

Yet Embree's thinking went well beyond what he had learned at Rockefeller. He had a deep-rooted understanding of the unique advantages of foundations and of their potential for effecting societal change. In a candid letter a decade and a half earlier, he had prefigured, and stated even more forthrightly, the perspective of "Timid Billions." A philanthropic trust was "in a remarkably strong and free position," he declared, not needing to shape programs to elicit gifts from individuals or public agencies, not responsible "for the doing of any particular type of thing." So long as it did not corrupt morals or overtly subvert the government, it was free to do whatever it thought best to advance human well-being. Such freedom and ample resources should lead foundations to "search out the really fundamental possibilities of human improvement, however radical, even bizarre, these might seem to the present generation." But, he lamented, an "obsession for superficial efficiency," the wish for immediate evidence of improvement, and the tendency to supervise recipients too closely had caused most foundations to engage in "trifling matters" rather than the kind of fundamental projects that might transform human history. Even so, if some fortunate coincidence brought together a group of trustees "willing to forego the pleasures of current mediocrity in order to attempt great social ventures," with one or more "resourceful, imaginative, and daring" officers, a foundation might "again do something spectacular and of incalculable benefit to mankind."[18]

Such an aspiration, articulated midway in his career, goes far to explain Embree's actions at the Rosenwald Fund. He never lost the hope of being that "resourceful, imaginative, and daring" executive who would do something spectacular. When he undertook to make his mark in the tangled thicket of race relations, he moved into the most daunting area of American life, where significant change was most sorely needed and most difficult to achieve. There, his imagination served him well. He was able to envision how financing the construction of an airstrip could advance the standing of African American men. He could see how underwriting the expansion of library services in the South could help to reduce discrimination. With no background in organized labor and affiliated with no religious body, he came to regard labor unions and church groups as allies in the fight against Jim Crow. He could recognize that the country's most impoverished region would prosper only with vast improvement in education, and though his chief concern was for the black population, reform would be severely limited unless whites were included in the effort. Embree had imagination in full measure; in an intellectual sense, he was resourceful. The same could not be said of him in a financial sense.

The Depression, which began in Embree's second year at Rosenwald, vastly reduced the financial resources he had planned to exploit. Had the fund's portfolio been diversified, instead of consisting entirely of Sears stock, the result might have been less calamitous. But had the stock retained all its value—or even if the fund's assets had rivaled those of Rockefeller and Carnegie—it is doubtful that, in the complicated area of race relations, Embree could have achieved "something spectacular and of incalculable benefit." The problems were too large, too monumental, too hard for ready resolution through large infusions of capital, no matter how wisely administered.

Black-white relations were not unlike an iceberg, a forbidding block of discriminatory practices and racist laws for all to see, supported beneath the surface by a far larger mass of ignorance, incomprehension, hostility, anger, and fear. Embree's task, as he saw it through the thirties and beyond, was to work at both levels. The deeper problems he attacked through a broadly conceived program of education and reform, aimed at a whole generation of white southern moderates, black leaders, municipal police, civic officials, and the general public. At the same time, he chipped away at the surface, using Rosenwald grants when possible to break down racist practices and expand opportunity for discrimination's sufferers, emphasizing all the while that racism worked to the disadvantage of all Americans.

Embree has been criticized for working within the strictures of southern segregation for most of his career. Such criticism, though not altogether misplaced, underestimates the depth and durability of racist sentiment. It gives far too little weight to the likely consequences had Embree tried to work outside those constraints, had he overtly opposed elected officials and the discriminatory laws they upheld. Had he done so, many schools would not have been built, access to library materials would not have improved, efforts to reform teacher education would have been stymied, forbiddingly long walks to consolidated schools would have discouraged more children from continuing, even the limited dialogue across racial lines would have been reduced. The chief losers in that circumstance would have been black communities, the chief victims an entire generation denied increased, though still far from equal, opportunity. Nor does such criticism take adequately into account the limited, but by no means insignificant, advances such as the creation of Dillard University, a development highly unlikely without the support of at least a portion of New Orleans' power structure. Embree did not hesitate to confront officials of that city on racial matters, most notably in regard to inequitable school funding. But, unlike his critics, he preferred a strategy of accomplishment to a tactic of non-accommodation unlikely to be productive. Given a choice between Embree's approach and that espoused by his detractors, it is improbable that many southern blacks at the time would have sided with the latter.

Moreover, such criticism fails to recognize Embree's considerable daring in racial matters, as in foundation policy. It was unprecedented in the thirties for a white man to write books portraying sympathetically America's minorities. It was daring over and over to criticize the South, in the South, for its inattention to higher education. It was daring repeatedly to assail Christian hypocrisy on race, and to pronounce the impending end of Western domination of the world. It took courage to defend and befriend Japanese Americans when anti-Japanese feeling across the country was at its height. A bold spirit underlay the decision to allocate funds for the Tuskegee airfield, making it possible for a thousand

African American men to make a long stride toward equality. Above all, it was daring, when bereft of significant financial resources, to move a foundation into a new mode of operation. By adopting the role of advocate, seeking to mold opinion by direct action, the fund under Embree's leadership became truly a pioneer. And to pioneer is to dare, to move beyond comfortable surroundings into uncharted territory.

* * *

The time of daring, the urge to break new ground is, for most people, long over by the time age sixty-five is reached. The life expectancy for American males in the mid-twentieth century did not extend much beyond that age and, particularly for financially secure professionals, attaining it typically signaled retirement. That was not the case with Edwin Embree. When the Rosenwald Fund closed, he could easily have withdrawn from active life without financial worries. His compensation had been ample over the years, the Rosenwald pension plan had been generous, and the Sears stock split in 1946 had substantially increased his wealth. Yet he remained physically and intellectually vigorous, energetic in his movements and creative in his thinking. Still well-connected, he continued to enjoy his associations with persons of national prominence. Never doubting that he still had much to contribute, he planned to continue working for another four or five years before retiring to Hawaii. The question was: What kind of position would enable him to continue to put his talents to good use?[19]

Some of Embree's closest friends believed that, by knowledge and experience, he was well suited for a university presidency.[20] Such an appointment would have been appropriate, for he was well acquainted with higher education, and there was a well-established pattern of foundation executives moving to and from university leadership. Embree had been considered for such posts, but had never pursued them. University presidencies he once described as "exceedingly unsatisfying jobs," involving the headaches of fund-raising, "grumbles and complaints of faculty, and the insurrections and tribulations of the students." Such posts required "a special temperament and a special set of abilities," and his own personality he thought better suited for foundation work.[21] Even so, the idea of a presidency had sometimes tempted him and, he confided to a southern newspaper editor, if a "really significant post" in the South or Southwest became open, it would interest him "a great deal."[22]

There were other options to be considered. His journalistic career had been brief and more than thirty years past, but editing a national magazine had not lost its appeal. One of his biggest disappointments at Rosenwald had come with the board's decision not to acquire *American Mercury,* and he still remembered his conversations with Ellery Sedgwick about assuming the editorship of the *Atlantic.* Yet such an opportunity was not now in the offing. Another possibility involved what would become the National Science Foundation. As Congress was in the process of creating that agency, Embree confided to his son that he was "being flirted with" regarding the position of founding director. Yet he expected the appointment to go to a chemist or physicist, preference being given to a natural scientist, rather than to someone with a social sciences background like himself.[23]

If he chose to remain in Chicago, political involvement might provide another avenue for useful work. After all, he had helped to craft national legislation, managed for a time the U.S. senatorial campaign of Paul Douglas, and been a prominent figure in the Independent Voters of Illinois and Americans for Democratic Action. His suitability for public office—specifically, the school board—had been publicized by the Chicago press, and such posts often served as a springboard to higher positions. He had a number of highly influential friends—most notably, Eleanor Roosevelt, Adlai Stevenson, Marshall Field, Paul Douglas— who could be expected to support him, and his long experience with the media would be helpful. In spite of these advantages, he never sought elective office. Perhaps his outspokenness and the controversy it generated, together with his reluctance to monitor his speech or downplay his convictions, served to rule out such an effort.

Perhaps the role for which Embree was best suited at that stage of life was international civil servant. His travels and studies had given him a breadth of perspective few could match. His acquaintance with a number of the world's peoples, his appreciation for varied cultures, his commitment to the advancement of developing nations would have served him well. There seems to have been some consideration of a post with the United Nations Educational, Scientific and Cultural Organization, but that did not materialize. He accepted instead a position that would draw on those same qualities, while allowing him to remain in philanthropic work in exciting new circumstances.[24]

His new position involved the Liberia Company, an investment firm created to develop and process forest products in that West African state. As a spin-off of the enterprise, the company established a foundation to spur improvements in the country's education and health. Embree, with his long-standing interest in Africa's oldest republic, was a natural choice to head the new philanthropy. His vision extended much further, however, and from the outset he urged the firm to think more boldly, to name the new philanthropy the "Africa Foundation," to signal an intention to invest more widely on the continent. Embree's view prevailed, for a month later the company did charter the separate Africa Foundation. Not surprisingly, the presidency of this second foundation was added to his portfolio.[25]

Embree was attracted to this new work for its own sake, but the position had an additional appeal—association with a man of influence. The originator of the enterprise was Edward R. Stettinius Jr. When informing friends and associates of his new position, Embree was careful to point out the central role in the firm of this former chair of U.S. Steel and former U.S. secretary of state. In the spring of 1948, he traveled with Stettinius and other company officials for an exploratory visit to Liberia.[26]

This was Embree's first trip to Africa but, inveterate traveler that he was, he could well expect there would be others. He had high hopes for the venture, seeing in it the possibility of "a magnificent program for the development of the African people."[27] Yet this was not to be, for financing difficulties, complicated by the serious illness of Stettinius, soon arose. Stettinius's death in 1949, still short of his fiftieth birthday, deprived the company of the prominent figure who had been expected to attract investors. Consequently, the two foundations, which were to be funded by 10 percent of the company stock and anticipated philanthropic contributions, never became firmly established. Embree had been concerned about adequate financing from the outset but, encouraged by assurances from the company's principals, had begun recruiting professional staff.[28] Soon recognizing the company's dimming prospects, however, he resigned from his twin presidencies in June 1949. While agreeing to help the foundations on a voluntary basis, he moved to establish himself as a professional consultant, "a kind of Elder Statesman, Incorporated," as he described the role.[29]

One of Embree's first clients was the John Hay Whitney Foundation, which allowed him to work with an endowment of $10 million, a portion of the foundation's assets. One of his major goals there was to create a program of what he called "opportunity fellowships." These were to be quite similar to the Rosenwald fellowship program, but extended to include not only African Americans, but Native Americans, Asian Americans, Hispanics, residents of U.S. territories, and even the children of recent immigrants. The grants were to be available to young persons of any group who had not had "an equal go at the Opportunities that are America."[30] Having accomplished this goal, he hoped then to move the foundation toward helping to improve teacher education.

Strengthening the preparation of teachers had long been a major interest. Relocation to New York in 1948 made it easier to work with the Sarah Lawrence staff in planning a year of graduate work for prospective teachers. At the same time, Embree participated in a project to reorganize the School of Education of New York University. Also at NYU, he became an informal advisor to the head of that institution's young Center for Human Relations Studies. Late in 1949, he initiated efforts to assemble a group to brainstorm on ways to improve teacher education. He drafted (but never published) for *Harper's Magazine* an article that he hoped might "be something of a Bible in the field."[31]

In further pursuit of that interest, Embree wrote to the Connecticut commissioner of education, F. E. Engleman, and Governor Chester Bowles, offering to help in that state's study of teacher education. In an act of audacity unusual even for him, Embree volunteered his services as a consultant, suggesting that his long experience in education and his national connections could be useful. Following up on these contacts, he corresponded with *Saturday Review* editor Norman Cousins, chair of the study commission, setting forth several "hypotheses" that needed to be examined. How this gratuitous advice, coming from someone who had resided outside the state for over thirty years, was received by the commission is not clear. Embree did talk with Engleman some six months after the initial contact, but no notable relationship developed.[32]Embree also continued his writing, publishing another book on race relations soon after returning from Africa. His original intention had been to produce a serious work, elaborating the content of the Earl Lectures he had given some months earlier at the Pacific School of Religion. Contacts with several publishing houses convinced him, however, that the market he had in mind had already been captured by Ruth Benedict and Gene Weltfish's *Races of Mankind*. He then decided to issue an inexpensive pamphlet for children, an even younger audience than he had targeted in *Indians of the Americas*.

Peoples of the Earth was essentially an attempt to explain differences among human groups and to encourage appreciation for cultural diversity. Cast as a series of letters from a kindly uncle to a young niece and nephew, the work traced the rise of civilizations from Egypt to the modern West, pointing out the contributions made by various peoples over several millennia. Though explaining the ascendancy of the West, the text pointed out that all civilizations have declined at some point, and that Western civilization, including the United States, was likely to follow a similar pattern. Indicative of this trend was the rapid industrialization of nonwhite nations, with a consequent increase in power and thirst for independence, signaling the opening of a new era. Recognition of this new era and understanding the long sweep of human history, the book suggested, should lead to declining cultural arrogance on the part of white people, more direct efforts to eliminate racial and ethnic discrimination, and more deliberate movement toward genuine democracy within the United States and around the world. With its seventy-five pages abundantly illustrated with drawings and over a dozen photographs, the pamphlet was well designed to appeal to a youthful readership.[33]

The book's message, however, aroused opposition. As the McCarthy era was getting under way, parents in a Chicago school district raised objections to the pamphlet, claiming it was Communist-inspired. The fund itself had earlier been called into question, with the congressional Reeves Committee charging it had been infiltrated by Reds. In 1952, a school principal in Rye, New York, ordered the book removed from an exhibit for National Brotherhood Week in the teachers lounge. As the principal's action became public, the district's superintendent and board supported him and banned the book from the district's schools. Two years after his death, Embree would be charged with "following a Communist line" and being associated with a dozen organizations listed by the House Un-American Activities Committee. Four years later, the banning of *Peoples of the Earth* again became a public issue in a local school board election. (In the meantime, the book reportedly was endorsed by University of Pennsylvania president Milton Eisenhower, brother of Dwight D. Eisenhower, the occupant of the White House.) The matter was laid to rest only when Embree's lawyer brother, Will, issued a statement outlining Embree's career, affirming his loyalty and patriotism, and pointing out that none of the named organizations was in fact subversive.[34]

* * *

With his involvement in controversies, his publications and civic activities, Embree was seldom far from the public eye, even after the fund closed its doors. In 1948, Howard and Fisk universities, both of which had been major beneficiaries of Rosenwald largesse, awarded him honorary degrees, personal recognition that he could not have accepted during the fund's lifetime.[35] That same year, he agreed to serve on the national council of the United Negro College Fund.[36] The publication in early 1949 of *Investment in People,* a history of the Rosenwald Fund co-authored with his research associate Julia Waxman, was the occasion for a luncheon in Embree's honor at New York's Pierre Hotel. Sponsored by the Bureau for Intercultural Education, the event attracted some sixty scholars, journalists, race relations authorities, and foundation representatives.[37] In the spring, at a black-tie dinner at the Waldorf-Astoria to honor Ralph Bunche for his mediation of an armistice between Israel and its Arab neighbors, Embree was one of several people selected to pay tribute to the former Rosenwald fellow and, a few months later, recipient of the Nobel Peace Prize.[38]

Such honorific occasions were not all that claimed Embree's attention. He continued his connections with higher education, primarily through new memberships on college boards. In 1948, Charles S. Johnson, his friend of more than twenty years, asked Embree to head the committee planning the four-day ceremony to inaugurate Johnson as president of Fisk University. As chair of the committee, Embree's duties included personally inviting the most distinguished guests, arranging for the presentation of several scholarly addresses, and then editing the papers for subsequent publication in a commemorative volume.[39] The list of invited guests was imposing: Eleanor Roosevelt, John D. Rockefeller Jr., U.S. Supreme Court justice Hugo Black, W. E. B. DuBois, Columbia University president Dwight Eisenhower, Marian Anderson, former Georgia governor Ellis Arnall. Participating in the program were sociologist Howard Odum, philanthropist Marshall Field, newspaper editor Mark Ethridge, philanthropy head and former Tuskegee principal Frederick Patterson—all race relations warhorses associated with the Rosenwald Fund. Honorary degrees were awarded to civil rights lawyer Charles H. Houston, industrial chemist Percy L. Julian, University of Chicago anthropologist Robert Redfield, and Swedish scholar Gunnar Myrdal, all of whom were linked to Johnson and Embree.[40] As in other situations, Embree's broad range of acquaintances in the scholarly, business, and foundation worlds enabled him to assemble an impressive array of dignitaries, speakers, and panelists.

During the occasion, Embree was elected to the Fisk board, a position he had declined more than twenty years earlier when at Rockefeller.[41] A similar avoidance of a conflict of interest had kept him off the board during the Rosenwald years, but with the fund's demise only weeks away, he agreed to accept the position.[42] His decision reflected his deep respect and friendship for the institution's new president, but it was perhaps quickened by the prospect of sharing membership with friends already on the board: longtime colleague Beardsley Ruml, Lessing Rosenwald, Fisk alumnus and former Rosenwald fellow John Hope Franklin. And he was undoubtedly gratified to be associated with the highly accomplished members of the university's art committee, which included artist Georgia O'Keeffe, painters and former Rosenwald fellows Jacob Lawrence and Aaron Douglas, writer-photographer Carl Van Vechten, and the New York City Ballet's Lincoln Kirstein.[43] His membership on the Fisk board, however, would last less than three years.

Another college board membership would be even briefer. In mid-1949, Wilbur K. Jordan, the president of Radcliffe College and an Embree friend from the Chicago days, invited him to become a trustee of that institution. With his long-standing interest in the education of women and probably attracted by the connection with Harvard, Embree readily agreed to serve. He was soon engaged in planning, with President Jordan and historian Arthur Schlesinger Sr., a large-scale study of the special higher education needs of women.[44] The project was ambitious and potentially important, but it never moved beyond the planning stage.

Embree's trusteeships provided regular occasions for travel, and other opportunities also put him on the road. At the end of 1949, he and Kate were in Puerto Rico, where they spent a week at the San Juan home of former Rosenwald associate Fred Wale and his wife. Early in January 1950, they renewed ties with Jaime Benitez, the chancellor of the University of Puerto Rico. The beginning of February found them in Tempe, Arizona, visiting an old friend. In the middle of the month, Embree journeyed to Chicago for a meeting of the Fisk board. The weekend of February 17–19 brought them to Princeton, New Jersey, for a conference. Daughter Edwina and her sociologist husband, Edward Devereux, then lived in the town, and Embree and Kate had a good family visit. On Monday, he was back at his midtown Manhattan office.[45]

On Tuesday, February 21, Embree had a typical workday. He spent the morning at his desk at the John Hay Whitney Foundation in the North Building of Rockefeller Center. At noon, he attended a luncheon sponsored by the NAACP, where he chatted with men he had long known, Channing Tobias of the Phelps Stokes Fund and Roger Baldwin of the American Civil Liberties Union.[46] He then returned to the office for the rest of the afternoon. After completing the day's business, he began his customary walk home to the Madison Hotel on Fifty-eighth Street, where he and Kate had taken up residence.

Having never learned to drive, Embree was accustomed to getting around town on foot or in taxicabs. During most of the years with Rockefeller, he and his family lived in a rented apartment in Brooklyn, and he routinely walked across the Brooklyn Bridge to the foundation's offices in lower Manhattan. In Chicago, when the fund was housed in a corner of the massive Sears, Roebuck warehouse, he took a cab to work. After the fund's headquarters moved to the Rosenwald mansion, and he and Kate had relocated to a lakefront residential hotel, he usually walked the mile and a half to the office and back again. Returning to New York, he had continued to get his exercise by walking to and from work.

But this time was different. On Fifth Avenue, Embree collapsed. Someone—a passerby, perhaps a hotel doorman—helped him up and escorted him the short distance to his hotel. A doctor was called. A heart attack was the unmistakable diagnosis. The three children were contacted—John in New Haven, Edwina in Princeton, Catherine in Washington. None would arrive in time. Only two hours after his collapse, never having reached a hospital, Edwin Embree was dead. He was sixty-six years old.

* * *

Embree's many friends were shocked by the suddenness of his death, for he had no chronic illnesses. He always seemed younger than his years, and he had looked well to those who had seen him recently.[47] He had not been under a doctor's care, nor had he complained of tiredness or any ailment. Though a smoker, he had never shown any sign of a heart problem. Three of his six older siblings would live into their eighties or beyond, as would both of his daughters. There was no reason to expect so swift an end to such an active life.

Obituary columns around the country reported Embree's passing. The *New York Herald Tribune* called attention to his theory of a "new race" emerging in the United States and to the national controversy stirred by his criticisms of the quality of collegiate education. The *Chicago Sun-Times* described him as a pioneer in race relations whose death was a loss to the nation, but whose labors had "immeasurably strengthened" American democracy. The *Philadelphia Inquirer* considered him "perhaps the country's foremost white authority on race relations" and traced the "record-breaking numbers" of southern black college students to Rosenwald's education efforts under his leadership.[48] Another Chicago newspaper spoke of Embree's "profound understanding" of racial tensions and of "that supreme confidence which enabled him to surmount the indignities, the exasperations, the illogic which crowds the race issue and keep it on the level where intelligence can do its work in order that tolerance in the end prevails." In a field characterized by awkwardness and embarrassment, bigotry and prejudice, "he had moved with gentle, good-humored, unruffled charm."[49]

Embree's family received phone calls, telegrams, and letters of condolence by the hundreds. They came from over half the states in the union and from every region of the country. They came from Toronto and Tokyo, London and Nassau, Caracas and Madrid and Vancouver. Over a dozen came from college and university presidents, both black and white, and almost twice as many from former Rosenwald fellows. They came from lawyers, scholars, medical doctors, music composers, foundation heads, business executives, U.S. senators, and presidential cabinet officers, from the librarian of Congress and the former First Lady, from the secretary of Hawaii and the undersecretary-general of the United Nations. They came from organizations that had benefited from Embree's counsel and Rosenwald's largesse: the Chicago Institute for Psychoanalysis, the Associated Negro Press, the American Missionary Association, the National Scholarship Service and Fund for Negro Students, the Federal Council of Churches, the Southern Regional Council, the United Negro College Fund, and municipal human relations councils. And, quite fittingly, they came from Jews and gentiles, and from white people and persons of Hispanic, African, and Japanese ancestry.[50]

Like the published obituaries, these messages called attention to Embree's dedication and effectiveness on behalf of race relations, but most sounded a more personal note. Several commented on the nature of his passing. Many old writers dragged on uselessly, one declared, but Embree had a kinder fate, going out "in a flame instead of a smolder."[51] One of Embree's siblings, recalling her brother's dread of old age and any lessening of his "capacity or zest for living," expressed gratitude that he had gone quickly and cleanly, never experiencing any reduction in his powers.[52] Several mentioned his commitment to his work, and one spoke of the "happy integration of enthusiasm and realism" in his personality.[53] A distinguished composer and former Rosenwald fellow testified that Embree "truly exemplified the spirit of brotherly love," and in the many years they had known each other, he had never felt that Embree belonged to one race and he to another.[54] Another fellow who knew him well wrote that Embree had made "wonderful contributions . . . not only by doing 'right things' but by daring other people not to do 'right things.'"[55]

A few weeks later, on a dismal late winter afternoon marked by driving rain mixed with snow, a memorial service was held on the University of Chicago campus. Among the almost 400 mourners who crowded the university's Bond Chapel, in addition to Kate, the couple's children, and their spouses, were Embree's two brothers and assorted nephews, nieces, and cousins. The service was organized and presided over by the prominent medical educator Franklin McLean, whose close association with Embree had begun more than a quarter-century earlier at the Peking Union Medical College. Eulogies were pronounced by five of his closest friends and associates: Roosevelt College president Edward James Sparling, University of Chicago anthropologist Robert Redfield, philanthropist and former Rosenwald trustee Marshall Field III, fund colleagues Will Alexander and Charles Johnson.[56]

The last and most moving tribute came from Johnson. Embree, he said, had been "a man disciplined to graciousness and integrity with an elemental honesty and sense of justice so instinctive that he was utterly unaware of it." No man in America had shown "greater understanding of and zeal for democracy—the kind of understanding and zeal that could carry one into the dark and dangerous backwaters of our national life." With "courage that matched his moral convictions," he had plunged into the "tangled emotional area of race in America," making himself a "target for demagogues." Edwin Embree, the Fisk University president concluded, had been a wise social statesman, "a generator of moving ideas, a writer of force and grace, an inspirer of youth, a prophet of the democratic ideal and practitioner of the art of democratic living, a man of charm, a civilized American."[57]

Also read at the service was a telegram from the Japanese American Citizens League, paying tribute to "a great American" and affirming that "[d]uring the trying war years, when our group of people were suspect[, Embree] was one of the first to express confidence in us and faith in America by becoming one of the national sponsors of our organization. We mourn his passing but the memory of him will sustain our faith that all people can live and work together."[58]

As a tribute to Embree, and as a means to promote the causes for which he had labored, the John Hay Whitney Foundation established a memorial lecture series at five higher education institutions, including

Berea College and Dillard University. Embree had been closely associated with both schools, having been reared on the campus of the first and instrumental in the creation of the second. During the three-year life of the lectureships, distinguished visitors spoke to audiences of students and townspeople about national and world issues that had concerned the man they commemorated. The lecturers were chosen for both their expertise and their personal knowledge of Embree: close collaborators Johnson and Alexander, University of Chicago president Robert Maynard Hutchins, humanities scholar and former Rosenwald fellow Sterling Brown, human rights champion Eleanor Roosevelt.[59]

Other tributes took different forms. Not long before his death, Embree had agreed to serve as a trustee of the National Scholarship Service and Fund for Negro Students, an organization he had helped to form. In his memory, a named scholarship was established to enable students to bridge the gap between their financial aid and overall college expenses; eight students benefited in the first year alone. In announcing the scholarships, Robert C. Weaver, who chaired the organization's Supplementary Scholarship Fund board, described Embree as "probably the most distinguished individual in interracial and intercultural affairs."[60] At fledging Roosevelt College, where the creation of a school of education had been approved in principle, the board voted to name the school after Embree, whenever it was established.[61]

* * *

Sometime in the 1940s, on an occasion when his wife and some friends were present, Embree had made a comment about what he would like done at the time of his death. The statement was probably offered half in jest. No one made anything of it at the time; nothing was ever written down. Yet his words, jocular as they may have been, were remembered, and they were followed to the letter.

Embree's body was cremated. His widow kept the ashes until their daughter Catherine was able to travel to Hawaii in 1955. On the island of Oahu, on what would have been her father's seventy-second birthday, Catherine and her husband ascended to the Nuuanu Pali lookout and, in view of the lush Koolau mountain range, scattered the ashes to the winds.[62] As they swirled in the air, then settled into the volcanic soil, the very private ceremony came to an end. But Catherine knew that, to fulfill her father's wish, one last duty needed to be performed.

* * *

Embree's father was buried in the Quaker cemetery in Newtown Square, Pennsylvania. Two of his sisters were interred in California, where they had lived for many years. The burial places of another sister, and of a brother who predeceased him, are unknown. The graves of his mother, his two other brothers, and his maternal grandparents are in the cemetery of the small Kentucky town where he was reared. But, appropriately for the restless world traveler he had been, a man who never had a fixed place he thought of as "home," Embree's ashes were scattered to the winds of the Pacific. As a consequence, no engraved stone slab chronicles Embree's life, and no bronze plaque pays tribute to his accomplishments. Several institutions that benefited significantly from his engagement with them seem unaware of his name. Today, threescore years after his death, persons with any living memory of him are few in number. Yet there are monuments of a sort and many things about his life well worth remembering.

One such monument is in New Orleans, another in Chicago. Embree's initiative, his persuasive efforts with two church bodies, his influence with men who became the institution's first officials, and the generous funding he arranged were critical to the birth of Dillard University. Without his midwifery, it is unlikely that institution would ever have come to life. Similarly, it was his willingness to join with James Sparling and Marshall Field III to create a college, and to sustain and nurture it through its early years, that gave downtown Chicago an institution open to all without regard to race, religion, ethnicity, or gender. Roosevelt University in the twenty-first century still exhibits the democratic ideals that Embree embodied. Equally notable is the sturdy endurance of several historically black institutions he consistently supported as centers of academic excellence. The reputations of Fisk, Howard, and the Atlanta confederation serve as reminders of how they were strengthened both by Rosenwald money and by numerous faculty members whose preparation owed much to Rosenwald fellowships.

These reminders in brick and stone point to Embree's legacy as a foundation executive. For over three decades, he served in that role, a length of tenure seldom matched then or since. His long experience and the fact that he entered on the mezzanine, if not the ground floor, of organized philanthropy put him in a position to contribute to the theory of the enterprise. In that connection, three things stand out. His opposition to perpetuities, deeply shared with Julius Rosenwald, called attention to the dangers of the "dead hand" and the importance of each generation seeking to solve its own problems with its own resources. While the approach he favored did not become the dominant foundation paradigm, the insistence with which he pursued the issue undoubtedly helped philanthropists and their agents to sharpen their thinking and to condition the terms on which a significant minority of trusts were established.

Objection to perpetuities was rooted in another of Embree's emphases, one fully expressed in his own actions. He envisioned scientific giving as a motor for moving society forward. Operating without a specific legal mandate, beholden to no constituency, largely free to deploy their resources as they saw fit, foundations in his view were uniquely positioned to promote positive social change. His complaint, beginning at Rockefeller and expanding thereafter, was that philanthropic organizations often became too bureaucratic and passive, failing to seize their opportunities and maximize their influence. Their timidity, traceable in large part to efforts to preserve endowments, he considered essentially a dereliction of duty. Reacting against that pattern, Embree was inclined always to push beyond traditional boundaries, to entertain the fresh idea and undertake the unconventional project. In his writings, he encouraged philanthropy officers to be more adventuresome; in his professional activities, as in his private life, he modeled such behavior.

That behavior was nowhere more pronounced than in the third key aspect of Embree's philanthropic legacy. When the Rosenwald Fund adopted the policy of direct action, it moved into altogether uncharted territory. It abandoned the safe ground of dispassionate disburser of money and entered the uncertain terrain of outspoken advocacy. Taking that road was, of course, consistent with Embree's vision of what a foundation should do, yet no trust up to that point had dared to do so. It was also in keeping with his understanding of what a philanthropic trust should be—a select group of well-informed, socially conscious citizens making up its board and a staff of imaginative, highly thoughtful individuals capable of work "comparable to that of a university." His conception had much in common with a contemporary think tank, but with the difference that the foundation had the financial resources to promote the ideas it generated and the social innovations it tested. Creating the model of the foundation *engagée* was arguably Embree's most distinctive contribution to philanthropic practice. Not widely adopted in his time, the model, with variations, became increasingly evident toward the close of the twentieth century.

Embree made his living as a foundation executive, but his legacy extends beyond the field of philanthropy. He was a social reformer, a visionary, but one with a vision tempered by realism and practicality. After almost a quarter-century of philanthropic work, he was not inclined to romanticize those he sought to help. The beneficiaries of such efforts, he wrote, were themselves "a baffling mixture of good and evil." Labor leaders sometimes concentrated on their own selfish purposes instead of the interests of those they represented. African Americans, "long persecuted and submerged," could display ignorance and prejudice like that of their oppressors. Irish Catholics, "long trampled upon in America, often trample on others when they have the chance." Trying to eliminate discrimination against Jews, one encountered among them "greed and stupidity and arrogance." And peoples in Africa and Asia under imperial domination might, after gaining independence, find themselves worse off under native rulers than under their occupiers. Such human frailties and disappointments notwithstanding, "substantial progress in human relations" had been made and would continue "step by faltering step."[63]

As Embree predicted, in the years since his death there have been striking changes in American behavior, in U.S. laws and institutions, that he helped to bring about, usually indirectly, often inconspicuously. Money from the Rosenwald Fund, the largest single source of financing for the NAACP's legal work, enabled that key organization to persist in challenges to racially segregated schools, culminating in the *Brown v. Board* decision four years after Embree's death. Much of the demanding intellectual effort leading to that decision was carried out by former Rosenwald fellows, beneficiaries of the program Embree created, then sustained through two challenging decades. Other fellows—trained in art and sociology, medicine and music, English and chemistry, every learned discipline—helped to prepare thousands of students for the wider world beginning to open to them after 1945. Certainly no less important, by their own accomplishments these scholars, scientists, and artists made evident the great reservoirs of intelligence and talent among America's black citizenry, forcing the majority population to recognize what they had long ignored. This consequence Embree had foreseen, and when circumstances became propitious, he showed white college officials how their faculties would be strengthened and their students benefited by highly qualified African American professionals. In launching this movement, which reached fruition only decades later, he led, as in other initiatives, without great fanfare. With equal parts sagacity and commitment, he mobilized prominent Americans to expose and combat the gross inequities in the nation's capital, leading in time to formal desegregation and increased opportunity.

These changes in policy and practice would not have occurred without an underlying change in consciousness on the part of many Americans. It is here perhaps that Embree's most important, but less obvious, contribution was made. In books and articles, in public addresses and private conversations, he tirelessly pointed out that racial discrimination was irrational and immoral, and that enforced segregation was ultimately unsustainable. In that approach, he appealed to his contemporaries' better natures, but he coupled it with a bluntly practical argument. The injustices imposed on citizens of color harmed the whole country; consequently, eliminating them was, for white America, basically a matter of "enlightened self-interest." Various forms of discrimination would end, desegregation would come, at varying paces around the country to be sure, but change was inevitable and should be recognized as such. His message often encountered opposition, but confident that his view was correct and would in time prevail, he did not relent.

Embree's confidence in his own views was in part a reflection of his optimistic nature, in part a manifestation of his ability to read major trends. Concluding in the early forties that legal segregation was moving toward disappearance and that overt racial discrimination would diminish perhaps required only modest foresight. That cannot be said of many of his other judgments. Recognizing even in the 1930s the unique virtues of African American culture, he believed the nation's life would be diminished if black institutions disappeared altogether, and if black citizens were totally assimilated to the majority's patterns. Months before Japanese planes appeared in Hawaii's skies, he saw, and determined to oppose, the threat to civil liberties that war and its aftermath would bring. He early discerned, and welcomed, the quickening pace of globalization, sensing that it would both require and facilitate changed relations among the earth's peoples. Alert to the postwar shift in the international power balance, he correctly predicted the increasing importance on the world stage of China and Japan, along with other areas still under colonial rule. Far earlier than most, he recognized the similarity between the aspirations of African Americans and those of subjugated peoples hungry for independence, and he warned that U.S. policies had to change in response. Such considerations, together with the crises of war and depression, led him to proclaim the coming end of Western domination, a conclusion premature, perhaps exaggerated, but certainly not entirely in error. His predictions struck some as threatening; others saw them as simply wrongheaded; still others, as clearly preposterous. Embree recognized the novelty and unpopularity of his pronouncements, but by calling attention to impending developments, he undoubtedly helped to ease the way through inevitably difficult transitions.

In one regard, his expectation was ostensibly mistaken. His idealism and optimism led him to overrate the possibilities of the new world order he championed. He underestimated the tenacity of nationalistic sentiment, and he did not foresee how quickly conflicting interests would divide the major powers in the Cold War. A citizen of the world and of the United States, he believed that those twin allegiances were completely compatible, and he expected the destruction and terror of contemporary warfare to lead most of the globe's population to share his perspective. International relations are still far from the situation he envisioned. This is not to say that, in the long term, Embree will be proved wrong. Perhaps in this, as in other regards, he was simply far ahead of his time.

* * *

Early in 1950, Embree, along with W. E. B. DuBois and the NAACP's Walter White, was asked to write a guest editorial to mark the fortieth anniversary of the *Pittsburgh Courier,* one of the nation's preeminent black newspapers. Embree chose as his title "Progress of the Half-Century of Human Relations." The 1,500-word statement was vintage Embree— informed by history, balanced in its current assessment, sanguine about the future.

Beyond the horrors of slavery, the cruelly betrayed promise of emancipation, and the myth of white supremacy that underlay both racial segregation and Western imperialism, the opening lines declared, the twentieth century had seen great progress, and more was in sight. Two world wars and the New Deal had dealt a fatal blow to false outlooks. Prejudice and discrimination were not yet dead, but at mid-century more than a million blacks held union cards, and fully a hundred black scholars were teaching in northern and western colleges, where 40,000 students of color were enrolled. In the North, hundreds of black doctors, nurses, police officers, and schoolteachers were part of the economic mainstream. Dozens of black people had been elected to public office at the municipal and state levels, and two sat in the U.S. Congress. To be sure, any African American, no matter how prosperous or cultivated, was still "liable to slight or insult any day in any city north as well as south." But now, in contrast to 1900 when white supremacy was almost universally accepted, millions of white Americans were as angry about such discrimination as the country's black citizens. "Today white imperialism is finished," Embree proclaimed, even if "vestigial traces" still remained.

> While glaring discriminations persist, they, too, are but remnants of an outgrown order. No intelligent man today claims the biological superiority of one race over another. Whatever the carry-over of old habits and practices, intelligent men today in America and the world over believe in equality. The triumph of the first half of the twentieth century is not yet seen in democratic practice, but it is a triumph nevertheless, a transformation in the minds of men.[64]

This piece, completed a scant three weeks before his death, was Embree's final testament.

In the course of a productive career, Embree had been a masterful facilitator. Seeing two entities that needed to be brought together, he undertook to join them. With his broad circle of contacts, he was able to bring unconnected individuals into useful relationship. In a racially divided nation, he introduced white Americans to their fellow citizens

of color. In the gap between the layperson and the specialist, he served
as a bridge, explaining complicated matters through his artful use of language. And to the country's most vexing problems, he sought to connect
the minds and money that might bring solutions. As one of his eulogists
declared, he had been "a sort of universal spare part in the limping machinery of American democracy."[65]

Embree had also been a teacher. When he joined the Yale administration, he had been appointed to an assistant professorship, a title in
which he took considerable pride. The title, however, only went with his
office; it involved no specified instructional responsibilities. Never professionally an educator, Embree nevertheless taught. He taught in what
he said. He taught in what he wrote. He taught in what he did. And most
notable, there was between his words and his actions an unmistakable
consistency. Maintaining such a consistency throughout an active public
life is an uncommon achievement. It is possible only for a thoroughly
integrated personality, a whole person, one who embodies what is called,
simply, integrity.

* * *

On the morning of July 31, 1955, the *Honolulu Advertiser* carried a most
unusual announcement. That afternoon, at the best hotel in Waikiki, the
Halekulani, there would be a celebration. Cocktails would be served.
There would be entertainment. The event was open to the general public.
All were invited.

When the appointed hour came, Catherine Embree Harris, back
from the Oahu highlands, and faithful to the last part of her father's wish,
greeted dozens of guests at the hotel. Some were family friends, others
complete strangers.[66] The affair, as Embree had stipulated, was open to
all—democratic in the broadest sense—racially mixed, socially varied,
representative of the rich diversity of the island's population. It was the
kind of gathering Embree himself had often hosted, a situation in which
he would have been completely at ease. The guests had come to a party,
with a three-piece Hawaiian band and a hula dancer, on a palm-shaded
patio in view of imposing mountains and rolling waves. But they had also
gathered to commemorate the life of a philanthropic trailblazer, a man
who had studied and valued distinctive cultures and whose unending

quest had been to discover how diverse peoples, on a rapidly shrinking globe, could live together in harmony and prosperity.

Throughout his adult life, Edwin Embree wrestled with the most perplexing issues facing American society: rapacious disease, inadequate education, virulent racism, insufficient economic opportunity, incomplete democracy. During his last decade, those efforts broadened to encompass a world desperate for peace, now open to new structures to prevent war and extend justice. He had known frustration and disappointment, but that did not cause him to become grim or bitter. He did not lose his enthusiasm, nor was there any crumbling of his bedrock belief that human intelligence could deal effectively with human ills.

Attracted to the good things of life, he had made it a point to have fun; in his sixties, he believed he had had more fun than anybody he knew. He enjoyed celebrations; he liked whatever was truly festive. With zest and earnest good humor, he was fond of entertaining. And when an appropriate occasion was at hand, he delighted in entertaining grandly. Those qualities found fitting expression in that posthumous party. That gala event was entirely suitable; it would have given Edwin Rogers Embree great pleasure.

NOTES

NCSNC   National Committee on Segregation in the Nation's Capital, SCRC
RAC   Rockefeller Archive Center, Sleepy Hollow, New York
RCCR   Roosevelt College Corporate Records, University Archives, Roosevelt University Library, Chicago
RFA   Rockefeller Foundation Archives, RAC
RG   Record Group
SCRC   Special Collections Research Center, Regenstein Library, University of Chicago
WCA   World Citizens Association
WCAP   World Citizens Association Papers, Central Committee Records, SCRC

1. FRONTIER OUTPOSTS, SINGULAR VILLAGE, PRESTIGIOUS UNIVERSITY

1. All descriptive material on Osceola and Polk County is from Osceola Centennial Book Committee.

2. Nellie Embree Rathbun Hill [ERE's sister] to ERE, 7/27/47, DEFP, in the possession of Embree's grandson, John Devereux of Madison, Wisconsin.

3. Ibid.

4. Ibid.; Royal Howard Embree [ERE's brother], in Ambler, vol. 1, 180–85.

5. Hill to ERE, 7/27/47.

6. Royal Howard Embree to ERE, 8/9/47, DEFP.

7. Ambler, 182–85.

8. William Dean Embree [ERE's brother], untitled two-page document, 6/61, DEFP.

9. The story of John G. Fee and the founding of Berea College has been told in print many times; see, for example, Wilson, *Berea College*. See also the chapter "Kentucky Crusader," in ERE, *Brown America*.

10. Wiebe, 2–6. Inevitably aware of their "island'" situation, the citizens of Berea had their uniqueness brought forcibly home soon after Edwin left for college. The Kentucky legislature in 1904 passed a law (the Day Law) forbidding the education of blacks and whites together. Since Berea College was the only institution in the state where interracial education took place, the law's target was evident. The college fought the law on constitutional grounds through the appellate courts, only to have the U.S. Supreme Court declare the law valid in 1905. Berea enrolled only white students until 1950, when relaxation of the Day Law again made a racially mixed student body possible.

11. CSJ, "*Phylon* Profile," 320.

12. ERE to Sadie Yancey, 6/1/48, f. 13, box 459, JRFA. Embree remembered his grandmother Matilda Hamilton Fee, in spite of old age, straitened family circumstances, and her husband's sternness, as a stylishly dressed, handsome woman who loved beautiful things. At every meal, there were flowers on the table. And at every meal, his grandfather removed them to a sideboard. ERE to Edwina Embree Devereux, 1/3/50, DEFP.

13. E. L. Allen, "Notes on Talk with ERE, October 17, 1944," attached to E. L. Allen to ERE, 10/17/44, f. 30, box 104, JRFA, 6–7. Allen was commissioned by Charles S. Johnson to gather material for an article on ERE to be published in *Phylon*.

14. Allen, "Notes"; Nellie Hill to ERE, 7/27/47.

15. Johnson, "*Phylon* Profile," 332; Catherine Embree Harris, personal communication to author, 8/14/06.

16. William Dean Embree to ERE, 3/22/28, EREP-SML, reel 2. Formed to lobby for anti-slavery legislation and to protect freed slaves from exploitation, the society came in time to emphasize the moral instruction and control of the behavior of the city's free black population. Rury, 231–33.

17. Wilson, *Berea College,* 15, 43.

18. Quoted in Dunn, 4.

19. Ibid., 4, 45.

20. In the twentieth century, other Fee descendants besides Edwin continued this family tradition of countering racial discrimination and promoting the interests of African Americans. Edwin's brother Will, a prominent member of the New York bar, was active in civil rights issues and in the establishment of the United Negro College Fund. Tucker, 423. And, like Edwin, he served on the board of an industrial school for blacks in Mississippi. A grandnephew, the nuclear physicist Robert R. Wilson, made special efforts to provide opportunities for African Americans during his years as the founding director of Fermi National Accelerator Laboratory outside Chicago. Explaining his convictions on racial matters, Wilson pointed to his family background, particularly the example of his great-grandfather Fee. Wilson, "Starting Fermilab."

21. ERE, *Brown America,* 69–70. Embree described his grandfather's convictions and his trials in a speech to a convention of the National Association for the Advancement of Colored People on June 27, 1929. In the same address, he praised African American citizens for their "Herculean labors and brilliant accomplishments" since emancipation, acknowledged that racial discrimination must still be combated, and, in words foreshadowing admonitions voiced a half-century later, challenged African Americans to continue to prove their worthiness through intellectual effort, "struggle without rest" or special favor, and responsible citizenship. "Citizens of a Common Country," reel 7, EREP-SML.

22. Laura Fee Embree, "A Day Behind the Counter," quoted in untitled and undated document by Nellie Hill, reel 2, EREP-SML.

23. Royal Howard Embree to ERE, 8/9/47, DEFP.

24. Laura Fee Embree to ERE, 5/8/03, reel 2, EREP-SML.

25. Johnson, *"Phylon* Profile," 321.

26. Wilson, *Berea College,* 146.

27. Johnson, *"Phylon* Profile," 322–23. The initial setback in his college plans apparently had no effect on his subsequent studies or on his career thereafter. It did, however, apparently condition his thinking about the nature and purpose of education. When he began to publish his educational views in the 1930s, he persistently inveighed against an undue emphasis on memorization.

28. Pierson, 4, 15, 37, 93, 127, 721.

29. Quoted ibid., 7–9, 404.

30. Ibid., 117.

31. ERE, "Rockefeller Programs: Early History," 7. Unpublished document [dated in pencil "1930"] in f. 3, box 1, EREP-RFA.

32. Ibid.

33. ERE, "Working One's Way through College," 309–13; Johnson, *"Phylon* Profile," 324.

34. ERE and Fowler, *History of the Class of 1906,* MAD-SML; clipping of wedding article, New Haven newspaper [unnamed], July 17, 1907, EREP-SML.

35. The notion of ethnocentrism apparently affected Embree profoundly, for it figured conspicuously in much of his mature writing. Other prominent Sumner ideas—opposition to popular sovereignty, strong capitalistic views, a belief that efforts at societal reform were useless—Embree rejected.

36. ERE, "Can College Graduates Read?" 4.

37. Pierson, vol. 1, 320. In a class election, Embree garnered five votes as the "biggest fusser," earning him a tie for twelfth place. ERE and Fowler, *History of the Class of 1906*, vol. 1, 11, 394, 417.

38. CSJ, "*Phylon* Profile," 324.

39. Catherine Embree Harris, personal communication to author, 2/4/06.

40. Catherine Embree Harris, personal communication to the author, 2/4/06.

41. ERE and Fowler, *History of the Class of 1906*, vol. 1, 156.

42. Clarence's brother George served as Yale University's treasurer, founded Yale University Press, and led a 1920s fund-raising drive. Both brothers were deeply engaged in alumni affairs.

43. ERE to Day [1931?], reel 2, EREP-SML. See also, for example, ERE to Day, 6/29/28, 8/30/28, 9/12/29, 9/20/29; Day to ERE, 6/22/28, all reel 2, EREP-SML.

44. ERE to Day [n.d.], f. 7, ERE to Day, 10/21/29, f. 8, both in box 59, CDP; ERE to George Day, 1/17/36, reel 2, EREP-SML; Frank L. Hayes, "Friend Recalls Day, Author, as a Paradox," *Chicago Daily News*, Feb. 16, 1940, reel 2, EREP-SML; Johnson, "*Phylon* Profile," 325. Day died in 1935.

45. ERE and Fowler, *History of the Class of 1906*, vol. 1, 156–57; EREOD, 4/3/23, RG 12.2.

46. Stokes to CSJ, 10/25/44, f. 30, box 104, JRFA.

47. ERE to William G. Frost, 2/8/12, Frost Papers, RG 303, 11-1, Berea College Archives, Berea, Kentucky.

48. ERE, *Life at Yale*.

49. By contemporary standards, the figures for student earnings and financial aid seem trivial, unless viewed in the context of an average student annual budget at the time of about $900. It should be kept in mind that the college's student body numbered fewer than 1,300, and tuition was $155 until 1914, when it

was raised to $160. Pierson, 411–13, 419.

50. Anson Phelps Stokes to CSJ, 10/25/44, f. 30, box 104, JRFA; ERE, "Rockefeller Programs: Early History," 8.

51. Pierson, vol. 2, 667–68. Embree may have met Vincent as early as 1908, when the older man visited the campus before deciding to decline the deanship of the Yale faculty. Pierson, vol. 1, 154. In any event, Vincent and Embree knew each other several years before they moved into a formal working relationship at the Rockefeller Foundation.

52. ERE, "Rockefeller Programs: Early History," 6. William Embree went on to a distinguished career as a partner in a prestigious Manhattan law firm (the future Milbank, Tweed, Hadley, and McCloy), as the president of both the New York County Bar Association and the Yale Law School Association, and with extensive involvement in civic affairs, civil rights issues, and philanthropic activities.

53. In his teens, Frederick Gates had to drop out of school to help support his family. See Gates, 46. Wallace Buttrick, the president of the General Education Board, had been a brakeman and postal clerk on an upstate New York railroad early in life. The son of an itinerant Kentucky peddler, Rockefeller Institute for Medical Research director Simon Flexner had been a drugstore clerk and a failed plumber's apprentice before entering medical training. Fosdick, *Story of the Rockefeller Foundation*, 11–12.

54. Harr and Johnson, 39.

2. LEARNING PHILANTHROPY

1. Harr and Johnson, 121; "Conference of Trustees of Rockefeller Foundation and General Education Board Held at Yale Club at Dinner," 12/4/18, f. 84, box 21, ser. 900, RG 3, RFA.

2. This outlook did not preclude steering such investigations in the direc-

tions that foundation executives considered critical. For an extensive analysis
of the ways that foundations sought to
mold opinion in support of capitalism, see
Slaughter and Silva, 55–86.

3. Sealander, 245. Though influenced
by Progressivism, Embree did not manifest all its typical characteristics. Like
many Progressives, he had been reared
in a fairly isolated village, but well before
1917 he had rejected the small town and
rural outlook that spawned the movement. Similarly, he was not looking backward nostalgically to some kind of golden
age of stability associated with a simpler
time, but forward to an evolving future
of increased opportunity and economic
justice, especially for minorities. Progressives tended to focus on changing institutions; Embree, for most of his career, gave
more attention to changing minds. In
that connection, he recognized, like most
Progressives but unlike his Rockefeller
colleagues, the importance of the media in
creating a climate for reform.

4. See, for example, exchanges with
Wycliffe Rose: ERE to Rose, 7/5/17, Rose
to ERE, 7/6/17, both f. 365; ERE to Rose,
7/11/17, 8/28/17, f. 366, all in box 21, ser. 1.1,
RG 5, EREP-RFA.

5. "Report upon Amendments of
Constitution and Bylaws," f. 251, box 25, RG
III.2.0, Office of the Messrs. Rockefeller,
Rockefeller Boards, RAC; "Embree, E. R.
1918," f. 476, box 27, ser. 1.1, RG 5, RFA, RAC.

6. EREOD, 8/19/22.

7. ERE, Family Journal no. 2, f. 6, box
59, CDP.

8. Simon Flexner Papers, Correspondence with Embree, Edwin R., no. 21, reel
33, Rockefeller Institute Papers, RAC.

9. ERE to Dr. Linsley R. Williams of
the Tuberculosis Commission, 5/27/20, f.
121, box 16, ser. 700, RG 1.1, RFA.

10. Family Journal no. 9, 9/3/20,
9/20/20; no. 10, 10/12/20, both in EREP-
SML; EREOD, 9/22/20, reel 1; Grant, 132.

11. ERE to N. F. Stoughton, 7/26/20, f.
121, box 16, ser. 700, RG 1.1, RFA; Family
Journal no. 3, attached to EREOD, 7/4/20,
reel 1.

12. Family Journal no. 9, 9/3/20,
EREOD, reel 1.

13. Exhibit A-3 [n.d.], EREOD, reel
1; Family Journal no. 9, 9/3/20; no. 10,
10/12/20; no. 8 [n.d.], all reel 1, EREP-
SML.

14. Family Journal no. 10, 10/12/20,
EREP-SML, reel 1.

15. Ibid.

16. ERE to GEV, 7/2120, 8/19/20, f.
121, box 16, ser. 700, RG 1.1, RFA. In the
parlance of the time, "general education"
commonly referred to the subjects introduced in the elementary schools and
offered in more advanced sequences in
higher grades (e.g., English, history, math-
ematics). The term distinguishes such
studies from specialized or vocational
education.

17. EREOD, "Report and Recommendations to Board of Trustees, 10/26/20,"
reel 1. See also attached Family Journal no.
1, 6/22/20.

18. Fosdick, *Adventure in Giving*,
84–86.

19. ERE, "Rockefeller Programs: Early
History: The Peking Union Medical Col-
lege" [1930 draft document], f. 3, box 1,
EREP-RFA.

20. EREOD, 5/16–17/21, reel 1.

21. ERE to Yale dean M. C. Winteritz,
6/10/21; GEV to ERE, 5/39/21; ERE to
GEV, 6/20/21, all in f. 380, box 54, CMB;
EREOD, 8/1/21, reel 1.

22. EREOD, 6/29/21–7/28/21, reel 1;
ERE to GEV, 8/20/21, f. 1023, box 44, ser.
2, RG 4.1, RFA.

23. EREOD, 7/29/21–8/22/21, reel 1.

24. EREOD, 8/2–22/21, reel 1.

25. ERE to GEV, 8/20/21, f. 1023, box
44, ser. 2, RG 4.1, RFA, RAC.

26. Bullock, *American Transplant*,
14–18.

27. Bowers, 424.

28. ERE, Family Journal no. 6, f. 6, box 59, CDP.

29. Ferguson, 52–53.

30. ERE to GEV, 8/20/21, f. 1023, box 44, ser. 2, RG 4.1, RFA, RAC; EREOD, 8/15–17/25; ERE to Houghton, 8/3/25, f. 1024, box 181, ser. 1, RG 4.1, CMB, RAC.

31. GEV to ERE, 5/9/22, f. 35, box 4, ser. 100, RG 1.1, RFA, RAC.

32. ERE to GEV, 7/14/22, f. 1023, box 44, ser. 1.2, RG 4, RFA, RAC; "Embree, Edwin R., 1920–1926," f. 35, box 4, ser. 100, RG 1.1, RFA; ERE, "Speech Made at Peking, 6/26/22," f. 380, box 54, CMB, RAC.

33. Family Journal for 1922, 6/1/22, reel 2, EREP-SML.

34. ERE to GEV, 6/18/22, f. 380, box 54, CMB, RAC.

35. "Recommendations, ERE to Trustees of PUMC, 8/10/22," f. 1023, box 44, ser. 1.2, RG 4, CMB, RAC.

36. Family Journal, 7/30/22, reel 4, EREP-SML.

37. ERE to Greene, 3/9/26, reel 4, EREP-SML; Greene to ERE, 3/10/26, ERE to Greene, 4/26/26, both in f. 1024, box 44, ser. 1.2, RG 4, RFA.

38. Family Journal no. 3 [n.d.], f. 6; Family Journal no. 8, 2/24/26, f. 7, box 59, CDP.

39. Family Journal no. 6, 7/21/21, reel 4, EREP-SML; Family Journal no. 8, 2/24/26, f. 7, box 59, CDP.

40. Family Journal no. 8, 2/24/26, f. 7, box 59, CDP.

41. EREOD, 12/30/22–1/22/23, 6/27/23; Family Journal no. 8, 7/27/23, reel 4, EREP-SML.

42. Family Journal no. 8, 8/12/23, reel 4, EREP-SML.

43. Family Journal no. 5, 10/10/23, EREP-SML.

44. Family Journal no. 5, 10/10/23, f. 6, box 59, CDP.

45. Catherine Embree Harris, personal communication to the author, 3/9/06;

Alexander, "The Education and Work of Edwin R. Embree," 5; ERE to Clarence Day, 12/1/27, reel 1, EREP-SML.

46. Alan Gregg, "Comments on Personalities Instrumental in Developing Original Programs and Policies of the Rockefeller Foundation; and Ideals Underlying Their Planning, Sept. 15, 1945," f. 174, box 23, ser. 900, RG 3.1, RFA, 17.

47. "Minutes of the Rockefeller Foundation," 12/5/23, f. 1, box 1, ser. 913, Division of Studies, RG 3.1, RFA; Kohler, Partners in Science, 46–48; Embree to GEV, 5/4/23, f. 1, box 1, ser. 913, RG 3, RFA, RAC; GEVOD, 10/22/23, reel 2, RG 12.1; ERE, "Rockefeller Programs: Early History" [1930], f. 3, box 1, EREP-RFA.

48. "Minutes of the Rockefeller Foundation," 12/5/23, f. 1, box 1, ser. 913, RG 3.1, RFA.

49. A similar lack of specificity appears in Embree's proposal for the division in ERE to GEV, 5/4/23, f. 1, box 1, ser. 913, RG 3.1, RFA. Even many months later, in discussing future foundation policy, Vincent emphasized to the board the importance of preserving "flexibility" and avoiding "crystallization." See untitled document excerpted from minutes of "Conference of Members and Officers, Princeton, NJ," 2/23–25/25, f. 165, box 22, ser. 900, RG 3.1, RFA, 9–10.

50. EREOD, 4/19–20/22, reel 1; 2/29/24, reel 2; "Expansion of Programs of Rockefeller Boards, 1/18/24," f. 165, box 22, ser. 900, RG 3.1, RFA, RAC.

51. Assuming new responsibilities did not mean that Embree surrendered all his old ones. He continued to be involved in explaining the foundation's policies to would-be beneficiaries and routing applicants to other Rockefeller boards. One such interview involved a proposed program to domesticate the musk ox. EREOD, 7/6/25, reel 2.

52. The movement also found expression early in the twentieth century in the

xenophobic reaction against immigrants from eastern and southern Europe and East Asia, embodied in the 1924 Immigration Act (Johnson-Reed Act).

53. "Memorandum of Membership of the Galton Society," f. 23, box 3, ser. 410A, RG 1.1, RFA, RAC.

54. Society secretary William K. Gregory to prominent eugenicist Madison Grant, 11/22/23, f. 23, box 3, ser. 410A, RFA. Grant subsequently affirmed to a key Rockefeller trustee that such a study was the best way to understand properly "the artificial conditions of selection now operating in civilized communities." Grant to Raymond B. Fosdick, 12/29/23, f. 23, box 3, RG 410A, RFA, RAC.

55. EREOD, 1/12/25, reel 2.

56. See his address in the Moody lecture series at the University of Chicago, 4/14/32, reel 7, EREP-SML. The argument for such sterilization is more fully developed in the chapter "Are Morons Sacred?" in Embree's *Prospecting for Heaven*, 54–61. By 1932, twenty-eight states had laws dealing with forced sterilization; a 1937 *Fortune* poll revealed that two Americans out of three favored such procedures for "mental defectives." Brunius, 72, 239. Some observers considered it contradictory to seek to educate and improve the health of poor and technologically backward people, while trying to limit their reproduction. Embree saw the two efforts as complementary. "We must help the higher groups to go on up. And we must discover new—possibly radical—techniques to advance human evolution," he wrote. "As I see it (a) the idea involved in world eugenics and (b) projects to give a boost to the most backward and unpromising groups are two aspects of a common idea." ERE to Clarence Day, 8/8/28, reel 2, EREP-SML. On this point, see also Sealander, 67–68.

57. "Expansion of Programs of Rockefeller Boards," 1/18/24, f. 165, box 22, ser.

900, RG 3.1, RFA; EREOD, 1/12/25, reel 1; interview with Dr. William F. Snow, 12/27/23; with National Research Council head Vernon Kellogg, 2/6/24; with Margaret Sanger, 3/27/24, all in EREOD, reel 2; address to McGill University alumni, Hamilton, Ontario, 2/11/24, f. 8, box 1, EREP-RFA. Embree's interest in mental health issues may have dated from 1908. The year after he returned to Yale, New Haven saw the establishment of the Connecticut Society for Mental Hygiene, presumed to be the world's first organization devoted to improving the treatment of the mentally ill and protecting the public's mental health. Of the fourteen charter members, four were associated with Yale, including Embree's mentor, Anson Phelps Stokes. See http://www.eugenics-watch .com.roots (accessed 3/28/08).

58. On Embree's interest in mental health research, see ERE to Wycliffe Rose, 2/14/17, f. 365, box 21, ser. 1.1, RG 5, EREP-RFA. Several key Rockefeller figures were closely associated with the American Eugenics Society (AES), a slightly younger, less blatantly racist organization than the Galton Society, with which it shared overlapping memberships. Rockefeller Jr. contributed regularly to the AES during the late 1920s, and several influential members of Rockefeller boards were on its advisory council in 1925: Ray Lyman Wilbur, Vernon Kellogg, William H. Welch, and Raymond B. Fosdick, along with former trustee Harry Emerson Fosdick, Raymond's brother and the Rockefellers' pastor at New York's Riverside Church. EREOD, 2/5/25, reel 2; file memorandum, f. 178, box 8, ser. III.2, Bureau of Social Hygiene, RAC. Rockefeller Jr. also contributed personally to the Eugenics Record Office at Cold Spring Harbor, donating $22,000 over a four-year period. Kevles, 55. For Raymond Fosdick's views on the population issue and the urgent need for action, see his commencement address at

Wellesley College, 6/20/22, in f. 257, box 25, RG III.20, Office of the Messrs. Rockefellers, Rockefeller Boards, RAC. Frederick T. Gates's deep concern about the genetic transmission of disease is evident in his *Chapters in My Life,* written for his children, 32–33.

59. EREOD, 2/13–26/24, reel 2; Flexner to ERE, 2/20/24, reel 34, no. 22, Simon Flexner Papers, RAC; "Minutes of the Rockefeller Foundation," 2/27/24, f. 23, box 3, RG 410A, RFA, RAC.

60. Peterson, 10.

61. Family Journal, 8/28/25, reel 4, EREP-SML; f. 33, box 4, ser. 915, RG 3, RFA; GEVOD, 2/10/25, reel 2. In the mid-twenties, Raymond Fosdick and Abraham Flexner, for example, envisioned Rockefeller support for studies in criminology, drug addiction, venereal disease, feeblemindedness, delinquency, and family structure, interrelated problems relevant to Embree's own concerns. Kohler, *Partners in Science,* 46–48.

62. That close association was evidenced on several occasions. When (future UNESCO director) Julian Huxley of the London Eugenics Education Society inquired about possible funding for research on the genetic heredity of paupers, Vincent and the heads of the GEB, IEB, and LSRM directed the matter to the Rockefeller Foundation through its "division of human biology." GEVOD, 1/15/26, reel 3, RG 12.1, RFA, RAC. The linkage is expressed in Embree's letter to Raymond Fosdick of 8/26/25 (f. 33, box 4, ser. 915, RG 3, RFA): "I am tremendously interested in the sciences of human biology, the possibilities of which we are beginning to explore. If it is possible to do anything in such matters as eugenics and a better understanding of mental processes, we shall be making contributions indeed." Similarly when Embree discussed with Clark Wissler a possible advisory committee for his division, of the fourteen men con-

sidered, six were members of the Galton Society, including five of the seven Americans (Wissler, Raymond Pearl, J. C. Merriam, Wingate Todd, E. L. Thorndike). EREOD, 4/14/24, reel 2.

63. Steve Sheldon, "Eugenics Popularization," http://www.eugenicsarchive.org (accessed 5/26/08). For Raymond Pearl's distrust of "eugenics propagandists," see EREOD, 3/17/27, reel 2. See also Abraham Flexner's warning to Embree to support only studies by university centers, avoiding direct foundation involvement in controversial topics like population and eugenics. EREOD, 1/6/25, reel 2.

64. ERE to G. Elliot Smith, 11/13/24, 12/11/24, f. 24, box 3, ser. 4110D, RG 1.1, RFA, RAC.

65. See, for example, ERE's datebook on the discussion following dinner and his overnight stay at Conklin's home. EREOD, 12/15/24, reel 2. Conklin was elected successively to the presidencies of the American Association of Zoologists, American Society of Naturalists, and American Association for the Advancement of Science.

66. For a discussion of Pearl's changing views and his influence, see Allen's "Old Wine in New Bottles," 231–61.

67. For summaries of Embree's conversations, see EREOD, reel 2: with Merriam, 12/1/24; with Bowman, 2/4/25; with Lillie, 12/3/24; with Davenport, 1/23/25 and 6/12/25.

68. "Minutes of the Rockefeller Foundation," 2/25/25, f. 33, box 4, ser. 915, RG 3, RFA, RAC.

69. Family Journal, 8/28/25, reel 4, EREP-SML. The two older children would return to Hawaii for part of their undergraduate work, and Catherine would spend more than two decades there following her retirement.

70. "Project Histories," f. 89, vol. 2, ser. 900, RG 3, RFA; f. 6, box 1, EREP-RFA.

71. EREOD, 3/29/26–4/11/26, reel 2.

72. GEVOD, 4/15/26, 4/23/26, 5/3/26, 10/18/26, all reel 3, RG 12.1; Flexner to ERE, 5/4/26, no. 23, reel 34, Simon Flexner Papers.

73. Vincent's way of dealing with controversial proposals is noted in Gregg, "Comments on Personalities," 20. See also GEVOD, 5/1/25, reel 2, and 11/5/26, reel 3, RG 12.1. Vincent's advice that Embree should be "well buttressed by appropriate experts" is recorded in GEVOD, 1/28/25, reel 2. For Embree's "buttressing," see "Conferences Concerning Human Biology," exhibit D, appended to the minutes of the Princeton conference, f. 165, box 22, ser. 900, RG 3.1. Embree's plea for greater presidential support, especially because he was a layman in a professional group, is recorded in GEVOD, 10/21/26, reel 3. All documents in RFA, RAC.

74. In the decision to eliminate the division, a key consideration was the view, advanced by Division of Medical Education director R. M. Pearce, that the exploration of new fields should be the responsibility of the foundation's president, not the head of one of its disbursing agencies. Pearce to Raymond B. Fosdick, 4/16/26, f. 121, box 17, ser. 900, RG 3.1, RFA. Another division head, Roger S. Greene, with whom Embree had clashed in 1921 over PUMC budgets, had warned earlier against new ventures that might jeopardize existing programs. Kohler, "Policy," 494. Vincent's views on the elimination of the division, on which he had pinned large hopes, are undocumented. Six months earlier, he clearly favored its continuation. See his letter to Raymond Fosdick, 5/24/26, with its attachment, "The Organization of the Foundation," f. 121, box 17, ser. 900, RG 3.1, RFA, RAC.

75. ERE, "Rockefeller Programs: Early History," f. 1, box 1, EREP-RFA.

76. Kohler, "Policy," 500. Kohler's judgment has been accepted and repeated by other historians of science, e.g., Diane B. Paul, "The Rockefeller Foundation," 264–65; and Gerald Jonas, *The Circuit Riders*, 125–53, 376. This is unfortunate for, in spite of its obvious value, the article contains factual errors and some questionable judgments. The biometrician Raymond Pearl was never a foundation trustee (as stated on 494). Nor apparently did Kohler understand the provenance of Embree's self-critique. It was not intended for Embree's "superiors" (stated on 500), but was a confidential document of which apparently only two copies were made. One went to Clarence Day for safekeeping (under an agreement the two close friends had made for "difficult" writings); the other was posthumously discovered among Embree's papers by his daughter, who deposited it with the RAC (f. 1, box 1, EREP-RFA). His characterization of Embree's personal traits offers strikingly slight documentation, and his description of Embree's administrative abilities seems to be based entirely on a confidential statement by Rockefeller trustee Raymond B. Fosdick. A careful search of Rockefeller files has revealed no evidence that Embree's other colleagues shared Fosdick's opinion. Nor does Kohler seem to be aware of other factors in the Fosdick-Embree relationship, as will be discussed in the next chapter.

77. See "Relation of Programs in Human Biology and in the Social Sciences," 2/2/25, f. 33, box 4, ser. 915, RG 3, RFA.

78. See, for example, entries for 6/13/24, 4/21/26, 5/14/26, 5/17/26, EREOD, reel 2. Embree's frustration is expressed in a personal letter to Vincent, in which he criticizes Rose for neglecting general education, the proper sphere for the IEB and GEB, while limiting the Rockefeller Foundation's access to the discipline of biology. ERE to GEV, 7/16/26, f. 122, box 17, ser. 900, RG 3.1, RFA. Vincent's impatience with the unresolved issue is hinted at in GEVOD,

10/25/26, reel 3. Embree's own frustration with Rose's magisterial manner was expressed in an ironic comment to a colleague: "There are two things which are complete and final at the moment of their inception: a described circle and a program formulated by Wycliffe Rose." ERE to Leonard Outhwaite, 3/10/28, f. 1141, box 112, ser. III.10, LSRM, RAC. Vincent also had trouble with Rose, perhaps based on a "fundamental antipathy," according to Raymond Fosdick, in Fosdick to Alan Gregg, 10/16/45, f. 174, box 23, ser. 900, RG 3.1, RFA.

79. Provost Gregory Foster to Rose, with attachment, 3/8/27, f. 433, box 30, ser. 1, IEB, RAC. See also attachment to G. Elliot Smith to ERE, 12/1/26, and 2/2/27. For the ensuing confusion, including the tension between Professor Smith and Provost Foster, see Alan Gregg to R. M. Pearce, 6/14/27, and Selskar M. Gunn to GEV, 6/17/27, all in f. 418, box 33, ser. 401A, RG 1.1, RFA.

80. Fosdick, Story of the Rockefeller Foundation, 232–33.

81. EREOD, 4/21–22/22, reel 1.

82. "Budget Estimates and Their Implications: A Statement by the President to the Trustees at the Meeting of November 7, 1924," f. 165, box 22, ser. 900, RG 3.1, RFA, RAC.

83. Conversation with Abraham Flexner, EREOD, 12/20/23, reel 1; with R. M. Pearce, EREOD, 4/17/25, reel 2; with Rose, 7/1/26, EREOD, reel 2. See also untitled and undated document in f. 33, box 4, ser. 915, RG 3, RFA, RAC.

84. See "Minutes of the Rockefeller Foundation," 5/27/25 (25144–45); 5/26/26 (26089–90), both in f. 33, box 4, ser. 915, RG 3, RFA.

85. GEVOD, 1/17–24/24, reel 2.

86. EREOD, 4/6/26, reel 2; see also ERE to Wilbur, 9/27/26, f. 1, box 1, ser. 913; RG 3; and 7/11/27, f. 33, box 4, ser. 915, RG 3, RFA. With Wilbur, Embree also discussed Vincent's pattern of withdrawing from board consideration projects that aroused opposition, a practice of which Wilbur disapproved (EREOD, 4/6/26, f. 5, box 120, JRFA).

87. GEVOD, 5/17/26, reel 3; Wilbur's letter of 5/21/26 is in f. 33, box 4, ser. 915, RG 3, RFA, RAC.

88. Fosdick, Story of the Rockefeller Foundation, 193. More than a year and a half into the DS, Embree in a jocular mood described his ignorance of the sciences as "wide and rich." Family Journal, 8/28/25, reel 4, EREP-SML. Alan Gregg opined that the trustees' enthusiasm for medicine and public health in the 1920s left Vincent and Embree—neither of whom were physicians—in their relationship to the board "more nearly in the position of announcers, commentators, and managers than players." "Comments on Personalities," 22. Recognizing that the board's medical contingent could impede expansion into new fields, Vincent had advocated staff appointments for "laymen" (nonphysicians) as a means to provide programmatic flexibility and "lay detachment." "Budget Estimates and Their Implications," f. 165, box 22, ser. 900, RG 3.1, RFA. Key portions of this document were also circulated at the meeting at which Embree outlined his plans for the Division of Studies. See, in the same folder, minutes of "The Conference of Members and Officers," held at Princeton, 2/23–24/25.

89. GEVOD, 10/21/26, reel 3.

90. In a subsequent publication, Robert Kohler conceded that Embree "probably blamed himself too much" and that "given the inherent difficulties," even a foundation executive more experienced than Embree probably could not have succeeded "with such an ill-defined and controversial field." Kohler, "Science, Foundations, and American Universities," 157, 160. See also Kohler's Partners in Science, 125–28.

91. In the mid-twenties, both Rockefeller Jr. and trustee Fosdick, like Embree, were concerned about intellectual stagnation in the foundation. See JDR Jr. to Fosdick, 12/28/25, f. 251, box 25, RG III.2.0, Office of the Messrs. Rockefeller, RAC.

92. ERE to Max Mason, 5/7/28, reel 3, EREP-RFA.

93. In this connection, compare the description of a type of sociobiology pursued during the 1920s and 1930s; Kingsland, 195–230. Were he alive today, Embree undoubtedly would be pleased by two current illustrations of his prescience. At Harvard, an early-twenty-first-century update of the life sciences concentration provided an introductory course sequence that combines three branches of biology with anthropology and psychology. And a 2007 symposium at that institution, convened to examine the cognitive components involved in complex decision making, brought together scholars from business, economics, medicine, public health, and psychology.

94. See Paul, 263; and Weindling, 130–31. For subsequent Rockefeller support for research in some of the fields Embree promoted—psychology, neurology, genetics, psychiatry, physiology—see Alan Gregg, "Confidential Monthly Report for the Information of Trustees," 120 (4/1/50), 21–23, RAC. Similarly, Rockefeller grants to the National Research Council's Committee for Research in Problems of Sex (which supported a project leading to the 1948 and 1953 Kinsey reports) were used in "a wide sweep of the investigation [involving] biology, physiology, psychology, psychopathology, sociology, and other disciplines." Fosdick, *Story of the Rockefeller Foundation*, 126.

3. SOMEONE TO KEEP JULIUS ROSENWALD STRAIGHT

1. Two other men held vice presidential titles in 1927, but they had only regional responsibilities. Embree's position had no such limitation. EREOD, 6/4/25, f. 164, box 2, EREP-RFA; ERE to Simon Flexner, 7/15/27, reel 34, Simon Flexner Papers, RAC.

2. ERE to Stokes, 7/1/26, A. P. Stokes Papers, MAD-SML.

3. EREOD, 5/4/26, reel 2.

4. To the same mid-1926 document, Embree appended several pages tracing the history of the foundation's activity in biology and suggesting the adoption of a third major emphasis, the biological sciences, as an appropriate complement to its traditional interests in public health and medical education. This obvious promotion of his own division was rejected by the committee a few months later. "The Rockefeller Foundation: Organization and Program" [n.d.], f. 122, box 17, ser. 900, RG 3.1, RFA.

5. "To the Board of Trustees of the Rockefeller Foundation," 11/1/26, f. 122, box 17, ser. 900, RG 3, RFA.

6. Fosdick to Agar, 10/28/26 [same letter to Flexner], f. 122, box 17, ser. 900, RG 3, RFA.

7. An analysis of the timing and the decision process makes clear how great was Fosdick's influence on the reorganization and how disinclined other trustees were to challenge his judgment. Completing the draft on Thursday, October 28, he sent copies to Agar and Flexner (and to foundation counsel Thomas Debevoise), who returned them within three days with only minor comments, mostly editorial in nature. The final report and recommendations were completed on Monday, November 1, 1926. The board met only four days later, on November 5, and the members probably received this document, along with other materials, immediately before the meeting. Of the foundation's thirteen trustees, four were absent, and a fifth, having been told by Fosdick the meeting would last only an hour, left for another

appointment before the vote was taken.
Thus only eight of the thirteen trustees
were available to vote. Three of the eight
were the committee that had formulated
the recommendations. Because his hand
would be strengthened, George Vincent
could be expected to approve, as could
Rockefeller Jr. Wycliffe Rose and Embree
had frequently disagreed over turf, but for
reasons unrelated to the Division of Studies, the GEB and IEB head opposed the
reorganization plan. Thus, probably only
two trustees—Vernon Kellogg and Julius
Rosenwald—approached the elimination
of the division with an open mind—if
they even had sufficient time to think
about it. Embree had not built a strong
case for his division, but even so, the ease
with which it was abolished is striking.
And when viewed in light of Fosdick's
stated low regard for Embree's abilities,
discussed below, the whole episode becomes even more remarkable. Straus to
Fosdick, 11/6/26; Fosdick to GEV, 11/8/26,
both in f. 122, box 17, ser. 900, RG 3, RFA.

8. "To the Board of Trustees of the
Rockefeller Foundation," 11/1/26, f. 122,
box 17, ser. 900, RG 3.1, RFA.

9. EREOD, 11/9/26, 2/14/27, reel 2.

10. Kohler, "Policy," 494.

11. GEVOD, 11/10/26, reel 3, RG 12.1,
RFA. It is possible that Vincent and Flexner expected Embree to leave Rockefeller,
and in these statements were merely being solicitous of his feelings. Subsequent
developments, however, indicated that
their expressed sentiments were genuine.
EREOD, 2/16–18/27, reel 2.

12. GEVOD, 9/30/26, reel 3, RG 12.1,
RFA.

13. Fosdick to GEV, 12/21/26, f. 35, box
4, ser. 100, RG 1.1, RFA.

14. GEV to Fosdick, 12/23/26, ibid.

15. ERE to GEV, 1/5/27, ibid.

16. Fosdick to Flexner, 1/12/27, ibid.

17. See his comments, in another context, reported in EREOD, 2/18/27.

18. Kohler, "Policy," 499–501.

19. Fosdick to Agar and Flexner,
10/28/26, f. 122, box 17, ser. 900, RG 3.1,
RFA.

20. GEVOD, 2/7/27, reel 3, RFA.

21. GEVOD, 2/16/27, 2/21/27, reel 3,
RFA.

22. On Fosdick's views, see Kohler,
"Policy," 499–500. In an early draft report
on the reorganization, Fosdick included
a paragraph, subsequently deleted to
shorten the document, that described the
president's office as the "nerve center of
the organization, sensitive to any growing rigidity in our machinery, alert to the
dangers of programs becoming stale, of
methods and technique[s] becoming fixed
and inelastic with the passage of time."
Apparent success "in certain limited
areas" today, he wrote, should not lead to
the assumption that the same work, conducted in the same way, would guarantee
future success. The chief danger of organizations like Rockefeller was "stagnation,
a reverence for our own machinery, an
absorption with details, a bureaucratic un-
willingness to embrace new ideas and new
ways of doing things" (f. 122, box 17, ser.
900, RG 3.1, RFA). There is no reason to
believe Embree ever saw this paragraph.
Yet in substance and sentiment it is the
identical twin of passages Embree himself
would write a year later. See ERE to Clarence Day, 12/1/27, reel 2, EREP-SML; and
the more extensive description, written
four years later, in his draft "Rockefeller
Programs: Early History" [1930], f. 3, box
1, EREP-RFA. The possibility of "dry rot"
also troubled Rockefeller Jr. His "growing
concern" was expressed at length in JDR
Jr. to Fosdick, 12/28/25, f. 251, box 25, RG
III.2.0, Office of the Messrs. Rockefeller,
RAC. Alan Gregg of the foundation's
Paris office was similarly concerned, as
reported in EREOD, 11/25/26, reel 2, RFA.

23. Alan Gregg in the thirties described Fosdick as "essentially partisan

in his sympathies and attitudes," a man who "presses hard for what he wants" and who was not above employing "various and perhaps devious means to obtain it." Quoted in Wheatley, 180. Though Fosdick's personal ambition seems the most likely explanation for his extraordinary effort to oust Embree, he may have been acting for the board's chair. Whether Rockefeller Jr. had lost confidence in the man he had recruited a decade earlier cannot be directly documented, but Embree's increasingly critical comments by 1926 may have caused offense. His resignation letter the following year offered what came close to an apology for being too forward. See ERE to Rockefeller Jr., 12/29/27, f. 258, box 25, RG III.2.0, Office of the Messrs. Rockefeller, RAC. Moreover, Embree had moved far from the pietistic and abstemious upbringing that may have attracted Rockefeller to him in the first place. An Embree public statement about Prohibition, misreported or misinterpreted, had brought unwelcome publicity to the foundation and the Rockefeller family. See *New York Times*, 4/11/23; ERE to JDR Jr., 4/14/23, f. 257, box 25, RG III.2.0, Office of the Messrs. Rockefeller, RAC. These developments may have raised doubts in Rockefeller Jr.'s mind, but whether they turned him against Embree altogether will probably remain unknown.

24. Family Journal [n.d.], reel 4, EREP-SML.

25. ERE to Day, 12/1/27, reel 2; ERE to Johns Hopkins zoologist Raymond Pearl, 3/4/28, reel 3, EREP-SML.

26. EREOD, 5/26/26, f. 183, box 2. RFA. Throughout the 1920s, the foundation remained publicity-shy, apparently seeking to avoid anything like the firestorm of negative attention that Rockefeller philanthropy had received some years earlier. Sealander, 276, n76.

27. A particularly frustrating situation arose in 1926 when Embree was asked to edit or co-edit a volume of essays on human biology. This was an opportunity to present the field to a wider public, and both E. V. Cowdry, the organizer of the project, and Edwin Conklin considered him the best man in the country to write the introduction. But, discouraged by President Vincent, Embree declined the assignment, and though importuned repeatedly by Cowdry, he felt compelled to dissociate himself entirely from the book. His interest remained lively, however, and soon after leaving Rockefeller he agreed to write the introduction to the volume. EREOD, 4/27/26, 5/1/26, 6/1/26, 10/27/26, 2/16/27, 10/24/27; ERE interviews, 11/10/28, f. 6, box 120, JRFA. Cowdry himself edited the book, which was published by P. B. Hoeber in 1930 as *Human Biology and Racial Welfare*.

28. EREOD, 3/18/18, 1/20/20, 3/14/20, 3/15/20, box 1, RFA.

29. Flexner to JR, 11/28/25, f. 2, box 15, JRP.

30. JR to Flexner, 10/12/27, ibid.

31. Flexner to JR, 12/1/23, 11/28/25; JR to Flexner, 10/21/27, all ibid.; Flexner to JR, 11/7/27, f. 31, box 104, JRFA. On ERE discussions with Flexner, see EREOD, 11/5/27.

32. ERE to JR, 11/7/27, reel 3; ERE to Day, 12/1/27, reel 2, both in EREP-SML; EREOD, 11/28–29/27, reel 2.

33. ERE to Day, 12/1/27, reel 1, EREP-SML.

34. EREOD, 11/30/27, 12/2/17; JR to ERE, 12/5/27, reel 3, EREP-SML.

35. Outhwaite datebook, 12/6/27, "Negro Problems Conference 1927–28"; Outhwaite to ERE, 12/12/27, both in f. 1023, box 101, sub-ser. 8, ser. III, LSRM, RAC. A decade later, Embree encountered what he called Princeton's "old-fashioned southern attitude" when he tried to arrange a postdoctoral appointment at the Institute for Advanced Study for a brilliant black mathematician. See the exten-

sive correspondence regarding William
W. S. Claytor in f. 6, box 402, JRFA. In the
1940s, Princeton movie theaters were seg-
regated, and stores did not allow African
Americans to try on clothing or shoes. See
Isaacson, 505.

36. "Participants in Inter-Racial Conference," f. 1023, box 101, sub-ser. 8, ser. III,
LSRM, RAC.

37. Outhwaite to ERE, 12/12/27;
"Schedule of Meetings and Subjects,"
both in f. 1023, box 101, sub-ser. 6, ser. III,
LSRM, RAC. There is an unsubstantiated
contention that James Weldon Johnson
suggested to Embree the idea of the fellowship program for black researchers and
artists that Embree implemented at the
Rosenwald Fund. Johnson and Embree
had talked ten days before the New Haven
conference, but Embree's diary mentions
only his hope that some younger black
men would attend (EREOD, 12/9/27,
RAC). Yet it is clear that, even before
the meeting, Embree was attracted by
philanthropic possibilities "in the field
of the arts, in which the Negro has already made important contributions and
through which he may most easily come
to recognition on his individual merits."
ERE to Outhwaite, 12/13/27, f. 1023, box
101, sub-ser. 8, ser. III, LSRM, RAC. As a
New York resident, he probably had some
familiarity with the flowering of African
American talent in Harlem, much of it
orchestrated by Charles S. Johnson. James
Weldon Johnson certainly reinforced and
sharpened Embree's thinking along these
lines, but he did not originate it. See ERE
interviews, 4/22/31, f. 7, box 120, JRFA.

38. ERE to JR, 12/27/27, f. 31, box 104,
JRFA.

39. Fosdick, Adventure in Giving, 238.

40. Several subsequent developments
indicate that Embree's hope to forge links
between the social and natural sciences
was shared by others. A year after he left
Rockefeller, there appeared in Paris the

first issue of Annales d'histoire économique
et sociale, a journal emphasizing research
in all the social sciences plus climatology,
linguistics, and medical science. The new
journal, and the school of interdisciplin-
ary scholarship which it fostered, would
revolutionize the field of history. During
the thirties, Rockefeller received at least
three funding requests for cross-disciplinary research projects involving elements
of Embree's plans for human biology. In
the same decade, Alan Gregg's Division of
Medical Sciences devoted almost three-
fourths of its expenditures to studies in
psychology and biology—the field then
called variously "psychobiology" or "mental hygiene" or "psychiatry" (see Paul, 263,
267–68). The period also saw the foundation mount the "new science of man" project, involving participation by its medical,
social science, and natural science divisions. These ventures, though probably
better conceived, were entirely in keeping
with the kind of investigations Embree
had envisioned for the Division of Studies.
A 2007 symposium, convened at Harvard
to examine the cognitive components
involved in complex decision making,
brought together scholars from business,
economics, medicine, public health, and
psychology. These developments, taken
together, suggest that Embree had his eye
on a far more promising, and ultimately
fruitful, enterprise than Raymond Fosdick was able to comprehend.

41. Gregg, "Comments on Personalities," 11.

42. During Ruml's five years on the
Rosenwald board, Embree relied on him
to second, and perhaps amplify, his own
views. The board had only three important standing committees—nominating,
finance, and executive—and there were
times when Ruml served simultaneously
on all three. DOB, MOT, 11/18/33, box 136,
JRFA.

43. Ascoli, 256, 299.

44. Stern to ERE, 7/10/28, f. 12. For an example of Stern's marginalization, see his correspondence in f. 13. Both folders are in box 129, JRFA.

45. Embree's apology for the faux pas is in ERE to Edgar Stern, 3/1/28, f. 5. Illustrative of the cordial relationship is ERE to Edith Stern, 3/4/30, and Edith Stern to ERE, 5/2/30, f. 6. For Julius Rosenwald's biographer, Embree suggested David Lawrence, but Lawrence apparently never undertook the assignment. Edgar Stern to ERE, 2/19/29, f. 5. All in box 140, JRFA.

46. The uncertainty was reflected in correspondence between the New Orleans Sterns and Alfred Stern. See Edith Stern to Alfred Stern, 10/12/28; Edgar Stern to Alfred Stern, 5/1/29; ERE to Edgar Stern, 5/4/29, all in f. 5, box 140; "Meeting of Members," 5/14/32, f. 12, box 80. In 1937, the board was again raised to thirteen members, and in 1941 to fourteen, while the family's membership, which was rotated among Rosenwald offspring and in-laws, remained at three. "Meeting of Members," 11/30/37, 11/14/41, f. 12, box 80, JRFA.

47. "Meeting of Members," 4/25/30, f. 11, box 80, JRFA.

48. By the 1940s, committee sessions had become quite informal. Though minutes were carefully kept and decisions properly documented, the meetings no longer were held in the fund's offices, but at private clubs over lunch or late afternoon cocktails. In such settings, with the time available for business apparently limited, the approval of Embree's recommendations tended to be pro forma.

49. MEC, 10/30/29, 1, f. 3, box 79.

50. EREOD, 11/10/27. After conducting studies for two years, Outhwaite was the best-informed official at Rockefeller headquarters on the circumstances of southern blacks.

51. ERE interviews, 2/17–24/28, f. 5, box 120, JRFA.

52. Also attending was Michael Davis, an authority on health service with whom Embree had worked at Rockefeller and who shared with trustee Franklin McLean an interest in pay clinics. ERE to Outhwaite, 4/19/28, f. 1141, box 112, ser. III.10, LSRM, RAC.

53. At the time, there were some 200 general-purpose foundations with a combined capitalization of approximately $1 billion; a new one was established every few weeks. Keppel, *Foundation*, vi; ERE, "Business of Giving," 322. In early 1928, four Carnegie endowments had a book value of $220 million; the Rockefeller trusts, $382 million. "Conference of Trustees and Guests, Julius Rosenwald Fund," 4/29/28, appendix A, box 135, JRFA, 1–4.

54. A copy of Rosenwald's remarks to the American Academy of Political and Social Science is in f. 17, box 32, JRP.

55. For one side of this disagreement, see Rockefeller Jr. to Thomas Applegate; to Raymond Fosdick, both 4/5/31, f. 302, box 29, ser. Rockefeller Boards, RG 2, Office of the Messrs. Rockefeller, RFA, RAC.

56. Keppel, *Foundation*, 4, 65.

57. Magda West, f. 3, box 89, JRFA; Keppel, *Foundation*, 4, 65.

58. "The Julius Rosenwald Fund: Report to June 30, 1928," f. 7, box 84, JRFA.

59. JR and Tobenkin, "Burden of Wealth."

60. Sedgwick to JR, 5/15/28, f. 6, box 3, JRP; JR, "Principles of Public Giving," 599–606. The finished piece was the work of William G. Rice, editor of the *Mining Gazette* of Houghton, Michigan, who had earlier ghost-written speeches for Rosenwald. JR to Rice, 1/5/29, 2/27/29; ERE to Rice, 11/22/28, all in f. 3, box 51, JRP; Ascoli, 318.

61. Pritchett, "Use and Abuse of Endowments."

62. JR, "Trend Away from Perpetuities"; ERE to *Atlantic Monthly*, 4/14/29,

f. 3, box 51, JRP; ERE to John H. Gray of American University, 6/13/29, f. 7, box 3, JRP. The Rosenwald Fund reprinted the article as an eleven-page pamphlet. A copy is in f. 10, box 3, JRP.

63. Many of these letters, including one from Henry Pritchett, are in f. 6, box 3, JRP. Embree was disappointed that, consistent with the publicity-shy Rockefeller Foundation's policy, Rockefeller Jr. would not allow his letter to be used publicly. Foundation president Vincent also refused initially, but relented under ERE's urging. ERE interview with JR, 6/30/30, f. 7, box 120, JRFA.

64. JR, "Trend Away from Perpetuities." As with the first *Atlantic* article, Embree had thousands reprinted and circulated widely (f. 10, box 3, JRP). Several weeks before the second *Atlantic* piece appeared, and with Embree's encouragement, Rosenwald had presented his ideas on perpetuities to the annual meeting of the American Hospital Association in New Orleans. Material for that address had been assembled by Embree, assisted by Michael Davis. ERE interviews, 9/11/30, 9/18/30, both f. 7, box 128, JRFA.

65. Keppel, *Foundation*, iv, 4, 33, 45–51, 56–57, 93. Even earlier, Keppel had criticized any effort by a philanthropic trust to mold public views. See his "Opportunities and Dangers," 6–7.

66. ERE, "Business of Giving," 321–29. Even before the piece appeared in print, Embree considered expanding it into a small book, in order to include information about current foundations and to recommend procedures for establishing such trusts. ERE conversation with Clarence Day, 6/8/30, f. 7, box 10, JRFA.

67. "Business of Giving," 321, 322, 329. The principles discussed and some of the language in this piece had appeared earlier in Embree's essay in the fund's annual report, "The Julius Rosenwald Fund: Review to June 30, 1929," f. 8, box

84, JRFA. The notion of creating new "social appetites" Embree probably got from George Bernard Shaw's essay "Socialism for Millionaires," which he quotes at the beginning of the article.

68. Pritchett's 1922 book was *A Science of Giving.* The quotation is from Keppel, "Opportunities and Dangers," 796.

69. ERE, "Negro Illness and Its Effect upon the Nation's Health."

70. ERE, "How Negro Schools Have Advanced under the Rosenwald Fund"; ERE, "Fewer and Better Nurses."

71. ERE, "What Is Organized Medicine?"

72. *New York Times,* July 7, 1929, 112.

73. ERE, "How the Foundations Fight Disease."

74. Eastman to JR, 6/21/29; ERE to Raymond Fosdick, 6/24/29, both in f. 6, box 3, JRP.

75. Cochran to JR, quoted in "Trend Away from Perpetuities," 4 and 8 in the reprint, f. 10, box 3, JRP.

76. Brookings in private conversation, reported in ERE, "Memorandum for Discussion by Mr. Rockefeller and Mr. Rosenwald" [1931?], f. 8, box 32, JRP. See Ross, "Philanthropy from the Viewpoint of the Sociologist." On Crane, see ERE to JR, 4/17/31, f. 9, box 33, JRP.

77. Mark M. Jones, quoted in ERE review of Alfred W. Anthony, ed., "Philanthropy for the Future," *Journal of Higher Education* 3, no. 5 (1931): 284.

78. Encouraged by U.S. ambassador Dwight Morrow, Embree was moving enthusiastically toward such commitments in Mexico, but turmoil following the assassination of President-elect Álvaro Obregón in July, together with skepticism from Mexican Catholics and nationalists about foreign involvement in the school system, disrupted the planning. Embree and Morrow continued to correspond about the project through 1929, but it never got under way. "A Report to the

Trustees of the Julius Rosenwald Fund," 7/6/28, f. 7, box 58, JRP. The Embree-Morrow correspondence is in f. 15, box 116, JRFA. For Embree's summary of the matter, see ERE to M. R. Werner, 9/27/37, f. 21, box 118, JRFA. On Nicaragua, see ERE interviews, f. 5; on the Mexico meeting with Hoover, 8/28/28, f. 6, both in box 120, JRFA.

4. SOUTHERN INITIATIVES, ASSET COLLAPSE, TRANSFORMATION

1. ERE to Clarence Day, 5/9/29, f. 8, box 58, CDP.
2. Embree and Waxman, 34.
3. "Conference of Officers of Rockefeller Foundation and International Health Board," 1/11/19, f. 164, box 21, ser. 900, RG 3; ERE to GEV, f. 121, box 16, ser. 700, RG 1.1, both in RFA, RAC; ERE to Walter MacDougall, 3/31/22, student records, Edwin R. Embree, RG 8, Berea College Archives, Berea, Kentucky.
4. Abraham Flexner served as an informal mentor for Embree and probably influenced his thinking about philanthropy more than any other figure. Embree sought his counsel repeatedly, especially during the early years at Rosenwald. Embree's views on philanthropic risk taking, the danger of foundations' sterility, the need for continuous intellectual renewal, foundations' support for the humanities, and the important work to be done in the South were all characteristic of Flexner. See *Abraham Flexner: An Autobiography*, 274 ff.
5. ERE to Stokes, 2/19/29, Anson Phelps Stokes Papers, MAD-SML; ERE interviews, 9/19/28, 6/28/29, f. 6, box 120, JRFA.
6. "Report to the Trustees, Annual Meeting," 11/16/29, box 135, JRFA; ERE to JR, 3/1/28, 2/14/29, both in f. 32, box 104, JRFA.
7. Attributed to key Rockefeller executive Frederick Gates, "scatteration"

suggests a failure to concentrate philanthropic funds on major issues, thereby diminishing their effectiveness.
8. DuBois's views on ending the dispersal of resources over scores of small, poor schools are described in Moss, 42, 48. Embree and officers of the GEB had agreed by 1928 that their efforts should be concentrated on university centers in Washington, Nashville, Atlanta, and New Orleans. "Conference of Trustees and Guests, Julius Rosenwald Fund," 4/29/28, 19; "Minutes of JRF," 5/11/29, 137, both in box 57, JRFA.
9. ERE to Frederick Brownlee (of the AMA), 3/2/28, f. 1141, box 112, ser. III.10, LSRM, RAC.
10. ERE interviews with Brownlee, 10/2/28; with Edgar Stern, 9/13/28, both in f. 6, box 120, JRFA; Embree and Waxman, 98–101.
11. ERE interviews, f. 7, box 120, JRFA.
12. Bond was one of Embree's favorite Rosenwald fellows, and the fund's president promoted his career at several points, agreeing to cover the costs of publishing his dissertation and almost elevating him to his first college presidency. Bond was a brilliant scholar and even without Embree's patronage would likely have established himself as the important educator and civil rights champion he became. In the 1930s, the Dillard faculty included biologist Charles Wesley Buggs, sculptor Elizabeth Catlett, historians Benjamin Quarles and Lawrence Reddick, and anthropologists Allison Davis and St. Clair Drake, all of whom had received Rosenwald fellowships.
13. Embree and Waxman, 263–69.
14. In some areas of the South, chagrin over the attractiveness of the new schools for black youth spurred local officials to erect new buildings for white children. Over 15,000 white schools used plans made available by the fund. Embree and Waxman, 56.

15. Concern about school boards' dependence on external funding was not unique to the fund; it emerged at the Rockefeller Foundation within the philanthropy's first few months. See Jerome D. Greene to Wallace Buttrick, 1/7/14, quoted in Anderson and Moss, 85. ERE to Frederick Brownlee, 3/2/28, f. 1141, box 112, ser. III.10, LSRM, RAC; ERE, "The Julius Rosenwald Fund: Review of Two Decades, 1917–1936," f. 3, box 85, JRFA, 15.

16. ERE, "Business of Giving," 329. Rosenwald and other philanthropies have been faulted for funding segregated institutions and, in the case of schools, cooperating with local, often racist, officials. See, for example, Stanfield, "Dollars for the Silent South." Such criticism is not without merit, but the critics have seldom suggested a viable alternative, nor have they offered a full discussion of the consequences for black southerners had such support not been forthcoming. It is notable that historian Carter G. Woodson, the father of black studies, defended such cooperation, pointing out that without the sanction of local white leaders, the new buildings would have been vulnerable to destruction by the Ku Klux Klan and other anti-black groups. Unpublished history of Rosenwald school-building program, chap. 5, 1–2, JRP. One Rosenwald school, in Mississippi County, Arkansas, was burned to the ground the night before it was to be dedicated. It was replaced in 1924; the new structure was of brick. Hoffschwelle, 119.

17. Embree and Waxman, 51, 55. One additional Rosenwald school was built after 1932. In response to a request from the White House, Embree agreed "reluctantly" (out of concern that it might appear that the program was being revived) to a school in Warm Springs, Georgia, the site of the treatment center for infantile paralysis patients where Franklin Roosevelt spent considerable time. The Eleanor Roosevelt School was dedicated in March 1937, with remarks by the president of the United States. Hoffschwelle, 277.

18. Embree and Waxman, 51–56.

19. According to one education official, the South's 9 million blacks constituted 24 percent of the region's population, but had access to only 245 high schools, fewer than 4 percent of those in operation. In the 1927 high school graduating class across the South, only about 7 percent of the students were African American. "Minutes of the JRF," 8/14/28, box 57, JRP, 39.

20. A balanced summary of the Jones report, free of the polemic that initially attended its publication, is in Anderson and Moss, 202–11.

21. "Minutes of the JRF," 8/14/28, box 57, JRP; ERE to Clark Foreman, 10/17/28, f. 10, box 105, JRFA.

22. Item IV, DOB, Executive Committee, 8/14/28; "Minutes of the JRF," 8/14/28, both in box 57, JRP; ERE to JR, 1/25/29, f. 32, box 104, JRFA; ERE to A. K. Stern, 11/16/31, f. 3, box 310, JRFA. For the importance of academic subjects in Embree's thinking, see the undated "Suggested Program of Studies for Pupils Taking Industrial Courses," f. 2, box 253, JRFA. The program, which covered grades seven through nine, called for three of the student's four courses each year to be academic. Carter G. Woodson, who had been the principal of an industrial high school for African Americans in Washington, D.C., shared Embree's view. He insisted that the black masses needed to be trained for work in an urban environment, and in 1930 he argued that such practical training was more needed than classical education. Goggin, 47, 160, 197. For another expression of the importance the fund attached to academic preparation, see Rosenwald agent George R. Arthur to Little Rock lawyer W. W. Booker, 12/17/28, f. 1, box 274, JRFA.

23. Projects were considered in several other cities, but with the exception of New Orleans, none was pursued very far. In the case of the Crescent City, Embree concluded, after face-to-face discussions, that school officials there were not genuinely committed to strengthening black education and could not be trusted to use funds wisely. These considerations, together with the failure of a local bond issue and the severe depletion of Rosenwald resources, doomed those negotiations. "Conference of Representatives of the Rosenwald Fund and the Orleans Parish School Board," 1/29/31; A. K. Stern to (superintendent of schools) Nicholas Bauer, 4/22/31; ERE to (school board member) Isaac Heller, 9/21/31, 11/9/31, all in f. 3, box 310, JRFA.

24. "Minutes of the JRF," 4/26/30, f. 1, box 5, JRP, 264–65; ERE to JR, 10/16/31; "Conspectus of Present and Future Activities of the JRF," 10/31/30, f. 5, box 58, JRP, 4–5.

25. ERE interviews with A. K. Stern, 3/11/30, 4/28/30, 3/24/31, all in f. 7, box 120, JRFA. Stern began to push industrial education in the months before Embree arrived at the fund. Hoffschwelle, 119–21. Embree's growing doubts about industrial education undoubtedly contributed to the cooling of what began as a warm relationship with Alfred K. Stern.

In several groundbreaking articles and a book, James D. Anderson has contended that northern philanthropic support of industrial education was basically intended to create a competent workforce of blacks to staff southern industry. Had that effort succeeded, the result, in his view, would have been youth trained for inferior, racially limited occupations and socialized to fit docilely into a repressive social order. Anderson's argument, accepted at least in part by various historians, is most fully developed in *The Education of Blacks in the South.* See also his "Education as

a Vehicle for the Manipulation of Black Workers," 17–18; and "Philanthropic Control over Black Higher Education," 156–57. In the chapter "The Black Public High School" in Arnove (206ff., particularly 207–208, 227–34), Anderson describes the Rosenwald Fund as assuming in 1928 the "vanguard role" in efforts to shape public secondary education for southern blacks.

Anderson's interpretation need not be rejected altogether, but note should be taken of significant inaccuracies regarding Embree and the Rosenwald Fund, involving a misunderstanding of Embree's motivations, the fund's priorities and policies, the personal dynamics among its executives, and the reasons for ending the school-building program. A comprehensive presentation of these inaccuracies would be out of place here, but two examples are indicative of the interpretive problems. First, Anderson's contention that, before 1932, Rosenwald, like other northern philanthropies, promoted industrial training at the expense of traditional schooling, thereby denying talented individuals access to higher education, flies in the face of Embree's statements and the board's actions. Moreover, it fails to take into account the Rosenwald fellowship program, which enabled almost 600 African American men and women to pursue advanced study. This program, of all the fund's initiatives, was the one to which Embree was most strongly committed and the one to which he devoted the most time and energy.

Second, Anderson seems to ignore the way that organizational priorities find expression in budget allocations. The figures are unusually revealing in this instance. During 1928–1932, the only time when the construction of industrial training facilities was supported, the fund's total expenditures for that purpose were $202,708. At a single meeting during that period, by contrast, the Rosenwald board on Embree's recommendation voted $959,000 for black higher education. Embree and Waxman, 263; "Minutes of Meeting of Trustees," 5/11/29, box 135, JRFA, 4–5, 9–15. Other meetings produced additional large allocations for colleges. Anderson's conclusions in other regards may be above reproach, but certainly Embree and the Rosenwald Fund cannot be made to fit the Procrustean bed to which he has consigned them.

26. Embree and Waxman, 60–61.

27. MEC, 6/4/40, f. 2, box 80, JRFA; Embree and Waxman, 63–65.

28. Embree and Waxman, 65–67. Library grants were used similarly to promote equal treatment even in private institutions. When the YMCA Graduate School in Nashville requested money to build up a collection of materials on African American life, the fund approved the request only with the stipulations that responsibility for selecting the items would be shared with Fisk University and that Fisk students would have full access to the collection. MEC, 9/18/29, f. 3, box 79, JRFA.

29. "Fellowships," 11/37, 28–29, f. 2, box 373; ERE to Robert C. Weaver, 12/20/40, f. 2, box 374, both in JRFA; Embree and Waxman, 156.

30. ERE interview with Alain Locke, 4/22/31, f. 7, box 120, JRFA; ERE to James Weldon Johnson, 4/4/29, f. 414, box 17, J. W. Johnson Papers, Beinecke Rare Book and Manuscript Library, Yale University; ERE interviews, 11/30/28, f. 6, box 120, JRFA.

31. "Minutes of Trustees," 11/1/28, f. 5, box 77, JRFA.

32. These two categories, obviously broad, seem designed to provide the maximum latitude for selecting recipients. "Special Meeting of Trustees," 5/11/29, box 135, JRFA, 18–20.

33. Ibid., 20. See also ERE to JR, 3/29/29, f. 32, box 104, JRFA. Additional

information on the fellowships in the arts can be found in Perkins, "Investment in Talent," 24–35.

34. Johnson was one of a few already prominent figures who received grants; others were W. E. B. DuBois and George E. Haynes. Johnson used the first of his twice-renewed grants to write *Black Manhattan,* the first history of Harlem; he also had in mind producing another volume of poems, a novel, and the text of an oratorio based on "God's Trombones." See f. 414, box 17, J. W. Johnson Papers. DuBois's award enabled him to write *Black Reconstruction,* a book he considered his most important scholarly work. Haynes's fellowship allowed the sociologist to observe native life in the colonies of Rhodesia, Angola, and the Belgian Congo. All three of these men were over fifty years old at the time; a later guideline prescribed that recipients usually be between twenty-two and thirty-four.

35. A complete list of fellowship recipients is in Embree and Waxman, appendix C.

36. Information on recipients' personal circumstances at the time of the award and its intended purpose is available in the individual fellowship folders at JRFA.

37. Embree, Johnson, and Alexander served on the committee throughout the life of the program and were certainly its most important members. After Moe's departure, additional members at various times were economist Robert C. Weaver, writer Arna Bontemps, Howard University dean Charles Thompson, editor Gould Beech, and Birmingham-Southern College president Raymond Paty. Embree and Waxman, 153. Three of these later members were African American, as was Charles S. Johnson. By the late twentieth century, such racially mixed standing committees did not seem exceptional; in the 1930s and 1940s, few, if any, could

be found beyond those of the Rosenwald Fund.

38. Raymond Paty to Fellowship Committee [1937], f. 2, box 374, JRFA.

39. "Negro Fellowships" [1932?], f. 10, box 57, JRP; Embree and Waxman, 150.

40. Moneys for such a program had been appropriated in 1929, but the Depression apparently prevented the expenditure. MEC, 5/11/29, f. 6, box 77, JRFA, 151; ERE to A. P. Stokes, 2/19/29, f. 310, box 19, A. P. Stokes Papers, MAD-SML.

41. ERE, "Julius Rosenwald Fund: Review for the Two-Year Period 1940–42," f. 7, box 85, JRFA, 17.

42. "Fellowships, Meeting of Trustees," 11/13–15/36, box 136, JRFA, 19.

43. "Fellowships," 11/37, f. 2, box 373, JRFA, 28–29; "Minutes of the JRF," f. 2, box 373, JRFA, 742; Embree and Waxman, 153. After the southern grants had been offered for a decade, Embree acknowledged that the white fellows lacked the "stellar quality" of the black, and one board member lamented that more fellows in a position to influence regional opinion had not been found. "Fellowship Program" [1947?], f. 10, box 76, JRFA; "Meeting of Trustees of the Julius Rosenwald Fund," 4/21/45, box 137, JRFA, 1013.

44. Program director William C. Haygood, "Memorandum to the Members of the Fellowship Committee," 6/43, f. 3, box 374, JRFA. Awards to whites totaled 538, representing 278 individuals. This number included a few social scientists who were not southerners, but whose research interested Embree. Embree and Waxman, 152, 252–59.

45. "Annual Meeting of Trustees," 11/16/29, box 135, JRFA; Embree and Waxman, 34–35.

46. Indicative of the widespread failure to comprehend the situation, Julius Rosenwald during these days feared the nation might soon face a labor shortage. Leuchtenburg, 105. Five months later,

Rosenwald did suggest that expansion into new areas be slowed. His expressed concern was not that the philanthropy could become financially overextended, however, but that Embree needed to be able to exercise proper oversight over the projects already under way. ERE interview with JR, 4/29/30, f. 7, box 120, JRFA.

47. "Annual Meeting of Trustees," 11/16/29, box 135, JRFA, 12–48.

48. Ascoli, 386. The fund's holdings in May 1932 were valued at $2,970,432. Its appropriations payable, together with a bank loan of $1,200,000, constituted liabilities of $3,782,914. Balance Sheet, 9/30/32, DOB, MOT, 11/12/32, f. 7, box 79, JRFA, 8.

49. "Conspectus of Present and Future Activities of the Fund," 7/23/30, f. 11, box 85, JRFA; "Recommendation to Limit Appropriations during the Next Year or Two," f. 5, box 58, JRP. Embree obviously had mixed feelings. Even as he recommended sharply reduced activity, he circulated to the board a four-page document warning against philanthropic timidity and bureaucratic routine, and affirming an obligation to pioneer in social reform. "Special Confidential Memorandum on the Kinds of Things That Should Be Supported by Foundations," 7/23/30, f. 12, box 85, JRFA.

50. ERE to JR, 11/27/31, f. 13, box 90, JRFA. Among the appropriations allowed to lapse was $2,700 for "Venereal Disease Control" in Alabama, which was the Tuskegee syphilis experiment. "Appropriations Allowed to Lapse," 5/14–9/30/32, f. 7, box 79, JRFA. Tuskegee was part of a six-state project testing methods of syphilis control across the South. As part of its effort to improve the health of African Americans, Rosenwald cooperated with the U.S. Public Health Service and state health departments in the experiment, providing about one-half of the funding during 1929–1931. The fund's financial support ended long before the introduction of

the practices that later made the Tuskegee project notorious, but during the thirties it did grant $13,000 to the Tuskegee venereal disease clinic for operating expenses. ERE to JR, 12/16/29, f. 32, box 104, JRFA; "Memorandum on Syphilis Control Demonstrations" [1931?], f. 10, box 57, JRP; DOB, MOT, 11/11/40, box 137, JRFA, 7.

51. ERE to Clark Foreman, 4/18/32, f. 10, box 105, JRFA.

52. In the last months of Rosenwald's life, Embree tried to persuade him to diversify the fund's endowment with an additional $5 million in non-Sears stock; his suggestion went unanswered. Ascoli, 374. The Depression had a major impact on Rosenwald's own wealth, in part because with great generosity he had backed the losses that some 300 employees had incurred on Sears stock. The settlement of his will revealed that he had borrowed $2 million from a Chicago bank and guaranteed loans of $150,000 to his synagogue and $210,000 to Embree. (How Embree used the loan money is not known.) *Chicago Daily Tribune,* Aug. 10, 1932, 1; ERE interviews, 4/12/32, f. 7, box 120, JRFA.

53. ERE and Lessing Rosenwald to Raymond Fosdick, 5/25/32, f. 2041, box 212, ser. I.2, GEB, RAC. This folder contains extensive correspondence on this matter. Like all philanthropies, the GEB was strained by the economic crisis, and given the unprecedented nature of Rosenwald's appeal, perhaps it can be pardoned for imposing such onerous conditions. Even so, the tone of its correspondence strikes the reader as unnecessarily brusque, smug, a bit superior. It is clear that the GEB's interest was in protecting the southern institutions, not aiding a sister philanthropy. See, for example, Max Mason to Trevor Arnett, 6/10/32; W. W. Brierley to ERE, 9/22/32; excerpts from Thomas Appleget's diary, 6/3/32; Appleget to (Rockefeller Jr.'s secretary) Janet M. Warfield, 7/29/32. One scholar who has

closely examined this episode characterizes it as a "thoroughly humiliating experience" for Embree and the fund. Ascoli, 392. When Rockefeller's approach is compared to Carnegie's, it is easy to conclude that this was not the former's finest hour.

54. Attachment to ERE to Trevor Arnett, 3/23/34, f. 2041, box 212, ser. I.2, GEB, RAC.

55. Embree and Waxman, 206–207; untitled report to board, MOT, 11/12/32, f. 7, box 79, JRFA. By 1937, the bank loan had also been repaid, and the fund's assets were valued at about $7 million. ERE, "Two Decades of the Julius Rosenwald Fund, 1917–1936," f. 3, box 85, JRFA, 7–8.

56. "General Statement," DOB, MOT, 11/18/33, box 136, JRFA, 9.

57. The fund's new orientation is described in a lengthy document written by Embree as part of the DOB, MOT, 11/12/32, box 135, JRFA.

58. Sealander, 22–23. The Rockefeller philanthropies in particular were publicity-shy, perhaps chastened by the doubts and opposition aroused when the foundation had sought a national charter from Congress two decades earlier.

59. For Embree's optimism about changing opinions and customs, see ERE to Clarence Day, 10/23/26, reel 2, EREP-SML. Though the Rosenwald precedent was not widely imitated at the time, such efforts to mold opinion were scarcely exceptional a half-century later. The National Committee on Responsive Philanthropy in a 1997 report called attention to a dozen philanthropies that, since the 1970s, have advanced an ideological agenda, using their resources to support conservative scholars, train a new generation of conservative leaders, finance think tanks and media outlets, and promote studies critical of liberal approaches and programs.

Philanthropy authority James Allen Smith has pointed out that such foundations operate on the fundamental assumptions that ideas matter, politics involve "an aggressive war of ideas," and ideas can be "propagated, marketed, and sold." Smith, "Foundations and Public Policy," 29–30. Similar assumptions were clearly embedded in Rosenwald's post-1932 orientation, and the late-twentieth-century uses of resources were foreshadowed by many of Embree's initiatives. Though traditional philanthropy executives may scoff at propagandistic measures, as some of Embree's counterparts perhaps did in private, their current influence can scarcely be denied. Embree, from the other side of the political spectrum, developed an early model of the foundation as an ideologically engaged organization. At the same time, the fund took on some characteristics of a contemporary think tank, conducting studies and articulating views to advance a social and political agenda.

60. "Conference of Trustees and Guests," 4/29/28, f. 1, box 57, JRP, 13. Three years later, Embree still averred, "Individual foundations can probably serve best by making investigations, experiments, and demonstrations." ERE, "The Julius Rosenwald Fund: Review for the Year 1931," f. 10, box 84, JRFA, 7. The Carnegie Corporation's Frederick Keppel, notably inclined to enunciate "foundation doctrine," had emphasized the same point. "Danger arises," he warned, "whenever any group with power in its hands, whether it be a state legislature, or the board of a university, or of a foundation, believes it to be its business to use its power to direct opinion." Any such group was dangerous, regardless of its intentions and whether acting consciously or unconsciously. Fortunately, he continued, foundations themselves were understanding more clearly "the distinction between the advancement of knowledge and the direction of opinion." "Opportunities and Dangers," 6–7.

61. DOB, MOT, 8/22/33, box 136, JRFA, 11–14. See also DOB, MOT, 11/12/32, box 135, 1–6. Embree defended the policy of "direct effort" and pointed out the special responsibilities entailed in "Two Decades," 10–11. He later linked the policy to the fund's founder, stating that Julius Rosenwald "was eager" to have the fund's officers "affect social policy directly as well as through financial contributions to specific agencies." DOB, MOT, 5/24/47 [no f.], box 137, JRFA.

62. Embree and Waxman, 182. Weaver's appointment marked the beginning of a long-term friendship with Embree. During the forties, they worked together closely on race relations issues, and Weaver served on the Rosenwald fellows selection committee. In the 1960s, Weaver became the first African American to hold a federal cabinet post, when President Lyndon Johnson appointed him secretary of the Department of Housing and Urban Development.

63. "Program of Conference on the Economic Status of the Negro," 5/11–13/33, f. 2047, box 213, ser. I.2, GEB, RAC. The conference attracted the attention of the New York Times (May 13, 1933, 25), which quoted addresses by Embree and W. E. B. DuBois at some length.

64. One of the more important Embree-arranged conferences, which took place in Chicago in 1944, resulted in the formation of the American Council on Race Relations. Another was a 1946 event, jointly sponsored by the Georgia Teacher Education Council and the Commission on Teacher Education of the American Council on Education, which brought together 170 delegates from thirty-five states to discuss rural education. DOB, MOT, 3/20/44, box 137, JRFA, 11–12; Embree and Waxman, 79–80.

65. See, for example, "Medical Costs to Suit Men of Moderate Means," New York Times, July 7, 1929, f. 3, box 89, JRFA, 112.

66. The value of favorable publicity was always on Embree's mind. During the Second World War, when anti-black riots erupted across the country, he appointed a board committee to consider how to persuade journalists to write more positive news about African Americans in uniform, including their role in combat. MOT, 11/13/43, f. 14, box 80, JRFA, 955–56. Later, when the fund commissioned a history of blacks in the war, the moneys appropriated to pay the two researchers were almost equaled by a separate appropriation to ensure "wide publicity" for their findings. MEC, 10/5/45, f. 7, box 80, JRFA.

67. DOB, MOT, 11/12/32, box 135; ERE to Frank Stubbs, 6/28/28, f. 24, box 129, both in JRFA.

68. Eleven of the thirty-three books dealt with financing medical care, a major interest of the fund during the early thirties. DOB, MOT, 5/18/35, box 136, JRFA, 24. In 1935 alone, for example, some 50,000 copies of the pamphlets "School Money in Black and White" and "Every Tenth Pupil" were distributed. DOB, MOT, 4/20/40, box 137, JRFA, 29. During 1942–1944, over 100,000 books and pamphlets were mailed. DOB, MOT, 11/20/44, box 137, JRFA, 13. To reach a younger group, Rosenwald in the mid-forties commissioned a book series for teenagers. Embree himself published two books aimed at that age group: *American Negroes: A Handbook* and *Peoples of the Earth*.

69. A chronological listing of Embree's books and articles appears in the bibliography.

70. During 1928–1931, the reviews appeared annually. The 1936 issue dealt with the first twenty years of the fund.

71. MEC, 10/30/29, f. 3, box 79, 12; DOB, MOT, 4/20/40, box 137, JRFA, 29. Embree's essays attracted considerable attention. His emphasis on black progress in the 1930 piece "The Negro Front" resulted in hundreds of newspaper comments and

more than a full column in the *New York Times*. That response helped him decide to write *Brown America*. ERE to JR, 12/18/30, 10/30/31, both in f. 9, box 33, JRP.

72. Of the four co-authored volumes, he was the principal author of three.

73. The breadth of Embree's interest in diverse cultures emerges even more forcefully when his unpublished manuscripts are considered. These included two on the peoples of the Pacific, another on cultural relations in the American Southwest, and a forty-eight-page sketch of a history of the Jews. Most are undated, but such writing projects were in mind no later than 1931. ERE to Clarence Day, 5/23/31, reel 2, EREP-SML.

74. See, for example, ERE to William H. Jackson, 12/5/46, f. 4, box 117, JRFA.

75. This was not Embree's first book; he had edited one and co-edited another at Yale. Published by the university press, both were noncommercial ventures aimed at Yale graduates, not the broad audience for which *Brown America* and later volumes were written.

76. ERE to Clarence Day, 4/14/31, 5/23/31, reel 2, EREP-SML; ERE to J. W. Johnson, 3/19/30, 1/29/31, 4/4/31, f. 414, box 17, J. W. Johnson Papers. Following its publication, Johnson wrote to express confidence that the "fine book" would "reach and affect a great many of the people who most need to be affected." Johnson to ERE, 10/11/3, J. W. Johnson Papers; ERE to DuBois, 4/25/31; DuBois to ERE, 5/12/31, both in Aptheker, 438–40.

77. ERE to John Embree, 11/27/31, 10/14/40, DEFP. See, for example, *New York Times,* Nov. 15, 1931; *New York Post,* July 2, 1932; *Chicago News,* Oct. 9, 1931; *International Journal of Ethics* 42, no. 3 (1932): 135; and *American Journal of Sociology* 37, no. 5 (Mar. 1932): 814.

78. Kenneth C. Kaufman, *Chicago Daily Tribune,* 11/21/43, C10; *Journal of Educational Sociology* 16, no. 6 (Feb. 1943): 396.

79. Joseph V. Baker, *Philadelphia Inquirer*, Mar. 1, 1950.

80. WorldCat, http://worldcat.org (accessed 5/26/07). Coinciding with the publication of *Brown America* was another fund initiative similarly intended to address widespread ignorance about African American life. Immediately after the book appeared, the Rosenwald board approved a $5,000 appropriation for fellowships for several researchers to prepare "materials on Negro life and work" for use in southern high schools and colleges. In recommending the project, Embree expected that instructors in "important teachers colleges" would develop such materials and ensure their incorporation into courses in English, history, and social studies. DOB, MOT, 11/7/31, f. 10, box 57, JRFA, 8, 11. What became of this venture, envisioned almost forty years before the black studies movement gained momentum, is unknown. It probably fell victim to the collapse of the fund's assets in the early thirties.

81. *Brown America*, 198.

82. Ibid., 209–11, 231f. The individual profiles were also published separately as ERE, "A Few Portraits in Sepia."

83. ERE, "Kentucky Crusader."

84. Embree, Johnson, and Alexander, *Collapse of Cotton Tenancy*. The study was funded by the Rockefeller Foundation and the Rosenwald Fund.

85. Attachment to ERE to Joseph Schaffner, 4/3/29, f. 8, box 59, CDP; ERE to JR, 3/1/28, f. 32, box 104, JRFA. Embree had known Hoover since the early twenties, when both had been involved in postwar relief efforts in Europe. EREOD, 1/23/23, reel 2. In 1927, he and Hoover had been two of four dinner guests at the home of financier Felix Warburg, where the back-to-the-soil movement in Russia was the main topic of discussion. EREOD, 11/5/27, f. 5, box 120. There were further conversations with Hoover during Embree's trip to Mexico the following year. ERE interviews, 8/28/28, f. 6, box 120, JRFA.

86. CSJ, untitled draft of a biographical sketch of Embree, f. 30, box 104, JRFA; Gilpin and Gasman, 110; ERE to Will Alexander, 12/11/35, f. 1, box 105, JRFA; Dunne, 10–11.

87. ERE, "Southern Farm Tenancy."

88. Scrapbooks, box 557, JRFA.

89. T. Lynn Smith, *Journal of Southern History* 2, no. 2 (1936): 287; Wilson Gee, *Southern Economic Journal* 2, no. 3 (Jan. 1936): 75–78.

90. E. Franklin Frazier, *Journal of Negro Education* 5, no. 2 (Apr. 1936): 273–75. For later commentary, see Thompson, 501–62; and Dunne, 1–34.

91. Dunne, 10–11. Yet even with the Bankhead-Jones bill passed and his good friend installed as head of the new agency, Embree was not satisfied. Believing that the issue of farm resettlement needed to be more widely understood, and impressed with *The Grapes of Wrath*, he considered getting a "first-rate novelist" to write a story of a rehabilitated sharecropper. In that connection, he thought of John Steinbeck, John Dos Passos, Edna Ferber, or Lillian Smith. He subsequently decided that both a scholarly treatise and a novel were needed, but neither was ever published. ERE to Alexander, 6/8/39; ERE to Alexander and CSJ, 6/22/39, both in f. 1, box 105, JRFA.

92. ERE to JR, 5/4/31, f. 9, box 33, JRP.

93. ERE, "Report to the Board, Meeting of Trustees," 11/16/29, box 135. See also ERE to (JRF southern office director) S. L. Smith, 3/6/35, 1/21/36, both in f. 32, box 105, JRFA.

94. ERE to Alexander, 10/28/36, f. 1, box 105, JRFA. Embree's optimism was based in part on the mistaken expectation that federal funding would soon be available for southern schools. DOB, MOT, 4/10/37, box 136, JRFA, 12–13. On

the council, Embree also enlisted the participation of the U.S. commissioner of education and the president of the American Council on Education. ERE, "The Julius Rosenwald Fund: Review for the Two-Year Period 1933–1935," f. 2, box 85, JRFA, 1, 16–19; "Members of the Meeting [of the Rosenwald Council on Rural Education]," 1/37, f. 2047, box 213, ser. I.2, GEB, RAC.

95. Embree's writing on elementary education in these years was not limited to the rural education project. Before the project got under way, he had surveyed educational practices in Samoa and the Dutch East Indies, publishing three articles on the former and co-authoring a book on the latter. Like his earlier assessment of schooling in Mexico, those two studies conditioned his thinking, for he was convinced that cross-cultural comparisons could yield valuable lessons for reform efforts in the American South. From his explorations, perhaps the two most notable insights gained had to do with (1) the importance of schooling closely linked to the student's practical experience and (2) the rural school as a center of community life. See "Schools in Mexico: A Report to the Trustees of the JRF," 7/6/28, appendix, f. 7, box 58, JRP, 1–2; "General Statement" [to Rosenwald board], 5/28/33, box 136, JRFA, 4.

96. ERE, "Rural Education and the Teacher," 144; ERE to (Harvard University press director) Dumas Malone, 6/28/38, f. 5, box 116, JRFA. A summary of Embree's views, and the problems the fund identified, can be found in his essay "Rural Education" in the fund's "Review for the Two-Year Period 1933–1935," f. 2, box 85, JRFA, 1–19.

97. ERE, "Education of Teachers," 427. This article was written at the invitation of American Scholar's editor, William A. Shimer. Shimer to ERE, 1/19/39, f. 1, box 107, JRFA.

98. Address to the Department of Superintendence of the National Education Association, 2/27/36. Published in American Scholar under the title "Education for All the People: Divided We Fall" and as a fund reprint.

99. "Education for All," reprint, 10, 14–15, in Biography: Embree, Edwin R., no. 62, Berea College Archives.

100. Talmadge during this time labeled the Rosenwald Fund "Jew money for niggers." Information on this episode is from Cook, "The Cocking Affair."

101. Chicago Daily Tribune, July 15, 1941, 5.

102. ERE to Ira Latimer of the Chicago Civil Liberties Committee, 9/3/41, f. 7, box 108, JRFA.

103. ERE to Trustees of the JRF, 7/15/41, f. ER 100 1941, box 739, Eleanor Roosevelt Papers: Correspondence, Personal Letters, FDRPL.

104. Cook, "Eugene Talmadge–Walter Cocking Controversy"; DOB, MOT, 11/7/42, f. 8, box 137, JRFA; Fred Wale to ERE, 2/27/45, f. 1, box 59, CSJP. During the 1942 campaign, Talmadge's supporters added to his campaign theme song two verses:

> Gene saved our college system
> From all the Rosenwalds
> Who sought to end traditions
> Which we know are dear to all
>
> We don't want all their millions
> And neither their advice
> On how to educate our youth,
> We Southerners think twice.

Quoted in Pinckney, 38.

105. ERE to Dr. and Mrs. Franklin C. McLean, 7/30/46, f. 21, box 105, JRFA. Talmadge, however, died before he could be inaugurated.

106. New York Times, Mar. 27, 1932, 5.

107. "Education in the South—Two Views," Birmingham News-Age-Herald, Jan. 6, 1935, 5.

108. *Birmingham News-Age-Herald,* Jan. 6, Mar. 3, Mar. 10, 1935. In 1938, Embree gave essentially the same address at commencement exercises at the University of Georgia, but that speech did not arouse the outcry of the earlier presentation. It did, however, win him a full column and a picture in a national newsmagazine. *Time* 31, no. 11 (June 27, 1938): 45, reel 6, EREP-SML. Not one to shrink from controversy, he once in a jocular mood described his conversational style as "promoting discussion by the effective method of insult." CSJ, notes for Embree biographical profile, f. 30, box 104, JRFA.

109. *Time* 25, no. 1 (Jan. 7, 1935): 34. Embree's words, in the "Educated Man" address, were: "We have avoided the recent absurdities of Fascist Italy and Hitlerite Germany but Huey Long is doing very nicely in Louisiana. In public life the demagogue and the blackleg carry the day in America quite as easily as in any other democracy."

110. ERE, "In Order of Their Eminence: An Appraisal of American Universities," 652. The dispute with Huey Long was reported in the *Time* issue of January 7, 1935.

111. Embree's ranking, in order, was Harvard, Chicago, Columbia, California, Yale, Michigan, Cornell, Princeton, Johns Hopkins, Wisconsin, Minnesota. He was struck by how much agreement there was no matter which of the measures were applied. "In Order of Their Eminence," 654–55. It is notable as well that those he ranked, and others he mentioned as promising, would likely be on anyone's list of the top twenty universities in the early twenty-first century.

112. Ibid., 664. The editor of the *Atlantic* later reported that the Embree piece sparked more controversy than any article on education published during his tenure. Edward Weeks to ERE, 3/3/47, f. 7, box 107, JRFA.

113. Strausbaugh, 3–4.

5. CHARACTER TO COPE WITH DISAGREEMENT

1. ERE interviews, 1/7/30, f. 7, box 120; 2/12/30, f. 4, box 79; EREOD, 7/11/27, 11/2/27, f. 5, box 120, all in JRFA.

2. Catherine Embree Harris, personal communication to the author, 1/8/07.

3. Alexander, "The Education and Work of Edwin R. Embree," 2.

4. *Ebony* 2, no. 1 (Nov. 1946): 40; see also Quincy Wright to Kate Embree, 3/1/50, DEFP.

5. Address to Southern Sociological Society, published under the title "Education and the Good South," 13. Asked to describe key aspects of her father's personality, the first term that occurred to Edwina Embree Devereux, then age ninety-four, was "festive." Author's interview, 10/23/05, Ithaca, New York.

6. Such guests in the early 1930s included poet-playwright James Weldon Johnson, socialist presidential candidate Norman Thomas, scholar W. E. B. DuBois, and actor Richard T. Harrison. ERE interviews, 3/7/31, 9/15/31, 1/4/32, f. 7, box 120, JRFA.

7. Embree mentioned this ideal in a letter to a prospective comptroller for the fund. ERE to Frank B. Stubbs, 6/28/28, f. 24, box 129, JRFA.

8. CSJ, notes for an article on Embree, f. 30, box 104, JRFA; fund staff member Hilda Reitzes, telephone interview by author, 2/13/06; staff member Elizabeth Allen to Kate Embree, 2/22/50, DEFP.

9. Elena Bossen to Edwina Embree Devereux, 12/6/[50?], DEFP.

10. Simon Flexner to ERE, 10/19/21, Correspondence with Embree, Edwin R., reel 33, Simon Flexner Papers, Rockefeller Institute Papers, RAC; Alan Gregg, "Comments on Personalities," f. 174, box 23, ser. 900, RG 3, RFA, RAC. Embree's ability to maintain a punishing schedule was typified by his activities during a week-long stint at universities in Nash-

ville in mid-January 1931. Early each day, he lectured to classes in both sociology and education at Vanderbilt and gave talks at the Vanderbilt School of Religion and the Peabody School of Education. At Fisk and Vanderbilt, on alternate afternoons throughout the six days, he led two-hour seminars on peoples of the Pacific. On three occasions, he held luncheon discussions with students and faculty, and there were similar conversations each of the six evenings. Between these public sessions, he discussed institutional affairs with the presidents of both Fisk and Vanderbilt, met with an officer of the Tennessee Department of Health, and conferred with officials at the fund's southern office (f. 7, box 120, JRFA). Embree arranged this teaching experience in order to learn firsthand what students were thinking and the quality of their intellects. ERE to Clark Foreman, 12/10/30, f. 10, box 105, JRFA.

11. Quoted in Sealander, 34.

12. GEB president Trevor Arnett to JR, 4/30/29, f. 25, box 15, JRP.

13. Hill, *One Man's Time*.

14. Catherine Harris, personal communication to the author, 5/23/06.

15. Later, when the show went on the road, the star, Richard Harrison, was honored at a dinner given by the governor of Texas. Embree used that event to emphasize the irrationality of racism, pointing out that Harrison could receive high official recognition during the evening but, a few hours later, be denied a Pullman berth when he left town. James Weldon Johnson. *Along This Way*, 406; ERE, *American Negroes*, 48–49.

16. Arna Bontemps to Langston Hughes, 8/16/43, in Nichols, 136; f. 9, f. 13, box 88, JRFA. For a description of Embree's parties, to which up to 500 people were invited, see "Rosenwald Fund Throws a Bangup Lawn Party," *Ebony* 2, no. 1 (Nov. 1945): 40–44.

17. Embree's optimism is evident in much of his writing, but particularly in *Prospecting for Heaven*. That work is organized as a set of imaginary discussions, involving Embree, his secretary, and a fictional Chinese philosopher, which center on five authorities—an educational psychologist, a sociologist, a psychiatrist, an international public health official, and a psychoanalyst—living persons whose ideas Embree had explored extensively. Essentially a vehicle for summarizing current work in the social sciences, the book conveys the message that steadily advancing research will enable individuals to lead "rich, full, satisfying lives." Arguably Embree's most imaginative book, it failed to find a substantial audience.

18. Alexander, "The Education and Work of Edwin R. Embree," 5. This address also describes Embree's lack of caution, his eagerness always to act.

19. Ibid., 6–7. Embree's boldness at Rosenwald may also reflect his association with Beardsley Ruml, who had impressed him with the extravagant commitment of Rockefeller moneys—roughly $25 million in seven years—to promote the social sciences. Embree later lamented that he had not acted with similar daring as Rockefeller's director of studies. ERE, "Rockefeller Programs: Early History," 12, f. 3, box 1, EREP-RFA; ERE to Catherine Embree Harris, 11/6/41, DEFP.

20. In 1923, the New York state superintendent of the Anti-Saloon League alleged that, in a luncheon address at Goucher College, Embree had expressed opposition to Prohibition. Apparently trying to divert attention from an ongoing investigation of his own financial procedures, the superintendent charged that their advisors sought to dissuade the Rockefellers from making private contributions to the league. Embree felt the need to issue a statement denying he had ever spoken publicly against Prohibi-

tion and to apprise Rockefeller Jr. of the content of his Goucher remarks. *New York Times,* Apr. 11, 1923, 3; ERE to Rockefeller Jr., 4/14/23, f. 257, box 25, Rockefeller Boards, RG III.2, Rockefeller Family Archives, RAC.

21. ERE to JR, 3/6/31, f. 32, box 104; ERE interviews, James Weldon Johnson, 11/30/28, f. 6, box 120, both in JRFA; ERE to J. W. Johnson, 12/1/28, f. 414, box 17, J. W. Johnson Papers; "Association for the Study of Negro Life and History" [1928?], f. 10, box 57, JRP; Willard Townsend, *Chicago Defender,* July 10, 1948. Embree's efforts to effect the merger of the NAACP and the NUL are described in Belles, "The NAACP, the Urban League and the Julius Rosenwald Fund."

22. There can be no doubt that Embree expected to arouse opposition. At his very first meeting with the fund's board, the point was made (presumably by Embree or new trustee Beardsley Ruml) that foundations "justified their existence only by courageous leadership and that if convinced of the wisdom of any action, they should be willing to go forward with experiments and demonstrations even if this resulted in attack by reactionary groups." Bound minutes of JRF, f. 16, box 57, JRP. Also in 1928, Ruml had persuaded the trustees of the Laura Spelman Rockefeller Memorial and the Rockefeller Foundation to affirm the policy of supporting the study of controversial issues in the social sciences. "Personal Memoranda, 1929," f. 3, box 5, Beardsley Ruml Collection, 8, SCRC. Almost a half-century later, Paul Ylvisaker of the Ford Foundation, perhaps unwittingly endorsing such views, contended that precipitating controversy was one way for foundations to speed up progress. Cited in Whitaker, *The Philanthropoids,* 74.

23. Embree's daughter Catherine could not remember her parents ever attending religious services, yet their tax returns in EREP-SML list annual contributions to three churches during the thirties and forties. Catherine Embree Harris, personal communication to the author, 4/20/06. Recalling his religious ancestry, Embree sometimes described himself as a Quaker, "though not in very good standing." ERE to Mrs. S. H. Stetson, 9/15/38, f. 10, box 47, JRFA.

24. Content and quotations from Embree's "Pure Religion and Undefiled." The article summarizes a pamphlet by John Haynes Holmes, the minister of Manhattan's Unitarian Community Church, that so impressed Embree he sent copies to Julius Rosenwald, Clarence Day, and Anson Phelps Stokes. ERE to JR, 8/10/28; ERE to Stokes, 5/15/28, both in A. P. Stokes Papers, MAD-SML; ERE to Day, reel 2, EREP-SML. Embree's religious perspective strikingly resembles that of Frederick Gates as published in his autobiography, *Chapters in My Life,* 205.

25. Anderson and Moss, 103.

26. Embree, Simon, and Mumford, *Island India,* 104–105. Broadening the audience for his critique, Embree published a similar paragraph in "Rebirth of Religion," 429.

27. William Hutchins to ERE, 10/8/32, Edwin R. Embree Papers, Special Collections, Hutchins Library, Berea College, Berea, Kentucky.

28. ERE to Hutchins, 4/3/34, ibid.

29. Embree, Simon, and Mumford, *Island India,* 105–106.

30. Ibid., 96–97.

31. ERE, *Indians of the Americas,* 241.

32. Embree's ambition is neatly captured in a letter to his son about John's possible career path. "If I were twenty-one and I had the feelings that I now have, I should certainly go into banking for it seems to me the most fascinating approach to controlling and influencing the world. It also seems to me to present interesting intellectual problems as well

as to offer substantially gratifying returns to him who is successful." ERE to John Embree, 1/27/31, DEFP.

33. During Embree's decade at Rockefeller, the foundation's board included among its luminaries eminent preacher Harry Emerson Fosdick; influential editor William Allen White; the presidents of Harvard, Yale, and Stanford; 1916 Republican presidential nominee Charles Evans Hughes; and 1924 Democratic nominee John W. Davis.

34. The Lincoln School was established, with heavy funding by the Rockefeller Foundation, as an educational experiment. It was modeled in part on a school formed in Louisville, Kentucky, by Abraham Flexner, before he became a key figure at the GEB.

35. Not limited to formal schooling, the educational experiences of the Embree children included extended stays in Hawaii, and in their teen years each enjoyed an overseas journey alone with both parents—John to Japan, Edwina to Britain and France, Catherine to Russia and the North Cape. These adventures stimulated a taste for international travel and living and were particularly important for John. After leaving Japan, he traveled alone to France, where he studied for several months before beginning his freshman year at McGill in Montreal. Later completing a doctorate in anthropology, he became one of the country's leading authorities on Japan and Southeast Asia. He was a member of the Yale faculty when he and his daughter were struck by a car and killed in December 1950, only ten months after his father's death.

An episode involving Catherine's college attendance reveals an important aspect of Embree's personality. Planning to attend an expensive private college in the East, she discovered she was eligible to receive institutional financial aid. Embree discouraged her from applying

for it, pointing out that, if she received a grant, a classmate who might need it more might be denied. While she had a right to apply, that right should not be exercised if it would put another student at a serious disadvantage. Sensitized by her father's explanation, Catherine did not seek the aid, leaving the Embree family to meet her expenses from its own resources. Catherine Embree Harris, personal communication to the author, 2/4/06.

36. That impression is conveyed by Embree's tendency to indulge them; he bought each one an automobile soon after they learned to drive, even though he himself never owned one. Even as his son was approaching thirty, Embree continued to foster his career advancement, mimeographing his doctoral dissertation, contacting university acquaintances on his behalf, recommending him as a book reviewer and as the possible author of a general interest book he suggested that Simon and Schuster publish. ERE to John Embree, 3/19/36, DEFP; ERE to Amy Loveman, 9/7/38, f. 20; see other letters, 10/6/43, 10/25/43, f. 19, all in box 117, JRFA.

37. Most of the extant correspondence is between Embree and John, and Embree and Edwina. Preserved by Edwina, the letters are held by her son John Devereux.

38. Trevor Arnett to ERE, 8/16/33, f. 2041, box 212, ser. I.2, GEB, RAC; ERE to Clark Foreman, 3/18/31, f. 10, box 105, JRFA. Though Embree considered insults to be an effective way to "spur on discussion," Robert Kohler, whose judgment of Embree is more than a bit dubious, has intimated that he was inclined to be sycophantic. Kohler considers only the Rockefeller years and even so he offers scant evidence of that trait ("Policy," 501). A more charitable, and probably more accurate, interpretation would see Embree's occasionally effusive language as an expression of his fundamental enthusiasm and positive outlook. His exuberance was

not directed toward his superiors alone, but is evident in letters to his fund associates and to his adult children.

39. Joanne Hill Styles, personal communication to author, 7/14/06. Late in life, when complimenting his wife and commenting on her personality, Embree told friends that Kate was a "most un-boring wife," that she "never permitted our married life to be dull." M. Schwarz to Kate Embree, 2/28/50, DEFP.

40. Embree and Waxman, 269–73.

41. William M. Kelley, "'Doc' Ferdinand Q. Morton Takes Over the Practice of Medicine," *Amsterdam News*, Dec. 17, 1930.

42. Ibid.

43. In his autobiography, DuBois later acknowledged the strength of arguments on both sides and proclaimed that he was equally for both. On this, see Lewis, *W. E. B. DuBois*, 291–92. For Embree's address, see "Negro Hospitals and Health," f. 10, box 58, JRP. For the same reasons advanced in this public statement, the fund supported the similarly segregated Provident Hospital in Chicago, not to further the separation of the races, but because most hospitals refused black physicians access to clinical facilities and up-to-date equipment. Using segregated institutions seemed at the time the only immediately practical way to improve medical care for the African American communities in the nation's two largest cities. In a candid letter to Clarence Day, Embree developed this argument more fully. There, he stated his objection to segregation, but averred that sometimes "convenience and the avoidance of friction, if not of riots," should take precedence over "any single abstract principle." He did not consider this view "too much of a compromise" for "a true ideal is a realistic facing of the facts. Realism, in my opinion, is about the finest ideal anyone can possess." ERE to Day, 12/18/30, reel 2, EREP-SML.

44. *New York Times,* Jan. 30, 1931. Born in Nebraska, reared in a racially integrated town in a border state, living all his adult life in the Northeast and Midwest, Embree was nevertheless labeled by some black critics a "southerner," inevitably implying racism. To racist whites such as Governor Talmadge of Georgia, on the other hand, he was a "Yankee agitator." In this regard, as in others, Embree was not easy to pigeonhole.

45. Embree and Waxman, 122–23.

46. CSJ, "The Social Philosophy of Edwin R. Embree," 63. Though more experiments and demonstrations were mounted in Chicago than in any other single location, similar activities took place in Boston, New York, Philadelphia, and Baton Rouge. Embree and Waxman, 126–29.

47. ERE interviews, 10/3/28, f. 6, box 120, JRFA.

48. *Chicago Daily Tribune,* Apr. 29, 1929, 1. Whether such a resolution was ever voted is not clear, but it is known that some society members supported the clinics publicly.

49. *Chicago Daily Tribune,* Oct. 23, 1929, 1. The topic was quickly pushed off the front pages, however, when prices on Wall Street plummeted the next day and the stock market collapsed within a week, as the Great Depression got under way.

50. *Chicago Daily Tribune,* June 20, 1929, 3; Oct. 12, 1929, 1; Oct. 24, 1929, 22.

51. N. S. Davis III, "A Reply," *Bulletin of the Chicago Medical Society,* Jan. 4, 1930, see particularly 28–32. Davis's obvious intent was not to argue with Embree, but to mobilize the medical community in opposition.

52. "Minutes of the JRF," 4/26/30, f. 1, box 58, JRP, 268–69; *Chicago Daily Tribune,* Sept. 4, 1930, 18; Oct. 21, 1930, 29. Praising Rosenwald's courage, Embree stated that, facing criticism of the clinics by "high and respectable sources," the fund's founder "never flinched—in fact

he enjoyed the fight." ERE to Raymond B. Fosdick, 3/19/32, f. 16, box 110, JRFA.

53. *Chicago Daily Tribune,* May 27, 1931, 23. Julius Rosenwald's personal gifts to Chicago dental clinics, beginning as early as 1912, apparently did not arouse the society's concern. See Ascoli, 106–109.

54. EREOD, 3/27/24; Family Journal: Russia in 1934, reel 5, EREP-SML; ERE to Raymond B. Fosdick, 3/9/32, f. 16, box 110, JRFA.

55. ERE interviews, 5/29/30, f. 7, box 120, JRFA; "Minutes of the Trustees," 4/26/30, f. 1, box 58, JRP, 257. Embree's persistence in this situation was probably in part a reaction to his frustration at Rockefeller when President Vincent, faced with doubts within his board, repeatedly withdrew his recommendations regarding the program in human biology. Though Embree denied support for the Chicago Birth Control League in 1930, his interest in population control did not wane. Several years later, he sought the trustees' approval to explore birth control possibilities in the rural South, again stressing its importance for advancing black welfare. DOB, MOT, 4/9/35 [f. 11/11/35], box 136, JRFA, 21–22. Though the fund's minutes provide little information about disagreements within the board, Lessing Rosenwald informed Embree's widow that "naturally" he and her husband had "frequently disagreed, but always with complete understanding and good faith." Rosenwald to Kate Embree, 2/26/50, DEFP.

56. "Conspectus of Present and Future Activities of the Julius Rosenwald Fund," 7/23/30, f. 4, box 28, JRP, 18.

57. On the American Nursing Association, see *Chicago Daily Tribune,* June 11, 1930. ERE to Raymond B. Fosdick, 3/9/32, f. 16, box 110, JRFA; ERE to Will Alexander, 12/1/36, f. 1, box 105, JRFA; Embree and Waxman, 128–31.

58. The results of the Samoa study were presented in a fund pamphlet and in

two articles: "A New School in America Samoa" and "Samoa Offers an Exchange." Embree's enthusiasm for exotic travel was palpable. His Samoa experience he described as "one of the finest I have had in any country." Seven months later, he reported that the Java trip provided "the most fascinating experiences a man ever had." ERE to Will Alexander, 9/7/32, 4/28/33, both in f. 1, box 105, JRFA.

59. DOB, MOT, 11/12/32, box 135, 21–22. Embree may very well have engineered this invitation (as he did a 1944 trip to Haiti under U.S. State Department auspices). He had been collecting information on the peoples of the Pacific for some time and was eager to write about them. Moreover, he was able to warn the board about a probable controversy, because he knew in advance that he would criticize the Dutch and other colonial governments for failing to preserve native cultures and for subordinating indigenous interests to their own economic and political concerns. He hoped that the study would create "new thinking and a significant shift in policy in the education of primitive peoples . . . living under the dominance of Western industrial powers." MEC, 12/7/32, f. 7, box 79, JRFA; ERE to Clarence Day, 5/23/31, reel 2, EREP-SML.

In the sections of the published study he wrote, Embree took the West to task for "blithe arrogance" in assuming that its superiority in arms, technology, and organization naturally meant superiority in all other aspects of life: religion, family practices, morality, societal systems. Embree, Simon, and Mumford, *Island India,* 72–73, 88–89, 96–97, 103–105. A truncated, less strident version of his critique appeared in the fund's 1931–1933 review in an essay titled "A World of Interesting Peoples," f. 1, box 85, JRFA, 17–18.

60. Embree had been thinking about a Chicago-based publication for some time. More than a year earlier, he had dis-

cussed with Raymond Fosdick, President Hutchins, and several university faculty the possibility of starting a journal in the social sciences. ERE interviews, 12/5/31, f. 7, box 120, JRFA. On that same trip, he formulated plans for a race relations institute linked to a university, which would engage in surveys, experimentation, and fellowships, essentially the model for the American Council on Race Relations started more than a decade later. Reel 4, EREP-SML.

61. ERE to Clarence Day, 8/14/33, f. 8, box 59, CDP. In the same letter, Embree played with the idea of leaving philanthropic work to edit a magazine full time, and he reported on a conversation with Ellery Sedgwick, in which the *Atlantic* editor intimated that Embree should join his staff with an eye to succeeding him.

62. All information in this and the next paragraphs is from "Proposal for a General National Magazine to Be Published in Chicago," Special Meeting of Trustees, 10/1/33, box 136, JRFA.

63. DOB, MOT, 5/19/34 [no f.], box 136, JRFA, 22. Two years later, Embree would comment wryly to Will Alexander that, in preparing for a forthcoming board meeting, "with tears streaming down my face, I finally decided not to present an item concerning a magazine for the Chicago area." ERE to Alexander, 10/30/35, f. 1, box 105, JRFA.

64. McArthur, 174–75. The chair of the presidential search committee was Harold Swift of the Chicago meatpacking family, who a year earlier had joined the Rosenwald board.

65. Embree's office diary records four extensive conferences with Hutchins during six months in 1929 and several sessions in each of the next two years. In 1930, even before presenting the matter to his faculty, Hutchins gave Embree a detailed explanation of his plan to reorganize the university. That effort was likely to result

in his first major fight, Hutchins predicted, but fortunately he had in his hands "a good many bludgeons, stilettos and aces." ERE interviews, 9/12/30, f. 7, box 120, JRFA. Among Embree's university friends, besides Ruml and McLean, were anthropologist Robert Redfield, political scientist Charles Merriam, and economist and future U.S. senator Paul Douglas.

66. Indeed, *Brown America* had so impressed officials of the NAACP that Embree was asked to help select the recipient of the association's Springarn Medal, an annual recognition of a highly accomplished African American. ERE interviews, 2/27/32, f. 7, box 129, JRFA. Adding to his reputation was the publication of two articles on the Soviet Union, following a 1934 trip: "Jews on the Steppes" and "Rebirth of Religion." Material for these pieces was gathered during a two-week trip to the USSR, much of it spent examining Jewish "colonies" in the Crimea, a project (heavily subsidized by Julius Rosenwald) to move urban Jews onto collective farms. One of his most fascinating family journals recorded his impressions; he emphasized the impossibility of obtaining a fair picture of such a vast and complex country, his surprise at the persistence of a money economy, and his dismay at the country's backward industrial infrastructure and social organization. ERE to Clarence Day, 6/28/34, f. 8, box 59, CDP; Family Journal: Russia in 1934, reel 5, EREP-SML.

67. The Chicago meeting brought together the American Statistical Association, American Sociological Society, American Economics Association, and American Political Science Association. *American Political Science Review* 29, no. 1 (Feb. 1935): 107; Lewis, *W. E. B. DuBois*, 234–35. During these years, his book reviews appeared in such diverse journals as *Scientific Monthly, Journal of Higher Education, American Journal of Sociology,*

and *Pacific Affairs*. The Hawaii degree recognized Embree's studies of cultural diversity. ERE to E. C. Carter of the Institute of Pacific Relations, 10/13/33, f. 12, box 253, JRFA. Embree's standing in scholarly circles is also evident in his membership on the directing boards of the Institute for Intercultural Studies, Institute for Pacific Affairs, and Southeast Asia Institute. In 1946, he declined an invitation to present a paper at the annual meeting of the intellectually high-powered Conference on Science, Philosophy, and Religion. ERE to conference organizer Louis Finkelstein, 12/30/46, f. 3, box 14, JRFA.

68. "Memorandum on the 'Julius Rosenwald Fund Review of Activities,'" f. 11, box 134, JRFA. Stern had left the board in 1932 but remained on the staff. In 1935, he was reelected to a three-year term that began in 1936.

69. Stern may have disagreed with Embree on other points, but probably on none more strongly than the program in industrial education. Stern was personally heavily invested in that program, and Embree's decision to drop it eighteen months after arriving at the fund may have begun their alienation.

70. MOT, 5/15–17/36, f. 6, box 133, JRFA.

71. ERE to (son and daughter-in-law) John and Ella, 8/7/37, DEFP; "Review of Activities and Future Program," MOT, 5/15–17/36, f. 12, box 82, JRFA. At the meeting, the board expressed continuing interest in medical services, but decided to phase the program down in the next few months. ERE to Will Alexander, 12/1/36, f. 1, box 105, JRFA.

72. ERE to John and Ella, 8/7/37, DEFP. In the same letter, he caricatured Hutchins as having "suddenly turned medieval and scholastic," now considering the contemplation of Aristotle and Euclid as "the only proper approach to education, to race relations, to form[al] economics, or to any aspect of human affairs."

73. ERE to John Embree, 7/1/36; ERE to John and Ella, 8/7/37, both in DEFP.

74. ERE to Will Alexander, 8/20/37, 9/29/37, f. 1, box 105, JRFA. The "rumbling" within the family trustees apparently came from both Alfred Stern and William Rosenwald, the youngest child of the founder. Stern, who was in the process of separating from the Rosenwalds' daughter Marion, resigned from the board in 1937, two years before his term expired. William Rosenwald, who as a member of the nominating committee wanted that body to be more active and to make decisions on general policy and strategy, left the board the following year when his term expired. From that point on, the family's participation on the board centered on perennial member Lessing Rosenwald, his sister Adele Rosenwald Levy, and their brother-in-law Edgar Stern. ERE to Will Alexander, 7/14/37, f. 1, box 105, JRFA.

75. ERE to John Embree, 5/20/36, 7/1/36, DEFP. Those steps included putting money regularly into a savings account for the first time in his life.

76. ERE to Will Alexander, 8/20/37, 9/29/37, both in f. 1, box 105, JRFA. The "wise southerners" elected to trusteeship included University of North Carolina sociologist Howard W. Odum in 1937, businessman Will W. Clayton in 1938, and Kentucky newspaper editor Mark Ethridge in 1939.

6. TOWARD "FULL DEMOCRACY"

1. Even the area of African American welfare was rather diffuse and open-ended, for it included subcategories of fellowships, university centers, health, other activities, and race relations. This diffusion can be partly explained as an attempt to preserve several established programs, while bringing some order to a wide dispersion of effort. It also seems likely that Embree deliberately avoided too much

specificity, lest he lose the freedom to attack targets of opportunity.

2. During 1930–1935, when financial restrictions imposed limits on the fund's projects, Embree published almost two dozen articles, wrote two books, and was the lead author of two others. During the next six years, until U.S. entry into World War II, he published a single book and only a baker's dozen of articles. During the war years, when the fund's activity again was curtailed, Embree had more time for writing. From 1942 until the fund's demise in 1948, his output consisted of fifteen articles, four books, a contribution to a fifth, and much of the text of the fund's history that appeared in 1949.

3. "This Glad New Year: Confessions of an Optimist," 1/20/40, DEFP. The content and quotations in the next paragraphs come from this unpublished document.

4. ERE letter of 6/5/40; ERE to Landon, 6/19/40, f. 11, box 114; ERE telegram to FDR, 6/8/40, f. 3, box 149, all in JRFA.

5. ERE to Congressman Rudolph G. Tenerowicz, 3/19/41; ERE to midwestern senators, 10/8/41; ERE telegram to Senator Richard Russell of Georgia, 11/7/41, all in f. 16, box 109, JRFA.

6. Embree had known Lindbergh since she was a girl, for the Embree and Morrow families had been neighbors in Englewood, New Jersey, right after Embree joined the Rockefeller Foundation. After the move to Rosenwald, he maintained a lively correspondence with Anne's father, Dwight Morrow, then U.S. ambassador to Mexico.

7. Untitled document, 3/41, f. 2, box 89, JRFA. The audience for this statement is not entirely clear. The personal tone and other internal evidence suggest it was intended not for publication, but for friends and acquaintances, especially in the Chicago area. An earlier, undated draft can be found in folder 1 of the same box; that

draft compares the Lindbergh approach to that of the Pharisee, who "walked by on the other side" of the road rather than help the man who had fallen among thieves.

8. Ibid. Embree's convictions about U.S. entry into the war left him in a quandary regarding conscientious objection. Active before and during the war in the Chicago Civil Liberties Committee, he was asked in 1940 to serve on a group dealing with men who refused the draft on grounds of conscience. He declined participation, stating, "I am really so mixed up in my mind on this whole topic that I would rather not get involved in any committee service." ERE to Charles W. Gilkey, 10/15/40, f. 7, box 108, JRFA.

9. ERE Family Journal no. 8, 2/15/26, 2/24/26, reel 4, EREP-SML. Hoping to counteract anti-Japanese sentiment, Embree considered the creation of a documentary film on Japanese family life, which he thought would have wide appeal across the United States. Interview with "Mr. Chorley," EREOD, 6/8/27. Embree's views toward Japan and Japanese–U.S. relations in the 1920s are plain; those of the 1930s are not. During the latter period, neither his official correspondence nor extant personal letters deal with the topic. The Japanese invasion of China undoubtedly dismayed him, belying his earlier belief that militarist influence in Japan would decline. His admiration of Japanese culture and affection for the people, however, apparently survived the war largely intact.

10. In an expression of patriotic solidarity, not free of transparent lobbying for a federal post, Embree wired the president on the day after Pearl Harbor: "If my knowledge and experience in Orient and East Indies can be of any service they are of course at your disposal. Also facilities and experience of the Julius Rosenwald Fund especially in interracial and international relations. We are proud to be at

your command." ERE to FDR, 12/8/41, f. 3, box 149, JRFA.

11. Catherine Embree Harris, *Dusty Exile*, vi. Though the relocation from the West Coast lacked the brutality of the Nazi pattern of minority removal, there were some depressing similarities: being forced against one's will to move with only a few days' notice, to take only what could be carried in one's hands, to sell at a huge loss all other possessions, to abandon one's home and community, to be transported to an undisclosed location, to endure constant uncertainty and anxiety. Though accurate figures may never be known, one estimate places the financial losses of the evacuees at over $400 million at 1942 values. "Japanese-American Citizens League: An All American Organization of American Citizens," f. 2, box 114, JRFA.

12. Telegram, ERE to Catherine Scott of Columbia University Press, 8/19/46, f. 2, box 109, JRFA.

13. The young woman who lived with John and Ella Embree was Miwa Kai; Kai, personal communication to the author, 8/30/06. The Embree family was deeply involved with Japanese Americans throughout the war. Anthropologist son John, with his Japanese-speaking wife, had spent a year of research in a Japanese village. The book on his observations there (*Suye Mura: A Japanese Village* [Chicago: University of Chicago Press, 1939]) was in 1941 the most current information in English on Japanese beliefs and customs. A few days after Pearl Harbor, the younger Embree's knowledge resulted in a call to government service, first with the Office of Strategic Services, then with the War Relocation Authority, the agency responsible for the evacuees. Embree and John, the latter in an official capacity, also visited an Arizona internment camp and saw the condition of the 18,000 evacuees firsthand. Harris, 2–3, 24, 36–37,

96. Embree undoubtedly also received information from his brother Howard, who in 1944 was a social worker at the Heart Mountain Relocation Center in Wyoming. Unsigned notes [ERE interviewer E. L. Allen?], f. 30, box 104, JRFA.

14. ERE to Clarence Pickett, 11/3/43; Teiko Ishida to ERE, 2/23/44; T. T. Yatabe to ERE, 3/2/45; Tats Kushida to ERE, 4/17/47; ERE to Tats Kushida, 11/4/47, all in f. 2, box 114, JRFA; *Nashville Tennessean*, July 6, 1944. It is striking that only one other foundation executive expressed solidarity with Japanese Americans by serving as a league sponsor: Will Alexander of the Rosenwald Fund. Embree's actions on behalf of Japanese Americans continued after the war. In 1947, he urged the U.S. attorney general to file an amicus curiae brief in a Supreme Court case involving discrimination against a Nisei fisherman, a case eventually decided in the appellant's favor. Tats Kushida to ERE, 6/8/48, f. 2, box 114, JRFA. That same year, he joined with scores of other prominent citizens to sponsor the Committee for Equality in Naturalization, a group formed to urge the repeal of the remaining provisions of the Oriental Exclusion Act. (In connection with the war effort, persons of Chinese, Filipino, and East Indian extraction had already been exempted from the act.) ERE to Richard J. Walsh, president of John Day Publishers, 1/31/47, f. 5, box 109, JRFA.

15. MEC, 6/6/45, f. 7, box 80; personnel documents in folders 1, 3, and 5, box 84, all in JRFA.

16. Dykeman and Stokely, 261–63.

17. ERE, "Foreword," in Weaver, *Race Relations in Chicago*, 2.

18. Embree accepted the chair "with reluctance, but with a deep sense of obligation." ERE to CSJ, 7/30/43, f. 3, box 59, CSJP. During its lifetime, this body, while retaining the same basic purpose, underwent several name changes. First called

the Mayor's Committee on Race Relations, it was soon renamed the Mayor's Commission on Human Relations. Since 1947, it has been a permanent part of the city's governing structure as the Chicago Commission on Human Relations. Herein the term "Commission" is used to refer to this organization.

19. Weaver, "City of Chicago: Mayor's Committee on Race Relations."

20. For a detailed account of the commission's work, see Embree's introduction to Wright, *Human Relations in Chicago;* and Wright, *The People of Chicago.* Both are in the municipal records housed in the Harold Washington Public Library, Chicago.

21. See City of Chicago, *City Planning in Race Relations;* and City of Chicago, *Home Front Unity.*

22. ERE to Detroit education official Marion Edman, 1/27/44, f. 1, box 528, JRP; Wright, *The People of Chicago,* 6–10, 30; Wright, *Human Relations in Chicago,* 31–35.

23. Accounting document, f. 4, box 84, JRP, 23–28.

24. The pageant took place at the Michigan Boulevard Garden Apartments, which had been financed by Julius Rosenwald and, for a time, was the home of boxing champion Joe Louis. Wright, *Human Relations in Chicago,* 26–27, 31–34.

25. DOB, MOT, 3/20/44 [no f.], box 137, JRFA, 11. The national organization that soon emerged was the American Council on Race Relations, which will be discussed in the following chapter. Even after Embree had ended his service as the chair and moved to New York, he continued to contribute to the commission's annual conference, recommending speakers, suggesting panel compositions, advising on fund-raising, and even returning in 1948 to deliver the keynote address. See ERE to Thomas Wright, 10/13/48 and 1/27/49, and his keynote address, "The Role of Education in Human Relations,"

all in reel 2, EREP-SML. For the 1948 conference, see Chicago Commission on Human Relations, "Recommendations of the Chicago Conference on Civic Unity," Municipal Records, Harold Washington Public Library, Chicago.

26. DOB, MOT, 4/21/45 [no f.], box 137, JRFA; Lelon, 458–59.

27. In 1954, the college became a university, and in 1959 it was rededicated to Eleanor and Franklin Roosevelt.

28. Frank McVey to ERE, 10/28/35, reel 1, EREP-SML.

29. ERE, "The New Civilization"; ERE to Iowa dean George D. Stoddard, 5/7/41, f. 113, box 14, JRFA; Elizabeth Weber, "The First Admission of Negro Students to Swarthmore," *Phoenix,* Apr. 12, 1996, www.sccs.swarthmore.edu/users/98/elizw/Swat.history (accessed 6/12/07). Embree's important academic presentations include keynote addresses given to the Tennessee College Association (1932), Southern Sociological Society (1940), and Southern Conference on Education (1941); several were a part of a series: the 1932 Moody Lecture at the University of Chicago, the Thirkield Lectures at Gammon Theological Seminary, and the Earl Lectures at the Pacific School of Religion (1945). Special gratification undoubtedly resulted from the last invitation and the chance to add his name to the list of illustrious Earl lecturers, which included Walter Rauschenbusch, H. Richard Niebuhr, G. Bromley Oxnam, Henry A. Wallace, William Allen White, and Theodore Roosevelt (Galen M. Fisher to ERE, 10/20/45, f. 2, box 117, JRFA). Many of his speeches found their way into print, but the manuscripts of some three dozen others apparently no longer exist. An incomplete list of his father's articles and addresses was prepared by Embree's son John, 3/21/50, reel 2, EREP-SML.

30. Embree accepted honorary degrees from the University of Hawaii (1936) and

University of Iowa (1941) because they were based on his research and writing, not on his philanthropic connections. Fisk and Howard awarded degrees to him in 1948, after the closure of the Rosenwald Fund removed any possible conflict of interest. In regard to university presidencies, see ERE to *Birmingham News* editor James Saxon Childers, 6/13/38, f. 10, box 108; and University of Cincinnati board chair George H. Warrington to ERE, 12/30/30, f. 7, box 120, both in JRFA. On declining invitations to join the boards of Yale, Howard, the New School for Social Research, and Fisk, see ERE conversation with George S. Fowler, 2/5/25, f. 164, box 2, EREOD; GEVOD, 6/4/26, reel 3, RG 12.1, RFA, RAC; EREOD, 6/16/27, reel 2; ERE interviews, 4/18/30, 6/15/30, both in f. 7, box 120, JRFA; ERE to Abraham Flexner, 7/23/30, f. 6, box 201, JRFA. In 1948, he joined the Fisk board after Charles S. Johnson became the university's president, and he became a trustee of Radcliffe College on the invitation of its president and his longtime friend from Chicago, Wilbur K. Jordan. Jordan to ERE, 6/21/49, reel 3, EREP-SML.

A rather bizarre incident involved the University of Hawaii. Six months after Pearl Harbor, Embree received a letter from Gregg M. Sinclair, a member of a faculty group advising the university regents on presidential selection, stating that Embree was under consideration for the Hawaii presidency. Embree responded promptly, expressing some interest. His letter crossed in the mail with another from Sinclair, informing him that Sinclair himself had been named to the position. Sinclair to ERE, 6/9/42; ERE to Sinclair, 6/16/42; Sinclair to ERE, 6/18/42, all in reel 1, EREP-SML. After Embree's death, Sinclair informed John Embree that he himself had nominated his father, that he considered Embree to be in a class with legendary university presidents Charles

W. Eliot and Andrew D. White, and that he had told Embree several times he would step down if Embree would assume the university presidency. Gregg M. Sinclair to John F. Embree, 3/6/50, DEFP.

31. Having some sense of the demands of the office and knowing his already-heavy obligations, Embree attempted to resign the chair after a month. When it was pointed out that his resignation would be interpreted as an expression of doubt about the college's future, he agreed to continue in the role. "Minutes of the Board," 5/24/45, RCCR.

32. The purchase of the historic ten-story building in the Loop relieved the city of a potential white elephant, while dramatizing the college's promise. Designed by Louis H. Sullivan, the building had been the home of the Chicago Symphony and the Chicago Lyric Opera Company. It had showcased circuses and vaudeville acts in its 4,200-seat auditorium, and Enrico Caruso, Amelita Galli-Curci, Feodor Chaliapin, Anna Pavlova, and Sarah Bernhardt had performed on its stage. It had also been the site of political conventions: Benjamin Harrison and Theodore Roosevelt had been nominated for the U.S. presidency there. *New York World-Telegram,* June 25, 1948.

33. E. James Sparling, "Annual Report of the President," 4/25/45–8/31/46 and 1947; "Minutes of the Board," 5/30/45, 6/19/45, 9/6/45, 9/26/45; "Minutes of Board Executive Committee," 4/24/46, all in RCCR; ERE to Robert O. Dibble, 9/27/45; ERE to Chaloner Prize Foundation, 5/21/46, both in Biographical Collection, Chairman Embree, RCCR; Weil, 46.

34. Embree had proclaimed that "democratic" organizational principles would be followed when the college was chartered. *Chicago Sun,* Apr. 27, 1945, 21. The college's affinity for the labor movement and the political prominence of the radical student group American Youth

for Democracy made it a target for Red-baiting groups before the institution was two years old. E. James Sparling, "Annual Report of the President," 1946–1947; "Progress: A Report from Roosevelt College" (Apr. 1950), both in RCCR.

35. The fund's initial appropriation was matched by $75,000 from the Field Foundation. Marshall Field III served on the Rosenwald executive committee after joining the board in 1941. He contributed significantly not only to Roosevelt College, but also to two race relations organizations started by Embree in the mid-forties. Only eight other schools—all but one historically black institutions—received greater funding, usually for limited purposes and over a far longer period. The grants to Roosevelt, by contrast, were for building costs and general operating expenses. Embree and Waxman, 266–75.

36. DOB, MOT, 4/21/45 [no f.], box 137, JRFA.

37. Ibid.; MEC, 10/5/45, f. 7, box 80; f. 4, box 84, all JRFA; Embree and Waxman, 275. Appreciation for Embree's service during the college's early years was expressed by both its students and its trustees. Soon after he left the board, the student body arranged an assembly to express gratitude to the college's three founders: Embree, Sparling, and Field. The formal invitation to the event was written by student body president Harold Washington; decades later, he was elected Chicago's first African American mayor. Washington to ERE, 12/48, reel 3, EREP-SML. In the month following Embree's death, the board voted that, when a school of education was established at some future date, it should be named after its first chair. Sparling to Kate Embree, 3/31/50, ERE, Biographical Collection: Correspondence, RCCR. This resolution was either lost or subsequently rescinded, for when the school of education was established in the mid-fifties, Embree's name

was not attached. No Roosevelt catalog lists the name, and university officials in 2007 had no knowledge of the 1950 action.

38. All that underlay the First Lady's decision to accept the trusteeship is not evident, but her views on racial issues and on the need for far-reaching change were clearly in close sympathy with the fund. Probably critical to her acceptance was the influence of Will Alexander, whose contacts with her and other key Washington figures exceeded Embree's in the thirties. In any event, soon after she became a board member, Embree persuaded her to invite Marshall Field III to Hyde Park, where together they prevailed on the publisher-philanthropist to join the board as well. ERE to Alexander, 5/18/41, f. 2, box 105, JRFA. The board had its full complement of thirteen members at the time, but the bylaws were changed to create a fourteenth position for Field to fill. ERE to Eleanor Roosevelt's secretary Malvine Thompson, 6/5/41; ERE to Eleanor Roosevelt, 10/20/41, 10/30/41, all in f. ER 100 1941, box 379, FDRPL. Soon after Field was elected to the board, Mrs. Roosevelt held a luncheon for her fellow trustees and the fund's executives at the White House. "Luncheon JRF," 11/10/41, f. 5, container 100, Office of Social Entertainments, FDRPL.

39. ERE to Mrs. Frank Sulzberger, 10/16/40; Embree script, 11/3/40, f. 6, box 109, JRFA.

40. The telegram was undoubtedly Embree's idea, and the wording probably was as well. He was connected to all the signers, a list that included author Pearl Buck, university presidents Ray Lyman Wilbur and Frank P. Graham, anthropologist Margaret Mead, NAACP president Walter White, and Urban League chief executive Lester Granger. A copy of the telegram is attached to ERE to Mrs. Roosevelt, 1/16/42, box 761, ER Papers w/ Correspondence 1933–1945, f. 100 Pers. Letters 1942, FDRPL.

41. ERE to Congressman Raymond S. McKeogh, 4/7/42, f. 16, box 109, JRFA.

42. The list of signers included former congressman Jerry Voorhis; magazine editors Frederick Lewis Allen, Norman Cousins, H. L. Mencken, Henry Seidel Canby; ministers Harry Emerson Fosdick, Adam Clayton Powell, G. Bromley Oxnam; Rabbi Stephen Wise; theologian Reinhold Niebuhr; and numerous authors: Archibald MacLeish, Bernard De-Voto, Pearl Buck, John P. Marquand, Carl Van Doren, and others. Collective letter to Richardson, 1/8/48, f. 9, box 106, JRFA.

43. ERE to Ickes and Knox, 7/17/42, f. 3, box 112, JRFA.

44. ERE to Ernest Grunsfeld, 1/9/42, f. 4, box 110, JRFA; *Chicago Daily Tribune,* Sept. 4, 1942, 13. When Douglas returned from military service after the war, he was elected to what would become a distinguished career in the Senate.

45. *Chicago Daily Tribune,* July 15, 1944, 7.

46. Ibid., Nov. 4, 1944, 1. Of the thirteen named here, almost half were black: Townsend, Frazier, Reid, Hughes, Hastie, Bethune.

47. Embree had a number of connections with the NCPAC leadership. Former fund staffer Clark Foreman was the organization's secretary, and college president Mary McLeod Bethune and YMCA official Channing Tobias were members of its board. ERE to NCPAC chair Elmer A. Benson, 7/26/45, f. 20, box 116; ERE to Sandburg, 2/16/48, f. 19, box 117, both in JRFA.

48. Independent Voters of Illinois stationery letterhead, "Board of Directors Minutes," 5/1/47, 5/27/48, both in f. 6, box 112, JRFA. Among the other organizers of the Chicago ADA were Paul Douglas, union official Willard S. Townsend, former California congressman Jerry Voorhis, and future Secretary of Labor and Supreme Court justice Arthur Goldberg. Edwin J. Kuh Jr. to ERE, 6/5/47, f. 4;

Vi McGrath to ERE, 2/18/47, f. 5, both in box 107, JRFA.

49. Humphrey was the youngest of the would-be U.S. presidents with whom Embree had notable interactions. Others were Charles Evans Hughes and John W. Davis (on the Rockefeller board), Henry Wallace (U.S. secretary of agriculture during the work on cotton tenancy), and Adlai Stevenson. Embree's relations with Presidents Hoover and Roosevelt were even more substantive than with these men, with the exception of Stevenson. Within Hoover's cabinet, Embree had extensive contacts with Ray Lyman Wilbur at Interior, Henry L. Stimson at State, and Robert P. Lamont at Commerce. His acquaintances in FDR's cabinet included not only Wallace and Stimson, but Secretary of Labor Frances Perkins and Secretary of the Interior Harold Ickes. With Truman's secretary of state, Edward R. Stettinius, he was extensively involved in 1948. Robert C. Weaver, Lyndon Johnson's secretary of housing and urban development, was a close friend. On the U.S. Supreme Court, Embree knew both Louis Brandeis and Stanley Reed. ERE to Brandeis, 10/3/31, f. 7, box 120; telegram, ERE to Reed, 2/23/40, f. 10, box 117, both in JRFA.

50. All quotations in this and the following paragraphs are from "Saturday Evening Session, 3/1/47, Proceedings of the ADA Committee, Congress Hotel, Chicago," f. 5, box 107, JRFA.

51. Frank Aydelotte to ERE, 10/27/37, 10/20/38, f. 11, box 117; ERE to Henry Sachs, 12/8/36, f. 19, box 117; ERE to Commissioner of Indian Affairs John Collier, 2/26/40, f. 19, box 110; W. W. Lockwood to ERE, 10/14/42, f. 13, box 253; ERE to Milton C. Rose, 5/20/46, f. 22, box 118; Clifton M. Utley to Clarence Carlson, 11/17/45, f. 11, box 113; Virginia Payne to ERE, 2/27/46, f. 26, box 117, all in JRFA. On Embree's suitability for the school board, see *Chicago Daily Tribune,* Aug. 19, 1946.

52. Guest lists, folders 9 and 13, box 88, JRFA.

53. Guest lists, folders 11 and 12, ibid.; ERE to daughter Catherine Harris, 10/30/42, copy in author's possession. The writer Arna Bontemps, who got home at 3:30 A.M., described the party as one of the two "fanciest" he had ever attended. "Champagne was served, along with all the lesser drinks. All in abundance. The barmen were worked to death. . . . And everybody happy. I mean HAPPY." Bontemps to Langston Hughes, in Nichols, 120.

54. Guest list, f. 8, box 88, JRFA; *Ebony* (Nov. 1946): 40–44.

55. Allison Davis fellowship file, f. 5, box 406, JRFA; *Who's Who in America, 1982–1983,* 42nd ed. (Chicago: Marquis, 1983). The son of a Washington postal worker and his wife, Davis had a younger, also brilliant, brother, John Aubrey Davis. A summa cum laude graduate of Williams, the younger Davis earned graduate degrees in political science at Wisconsin and Columbia, using three years of Rosenwald fellowships for that study. Active in civil rights work beginning in his twenties, he was the founder and executive director of the American Society of African Culture, served several years on the executive committee of the American Political Science Association, and was elected vice president of that body. In the preparation of the NAACP's second brief in the *Brown v. Board* case, he organized and coordinated all the nonlegal research. For the last, see Perkins, "Welcome Consequences."

56. DOB, MOT, 3/28/41 [no f.], box 137, JRFA. Underwriting a salary to promote the hiring of a black person to an all-white staff was a well-established practice at the Rosenwald Fund. It had been introduced as early as 1930 to encourage the creation of positions for building agents and vocational supervisors in southern school districts and for public health officers and nurses in seven southern states.

Early in the Roosevelt administration, the practice had been extended to facilitate the appointments of African American professionals to federal agencies. ERE interviews, 2/3–4/30, f. 7, box 129, JRFA.

57. ERE to Eleanor Roosevelt, 2/10/42, f. ER 100 1942, box 1639, Eleanor Roosevelt Papers: White House Correspondence, 1933–1945, FDRPL. Concerned about opposition from the two influential family trustees, Embree was careful the night before the meeting to line up vigorous support from key board members Will Alexander, Charles Johnson, Mark Ethridge, and Eleanor Roosevelt. Telegram, ERE to Mrs. FDR, 3/3/42, f. ER 100 1942, box 1639, Eleanor Roosevelt Papers: White House Correspondence, 1933–1945, FDRPL; DOB, MOT, 4/10/42 [no f.], box 137, JRFA, 13–14.

58. Davis earned the distinction Embree expected. He spent the rest of his career at Chicago, was named John Dewey Distinguished Service Professor there, and had other teaching stints at Columbia, Michigan, Illinois, and Berkeley. He published several books, was nationally recognized as an authority on socialization and the personality development of children, and was among the first to challenge standardized tests on the grounds of cultural bias. He was the first person, black or white, in the field of education to be elected to the American Academy of Arts and Sciences. In 1994, a decade after his death, he was honored by the U.S. Postal Service with a stamp in its black history series. U.S. Postal Service, *1994 Yearbook* (Washington, D.C.: USPS, 1995).

59. Sarah Lawrence president Harold Taylor to ERE, 9/14/45, f. 16, box 114; MEC, 6/4/46, f. 8, box 80, both in JRFA; Embree and Waxman, 276. Information on the salary subsidies at Black Mountain College is in MEC, 6/6/45, f. 7, box 80, and f. 4, box 84, both in JRFA. Embree also used a salary subsidy to facilitate the

desegregation of the faculty of Chicago's Parker School, the private secondary institution that daughter Catherine had attended. DOB, MOT, f. 4, box 84, JRFA, 25. In addition, he devised a plan which enabled black children living on Chicago's south side to attend the Parker School, located on the north side. Flora J. Cooke to Kate Embree, 2/28/50, DEFP. Steps were also taken to engage two African American apprentice teachers in the public schools of the Chicago suburb Winnetka and at the private Winnetka Country Day School. ERE to Catherine Harris, 10/30/42, copy in author's possession.

60. Several such appointments were made at Roosevelt College. MEC, 6/4/46, f. 8, box 80; DOB, MOT, 11/8–9/47 [no f.], box 137, both in JRFA; Belles, "The College Faculty, the Negro Scholar, and the Julius Rosenwald Fund." The integration campaign is described by the fund's education director Fred G. Wale in "Chosen for Ability." In late 1945, the fund also undertook to help returning veterans find jobs by establishing a clearinghouse for information on openings and publicizing the service to race relations agencies across the country (f. 14, box 126, JRFA). When the State Department expressed an openness to appointing African Americans as cultural attachés in U.S. embassies in Ethiopia and Liberia, Embree was ready with recommendations of two "well-qualified former [Rosenwald] fellows." ERE to Will Alexander, 4/26/45, f. 2, box 105, JRFA.

61. August Meier, review of William Darity Jr., ed., *Race, Radicalism, and Reform: Selected Papers,* in *Journal of American History* 76, no. 3 (Dec. 1989): 968.

7. ON THE NATIONAL STAGE

1. Statement at the American Missionary Association's "Seminar on American Racialism," New York, 1/16/42, f. 2, box 163, JRFA. Embree had long been

alert to how war could change race relations. In the closing months of World War I, he called attention to the fact that, through the military draft, black men were required to meet "their full duties" as citizens. "With this experience," he wrote, "is it likely we shall ever again be willing to treat these colored citizens quite as we have before? Shall we be willing to slight and insult those we have called upon to defend us? . . . [I]s it too much to hope that the two races may learn to live together in substantial friendliness in this free and democratic country?" ERE, "With the Negro Troops," 538.

2. ERE to Secretary to the President Marvin H. McIntyre, 2/3/42, f. Colored Matters (Negroes) 1942 Mar.–Apr., box 4, FDRPL. Embree's list consisted primarily of his friends and associates, including Will Alexander, Charles S. Johnson, and Rosenwald trustee Mark Ethridge.

3. Roosevelt to ERE, 3/16/42, ibid. A year later, Embree, Commissioner for Indian Affairs John Collier, Will Alexander, and Charles Johnson considered asking President Roosevelt to appoint a national committee to ensure the protections of the Bill of Rights, particularly for minorities, during the war. ERE to Johnson and Alexander, 6/16/43, f. 2, box 60, CSJP.

4. ERE to Will Alexander, 4/14/42, f. 2, box 105, JRFA. The board had voted in 1940 to close the fund at the end of 1945. A year after approving the Division of Race Relations, the board, over the objections of chair Lessing Rosenwald, rescinded the 1940 resolution. "Life of the Fund," DOB, MOT, 11/20/44 [no f.], box 137, JRFA, 26.

5. Gilpin and Gasman, 170–73. During the war years, Alexander spent most of his time in Washington, D.C., serving in various governmental, advisory, and volunteer posts. Johnson's appointment became possible only at the end of 1942, after a three-institution agreement to share his services had been reached.

While going on the fund's payroll, he would continue to head Fisk University's Department of Race Relations, recently established with Rosenwald money. He would also lead a new Division of Race Relations of the American Missionary Association, to be based at Fisk. As part of this unusual arrangement, Embree agreed that the fund would assume the costs of a midwestern office for Johnson and cover most of his salary.

6. In response to an inquiry from the head of the Associated Negro Press, Embree pointed to an advantage he saw for African Americans in racial separation, notably the opportunity to preserve and develop their own distinctive qualities in churches, colleges, the press, businesses, and cultural institutions. At the same time, he affirmed his commitment to "the theory of equal rights for all races, throughout the country." ERE to Claude A. Barnett, 12/11/33, cited in Belles, "The Julius Rosenwald Fund: Efforts in Race Relations," 248.

7. ERE to Charles Hamilton Houston, 9/30/47, f. 4, box 134, JRFA. In a chapter marred by numerous errors of fact and dubious judgments, historian John H. Stanfield speaks of the fund spending "most of its years servicing Jim Crow institutions" and of Embree's "gradual shift from traditional belief in racial segregation to racial integration." *Philanthropy and Jim Crow,* 97, 108. Though in other passages he compliments Embree, Stanfield seems not to understand Embree's fundamental beliefs, his realistic assessment of the most effective means to enable the black population in the South to advance, and his equally realistic recognition that the war made possible—and urgent—a direct attack on segregation that earlier would almost certainly have been counterproductive. In this connection, it should be noted that the Embree-Alexander-Johnson decision to attack Jim

Crow preceded by several months the publication of the Durham Manifesto, a pivotal anti-segregation statement issued by some seventy-five black leaders from the South. Contrary to Stanfield's characterization, Embree and his colleagues were in the forefront of the anti-segregation movement.

8. See, for example, MEC, 3/3/43, f. 5, box 80, 922; "Draft of Memorandum on Race Relations for Trustees Docket" [11/44?], f. 6, box 60; "The General Problem of Segregation," 11/16/45, Supplementary Docket, Board of Trustees, 11/16/45 [no f.], box 137, all in JRFA.

9. Tuskegee trained 994 pilots through 1946. See http://www.Tuskegee-airmen.org (accessed 12/15/08). On ERE's address, see f. 7, box 117, JRFA.

10. F. D. Patterson to ERE, 7/6/43, attached to "ERE to Trustees of the JRF," 7/16/43, f. ER 100 1943, FDRPL. In the letter, Patterson mentions a loan of $130,000, but in a published article he set the figure at "more than $200,000." Frederick D. Patterson, "Foundation Policies in Regard to Negro Institutions of Higher Learning," *Journal of Educational Sociology* 32, no. 6 (Feb. 1959): 291. The larger sum indicates a supplementary allocation by the fund, bringing the total to well over half of Tuskegee's investment in aviation during the war years.

11. "ERE to Trustees of the JRF," 7/16/43; ERE to Will Alexander, 12/3/42, both in f. 2, box 105, JRFA. Some black leaders, notably William H. Hastie (then a civilian aide to Secretary of War Henry Stimson), were reported to consider the loan unnecessary and perhaps unwise, believing it relieved the army of an obligation it otherwise would have been required to meet. Moreover, because the airstrip would be used only by black pilots, its creation could be seen as extending the separation of the races. The issue is reminiscent of the earlier dispute

over the fund's support for expanded hospital facilities in Harlem: was it preferable to act to advance African American welfare immediately even in segregated circumstances, or to postpone indefinitely such improvements lest segregation be strengthened? In these instances, as in the fund's cooperation with southern school boards in building schools for rural black youth, Embree consistently favored the former option.

12. In 1945, when the War Department established a commission of generals to plan the elimination of racial discrimination in the armed services, Embree was asked to confer with the group. "Supplementary Docket: Topics for General Discussion," DOB, MOT, 11/16/45 [no f.], box 137, JRFA. Earlier, he had expressed concern about the denial of equal opportunity to black men and women in military service. See ERE to Will Alexander, 3/9/43, f. 2, box 105, JRFA. In 1943, the fund's board approved a committee of three—Embree, Alexander, Eleanor Roosevelt—to investigate and report on the extent to which blacks were being used in combat. MEC, 6/4/43, f. 5, box 80, JRFA. Embree and Alexander also visited a WAC training facility to assess conditions there. "Report of Informal Visit to Training Camp for WAAC's [sic], Des Moines, Iowa," 9/21/45, attached to ERE to Eleanor Roosevelt, 9/23/42, ER Corres. ER 100 1942, f. Edwin Embree, box 721, FDRPL.

13. Indicative of Embree's sensitivity to racial tensions and his farsightedness was an initiative he took early in June 1943. Using philanthropy's power to bring together thoughtful and influential people, he hosted a one-day conference to consider the current problems of black workers and to determine how wartime gains could be extended after the war. The meeting apparently had been planned before the Mobile violence, for the group

met in Chicago only ten days after the beginning of that outbreak and before Beaumont and the other cities experienced any rioting. "Minutes of Special Committee called by the Rosenwald Fund," 6/3/43, f. 5, box 80, JRFA.

14. MEC, 7/6/43, f. 5, box 80, JRFA; Gilpin and Gasman, 176–77. Continuing to lobby the president, Embree encouraged Will Alexander to suggest that Roosevelt use a fireside chat to recommend that other cities create race relations commissions like the one getting under way in Chicago. ERE to Will Alexander, 7/30/43, f. 2, box 105, JRFA.

15. A combined total of almost 1,000 copies were bought and distributed by the American Council on Race Relations and the American Missionary Association each month. Gilpin and Gasman, 177. When it is recalled that the ACRR was essentially Embree's creation and that Charles S. Johnson was the director of race relations of the AMA, the interlocking and mutually supporting relationships of these groups becomes obvious.

16. Gilpin and Gasman, 159–60, 177; Gilpin, 199. Though at the outset Johnson had admonished his staff that the presentation of material should be "orderly and objective," within three years he and Embree were prepared to use the *Monthly Summary* information for advocacy. Their plan was to have their strategically placed reporters survey legitimate theaters in the North and West to determine which ones discriminated against minorities in their admissions policies and then use the results to persuade members of the Actors' Equity Association to refuse to play in those venues unless the policy were changed. ERE to CSJ, 7/16/46, f. 16, box 105, JRFA. Actors' Equity did issue such an ultimatum in June 1947 to the only full-time legitimate theater in Washington, D.C., which then ended its discriminatory policy.

17. Alexander seems to have selected the dozen invited guests. "Dinner and Meeting on Race Relations," 12/14/43, box 110, Office of Social Entertainments, FDRPL.

18. ERE to Franklin McLean, 5/19/44, f. 21, box 105, JRFA. Seeking to garner the "considerable prestige" he envisioned for the organization, Embree made special, but unsuccessful, efforts to persuade John D. Rockefeller Jr. and 1940 Republican presidential nominee Wendell Willkie to attend. ERE to Rockefeller Jr., 3/3/44, f. 399, box 37, ser. P Welfare General, RG 2, Office of the Messrs. Rockefeller, Rockefeller Family Archives, RAC; ERE to Willkie, 2/10/44, f. 1, box 89, ACRR. Embree had discussed such a meeting with his executive committee but, indicative of his latitude within the fund, he informed the full board only on March 20, one day before the conference was to convene. DOB, MOT, 3/20/44, box 137, JRFA, 11–12.

19. ERE to Franklin McLean, 5/19/44. See also ERE to Bishop R. R. Wright Jr., 3/29/44, f. 1, box 89, JRFA.

20. ERE, "The American Council on Race Relations." Apparently little was made of the fact that, of the twenty-two participants in the second meeting, almost two-thirds were from either Chicago or New York, which is suggestive of little nationwide interest in the venture.

21. "Board Minutes," 5/20/44, f. 10, box 27, ACRR. The fund contributed a total of $125,000 for the council's first two and a half years. MEC, 10/3/46, f. 8, box 80, JRFA. The bylaws of the ACRR are in f. 9, box 27.

22. Alexander also served as the council's treasurer and presided at executive committee meetings on the frequent occasions when the Philadelphia-based president, Clarence Pickett, could not make the trip to Chicago. Pickett was the executive secretary of the American

Friends Service Committee, board chair of the Doris Duke Foundation, and a member of the Field Foundation's board. Untitled document [n.d.], f. 363, reel 3, EREP-SML; "Minutes, Board of Directors," 5/20/44, f. 10, box 27, ACRR.

23. ACRR bylaws, f. 9, box 27; "Recapitulation of Publications Distributed from January 1 to April 30, 1947" [no f.], box 28, both in ACRR.

24. In addition to its large subsidies to the ACRR, the fund separately provided at least $5,000 of a $10,000 budget for a radio series on the problems of minorities on the West Coast. Charles S. Johnson also arranged for $2,000 from the AMA. MEC, 7/25/45, f. 7, box 80, JRFA.

25. "Facts about Japanese-Americans" [n.d.]. Wayne Coy Papers, FDRPL; "Executive Committee Minutes," 3/6/46, f. 1; "Minutes of the Board," 5/17/46, f. 2, both in box 28, ACRR.

26. "Board Minutes," 5/17/46, f. 1, box 28, ACRR. The Rosenwald board made a special allocation of $2,000 to fund Houston's committee. When the Southern Regional Council decided to examine the administration of the GI Bill in the South, an additional $15,000 to cover the study director's salary and travel expenses was appropriated. MEC, 6/6/45, f. 7, box 80, JRFA. The telegrams (5/19/45) from the ACRR board of directors to Truman and Stettinius are in f. 1, box 28, ACRR.

27. ERE to Will Alexander, 7/30/45, f. 2, box 105, JRFA. By the third annual meeting of the board, only eleven of the thirty-three members attended. "Executive Committee Minutes," 6/14/46, 9/18/46; "Board of Directors Minutes," 11/15/46, all in f. 1, box 28, ACRR. Embree and others opposed political activism in part due to fear of losing the ACRR's tax-exempt status. See Louis Wirth's "Progress Report," 4–9/49, f. 4, box 28, ACRR.

28. "Board of Directors," f. 5, box 4, Robert Redfield Papers, SCRC, Univer-

sity of Chicago. There is even evidence that some ACRR board members actually undercut fund-raising efforts. See, for example, the discussion of Rockefeller official Dana S. Creel with ACRR board member Donald Young. "Memorandum: American Council on Race Relations," 8/21/47, f. 399, box 37, ser. P Welfare General, RG 2, Rockefeller Family Archives, RAC. Because board members like Lester Granger of the NUL and Walter White of the NAACP saw the ACRR as competition with their own organizations, particularly for donors, it is hard to imagine they were enthusiastic supporters. MEC, 10/3/46, f. 8, box 80, JRFA. For Granger's view, see Arthur W. Packard's memorandum on the ACRR, 5/18/44, in f. 399, box 37, ser. P, Welfare General, RG 2, Office of the Messrs. Rockefeller, Rockefeller Family Archives, RAC.

29. The new university committee included two Embree friends, the anthropologists Robert Redfield (already an ACRR director) and Allison Davis. "Minutes of the Board," 11/15/46, 3/7/47; "Minutes of the Executive Committee," 1/1/47, all in folders 1 and 2, box 28, ACRR.

30. See the council's final report, 8/50, f. 8, box 36, ACRR. For a discussion of other ACRR difficulties—personnel cutbacks, staff unionization, a protest from the ACLU—see "Special Meeting of the Board," 3/7/47, and "Meeting of the Chicago Members of the Executive Committee," 9/18/47, both in f. 2, box 328, ACRR.

31. Though organizational documents do not sustain the charges, one disgruntled board member later reported that Embree and Field had run the ACRR, that Embree had dominated policy decisions and, after the reorganization, occasionally undermined President Louis Wirth, whom he allegedly disliked. Donald Young interview with Dana S. Creel, "Memorandum," RAC. It appears that,

by late 1945 or early 1946, Embree had become so disillusioned with the ACRR that he had begun to consider the formation of another high-powered organization devoted exclusively to research and leadership development in human relations. See draft statement, "Council on Human Relations" [n.d.], reel 7, EREP-SML.

32. ERE to Robert C. Weaver, 7/18/46, f. 3, box 106, JRFA; Embree and Waxman, 184–85. Embree also served on the bureau's board.

33. "Federal Council of Churches of Christ in America," MEC, 10/31/44, f. 6, box 80; "Educational Programs through the Church and Labor," DOB, MOT, 5/18/46 [no f.], box 137; "The Race Relations Program of the Fund, 1946," f. 2, box 60, all in JRFA; Embree and Waxman, 194–95, 274. It is notable that the Federal Council of Churches' commission was chaired by Will Alexander.

34. "Race Relations: General Program," 4/17/43 [no f.], box 137, JRFA.

35. Until 1948, when the fund expired, its grants to the Legal Defense and Educational Fund totaled $33,500, one-third of all the NAACP's litigation expenditures aimed at school desegregation through the *Brown* decision. The fund's indirect role in that decision, through the fellowships that allowed almost a dozen men and women to get the graduate training needed to contribute later to the NAACP brief, is described in Perkins, "Welcome Consequences," 344–56.

36. Examples of the invitations Embree received are in the thirty folders in box 116, JRFA.

37. Many of the institute's faculty during these years were connected to the Rosenwald Fund: Will Alexander, Clark Foreman, lawyer Charles Hamilton Houston, Howard University dean Charles H. Thompson, and former fellows Allison Davis, Ira DeA. Reid, and C. Vann Woodward. Others were linked to Embree and

Johnson through the Chicago mayor's commission, the ACRR, or the University of Chicago: Robert C. Weaver, CIO official Willard Townsend, Chicago professors Ellsworth Faris, Robert Redfield, and Louis Wirth. For a detailed description of the institute, see Gilpin and Gasman, 183–200.

38. "Far East Can Mean Peace or War, Declares Embree," *Nashville Tennessean,* July 5, 1944, 22. In remarks at the institute a few days later, with anti-Japanese sentiment high across the country, he urged that Americans of Japanese descent be returned soon to their West Coast homes and to fair treatment by their neighbors.

39. "The Challenge of the Future," f. 1, box 37, CSJP. In a follow-up presentation, "Education for the New World," Embree pointed to the failure of American education to develop students' appreciation of cultural differences. And in a point publicized particularly by the Associated Negro Press, he took historically black colleges to task for reducing the appointments of white professors, thereby denying their students opportunities to come into "friendly and scholarly contact with white teachers." Unidentified newspaper clipping, f. 459, box 65, Educational Interest Service: Fisk Univ. file, RG 2, Office of the Messrs. Rockefeller, Rockefeller Family Archives, RAC.

40. This is Charles S. Johnson's characterization in "The Future That Is Here," in *The Edwin R. Embree Memorial Lectures, 1954–1955* (New Orleans, La.: Dillard University, 1955), 68.

41. "Metamorphosis?" *Nashville Banner,* July 5, 1945, quoted in Gilpin and Gasman, 186.

42. The warning is mentioned, without details, in Johnson's "The Future," 68.

43. Gilpin and Gasman, 188–89.

44. "Race Relations in One World." Yet even as Embree praised the "Christian principle" of brotherhood, he reiterated in

another lecture ("Peoples of the Earth") the view published years earlier that, far from encompassing Christianity, Western civilization contradicted it. Christianity had never been widely practiced in the West, he asserted. Summaries of both addresses are in f. 4, box 37, CSJP. Commenting on the address, Arna Bontemps wrote that Embree "twisted the tiger's tale as usual." Bontemps to Langston Hughes, in Nichols, 209. For newspaper coverage, see James Pilkington, "Race Relations Meeting Opens at Fisk University," *Nashville Banner,* July 2, 1946, and "Rosenwald Fund Head Predicts a 'New Order' at Fisk Sessions," July 3, 1946; and *Nashville Tennessean,* July 3 and 4, 1946. Clippings available in f. 3, box 37, CSJP. A few weeks prior to his keynote address at the institute, Embree gave essentially the same speech to the National Conference of Social Work, which was meeting in Cleveland. Kathleen McLaughlin, "Warns the Whites of Race Bias Peril," *New York Times,* May 27, 1946, 18.

45. The complete citations for these works are in the bibliography.

46. These pages (237–43) echoed a point Embree had made earlier in Embree, Simon, and Mumford, *Island India.*

47. The *Saturday Review* and *New York Times* reviews are quoted in the initial pages of the reissue of the second edition. See also *Social Forces* 19, no. 1: 18; *American Antiquity* 7, no. 2: 189; *Social Studies* 31, no. 6: 282; *American Journal of Sociology* 46, no. 1: 108; *Hispanic American Historical Review* 20, no. 4: 822.

48. ERE to H. Scudder Merkel, 5/17/40, f. 3, box 530, JRFA. According to Deloria, Embree had been one of the few observers to discern the importance of the 1934 Indian Reorganization Act, and his had been "one of the first attempts to place the new Indian policy in an intelligent light." His important contribution had been to help defend tribal cultures

and governments at a time "when they sorely needed defense." Moreover, he had some understanding of the "soul" of Native Americans and, rejecting the great melting-pot concept dominant in his day, had foreseen America as "a great pageant of diverse peoples." Introduction to the second edition of *Indians of the Americas* (New York: Macmillan, 1970), viii–xiii.

49. ERE, *American Negroes,* 68–69. This was neither the first nor the last time that Embree used these thought-provoking words to argue against racial injustice. They had been adumbrated in *Brown America,* 22; and the Yale Graduate Sociology Club had heard them two years earlier. *New York Times,* Jan. 11, 1941, 15.

50. ERE, *Brown Americans,* 230–33.

51. Carey McWilliams, *Lawyers' Guild Review* (Nov.–Dec. 1943); Kenneth C. Kaufman, *Chicago Daily Tribune,* Nov. 21, 1943, C10; Linwood T. Coles, *Norfolk Journal and Guide,* Feb. 9, 1944; C. A. Franklin to ERE, 2/24/44, all clippings in f. 12, box 529, JRFA.

52. Fosdick to ERE, 11/24/43; Weaver to ERE, 11/24/43, both in f. 11; Wormley to ERE, 3/9/44; Ellsworth Shaw to ERE [n.d.]; Louis Mercier to ERE, 12/16/44, all three in f. 12. For a less positive response, see the exchange between Embree and a Mississippi lawyer: Kenneth G. Price to ERE, 1/11/44, 1/28/44; ERE to Price, 1/19/44, all in f. 12. All documents in this note in box 529, JRFA.

53. ERE to CSJ, 10/26/42, f. 2, box 534, JRFA. Portraying fully rounded figures and arriving at just the right tone were not without difficulty. Even after the book was in galley proof, the head of Viking Press asked Embree to reconsider some wording he thought patronizing, to avoid "apologizing or pussyfooting" about the radical views of three of his subjects, and to explain whether he agreed or disagreed with quoted comments, some of which he considered "particularly violent" and po-

tentially libelous. Marshall Best to ERE, 11/4/43, f. 1, box 534, JRFA.

54. Telegram, ERE to Robert L. Hatch of Viking Press, 11/29/43, f. 1, box 534, JRFA. A tie vote forced Embree to raise the number of subjects from the expected twelve to thirteen, thus preventing an even more direct play off the title of William Bolitho's well-known *Twelve against the Gods.* Embree took pride in devising catchy titles, typified in *Thirteen* by such chapter headings as "Amazon of God," for college founder Mary McLeod Bethune, "Sweet Potato Wizard," for scientist George Washington Carver, and "Shakespeare in Harlem," for writer Langston Hughes. He also proposed the titles of all the popular books of his friend Clarence Day, and advised James Weldon Johnson on the title of his biography. ERE to Johnson, 7/7/31, f. 6, box 561, JRFA; Johnson to ERE, 7/11/31, f. 414, box 17, both in J. W. Johnson Papers.

55. ERE to publisher Marshall Best, 6/29/44, f. 1, box 534, JRFA.

56. Marshall Best to ERE, 7/12/44, 3/20/45, both in f. 1, box 534, JRFA. With its human interest and lively style, the book continued to attract the public long after the subjects and the author had passed away. Reissued in 1968, when the civil rights movement was at its height, the volume found its way onto the shelves of several hundred additional libraries and into the hands of countless readers. WorldCat, http://worldcat.org (accessed 6/7/07).

57. Frank H. Hankins, *American Sociological Review* 9, no. 3 (June 1944): 330; DuBois to ERE, 2/2/44; Dorothy Canfield, Book-of-the-Month Club review, Mar. 1944; Wallace to ERE, 11/8/44, all in f. 15, box 534, JRFA.

58. Samuel M. Strong, *American Journal of Sociology* 50, no. 2 (1944): 159; A. C. Powell, *The People's Voice,* Feb. 19, 1944; Bilbo to Viking Press, 11/21/45, all in f. 1, box 534, JRFA.

59. Late in the war, Embree was asked by the Writers' War Board to contribute an article for the magazine *Army Talk,* which was distributed to troops in Europe. He drafted a piece, but a month later conceded he could do no better than the article "Balance Sheet in Race Relations" which had been published in the May 1945 *Atlantic.* In the draft, he stated bluntly, "Young Negroes coming back from war experiences will never again fit into the serfdom of southern feudalism or into second class status in northern industrial cities" (f. 2, box 120, JRFA).

60. ERE to Richard Walsh Jr., 3/9/42, f. 8, box 528, JRFA. Reflecting the expectation of personal success he had imbibed at Yale, Embree acknowledged to his board on one occasion that it was largely his desire for "personal influence in education and human relations" that had brought him to Rosenwald from Rockefeller. DOB, MOT, 5/24/47 [no f.], box 137, JRFA, 37.

61. "Radio Series on the Negro," MEC, 6/4/40, f. 2, box 80, JRFA. The idea for the series came from 1932 Rosenwald fellow Ambrose Caliver, the Education Office's specialist in African American education.

62. Personal communication, Catherine Embree Harris to the author, 1/28/06; ERE to Clarence Day, 6/29/28. reel 2, EREP-SML.

63. Dalfiume, 100.

64. ERE to Lesser, 9/15/42; Lesser to ERE, 9/22/42, both in f. 11, box 114, JRFA.

65. ERE to Jackson Leighter, 3/9/43, f. 11, box 114, JRFA.

66. MEC, 6/27/44, f. 6, box 80, JRFA; Embree and Waxman, 277. Five of the committee members, including most prominently Charles S. Johnson, Langston Hughes, and the proposed director, poet Owen Dodson, were former Rosenwald fellows, and a sixth member would later receive a fellowship.

67. Hatch, 127–30.

68. ERE to Columbia Foundation executive Marjorie Elkus, 11/13/49, reel 2, EREP-SML.

69. "Guide to the World Citizens Association Central Committee Records, 1939–1953," WCAP. Embree's commitment to closer cooperation in world affairs was apparently crystallized by the Second World War. In 1941, before the United States became formally engaged, he declared to a professional group that the conflicts in Europe and Asia had renewed interest in a world organization that would "end or mitigate" the trend toward frequent and ever more destructive wars. Thoughtful people all over the world were beginning to realize that "some sort of planned world order must replace the current haphazard map of nationalistic governments and economic barriers." ERE, *Living Together* [no p.].

70. Wilbur to ERE, 1/30/39; ERE to Blaine, 2/2/39, both in f. 1, box 119, JRFA. Wilbur and Embree also had known each other since the Rockefeller years. Greene was initially the director of the WCA, but he left after 1939 to lead the Japanese Non-Aggression Committee in Washington. Greene to ERE, 2/2/39; Blaine to Cordell Hull, 3/5/40, both in f. B5, box 7, ser. VII, WCAP.

71. A career diplomat, Davies had been an economic advisor at the 1919 Paris peace conference and had served as U.S. ambassador to both the USSR and Belgium. Also nominated, but declining committee membership, were future secretary of state John Foster Dulles, prominent jurist Grenville Clark, University of Wisconsin president Clarence Dykstra, and *Louisville Courier-Journal* editor and Rosenwald trustee Mark Ethridge. Greene to Cassels, 7/11/39, f. A1, ser. VII; f. B2, ser. VIII, both in WCAP.

72. Embree was apparently the only member of the executive committee to take such initiative (f. 5, box 10, WCAP).

73. "List of February 14, 1941," f. A2, box 6, ser. IV, WCAP.

74. ERE to Henri Bonnet, 11/5/41, f. 6, box 10, ser. XV, WCAP.

75. ERE to Edwin M. Clough, 11/4/40, f. B5, box 7, ser. VIII, WCAP.

76. Independent of the WCA, Embree by 1943 began to plan a hundred-person conference on Africa that also was never held. ERE to Secretary of the Institute of Pacific Relations E. C. Carter, 4/26/43, f. 3, box 113, JRFA.

77. See various documents in f. 2, box 119, JRFA, particularly ERE to Blaine, 2/20/45.

78. Embree, Blaine, Cassels, Waymack, and Wright, *World at the Crossroads*, 10–13.

79. Undated report, f. B16, box 5, ser. III, WCAP.

80. For a sampling of reviews, see f. B17, box 5, ser. III, WCAP.

81. Gross, *Roosevelt University*, 40–41; E. James Sparling, "Report of the President," 1946–1947, RCCR.

82. Sparling, Report, 1946–1947; Sparling to ERE, 4/29/49, Embree, Edwin R., Roosevelt University Biographical Collection: Correspondence, University Archives, Roosevelt University Library. Several times during this period, Embree used public occasions to denounce, by implication, both Reds and Red-baiters. At the Rosenwald gala in mid-1948, he repeated his words from the ADA dinner the year before, declaring that anyone who would throw over America's heritage of health, prosperity, democracy, and opportunity was "either a fool or a traitor or probably both." In his keynote address at the Conference on Civic Unity a few months later, he decried the "witch-hunt" directed against Roosevelt College and the University of Chicago (reel 2, EREP-SML).

83. MEC, 10/31/46, f. 8, box 80, JRFA; Landis, 93.

84. The research subcommittee consisted of Robert C. Weaver, Will Alexander, Joseph Lohman, E. Franklin Frazier, Charles Hamilton Houston, and ACRR board members Charles Dollard, Donald R. Young, and Louis Wirth. Lohman to Isador Lubin, 11/11/46, National Committee on Segregation in the Nation's Capital, Isador Lubin Papers, Personal Correspondence, 1935–1971, box 70, FDRPL.

85. MEC, 10/31/46, f. 8, box 80, JRFA; ERE to Lohman, 12/10/48, reel 3, EREP-SML; Embree and Waxman, 277. The NCSNC later shared space at 4901 S. Ellis Avenue with the ACRR.

86. Gertrude Martin, *Chicago Defender*, Jan. 1, 1949, 7.

87. Lohman and Embree, "The Nation's Capital," 33.

88. Ibid., 33–37.

89. ERE to NCSNC chair George N. Shuster, 12/10/48; Lohman to ERE, 9/16/48. The President's Committee on Civil Rights recommended legislation to eliminate segregation in the district's public schools, hospitals, recreational facilities, housing projects, and welfare agencies, and the enactment of a fair employment practices act for the district. All the issues addressed by these recommendations were highlighted in "The Nation's Capital" and in the NCSNC's report. Lohman, "Recommendations for the Consideration of the NCSNC," 12/12/48. For members of the "Executive-Continuation Committee," see Lohman to ERE, 1/19/49. All documents on reel 3, EREP-SML.

8. CELEBRATIONS, PROCLAMATIONS, TRIBUTES

1. Financial statement, 12/28/39, f. 1, box 80, JRFA.

2. MEC, 12/28/39, f. 1; 7/26/46, f. 8, both in box 80, JRFA.

3. Resolution quoted in DOB, MOT, 11/20/44 [no f.], box 137, JRFA, 26.

4. "Life of the Fund," ibid.

5. MEC, 7/43, 11/43, 1/44, all in box 80, JRFA. These grants illustrate the interconnectedness of race-concerned organizations at this point in the fund's life. Embree's brother Will headed the foundation committee of the UNCF, while John D. Rockefeller Jr. chaired the organization. The SRC, which succeeded the Will Alexander–led Commission on Interracial Cooperation, was presided over by University of North Carolina sociologist Howard W. Odum, who had just completed six years as a fund trustee. The chair of its executive committee was Charles S. Johnson. Egerton, 311.

6. MEC, 5/24/47, f. 9; 3/4/48, 5/11/48, both in f. 10, all in box 80, JRFA.

7. *Phylon* 9, no. 3 (1948): 195. This issue of *Phylon* is largely devoted to the fund's gala.

8. DuBois to JRF, 12/14/35, f. 5, box 409, JRFA. Dubois's respect for Embree is indicated by the fact that, as an anniversary present, he gave his wife a copy of *Brown America*. DuBois's address traced the history of race relations in the United States during the life of the Rosenwald Fund, emphasizing the progress made on multiple fronts, but concluding that greater tolerance of cultural diversity was still urgently needed. His address was far more notable than that of Myrdal, who explained he was no longer in close touch with the American scene. Both papers were published in *Phylon* 9, no. 3.

9. ERE to Myrdal, 2/4/48, f. 5, box 88; f. 6, box 84, both in JRFA. Conspicuous among Myrdal's collaborators were political scientist Ralph Bunche, sociologists Charles S. Johnson and E. Franklin Frazier, and anthropologist W. Allison Davis. Also involved as a researcher was newly minted Ph.D. Kenneth B. Clark, whose rise to prominence came only with the *Brown v. Board* decision. Had education authority Horace Mann Bond been

able to accept Myrdal's invitation to write a monograph, he too would have been added to this distinguished roster.

10. The descriptions in this and the following paragraphs, including the quotations, are drawn from *Phylon* 9, no. 3. On the fellowship to Primus, see Nichols, 232.

11. "Rosenwald Fund's Big Benefits," *Chicago Daily News*, May 29, 1948, 6.

12. Only a few days before this issue appeared, Harper published Embree's (and Julia Waxman's) history of the Rosenwald Fund, *Investment in People*. Chapter 12 of that book contains much of the content and language of the magazine article.

13. ERE, "Timid Billions," 30.

14. Ibid., 31–32.

15. Ibid., 34–37. Not surprisingly, human relations and world peace received the lengthiest treatment. The latter claimed a full page in the ten-page article, reflecting an Embree preoccupation in the forties and, in a larger sense, his decades-long concern with the question of how peoples of diverse backgrounds could live together in harmony and prosperity. Foundation support of the arts he had championed since his early Rockefeller days, and "human studies" was essentially human biology under another name. The need for teacher education reform and a great southern university were, of course, themes he had often sounded years earlier.

16. See reel 7, EREP-SML, which contains about seventy-five letters in response to the article.

17. Rosenwald expenditures did not always reflect some of these principles. Will Alexander's Commission on Interracial Cooperation, for example, received an annual $10,000 subsidy throughout the 1930s. Similarly, the NAACP for five years received small grants—$1,000–$2,500— obviously insufficient to make a large difference, but perhaps enough in the Depression to help the organization survive.

MEC, 12/28/39, f. 1, box 80; 9/21/31, f. 6, and 3/22/32, f. 7, both in box 79, JRFA. Considered individually, such small grants—and they are numerous—seem to be "retail" philanthropy. But if improving race relations is seen as the overarching fund purpose, collectively they may be regarded as a "wholesale" approach.

18. "More Thoughts about Foundations," attachment to ERE to Clarence Day, 11/5/34, reel 2, EREP-SML. In the cover letter, Embree said he had considered "burying [this and related documents] in Day's files," as they had discussed doing with other pieces likely to generate great controversy if published.

19. ERE statement, attached to "Report of Yale Class of 1906 Dinner, 1949," reel 4, EREP-SML.

20. Alexander, "The Education and Work of Edwin R. Embree," 3.

21. ERE to John Dollard, 10/1/40, f. 3, box 110, JRFA.

22. ERE to James Saxon Childers, 6/13/38, f. 10, box 108, JRFA.

23. ERE to John Embree, 7/29/47, reel 2, EREP-SML.

24. Family Journal, 4/12/48, DEFP; ERE to John Embree, 7/29/47, reel 2, EREP-SML.

25. As early as 1923, Embree had begun to attend meetings of the American-Liberian Board (formerly the New York State Colonization Society), a group primarily concerned with education in Liberia. Soon becoming a trustee of the organization, he was elected to its presidency in 1928. EREOD, 5/3/23, reel 2; ERE to JR, 11/6/28, f. 32, box 104, JRFA; ERE to A. P. Stokes, 1/16/28, A. P. Stokes Papers, MAD-SML. On the creation of the Africa Foundation, see ERE to [Liberia Company president] Blackwell Smith, 3/10/48, 3/11/48; Smith to ERE, 4/22/48, all in reel 3, EREP-SML.

26. Family Journal, 4/12/48, reel 4, EREP-SML.

27. ERE to [Liberia Company vice president] David Sulzberger, 4/22/48, reel 3, EREP-SML.

28. Stettinius to ERE, 4/26/48; ERE to Dr. Stanley J. Leland, 5/11/48, both in reel 3, EREP-SML.

29. ERE to E. James Sparling, 6/21/49, 12/17/49, Embree, Edwin R., Biographical Collection: Correspondence, University Archives, Roosevelt University. That same year, Sparling nominated Embree for the presidency of the American Council on Education, but Embree declined consideration on the grounds that the organization needed a younger man. ERE to Sparling, 12/17/49, Edwin Rogers Embree Papers, University Archives, Roosevelt University Library, Chicago. Embree described his new role in ERE to Family Journalists, 6/28/49, reel 2, EREP-SML.

30. ERE to Marjorie Elkus, 10/13/49; ERE to Family Journalists, 6/28/49, both in reel 2, EREP-SML. Deeply concerned about the disappearance of such fellowships when the fund closed, Embree had pointed John Hay Whitney's representatives in that direction even before becoming associated with the philanthropy. ERE to A. C. Campbell, 5/21/48, reel 3, EREP-SML; ERE to William H. Jackson, 12/5/46, f. 4, box 117, JRFA.

31. ERE to Wilbur K. Jordan, 9/21/49, reel 3, EREP-SML.

32. ERE to Engleman, 3/7/49, 3/11/49; ERE to Bowles, 3/7/49, 4/12/49; ERE to Cousins, 4/27/49, all on reel 2, EREP-SML.

33. ERE, Peoples of the Earth.

34. Stanfield, Philanthropy and Jim Crow, 97; Jeanne C. Webber to School Board, 3/8/52; Port Chester Daily Item, Apr. 30 and May 1, 1956; Webber to William Dean Embree, 5/25/56; W. D. Embree to Webber, 5/29/56, all in DEFP. The effect of such opposition on the book's sales cannot be determined, but Embree's interest was in affecting opinion, not in sales per se. Like his other books, Peoples

was written for educational purposes, not for personal profit. All royalties from the book went, not to the author nor to the expiring Rosenwald Fund, but to the New York–based Bureau for Intercultural Education.

35. These were Embree's third and fourth honorary degrees, adding to those awarded by the University of Hawaii in 1936 and the University of Iowa in 1941.

36. ERE to UNCF chair John D. Rockefeller Jr., 1/27/49, reel 3, EREP-SML.

37. *New York Sun*, Feb. 16, 1949; ERE to Leslie Guingard, 2/18/49, reel 1, EREP-SML.

38. Bunche had been one of Embree's favorite fellows and was arguably the most distinguished of them all. Embree's statement at the dinner, which was sponsored by the American Association for the United Nations, 5/4/49, is on reel 1, EREP-SML.

39. The volume was *Build the Future*.

40. *Nashville Tennessean*, Nov. 8, 1948. Percy Julian was one of the most conspicuously successful Rosenwald fellows; he served as vice chair of the Roosevelt College board while Embree was the chair.

41. GEVOD, 6/4/26, reel 3; EREOD, 6/16/27, reel 2, both RFA, RAC. Embree's connection to Fisk had been continuous from the mid-twenties. In 1932, he gave the principal address at ceremonies honoring lyric tenor Roland Hayes, the first recipient of a Fisk honorary degree. ERE interview with Fisk president Thomas Elsa Jones, 4/14/32, f. 7, box 120, JRFA.

42. A concern to avoid conflicts of interest also led Embree to decline membership on the boards of the New School for Social Research and Howard University. ERE interviews, 4/18/30, 6/15/30, both in f. 7, box 120, JRFA.

43. Gilpin and Gasman, 224; CSJ to ERE, 5/31/49, reel 2, EREP-SML.

44. Jordan to ERE, 6/21/49, reel 3, EREP-SML.

45. Wale to Kate Embree, 5/19/50; Benitez to Kate Embree, 3/10/50; Rose H. Alshuler to Kate Embree, 2/22/50; Fisk trustee Dan May to Kate Embree, 2/22/50; ERE to Edwina Devereux, 2/20/50, all in DEFP.

46. Tobias to Kate Embree, 2/23/50; telegram, Baldwin to Kate Embree, 2/22/50, both in DEFP.

47. Bruno Lasher to John Embree, 2/25/50; Quincy Wright to Kate Embree, 3/1/50, both in DEFP.

48. *New York Herald Tribune*, Feb. 22, 1950; *Chicago Sun-Times* (reprinted in *Chicago Defender*, Mar. 4, 1950); *Philadelphia Inquirer*, Mar. 1, 1950. Embree's disciplinary specialty was a source of some confusion. The *New York Times* labeled him a sociologist, the *St. Louis Post-Dispatch*, an anthropologist. He probably would have claimed professional status in neither field.

49. Unidentified newspaper clipping [n.d.], DEFP.

50. The DEFP contains some 350 notes, telegrams, and letters of condolence, most dated the last week of February 1950.

51. Louise Prentice to Kate Embree, 6/1/50.

52. Nellie Matilda Embree Hill to Edwina Devereux, 4/8/50, DEFP.

53. Bruno Lasher to John Embree, 2/25/50; Quincy Wright to Kate Embree, 3/1/50, both in DEFP.

54. William Grant Still to Kate Embree, 3/9/50, DEFP.

55. Allison Davis to Kate Embree [n.d.], DEFP.

56. William Dean Embree, "Memorandum for Members of the Family," 3/31/50; *Edwin Rogers Embree: Memorial Services*, 3/11/50 (a brochure produced after the service), both in DEFP.

57. Copy of statement sent to Edwina Embree Devereux, 3/15/50, DEFP.

58. *ERE: Memorial Services*. The brochure contains the telegram's message and the remarks of the five eulogists.

59. The idea of the lectureships may have originated with Whitney Foundation director Robert C. Weaver, who had worked so extensively with Embree in the 1940s.

60. National Scholarship Service and Fund for Negro Students press release, 6/30/50, DEFP.

61. E. J. Sparling to Kate Embree, 3/31/50, Edwin Rogers Embree Papers, University Archives, Roosevelt University Library, Chicago.

62. Catherine Embree Harris, personal communication to author, 1/29/06.

63. "This Glad New Year," 1/20/40, DEFP, 12.

64. "Progress of the Half-Century of Human Relations," reel 7, EREP-SML.

The piece had been scheduled to run on March 11, the day of the memorial service in Chicago. But the *Courier* chose to postpone publication, carrying instead a no less eloquent statement published almost a decade earlier: ERE, "American Democracy and the Negro."

65. The words are from Robert Redfield's eulogy. Redfield also described Embree as "like an understanding and generous host at a party attended by all mankind, moving about from group to group, drawing out of each what was interesting, directing the attention of one to what would be sympathetically received by another." *ERE: Memorial Services.*

66. Catherine Embree Harris, personal communication to author, 1/29/06.

BIBLIOGRAPHY

PUBLISHED WORKS OF EDWIN ROGERS EMBREE

This list draws on an incomplete document prepared by John Embree soon after his father's death and on an anonymous and undated document prepared at Fisk University, to which have been added other titles discovered by the author. Of the articles, only original publications are listed, not republications in a second or, occasionally, a third periodical. Not included are Embree-written book reviews, which number in the dozens. The list is divided by genre and then arranged chronologically to indicate the issues Embree sought to bring to public attention at various points in his career.

Books

History of the Class of 1906, Yale College. Ed. (with George Starkweather Fowler). 2 vols. New Haven, Conn.: Yale University Press, 1906, 1919.

Life at Yale. Ed. New Haven, Conn.: Yale University Press, 1912.

Reviews of the Julius Rosenwald Fund. Chicago: Julius Rosenwald Fund, 1928, 1929, 1930, 1931, 1933, 1935, 1936, 1938, 1940, 1942, 1944, 1946, 1948. (The 1936 publication is a retrospective for the period 1917–1936.)

Brown America: The Story of a New Race. New York: Viking, 1931.

Prospecting for Heaven: Some Conversations about Science and the Good Life. New York: Viking, 1932.

Island India Goes to School (with Margaret Sargent Simon and W. Bryant Mumford). Chicago: University of Chicago Press, 1934.

The Collapse of Cotton Tenancy (with Charles S. Johnson and Will W. Alexander). Chapel Hill: University of North Carolina Press, 1935.

Indians of the Americas: Historical Pageant. Boston: Houghton Mifflin, 1939.

American Negroes: A Handbook. New York: John Day, 1942.

Brown Americans: The Story of a Tenth of the Nation. New York: Viking, 1943. (Also published as *Negrene i Amerika: En Tiendedel af Nationen*. Copenhagen, 1947.)

Thirteen against the Odds. New York: Viking, 1944.

World at the Crossroads (with Anita Blaine, Edwin H. Cassels, W. W. Waymack, Quincy Wright). Chicago: World Citizens Association, 1946.

Peoples of the Earth. New York: Hinds, Hayden, and Eldredge, 1948.

Build the Future: Addresses Marking the Inauguration of Charles S. Johnson. Ed. and intro. Nashville, Tenn.: Fisk University Press, 1949.

Investment in People: The Story of the Julius Rosenwald Fund (with Julia Waxman). New York: Harper, 1949.

Articles, Book Chapters, Published Addresses

"Working One's Way through College." *Munsey's Magazine,* June 1911, 309–13.

"Yale Changes in Fifteen Years." *Yale Alumni Weekly,* 1913, 355.

"Yale and the South." *Yale Alumni Weekly,* 1914, 879.

"An All-Yale Class-Record Series." *Yale Alumni Weekly,* Feb. 1915.

"With the Negro Troops." *Survey* 40 (Aug. 19, 1918): 537–38.

"The Wonder of the French." *Yale Alumni Weekly,* Nov. 15, 1918.

"Impressions from a Visit to Changsha." *Yale Alumni Weekly,* 1923, 951.

"Two Leaders of the New China." *Asia* 24 (Oct. 1924): 805+.

"Football in the Mid-Pacific." *Yale Alumni Weekly,* 1926, 283.

"Negro Illness and Its Effect upon the Nation's Health." *Modern Hospital* 30, no. 4 (Apr. 1928): 49–54.

"How Negro Schools Have Advanced under the Rosenwald Fund." *Nation's Schools* 1, no. 5 (May 1928): 37–44.

"Fewer and Better Nurses." *Survey* 60 (July 15, 1928): 434–35.

"Pure Religion and Undefiled." *Survey* 41, no. 3 (Nov. 1, 1928): 178–80.

"What Is Organized Medicine?" *Modern Hospital* 33, no. 2 (Aug. 1929): 49–53.

"How the Foundations Fight Disease." *Survey* 63, no. 7 (Jan. 1, 1930): 413–17.

"Introduction." In *Human Biology and Racial Welfare,* ed. E. V. Cowdry. New York: Hoeber, 1930, vii–xiv.

"The Business of Giving Away Money." *Harper's Magazine,* Aug. 1930, 320–29.

"A Conversation in Peking." *Atlantic,* Nov. 1930, 561–68.

"Kentucky Crusader." *American Mercury,* Sept. 1931, 98–107.

"A Few Portraits in Sepia." *Atlantic,* Oct. 1931, 489–97.

"Challenge to the Schools." In *Our Children,* ed. S. Gruenberg and D. Canfield. New York: Viking, 1932, 195–203.

"Libraries and the Southern Renaissance." *School and Society* 36 (July 23, 1932): 103–106.

"Shall the South Accept Mediocrity?" *American Scholar* 1 (Oct. 1932): 413–17.

"A New School in American Samoa." *Survey Graphic* 22, no. 2 (Feb. 1933): 102–105.

"Samoa Offers an Exchange." *Social Forces* 11, no. 4 (May 1933): 559–69.

"Uses of Leisure." *Library Journal* 58, no. 15 (Sept. 1, 1933): 680–81.

"In Samoa the Moon Is Setting." *Asia* 34, no. 1 (Jan. 1934): 11–18.

"Objectives of Colonial Education." *Political Quarterly* 5, no. 2 (Apr.–June 1934): 221–35.

"Facing East." *Atlantic,* Sept. 1934, 349–59.

"Every Tenth Pupil: The Story of the Negro Schools in the South." *Survey Graphic* 23 (Nov. 1934): 538–41.

"Jews on the Steppes." *Survey Graphic* 24 (Jan. 1935): 11–15.

"Our Southern Farm System and the School." *Progressive Education* 12 (May 1935): 302–308.

"In Order of Their Eminence: An Appraisal of American Universities." *Atlantic,* June 1935, 652–64.

"Rebirth of Religion in Russia." *International Journal of Ethics* 45, no. 4 (July 1935): 422–30.

"Rural Education." *School and Society* 42 (Nov. 2, 1935): 585–603.

"Southern Farm Tenancy: The Way Out of Its Evils." *Survey Graphic* 25 (Mar. 1936): 149–53+.

"Education for All the People: Divided We Fall." *American Scholar* 5 (May 1936): 312–22.

"Education for Rural Life." *Journal of Negro Education* 5, no. 3 (July 1936): 439–47.

"The New Civilization: A Mingling of East and West." *University of Hawaii Bulletin* 15, no. 9 (July 1936): 1–9.

"Rural Education and the Teacher." *Educational Record* 17 (Oct. 1936): 130–51.

"Negro, The American" and "Philanthropy." In *Encyclopedia Britannica*, 14th ed. 1929– (1937 and 1939 printings): 194–96.

"Little Red Schoolhouse: 1938 Model." *Atlantic*, Nov. 1937, 636–43.

"Can College Graduates Read?" *Saturday Review of Literature*, July 3, 1938, 3–4.

"The Education of Teachers." *American Scholar* 8, no. 4 (Autumn 1939): 422–30.

"Illiteracy" and "The Julius Rosenwald Fund." Britannica Book of the Year, 1938–1947.

"Education for Rural Life." *1940 Yearbook of Agriculture*, 1033–41.

"Education and the Good South." *Social Forces* 19 (Oct. 1940): 12–16.

Living Together. Chicago: Institute for Psychoanalysis, 1941.

"Place of the Universities in the Southern Renaissance." *Southern Conference on Education: Proceedings of the Fourth Conference* (1941): 33–39.

"American Democracy and the Negro." *Opportunity*, June 1941, 174–75.

"The Status of Minorities as a Test of Democracy." *Journal of Negro Education* 10, no. 3 (July 1941): 453–58.

"Half Slave, Half Democrat." *American Mercury*, Mar. 1942, 323–30.

"For Whose Freedom?" *Asia* 42 (Apr. 1942): 221–24.

"Negroes and the Commonweal." *Survey Graphic* 31 (Nov. 1942): 490–94.

"It's Friendship with Colored Peoples or Chaos." *Nation's Schools*, Apr. 1943, 18–19.

"The Educational Process as Applied in America." *American Journal of Sociology* 48, no. 6 (May 1943): 759–64.

"Negro and the North." *American Mercury*, Aug. 1944, 713–17.

"The American Council on Race Relations." *Journal of Negro Education* 13, no. 4 (Autumn 1944): 562–64.

"Color and Christianity." In *Religion in the Post-War World*, ed. Willard L. Sperry. Cambridge, Mass.: Harvard University Press, 1945, vol. 3, 41–60.

"Schools in the Modern World." In *Days of Dedication*. Germantown, Pa.: Germantown Friends School, 1945.

"Balance Sheet in Race Relations." *Atlantic*, May 1945, 87–91.

"Education for One World." *Journal of Negro Education* 15, no. 3 (Summer 1946): 571–78.

"The Nation's Capital" (with Joseph D. Lohman). *Survey Graphic* 36, no. 1 (Jan. 1947): 33–37.

"*Phylon* Profile XVII: Julius Rosenwald, Philanthropist" (with Julia Waxman). *Phylon* 9, no. 3 (1948): 215–28.

"We Pass the Torch." *Phylon* 9, no. 3 (1948): 254–56.

"Democracy through the Schools." *High School Journal* 31 (Jan. 1948): 17.

"Timid Billions: Are the Foundations Doing Their Job?" *Harper's Magazine*, Mar. 1949, 28–37.

"Human Relations: Mid-Century." *Journal of Educational Sociology* 23, no. 6 (Feb. 1950): 363–69.

"Fellowships Are My Business." *Negro Digest*, May 1950, 45–49.

Essays Published in Julius Rosenwald Fund Reports

1928	"The Julius Rosenwald Fund"
1929	"The New Philanthropy"
1930	"Medical Economics"
	"The Negro Front"
1931	"The Place of Universities in the Southern Renaissance"
	"Social Planning and the Foundation"
1933	"Julius Rosenwald"
	"A World of Interesting Peoples"

1935   "Medical Economics"
       "Rural Education"
1937   "Eight Years Work in Medical
       Economics—1929–36"
1938   "The Education of Teachers"
1940   "Three Ramparts We Watch"
1942   "Color and Democracy"
1944   "Race Relations Balance Sheet"
1948   "Human Relations in America"

ARCHIVAL MATERIALS

Berea College Archives, Berea, Kentucky
  Edwin Rogers Embree Papers
  William Goodell Frost Papers
City of Chicago Municipal Records,
  Harold Washington Public Library,
  Chicago, Illinois
  Mayor's Commission on Human
  Relations
Devereux-Embree Family Papers, private
  collection
Franklin Delano Roosevelt Presidential
  Library, Hyde Park, New York
  Eleanor Roosevelt Papers
  Isadore Lubin Papers
  Wayne Coy Papers
John Hope and Aurelia E. Franklin
  Library, Fisk University, Nashville,
  Tennessee
  Charles S. Johnson Papers
  Julius Rosenwald Fund Archives
New York Public Library, Manuscripts and
  Archives Division, New York, New York
  Clarence Day Papers
Rockefeller Archive Center, Sleepy Hollow,
  New York
  Bureau of Social Hygiene Records
  China Medical Board, Inc., Records
  Edwin Rogers Embree Papers
  General Education Board Archives
  Laura Spelman Rockefeller Memorial
  Archives
  Office of the Messrs. Rockefeller, Rock-
  efeller Boards
  Rockefeller Foundation Archives
  Simon Flexner Papers

Roosevelt University, University Ar-
  chives, Chicago, Illinois
  Corporate Records, Roosevelt College
  Edwin Rogers Embree Papers
University of Chicago, Special Collec-
  tions Research Center, Regenstein
  Library, Chicago, Illinois
  Beardsley Ruml Papers
  Julius Rosenwald Papers
  National Committee on Segregation in
  the Nation's Capital, Records
  Robert Redfield Papers
  World Citizens Association, Records
Yale University, New Haven, Connecticut
  Anson Phelps Stokes Papers, Manu-
  scripts and Archives Division,
  Sterling Library
  Edwin Rogers Embree Papers, Manu-
  scripts and Archives Division,
  Sterling Library
  James Weldon Johnson Papers, Bei-
  necke Rare Book and Manuscripts
  Library

BOOKS AND ARTICLES

Adams, David W. "Philanthropists, Pro-
  gressives and Southern Black Educa-
  tion." *History of Education Quarterly* 23
  (1983): 99–111.
Alexander, William W. "The Education
  and Work of Edwin R. Embree." In *The
  Edwin R. Embree Memorial Lectures,
  1952–1953.* New Orleans, La.: Dillard
  University, 1953.
———. "Our Conflicting Racial Policies."
  Harper's 190 (Jan. 1945): 172–79.
Allen, Garland E. "Old Wine in New
  Bottles: From Eugenics to Popula-
  tion Control in the Work of Raymond
  Pearl." In Benson, Maienschein, and
  Rainger, 231–61.
Ambler, Robert, comp. and ed. *Embree Foot-
  prints: Genealogy and Family History of
  the Embree Descendants of Robert of New
  Haven and Stamford, Connecticut, 1643–
  1656.* 4 vols. Privately published, 1997.

Anderson, Eric, and Alfred A. Moss Jr. *Dangerous Donations: Northern Philanthropy and Southern Black Education, 1902–1930.* Columbia: University of Missouri Press, 1999.

Anderson, James D. "Education as a Vehicle for the Manipulation of Black Workers." In *Work, Technology and Education: Dissenting Essays in the Intellectual Foundation of American Education,* ed. Walter Feinberg and Henry Rosemont Jr., 15–40. Urbana: University of Illinois Press, 1975.

———. *The Education of Blacks in the South, 1860–1935.* Chapel Hill: University of North Carolina Press, 1988.

———. "Northern Foundations and the Shaping of Southern Black Rural Education, 1902–1935." *History of Education Quarterly* 18 (Winter 1978): 371–96.

———. "Northern Philanthropy and the Training of Black Leadership: Fisk University, a Case Study, 1915–1930." In *New Perspectives on Black Educational History,* ed. Vincent P. Franklin and James D. Anderson, 97–111. Boston: Hall, 1978.

———. "Philanthropic Control over Black Higher Education." In Arnove, 147–77.

Aptheker, Herbert, ed. *The Correspondence of W. E. B. DuBois.* 3 vols. Amherst: University of Massachusetts Press, 1973, 1976, 1978.

Arnove, Robert F., ed. *Philanthropy and Cultural Imperialism: The Foundations at Home and Abroad.* Boston: Hall, 1980.

Arthur, George R. *Life on the Negro Frontier.* New York: Association Press, 1934.

Ascoli, Peter M. *Julius Rosenwald: The Man Who Built Sears, Roebuck and Advanced the Cause of Black Education in the American South.* Bloomington: Indiana University Press, 2006.

Beilke, Jayne. "Nineteenth-Century Traditions of Benevolence and Education: Toward a Conceptual Framework of Black Philanthropy." In *Uplifting a People: African American Philanthropy and Education,* ed. Marybeth Gasman and Katherine V. Sedgwick. New York: Lang, 2005.

Belles, A. Gilbert. "The College Faculty, the Negro Scholar, and the Julius Rosenwald Fund." *Journal of Negro History* 54, no. 4 (Oct. 1969): 383–92.

———. "The Julius Rosenwald Fund: Efforts in Race Relations, 1928–1948." Ph.D. diss., Vanderbilt University, 1972.

———. "The NAACP, the Urban League, and the Julius Rosenwald Fund." *Crisis* 86 (1979): 97–106.

Benson, Keith R., Jane Maienschein, and Ronald Rainger, eds. *The Expansion of American Biology.* New Brunswick, N.J.: Rutgers University Press, 1991.

Black, Edwin. *The War against the Weak: Eugenics and America's Campaign to Create a Master Race.* New York: Four Walls Eight Windows, 2003.

Bontemps, Arno, ed. *The Harlem Renaissance Remembered.* New York: Dodd, Mead, 1972.

Bowers, John Z. "The Founding of the Peking Union Medical College: Policies and Personalities." *Bulletin of the History of Medicine* 45, no. 5 (Sept.–Oct. 1991): 409–29.

Brown, E. Richard. "Rockefeller Medicine in China: Professionalism and Imperialism." In Arnove, 123–46.

Brunius, Henry. *Better for All the World: The Secret History of Forced Sterilization and America's Quest for Racial Purity.* New York: Knopf, 2006.

Bullock, Henry A. *A History of Negro Education in the South.* Cambridge, Mass.: Harvard University Press, 1970.

Bullock, Mary B. *An American Transplant: The Rockefeller Foundation and Peking Union Medical College.* Berkeley: University of California Press, 1980.

Caliver, Ambrose. "Some Significant Developments in the Education of Negroes in the Past Generation." *Journal of Negro History* 35, no. 3 (Apr. 1951): 111–34.

Carnoy, Martin. *Education as Cultural Imperialism.* New York: McKay, 1974.

Cook, James F. "The Cocking Affair." In *New Georgia Encyclopedia.* http://www.georgiaencyclopedia.org (accessed June 15, 2007).

———."The Eugene Talmadge–Walter Cocking Controversy." *Phylon* 35, no. 2 (1974): 181–92.

Cowdry, E. V., ed. *Human Biology and Race Welfare.* New York: Hoeber, 1930.

Dalfiume, Richard M. "The 'Forgotten Years' of the Negro Revolution." *Journal of American History* 55, no. 1 (June 1968): 90–106.

Davis, Larry. *A Clashing of the Soul: John Hope and the Dilemma of African American Leadership and Higher Education in the Early Twentieth Century.* Athens: University of Georgia Press, 1990.

Deloria, Vine. Introduction to Embree, *Indians of the Americas,* 2nd ed. New York: Macmillan, 1970.

Dunn, Durwood. *An Abolitionist in the Appalachian South: Ezekiel Birdseye on Slavery, Capitalism and Separate Statehood in East Tennessee, 1841–1846.* Knoxville: University of Tennessee Press, 1997.

Dunne, Matthew W. "Next Steps: Charles S. Johnson and Southern Liberalism." *Journal of Negro History* 83, no. 1 (Winter 1948): 1–34.

Dykeman, Wilma, and James Stokely. *Seeds of Southern Change: The Life of Will Alexander.* New York: Norton, 1976.

Egerton, John. *Speak Now against the Day: The Generation before the Civil Rights Movement in the South.* Chapel Hill: University of North Carolina Press, 1995.

Ferguson, Mary E. *China Medical Board and Peking Union Medical College: A Chronicle of Fruitful Collaboration, 1914–1951.* New York: China Medical Board of New York, 1970.

Flexner, Abraham. *Abraham Flexner: An Autobiography.* New York: Simon and Schuster, 1960.

Flexner, Abraham, and Esther S. Bailey. *Funds and Foundations: Their Policies Past and Present.* New York: Harper, 1952.

Fosdick, Raymond B. *Adventure in Giving: The Story of the General Education Board.* New York: Harper, 1962.

———. *Chronicle of a Generation: An Autobiography.* New York: Harper, 1958.

———. *The Story of the Rockefeller Foundation.* New York: Harper, 1952.

Franklin, John Hope. "The American Negro Scholar." In *Soon, One Morning,* ed. Herbert Hill, 74–76. New York: Knopf, 1963.

Gasman, Marybeth, and Katherine Sedgwick, eds. *Uplifting a People: African American Philanthropy and Education.* New York: Lang, 2005.

Gates, Frederick. *Chapters in My Life.* New York: Free Press, 1977.

Gilpin, Patrick J. "Charles S. Johnson and the Southern Educational Reporting Service." *Journal of Negro History* 63, no. 3 (July 1978): 197–208.

Gilpin, Patrick J., and Marybeth Gasman. *Charles S. Johnson: Leadership beyond the Veil in the Age of Jim Crow.* Albany: State University of New York Press, 2003.

Goggin, Jacqueline. *Carter G. Woodson: A Life in Black History.* Baton Rouge: Louisiana University Press, 1993.

Goodwin, Doris Kearns. *No Ordinary Time: Franklin and Eleanor Roosevelt: The Home Front in World War II.* New York: Simon and Schuster, 1974.

Grant, R. G. *Flight: 100 Years of Aviation.* New York: DK, 2002.

Gross, Theodore L. *The Rise of Roosevelt University: Presidential Reflections.* Carbondale: Southern Illinois University Press, 2005.

———. *Roosevelt University: From Vision to Reality, 1945–2002*. Chicago: Roosevelt University, 2002.

Harr, John Ensor, and Peter J. Johnson. *The Rockefeller Century*. New York: Scribner's, 1988.

Harris, Catherine Embree. *Dusty Exile: Looking Back at Japanese Relocation during World War II*. Honolulu, Hawaii: Mutual, 1999.

Hatch, James V. *Sorrow Is the Only Faithful One: The Life of Owen Dodson*. Urbana: University of Illinois Press, 1993.

Hill, Roger. *One Man's Time and Chance: A Memoir of Eighty Years, 1895–1975*. Privately printed. Hutchins Library Special Collections, Berea College, Berea, Ky.

Hoffschwelle, Mary. *Rosenwald Schools of the American South*. Gainesville: University Press of Florida, 2006.

Hofstadter, Richard. *The Age of Reform: From Bryan to Roosevelt*. New York: Random House, 1955.

Hoss, E. E. *Elihu Embree, Abolitionist*. Nashville: University of Tennessee Press, 1897.

Howe, Barbara. "The Emergence of Scientific Philanthropy, 1900–1920." In Arnove, 25–54.

Isaacson, Walter. *Einstein: His Life and Universe*. New York: Simon and Schuster, 2007.

Johnson, Charles S. *The Negro in American Civilization*. New York: Holt, 1930.

———. "*Phylon* Profile X: Edwin Rogers Embree." *Phylon* 7, no. 4 (1946): 317–24.

———. "The Social Philosophy of Edwin R. Embree." In *The Edwin R. Embree Memorial Lectures, 1954–1955*. New Orleans, La.: Dillard University, 1955.

Johnson, James Weldon. *Along This Way: The Autobiography of James Weldon Johnson*. New York: Viking, 1933.

Jonas, Gerald. *The Circuit Riders: Rockefeller Money and the Rise of Modern Science*. New York: Norton, 1989.

Jordan, John M. *Machine-Age Ideology: Social Engineering and American Liberalism, 1911–1939*. Chapel Hill: University of North Carolina Press, 1994.

Kay, Lily E. *The Molecular Vision of Life: Cal Tech, the Rockefeller Foundation, and the Rise of the New Biology*. New York: Oxford University Press, 1991.

Kellogg, Charles F. *NAACP: A History of the National Association for the Advancement of Colored People*. 2 vols. Baltimore, Md.: Johns Hopkins University Press, 1967, 1968.

Keppel, Frederick P. *The Foundation: Its Place in American Life*. New York: Macmillan, 1930.

———. "Opportunities and Dangers of Educational Foundations." *School and Society* 22, no. 574 (Dec. 26, 1925): 793–99.

Kevles, Daniel J. *In the Name of Eugenics*. New York: Knopf, 1985.

Kingsland, Sharon E. "Toward a Natural History of the Human Psyche: Charles Manning Child, Charles Judson Herrick, and the Dynamic View of the Individual at the University of Chicago." In Benson, Maienschein, and Rainger, 195–230.

Kohler, Robert. *Partners in Science: Foundations and National Scientists, 1900–1945*. Chicago: University of Chicago Press, 1991.

———. "A Policy for the Advancement of Science: The Rockefeller Foundation, 1924–29." *Minerva* 16, no. 4 (Dec. 1978): 480–515.

———. "Science, Foundations, and American Universities in the 1920s." *Osiris* 2, no. 3 (1987): 135–64.

Lagemann, Ellen, ed. *Philanthropic Foundations: New Scholarship, New Possibilities*. Bloomington: Indiana University Press, 1999.

Landis, Kennesaw M., II. *Segregation in Washington: A Report of the National Committee on Segregation in the Nation's Capital*. Washington, D.C.: National

Committee on Segregation in the Nation's Capital, 1948.

Leavell, Ullin Whitney. *Philanthropy in Negro Education.* Nashville, Tenn.: George Peabody College for Teachers, 1930.

Lelon, Thomas Charles. "The Emergence of Roosevelt College of Chicago: A Search for an Ideal." Ph.D. diss., University of Chicago, 1973.

Leuchtenburg, William E. *Herbert Hoover.* New York: Holt, 2009.

Lewis, David Levering. *W. E. B. DuBois: The Fight for Equality and the American Century, 1919–1963.* New York: Holt, 2000.

———. *When Harlem Was in Vogue.* New York: Knopf, 1981.

Link, Arthur S. "What Happened to the Progressive Movement in the 1920s." In *Progressivism: The Central Issues,* ed. David M. Kennedy, 147–63. Boston: Little, Brown, 1971.

Ludmerer, Kenneth. *Genetics and American Society: A Historical Appraisal.* Baltimore, Md.: Johns Hopkins University Press, 1972.

Luker, Ralph E. *The Social Gospel in Black and White: American Racial Reform, 1885–1912.* Chapel Hill: University of North Carolina Press, 1991.

Macrakis, Kristie. "The Rockefeller Foundation and German Physics under National Socialism." *Minerva* 27 (1989): 33–57.

Mays, Benjamin E. *Born to Rebel: An Autobiography.* New York: Scribner's, 1971.

McArthur, Benjamin. "A Gamble on Youth: Robert M. Hutchins, the University of Chicago and the Politics of Presidential Selection." *History of Education Quarterly* 30, no. 2 (Summer 1990): 161–86.

McPherson, James M. *The Abolitionist Legacy: From Reconstruction to the NAACP.* Princeton, N.J.: Princeton University Press, 1975.

Moss, Alfred A., Jr. *The American Negro Academy: Voice of the Talented Tenth.* Baton Rouge: Louisiana State University Press, 1981.

Myrdal, Gunnar. *An American Dilemma.* New York: Harper and Row, 1944.

National Committee on Responsive Philanthropy. "The Strategic Philanthropy of Conservative Foundations: Moving a Public Policy Agenda" (1997), 1–3. http://www.mediatransparency.org /conservativephilanthropy.php (accessed Aug. 19, 2007).

Nichols, Charles, ed. *Arna Bontemps–Langston Hughes Letters 1925–1967.* New York: Dodd, Mead, 1980.

Osceola Centennial Book Committee. *Osceola: 1871–1971.* Osceola, Nebr.: Osceola Centennial Book Committee, 1972.

Paul, Diane B. "The Rockefeller Foundation and the Origins of Behavior Genetics." In Benson, Maienschein, and Rainger, 262–83.

Peeps, J. M. Stephen. "Northern Philanthropy and the Emergence of Black Higher Education: Do-Gooders, Compromisers or Co-Conspirators?" *Journal of Negro Education* 50 (1981): 251–69.

Perkins, Alfred. "An Apprenticeship in Philanthropy: Edwin Rogers Embree and the Rockefeller Foundation, 1917– 1927." http://www.rockarch.org/publications/resrep (accessed Dec. 12, 2008).

———. "Investment in Talent: Edwin Rogers Embree and the Julius Rosenwald Fellowships." In Schulman, 25–35.

———. "Welcome Consequences and Fulfilled Promise: Julius Rosenwald Fund Fellows and *Brown v. Board of Education.*" *Journal of Negro Education* 72, no. 3 (Summer 2003): 344–56.

Peterson, Nicholas. "Studying Man and Man's Nature: The History of the Institutionalisation of Aboriginal Anthropology." *Australian Aboriginal Studies* 2

(1990): 7–18.

Pickens, D. K. *Eugenics and the Progressives.* Nashville, Tenn.: Vanderbilt University Press, 1968.

Pierson, George Wilson. *Yale College: An Educational History, 1871–1921.* 2 vols. New Haven, Conn.: Yale University Press, 1952.

Pinckney, Darryl. "Writers and the Julius Rosenwald Fund." In Schulman, 37–49.

Pritchett, Henry S. "The Use and Abuse of Endowments." *Atlantic Monthly,* Oct. 1929, 517–24.

Pumphrey, Ralph E. "Michael M. Davis and the Development of the Health Care Movement." *Societas: A Review of Social History* 2, no. 1 (Winter 1972): 27–41.

Richardson, Joe M. "Edgar B. Stern: A White New Orleans Philanthropist Helps Build a Black University." *Journal of Negro History* 82, no. 3 (Summer 1997): 328–42.

Robbins, Richard. *Sidelines Activist: Charles S. Johnson and the Struggle for Civil Rights.* Jackson: University Press of Mississippi, 1996.

Rogers, Elizabeth Embree. *Full Forty Years of Shadow and Sunshine: A Sketch of the Family Life of the J. A. R. Rogers Family.* Privately printed, 1896. Hutchins Library Special Collections, Berea College, Berea, Ky.

Rosen, Christine. *Preaching Eugenics: Religious Leaders and the American Eugenics Movement.* New York: Oxford University Press, 2004.

Rosenwald, Julius (as told to Elias Tobenkin). "The Burden of Wealth." *Saturday Evening Post,* Jan. 5, 1929, 12+.

———. "The Principles of Public Giving." *Atlantic Monthly,* May 1929, 599–607.

———. "The Trend Away from Perpetuities." *Atlantic Monthly,* Aug. 1930, 141–49.

Ross, Edward Alsworth. "Philanthropy from the Viewpoint of the Sociologist." In *Intelligent Philanthropy,* ed. Ellsworth Faris, Ferris Laune, and Arthur J. Todd, 225–42. Chicago: University of Chicago Press, 1930.

Rury, John L. "Philanthropy, Self-Help, and Social Control: The New York Manumission Society and Free Blacks, 1785–1810." *Phylon* 46, no. 3 (1985): 231–41.

Schulman, Daniel, ed. *A Force for Change: African American Art and the Julius Rosenwald Fund.* Evanston, Ill.: Northwestern University Press, 2009.

Sealander, Judith. *Private Wealth and Public Life: Foundation Philanthropy and the Reshaping of American Social Policy from the Progressive Era to the New Deal.* Baltimore, Md.: Johns Hopkins University Press, 1997.

Sheldon, Steve. "Eugenics Popularization." http://www.eugenicsarchive.org (accessed May 26, 2008).

Slaughter, Sheila, and Edward T. Silva. "Looking Backwards: How Foundations Formulated Ideology in the Progressive Era." In Arnove, 55–86.

Smith, James Allen. "Foundations and Public Policy: A Historical Perspective." University of Southern California (2002). http://www.usc.edu/schools (accessed Aug. 7, 2008).

Stanfield, John H. "The Cracked Back Door: Foundations and Black Social Scientists between the Wars." *American Sociologist* 17 (1982): 193–204.

———. "Dollars for the Silent South: Southern White Liberalism and the Julius Rosenwald Fund, 1928–1948." In *Perspectives on the American South: An Annual Review of Society, Politics and Culture,* ed. Merle Black and John Shelton Reed, vol. 2, 117–38. Chapel Hill: University of North Carolina Press, 1948.

———. *Philanthropy and Jim Crow in American Social Science.* Westport, Conn.: Greenwood, 1985.

Strausbaugh, John A. "Cooperation in Georgia." *South Atlantic Bulletin* 6, no. 3 (Apr. 1940): 3–4.

Thompson, Edgar T. "Economic Problem No. 1." *Social Forces* 17, no. 4 (May 1939): 501–62.

Tucker, Shauna K. "The Early Years of the United Negro College Fund, 1943–1960." *Journal of African American History* 87 (Autumn 2002): 416–32.

Urban, Wayne J. *Black Scholar: Horace Mann Bond.* Athens: University of Georgia Press, 1992.

———. "Philanthropy and the Black Scholar: The Case of Horace Mann Bond." *Journal of Negro Education* 53 (1989): 478–93.

Veevers-Carter, Wendy. *Clarence Day, an American Writer.* New York: Gardners, 2007.

Wale, Fred G. "Chosen for Ability." *Atlantic Monthly,* July 1947, 81–85.

Weaver, Robert C. "City of Chicago: Mayor's Committee on Race Relations." *Journal of Negro Education* 13, no. 4 (Autumn 1944): 560–62.

Weil, Rolf A. *Through These Portals: From Immigrant to University President.* Chicago: Privately published, 1991.

Weindling, Paul. "The Rockefeller Foundation and German Biomedical Sciences, 1920–40: From Educational Philanthropy to International Science Policy." In *Science Politics and the Public Good: Essays in Honor of Margaret Gowing,* ed. Nicolaas A. Rupke, 119–40. London: Macmillan, 1988.

Werner, M. R. *Julius Rosenwald: The Life of a Practical Humanitarian.* New York: Harper, 1939.

Wheatley, Steven C. *The Politics of Philanthropy: Abraham Flexner and Medical Education.* Madison: University of Wisconsin Press, 1988.

Whitaker, Benjamin. *The Philanthropoids: Foundations and Society.* New York: Morrow, 1974.

Wiebe, Robert. *The Search for Order, 1877–1920.* New York: Hill and Wang, 1967.

Wilson, Robert R. "Starting Fermilab." *About Fermilab: History and Archives Project.* http://www.history.fnal.gov (accessed Sept. 27, 2005).

Wilson, Shannon H. *Berea College: An Illustrated History.* Lexington: University Press of Kentucky, 2006.

Winston, Michael R. "Through the Back Door: Academic Racism and the Negro Scholar in Historical Perspective." *Daedalus* 100, no. 3 (Summer 1971): 678–719.

Woodson, Carter G. Chapter 5 of unpublished history of Rosenwald school-building program. Julius Rosenwald Papers, Special Collections Research Center, Regenstein Library, University of Chicago.

Wright, Eleanor, ed. *The People of Chicago: Five-Year Report, 1947–1951.* Municipal Records, Harold Washington Public Library, Chicago, Ill.

Wright, Thomas H. *Human Relations in Chicago: Report of the Mayor's Commission on Human Relations for 1946.* Municipal Records, Harold Washington Public Library, Chicago, Ill.

INDEX

Page numbers in italics indicate illustrations.

Actor's Equity Association, 324n16

Acts 17:26, 243

Africa, ERE travel in, 262, 264

Africa Foundation, 262

African Americans: appointment to federal positions, 321n56; black studies movement, 305n80; educational limitations in the South, 298nn19,22; ERE writings on, 117–121; health care issues, 91; JRF philanthropy toward, 73; New Haven black-white relations conference, 76–77; northern migration, 120, 125, 188, 213; racial integration of Berea, Ky., 7–8; representation on JRF Board, 81; representation on JRF staff, 82; Tuskegee syphilis experiment, 301n50; WWI military service, 322n1; WWII combat role, 304n66; WWII morale and loyalty, 237–239

Agar, John G., 65–66

Agnes Scott College, 131

agriculture. *See* land/land ownership

Alexander, Will W.: co-director of JRF Division of Race Relations, 215; election to JRF Board, 81, 162; as ERE associate, 82, 96, 116, 160; as ERE co-author, 121–124; ERE introduction to, 76; ERE lecture series speaker, 271; eulogy to ERE, 270; NAACP tribute to, 254; NCSNC member, 245, 250–251; president of Dillard University, 99; role

in ACRR, 220–221; selection committee for JRF fellows, 107

All Quiet on the Western Front (Remarque), 118

Allen, Frederick Lewis, 320n42

America First Committee, 185–186

American Antiquity, 231

American Association for the Advancement of Science, 288n65

American Association of Zoologists, 288n65

American Council on Education, 209, 303n64, 332n29

American Council on Race Relations (ACRR), 220–225, 251, 303n64, 324n15, 325nn20,27,28, 326n31

An American Dilemma (Myrdal), 252

American Eugenics Society, 287n58

American Film Center, 238

American Hospital Association, 91, 151–152, 153

American Journal of Sociology, 231

American Labor Education Service, 226

American Mercury, 118, 155–156, 230, 261

American Missionary Association, 7, 98–99, 269, 322n5

American Museum of Natural History (New York), 50

American Negroes: A Handbook (Embree), 231–232

American Nursing Association, 153

American Red Cross, 107

22; nicknames, 13, 14, 21; obituary and eulogies, 268–271, 333n48, 334n65; personal attitudes and ambitions, 141–147; photographs, *167–174, 177–179, 181;* physical description and work ethic, 134–137; post-JRF career, 260–265; 65th birthday, 248. *See also* education; employment of ERE

Embree, Edwina Rogers (daughter), 24–25, 41, 46, 267

Embree, Elihu (distant relative), 12

Embree, Ella (daughter-in-law), 187

Embree, Hallie (sister), 96

Embree, Howard (brother), *167,* 316n13

Embree, John Fee (son), 24, 55–56, 144–145, *172,* 187, 309n32, 310n35, 316n13

Embree, Kate Clarke (wife), *172;* entertaining friends in Chicago, 137–138, 206; ERE compliment of, 311n39; fulfilling ERE final wishes, 271–272; marriage to ERE, 22; personality and child rearing, 146; separations due to ERE's travels, 33, 41, 145; travels with ERE, 46, 55–56

Embree, Laura Fee (mother), *166;* death of, 14–15, 47; illness from malaria, 5; influence on ERE, 13–14; pregnancy and birth of ERE, 3; return to parents' home in Kentucky, 5

Embree, Lawrence (distant relative), 11

Embree, Raymond (brother), *167*

Embree, Robert (family progenitor), 16

Embree, Thomas (distant relative), 12

Embree, William Dean (brother), *167, 169;* defense of ERE loyalty, 265; as N.Y. lawyer, 27, 283n20, 284n52; as school trustee, 96; as student at Yale, 16

Embree, William Norris (father): employment by Union Pacific, 2–4; failing health and death, 5; views on slavery, 11

Emory University, 131

employment of ERE: at JRF, 73–76; as *N.Y. Sun* reporter, 22–23; post-JRF career, 260–265; at RF, 26–29; as student, 19–20; at Yale University, 23–26

Empress of Asia, 41

Encyclopedia Britannica, 159

endowments, perpetual. *See* philanthropy, practice and philosophy of

Engleman, F. E., 263

entertaining/entertainment industry: ERE contacts in, 206–207; ERE interracial gatherings, 138–139, 321n53; ERE posthumous party, 278–279; JRF termination celebration, 251–254; racial discrimination, 324n16; Waldorf-Astoria dinner for Ralph Bunche, *181,* 265. *See also* media and motion pictures

equality of opportunity, ERE view on, 203

Essay on the Principle of Population (Malthus), 51

ethnic diversity/discrimination: democracy, ERE views on, 203–205; ERE legacy, 268–269, 278–279; ERE writings on, 118–119, 121, 191, 235–236, 264–265, 304n73; Hispanic, 219, 222; Jewish, 148, 192, 274; "opportunity fellowships," 263; Soviet Union, 313n66. *See also* race relations; racial discrimination

Ethridge, Mark, 116, 266, 314n76, 321n57, 329n71

eugenics, 50–54, 287nn56,57,58, 288n62

Eugenics Record Office, 287n58

"Facts about Japanese-Americans" (ACRR), 222

Falk Fund (Pittsburgh), 110

"family journals," 34–35, 72

family planning, 24, 152. *See also* population growth/control

fascism, ERE comments on, 183, 202

Fax, Mark, 211

Federal Council of Churches, 226, 269

Fee, John Gregg (ERE maternal grandfather), *164;* abolitionist roots and ordination, 5–6; anti-slavery opposition, 7–9; commitment to racial equality, 12, 139–140; ERE book dedication to, 121; influence on ERE, 9–13, 243; marriage, 7

Fee, Matilda Hamilton (ERE maternal grandmother), 282n12

ALFRED PERKINS has taught history at Upsala, Maryville, and Berea colleges, and served as academic dean and vice president of all three institutions. His most recent publications have appeared in *Catholic Historical Review, Appalachian Heritage, Journal of Negro Education,* and *Rockefeller Archive Center's Research Reports.* Now retired, he lives in Florida, where he enjoys bicycling, kayaking, and beach walking.

www.ingramcontent.com/pod-product-compliance
Lightning Source LLC
Chambersburg PA
CBHW060324100426
42812CB00003B/877